Black Frankenstein

D1338891

America and the Long 19th Century

GENERAL EDITORS
David Kazanjian, Elizabeth McHenry, and Priscilla Wald

Black Frankenstein: The Making of an American Metaphor
Elizabeth Young

Black Frankenstein

The Making of an American Metaphor

Elizabeth Young

NEW YORK UNIVERSITY PRESS
New York and London

Leeds Trinity University

NEW YORK UNIVERSITY PRESS
New York and London
www.nyupress.org

© 2008 by New York University
All rights reserved

Extract from "Dreaming Frankenstein" from *Dreaming Frankenstein and Collected Poems* by Liz Lochhead is reproduced by permission of Polygon, an imprint of Birlinn Ltd. (www.birlinn.co.uk).

A portion of chapter 4 originally appeared in "Here Comes the Bride: Wedding Gender and Race in *Bride of Frankenstein*," *Feminist Studies* 17:3 (fall 1991): 403–37.

LIBRARY OF CONGRESS CATALOGING-IN-PUBLICATION DATA
Young, Elizabeth.
Black Frankenstein : the making of an American metaphor / Elizabeth Young.
p. cm.   Includes bibliographical references and index.
ISBN-13: 978-0-8147-9715-0 (cloth : alk. paper)
ISBN-10: 0-8147-9715-6 (cloth : alk. paper)
ISBN-13: 978-0-8147-9716-7 (pbk. : alk. paper)
ISBN-10: 0-8147-9716-4 (pbk. : alk. paper)
1. American literature—White authors—History and criticism.
2. American literature—African American authors—History and criticism. 3. African Americans in literature. 4. Race in literature.
5. Race relations in literature. 6. Frankenstein (Fictitious character) in literature. 7. Frankenstein (Fictitious character)—Political aspects.
8. Monsters in literature. 9. Metaphor in literature. 10. Monsters in motion pictures.   I. Title.
PS173.N4Y68   2008
810.9'352996073—dc22   2008008049

New York University Press books are printed on acid-free paper, and their binding materials are chosen for strength and durability. We strive to use environmentally responsible suppliers and materials to the greatest extent possible in publishing our books.

Manufactured in the United States of America

c 10 9 8 7 6 5 4 3 2 1
p 10 9 8 7 6 5 4 3 2 1

810. 9352996073 You
3382579

To Laura M. Green and William A. Cohen

Contents

List of Illustrations		ix
Acknowledgments		xi
	Introduction	1
1	United States of Frankenstein	19
2	Black Monsters, Dead Metaphors	68
3	The Signifying Monster	107
4	Souls on Ice	159
	Afterword	219
	Notes	231
	Index	293
	About the Author	308

Illustrations

1. Frank Bellew, "The Modern Frankenstein" — 39
2. Henry Louis Stephens, "The New Frankenstein" — 49
3. Atlanta University *Bulletin* — 61
4. Peter Newell, "In the Laboratory" — 85
5. Edison *Frankenstein* — 164
6. Edison *Frankenstein* — 165
7. Edison *Frankenstein* — 166
8. Edison *Frankenstein* — 167
9. *Birth of a Nation* — 171
10. *Bride of Frankenstein* — 178
11. *Bride of Frankenstein* — 185
12. *Blackenstein* — 191
13. *Blackenstein* — 193
14. *Blackenstein* — 194
15. *Blackenstein* poster — 195
16. Jerry Yulsman, Dick Gregory photograph — 205
17. Milton Glaser, *Dick Gregory's Frankenstein* — 214
18. Glenn Ligon, *Study for Frankenstein #1* — 223

Acknowledgments

Many friends, colleagues, and institutions have supported this project over the long period of its gestation. I began thinking about *Frankenstein* many years ago, under the expert tutelage of Catherine Gallagher, and I thank her for this. Most recently, New York University Press has welcomed this project, and I am grateful to Eric Zinner, Emily Park, Despina Papazoglou Gimbel, Andrew Katz, Martin Tulic, two anonymous readers, and others at the Press. A fellowship from the George A. and Eliza Gardner Howard Foundation provided crucial sabbatical support. Along the way, others have published, reprinted, or otherwise encouraged my writing on topics related to *Frankenstein*, most of which is not in this book but all of which influenced it: Rhona Berenstein, Ken Gelder, Barry Keith Grant, Jon Lewis, Eric Smoodin, and the editors of *Camera Obscura* and *Feminist Studies*.

Many people at Mount Holyoke College have advanced this project. I thank the office of the Dean of Faculty—including Donal O'Shea and Penny Gill—for substantial support, including a Faculty Fellowship. I thank my colleagues in English, Gender Studies, Film Studies, and American Studies, particularly Christopher Benfey, Robin Blaetz, Anthony W. Lee, Amy Martin, Mary Renda, Ajay Sinha, Paul Staiti, Thomas Wartenberg, and Donald Weber. Local colleagues Bettina Bergmann, Anna Botta, Darcy Buerkle, Barbara Kellum, and, especially, Dana Leibsohn greatly assisted with the analysis of visual material. The Nineteenth-Century American Women Writers Study Group has provided great collegiality. Staff at the Mount Holyoke College Library, Smith College Library, American Antiquarian Society, Atlanta University Library, Harvard Theatre Collection, British Library, and Museum of Modern Art have been very helpful. Invaluable assistance was provided by James Gehrt and Aime DeGrenier of Mount Holyoke Library and Information Technology Services and by Hamenth Swaminathan.

Double thanks go to Judith Frank for her indispensable friendship and support of this and previous projects. For assistance of various kinds, I am grateful to the following colleagues and friends: Awam Amkpa, Sabrina Barton, Lisa Beskin, Ian Conrich, Simone Davis, Don Dingledine, Elizabeth Garland, Nina Gerassi-Navarro and Ernesto Livon-Grosman, Susan Gillman, Teresa Goddu, Bruce L. Hay, Karen Jacobs, Amy Kaplan, Carolyn Karcher, Jonathan D. Katz, Annette Kuhn, Caroline Levander, Robert Levine, Mary Loeffelholz, Lisa Long, Susan Lurie, Tania Modleski, Christen Mucher, Samuel Otter, Shirley Samuels, Karen Sánchez-Eppler, Jackie Stacey, Michelle Stephens, and Trysh Travis. I greatly appreciate the vital encouragement given by Janice Dumond, Elissa Forman, Karen Heath, Lisa Hunter, Marion Kozak, Candida Lacey, Bridget Ryan, the Systors, and Dorothy Wedderburn. I have received much sustenance from family: Alfred, Marilyn, Sarah, Thomas, Emily, Jeff, Noah, Ruby, Davia, Isabel, and Frankie.

The dedication is to Laura M. Green and William A. Cohen—brilliant readers, steadfast supporters, excellent friends—without whom this book would never have come to be.

Introduction

You can teach an old metaphor new tricks. In the Frankenstein story, first introduced in the novel by Mary Shelley in 1818 and made famous on film by James Whale in 1931, a monster, assembled from corpses and reanimated, rebels violently against his creator. The Frankenstein story has a long history of being used as a political metaphor, and at the start of the twenty-first century, it continues to shape political debate. Consider, for example, critiques of U.S. foreign policy in the wake of 9/11. In "We Finally Got Our Frankenstein," filmmaker Michael Moore compares Iraqi leader Saddam Hussein to the Frankenstein monster: "We had a virtual love fest with this Frankenstein whom we (in part) created. And, just like the mythical Frankenstein, Saddam eventually spun out of control. He would no longer do what he was told by his master. Saddam had to be caught." Moore considers Hussein one of many monsters created by the U.S. government, including Osama bin Laden—"Our other Frankenstein"—and a roster of right-wing dictators: "We liked playing Dr. Frankenstein. We created a lot of monsters—the Shah of Iran, Somoza of Nicaragua, Pinochet of Chile—and then we expressed ignorance or shock when they ran amok and massacred people."[1]

Moore uses the Frankenstein metaphor to condemn the U.S. government for "playing Dr. Frankenstein," conducting a scientific experiment that is also a "love fest" gone wrong. Novelist Carlos Fuentes offers a similar cautionary tale but links the monster to a familial metaphor: "Saddam Hussein was Saddam Hussein because the United States gave him all possible support. The United States is extraordinarily gifted in creating monsters like Frankenstein. Then one fine day they discover that these Frankensteins are dreadful. However, for twenty years they were the spoilt children, their proteges, and the babies of the United States."[2] Journalist Maureen Dowd invokes the idea of religious overreaching when she condemns Vice President Dick Cheney "and his crazy-eyed Igors at the Pentagon [for] their hunger to remake the Middle East. It's often seen in scary movies: you play God to create something in your own image, and the monster you make ends up coming after you." She renames the vice president "Dr. Cheneystein."[3]

Even when the metaphor is not directly named, *Frankenstein* informs contemporary critiques of U.S. foreign policy. "Blowback" is the term popularized by Chalmers Johnson to describe contemporary violence against the United States that results from its foreign policy: "The most direct and obvious form of blowback often occurs when the victims fight back after a secret American bombing, or a U.S.-sponsored campaign of state terrorism, or a CIA-engineered overthrow of a foreign political leader."[4] With its plot of boomerang violence, *Frankenstein* is the embodiment of blowback, or as another commentator summarizes the theory, "Now the monster has turned on its creator."[5] In *Multitude: War and Democracy in the Age of Empire* (2004), Antonio Hardt and Michael Negri extract a different political lesson from *Frankenstein*. They open the volume, the sequel to their influential *Empire* (2000), with a discussion of the Frankenstein monster and the golem, another fictional monster who rebels against his creator. Writing "under the cloud of war . . . between September 11, 2001, and the 2003 Iraq War," Hardt and Negri suggest that both monster and golem are "whispering to us secretly under the din of our global battlefield . . . a lesson about the monstrosity of war and our possible redemption through love."[6] Later in the volume, Hardt and Negri use the Frankenstein monster as the affirmative symbol of the "multitude," their model of a global democratic proletariat. Since "Frankenstein is now a member of the family," they assert, "[t]he new world of monsters is where humanity has to grasp its future."[7] Hardt and Negri are vague on the details of this vision, but they are clearly faithful to Mary Shelley's own depiction of the monster as a sympathetic figure. The "love fest" of Moore's "We Finally Got Our Frankenstein" has become the "redemption through love" prompted by monsters.

These are disparate examples, varying in tone, sophistication, and target. My interest is in the metaphoric figure they employ as much as the political ground they occupy—or rather, in the way the figure shapes the ground. Metaphors matter to culture and thought, and these examples all suggest the continuing vitality of the Frankenstein metaphor for shaping contemporary political critique and, in particular, for voicing dissent against elites whose policies are seen as misguided in intention and disastrous in effect. Critiques of U.S. power are one inheritance of the Frankenstein story in a post-9/11 world; expressions of sympathy for the monstrous violence that defines that world are another. What we might call the "blowback" and "sympathy" themes of the Frankenstein story extract different but complementary meanings from it, using it to criticize monster-makers and to explain monstrous violence, if not to defend monsters themselves.

Highlighting some contemporary political uses of the Frankenstein metaphor, these examples also suggest some ambiguities intrinsic to this metaphor. Moore employs "Frankenstein" to signal both monster and monster-maker, whereas in Shelley's novel "Frankenstein" refers only to the maker, who is a university student, not a doctor; Fuentes's image of Hussein as a long-time "spoilt baby" has no correspondence to the plot of the novel, in which the creature is abandoned from birth; Dowd's reference to Igor, the scientist's assistant, is to the film version of *Frankenstein*. Such changes themselves have a long history: the term "Frankenstein" migrated from creator to monster as early as the 1830s, and the assistant character was added to theatrical productions in the 1820s.[8] Combining different elements of the Frankenstein story, these writers do not so much replace older versions with newer ones as reanimate elements in place since the early nineteenth century. In these processes of recombination and reanimation, they mimic the actions of Victor Frankenstein within the story, a self-reflexivity that Mary Shelley had set in motion in her 1831 preface to the novel, in which she aligned monster and book: "I bid my hideous progeny go forth and prosper."[9] The piecing-together process by which "Frankenstein" becomes "Cheneystein" is part of a longer, and indeed prosperous, history in which commentators on *Frankenstein* reprise the monster-making in the novel itself.

There are, of course, many other strands of Frankenstein imagery in contemporary political culture, including references to the story in discussions of stem-cell research, cloning, cosmetic surgery, and genetically modified foods.[10] These discussions draw on the implications of the idea of "Frankenstein" as monstrous creation, an idea embodied in the neologisms drawn from the word itself. Thus, a judge ruling in a lawsuit against McDonald's Chicken McNuggets condemns this product as "a McFrankenstein creation"; opponents of a cellphone tower designed to look like a fir tree term it "Frankenpine."[11] Whereas these examples provide a verbal analogue to hybrid monsters, others also make the connection to monster-makers. For example, campaigners against "frankenfoods" attack genetically modified foods as monstrous creations, while also targeting the corporations that produce these foods, like Monsanto, as both monster-makers and monsterlike agribusiness giants.[12] Moreover, the metaphor is used by those on the political right as well as the left. For example, Leon Kass, former chairman of President Bush's Council of Bioethics, has excoriated cloning for what he sees as its place on a slippery slope of social wrongs including feminism, single-parenting, gay rights, sex with animals, cannibalism, and the desecration of corpses. Counseling "the wisdom of repugnance" against cloning, Kass condemns "the Frankensteinian hubris to create human life and increasingly to control its destiny."[13]

But if the Frankenstein metaphor is so protean that it sometimes seems to defy categorization, it does have particularly significant forms. I have chosen to begin with examples from left-wing discussions of U.S. foreign policy because they highlight the vitality of the Frankenstein metaphor, in a context far removed from its specific plot of bodily animation, as a contemporary language of political dissent. This book investigates one prehistory of such political critiques, tracking the Frankenstein metaphor in U.S. literature, film, and culture of the past two centuries in relation to the interdependent themes of race and nation. These themes converge in the sustained, multivalent, and revelatory imagery of a black American Frankenstein monster.

Writing in 1860 on the eve of Civil War, Frederick Douglass declared, "Slavery is everywhere the pet monster of the American people."[14] A century later, in the midst of the second Civil War launched by the civil rights movement, comedian and activist Dick Gregory specified the legacy of that "pet monster." When he saw James Whale's *Frankenstein* as a child, Gregory remembered, he realized that "[h]ere was a monster, created by a white man, turning upon his creator. The horror movie was merely a parable of life in the ghetto. The monstrous life of the ghetto has been created by the white man. Only now in the city of chaos are we seeing the monster created by oppression turn upon its creator."[15] In the "now" of 1968, Gregory saw the African American urban uprisings of the era in terms of the monster's revenge against his creator. In the sphere of domestic U.S. race relations, as in that of U.S. foreign policy, *Frankenstein* was the story of blowback.

This study fleshes out the genealogy from Douglass to Gregory and beyond, arguing for the importance of the metaphor of the black Frankenstein monster in nineteenth- and twentieth-century U.S. culture. *Frankenstein* and its legacy have been the subject of substantial amounts of scholarly and popular writing, but little serious attention has been paid to the historical specificities of its place in American culture, and virtually none to its racial resonances in the United States.[16] I take up the question of what happens to the Frankenstein story in America, defining that story in its most basic form as having three distinct elements: a monster is amalgamated from body parts; a monster is reanimated from corpses; and a monster engages in revolt against a creator.[17] Drawn from these elements, the figure of a black Frankenstein monster appears frequently throughout nineteenth- and twentieth-century American culture, in fiction, essays, oratory, film, painting, and other media, and in works by both whites and African Americans. Described as yellow in the novel, painted blue in nineteenth-century stage incarnations, and tinted green in twentieth-century cinematic ones, the monster's color nonetheless signifies symbolically, on the domestic American scene, as black.

In this genealogy of black Frankenstein stories, the figure of the monster is consistently intertwined with fantasies and anxieties about masculinity, relations between men, and the male iconography of the American nation. Within this terrain of masculinity, the Frankenstein metaphor is mutable in its politics. It is sometimes invoked by political conservatives, but it has tended to serve more effectively as a radical condemnation of those in power for making monsters or as a defense of monsters themselves. In a racist culture that already considered black men monstrous and contained them within paternalist rhetoric, the Frankenstein story, with its focus on the literal making of monsters and the unmaking of fathers, provided a stylized rhetoric with which to turn an existing discourse of black monstrosity against itself. Black Frankenstein stories, I argue, effected four kinds of antiracist critique: they humanized the slave; they explained, if not justified, his violence; they condemned the slaveowner; and they exposed the instability of white power.

These arguments about black Frankenstein stories are organized chronologically in four chapters, with an emphasis on the turn of the twentieth century, when fiction by Stephen Crane and Paul Laurence Dunbar articulated the literary possibilities of the black Frankenstein monster most fully. My aim is less to offer a comprehensive historical survey than to trace a network of affiliations clustering at particular historical moments and across literary, cinematic, and other cultural forms. In chapter 1, I show that the imagery of the Frankenstein story is central to U.S. discussions of race and nation in the nineteenth century. The Frankenstein monster served as the dystopian specter of a body politic tenuously assembled from disparate parts, as well as the embodiment of racial uprising in a nation rhetorically founded on the imagery of filial revolt. Beginning with connections forged between the Frankenstein story and accounts of the Nat Turner revolt, I argue for the importance of this story in antebellum writing by Margaret Fuller, John Van Evrie, Herman Melville, and Frederick Douglass; in literary and visual accounts of the rebellious Confederacy by Douglass, Henry Louis Stephens, and Charles Sumner; in the newly codified postwar rhetorics of miscegenation and interracial rape; and in the turn-of-the-century language of African American racial uplift.

I turn in chapters 2 and 3 to more explicitly literary representations of a black Frankenstein monster in turn-of-the-century fiction by Stephen Crane and Paul Laurence Dunbar. In chapter 2, I focus on Crane's *The Monster* (1898), arguing that this novella intertwines a thematic focus on a black monster with an aesthetic inquiry into the resemblance between monsters and metaphors. Situating *The Monster* in the context of late-nineteenth-century rhetoric about metaphor as well as monstrosity, I argue that attention to the novella's figurative surface transforms our understanding of its racial themes as well as of metaphor itself. In chapter 3, I analyze Dunbar's novel *The Sport of the Gods* (1902), which explicitly names its violent black protagonist as a Frankenstein monster, along with other works from throughout Dunbar's career. I argue that Dunbar's writing pivots on the question of parody, a form that is extensively thematized within Shelley's *Frankenstein*, as well as within the African American signifying tradition from which Dunbar drew. Dunbar and Crane, I show, self-reflexively adapt a novel in which the Frankenstein monster is already both a dead metaphor brought to life and a debased and debasing parody of an original.

Twentieth-century black Frankenstein stories, the subject of chapter 4, are dominated by the visual translation of the story into film. I begin by suggesting the aesthetic connections between film form and the Frankenstein monster in two silent films: the Edison *Frankenstein* (1910), the first film version of the novel, and D. W. Griffith's *The Birth of a Nation* (1915), the founding cinematic depiction of blackness as monstrous. I argue that the most famous of *Frankenstein* films, James Whale's 1931 *Frankenstein* and 1935 *Bride of Frankenstein*, are implicit black Frankenstein stories, which update the homoeroticism of Shelley's novel and the Edison *Frankenstein*, while rejecting the racist vocabulary of cinematic monstrosity initiated by Griffith. The film *Blackenstein* (dir. William Levey, 1973) makes explicit the racial implications of the Whale films by situating the monster within the self-parodying aesthetics of blaxploitation horror. Turning in the second half of this chapter to works by black writers, I argue that the figure of a black Frankenstein monster indirectly structures nonfiction of the civil rights and Black Power eras by James Baldwin and Eldridge Cleaver and directly shapes the autobiographies, essays, and performances of Dick Gregory. Gregory brings the oppositional possibilities of a black Frankenstein monster to fruition, moving him from Europe to America via Africa and from white man's gothic specter to black man's comic satire.

In an afterword, I turn to a recent painting by Glenn Ligon, which brings together visual and verbal modes of representing the Frankenstein story in new ways. In so doing, Ligon suggests new configurations of race and sexuality in the black Frankenstein metaphor, while drawing attention to the limits of visibility, of verbalization, and of metaphor as a whole.

Apart from addressing a surprising absence in the scholarship on *Frankenstein*, this book has three major goals. First, this study uses the black Frankenstein metaphor to recast the study of race in U.S. literature and culture. Slavery and its unresolved aftermath have long been understood as a central conflict within American literature, indirectly shaping the works of such canonical white writers as Poe, Melville, Fuller, and Twain, directly organizing the works of such canonical black writers as Douglass, Wright, Ellison, Baldwin, and Morrison, and dominating the popular phenomena of Stowe's *Uncle Tom's Cabin*, Griffith's *Birth of a Nation,* and Mitchell's *Gone with the Wind.* These dozen figures all make appearances in the following pages. *Frankenstein*, I suggest, looks like a quintessentially domestic story once it is brought into, or back into, the United States. The Frankenstein story of monstrous sons and haunted fathers throws U.S. racial formations into high relief and, in so doing, illuminates how these formations have been shaped, reinforced, and opposed in American culture.

This recasting of *Frankenstein* both confirms and complicates Toni Morrison's influential argument, in *Playing in the Dark: Whiteness and the Literary Imagination*, that studying the "Africanist presence" in works by white American authors provides important insight into the construction of whiteness. Images of blackness reveal the contours of whiteness, or in Morrison's phrase, "the subject of the dream is the dreamer."[18] The Frankenstein monster appears at the start of Morrison's study, in a list of literary characters she admires: "I am in awe of the authority of Faulkner's Benjy, James's Maisie, Flaubert's Emma, Melville's Pip, Mary Shelley's Frankenstein."[19] Shelley's *Frankenstein* does not appear again in *Playing in the Dark*, which exclusively analyzes American literature, but I will draw

Shelley into the orbit of Morrison's analysis. *Frankenstein* responds to the terms of *Playing in the Dark*, while extending them to a work that is British in origin and manifestly unfocused on either blackness or whiteness. That the Frankenstein narrative is fantastic as well as foreign increases, rather than impedes, its racial significance to American culture. The English story of a monster made in a European laboratory, I argue, has as domestic a claim on American literary culture as that of the slave in his cabin.

If this study makes a case for the American dimensions of the black Frankenstein story, it also uses *Frankenstein* to situate U.S. culture in an international frame. The field of American Studies has expanded in the last generation from its initial attention to U.S. literature and culture within a domestic context to transatlantic, circumatlantic, transnational, transamerican, hemispheric, and imperialist frameworks.[20] In moving *Frankenstein* into U.S. culture, I also confirm the necessity of keeping it in a transatlantic orbit. As mobile in the early nineteenth century as now, these black Frankenstein accounts journey reciprocally between England and the United States, and among continental Europe and Africa. Such journeys inform the black Frankenstein story at every stage, starting within the novel itself. The transatlantic connection that these chapters chart is not a one-way journey in which race is "added" to *Frankenstein* as it reaches America, but rather a series of criss-crossings in which U.S. representations of the Frankenstein story make visible, and further transform, the complex representations of New World slavery already refracted in the novel.

In charting such crossings, this study contributes to the developing understanding of the orbit that Paul Gilroy has influentially formulated as the "black Atlantic," a hybrid space linking British, American, Caribbean, and African cultures, in which movement among these cultures is mobile and reciprocal.[21] The African American authors under discussion here articulate a black Atlantic sensibility in several registers: Douglass, for example, develops his monster metaphors in dialogue with British abolitionism, whereas Dunbar adapts African cultural forms in his fiction. The resonance of *Frankenstein* with these and other African American writers suggests that a novel by a white British writer has been an important stop in the circulation of the black Atlantic.

In its discussions of white authors responding to slavery, this is also a project in what we might call the "white Atlantic," which I consider less the diacritical opposite to Gilroy's term than a frame overlapping with it.

Marcus Wood has emphasized the mixture of "masochism, paranoia, self-delusion, hypocrisy, anxiety, anger, terror, guilt, horror, and envy which lie, frequently disguised, within English attempts to respond to the legacy of Atlantic slavery."[22] We might call this list a taxonomy of the "white Atlantic" in its most anxious mode, and it is an apt summary both of Victor Frankenstein's own responses to the monster he creates and of the responses to slavery of some of the white American writers under discussion here, such as Thomas Dew and Thomas Dixon. Other authors and artists, however, are not reducible to a language of white anxiety, as with Stephen Crane, and still others criticize this language, as with James Whale. Collectively, these works by whites and African Americans show the transatlantic circulation of Frankenstein imagery in Anglo-American expressions of white anxiety and in African American accounts of antiracist resistance, and also in works, across race, that reflect hybrid mixtures of anxiety and resistance. The black and white Atlantic stories generated in the wake of *Frankenstein* simultaneously suggest the novel's fit with U.S. narratives of race and nation, and the interdependence of those traditions with a broader Atlantic world.

Like Harriet Beecher Stowe's Uncle Tom, the Frankenstein monster is an iconic figure created by a woman writer. As a study in cultural constructions of race—both nationally specific and transatlantically organized—this is, necessarily, an investigation of gender and sexuality in U.S. culture. As more than a quarter century of feminist criticism has shown, Shelley's *Frankenstein* uses its male-centered plots to explore questions about women, including female authorship, maternity, sexuality, and the very field of feminist criticism, which has heavily emphasized Shelley's novel at different stages of its own academic development.[23] *Black Frankenstein* enters this critical genealogy at the juncture of feminist criticism with studies of masculinity. The majority of the works under discussion are by men and about men, and they extend what Bette London terms *Frankenstein*'s own "insistent specularization of masculinity, its story of the male creator making a spectacle of himself."[24] As a study of the spectacle of masculinity, this book is, at times, a study of the spectacle of misogyny; for example, women are sometimes silenced, assaulted, and murdered in these texts. The majority of the works in the black Frankenstein genealogy, that is, replicate *Frankenstein*'s focus on men without actively pursuing its critique of masculinity. In so doing, some of the works in this genealogy confirm some of the sexist gender patterns in American literature first identified by feminist critics. With their plots of men who want,

like Victor Frankenstein, to "penetrate the secrets of nature," these works
—like American classics looking westward to "virgin land"—focus on the
lay of the land. When their creator-figures are undone, these, too, become
melodramas of beset manhood.[25]

Moreover, as a study of men locked in intimate relation to each other,
this project confirms and extends the sexual connotations of Shelley's
Frankenstein on the terrain of American culture. Eve Kosofsky Sedgwick
first identified the organizing tableau of Shelley's *Frankenstein* as that of
"two men chasing one another across a landscape. It is importantly undecidable in this tableau . . . whether the two men represent two consciousnesses or only one; and it is importantly undecidable whether their bond
. . . is murderous or amorous."[26] These stories expand on the novel's interest in relationships between men, from the homoerotic to the homophobic. Panic about sexual intimacy between men conjoins, in the black
Frankenstein tradition, with racist constructions of black sexuality and,
later, with more affirmative accounts of gay possibility. In these dynamics
between men, the black Frankenstein tradition highlights the interracial
male "buddy story" so central to American culture. Some of the stories
under discussion present both creator and creation as African American, but most emphasize a cross-racial contrast between white creator
and black creation. In so doing, they both reveal the anxiety behind the
interracial buddy plots of American culture and suggest tools for radical
inversions of these plots. In the black Frankenstein tradition, white and
black men together are not so much Huck and Jim as Huck and Frank, an
antagonistic pairing in which the black man uses the body made by the
white man as a lethal weapon against him.[27]

My first goal in *Black Frankenstein*, then, is to show how the black
Frankenstein metaphor affirms, and at the same time challenges, structures of race and masculinity in U.S. culture. My second goal is to offer a study in form, for the project is as much about the making of the
Frankenstein metaphor in aesthetic terms as in cultural ones. I explore
the formal elements of this project of metaphor-making at several levels.
At the level of genre, in tracing a genealogy of black Frankenstein stories across nineteenth- and twentieth-century literature and into film, I
bring together the critical frameworks surrounding different forms of the
gothic. Race is now often at the center of studies of nineteenth-century
gothic American literature, but the gothic in twentieth-century literature
is generally routed regionally into discussions of the South, and interpretations of film horror seldom focus on race.[28] Emphasizing racial themes

throughout these different gothic media, I draw particular attention to the centrality of African American writing in and about the gothic. The "black gothic" writers whom I discuss here—Douglass, Dunbar, Baldwin, Cleaver, and Gregory—consistently use the genre to effect a resistant strategy that Teresa Goddu has called "haunting back."[29]

The gothic is not the only genre under transformation here: as the "Frankenfoods," "McFrankenstein," "Frankenpine," and "Cheneystein" examples all suggest, the Frankenstein story often moves from horror into humor. It is no accident that the genealogy of black Frankenstein stories that I trace culminates in the work of a comedian, Dick Gregory. In *Frankenstein*'s theatrical and popular history, humor has often blunted the voice of the monster, but humor has also been used to dismember the story's language of demonization and turn it back against symbolic monster-makers. In this case, comedy provides a form of leverage against racism, a way of laughing back as well as haunting back. The black Frankenstein genealogy, I suggest, forces a rethinking of "black comedy," suggesting that it is a mode as insistently connected to U.S. racial questions as the "blackness" of the gothic.

In addition to questions of genre, issues of form are intrinsic to the Frankenstein story in more structural ways as well. Allegory, for example, is one framework for the readings that follow—I read many of these Frankenstein stories as racial allegories—and allegory itself, as a rhetorical form, has some similarities to the Frankenstein monster. Allegory has often been devalued as flat, artificial, or mechanical—terms that have been applied to the monster too. In Angus Fletcher's influential characterization, allegorical characters seem to act as though possessed by "daemons" and as though they are "robots," a combination for which he explicitly names Shelley's Frankenstein monster one of several "prototypical creations."[30] Allegory has been reexamined in recent literary theory, its pejorative terms both revalued and historicized; in her study of nineteenth-century American literature, for example, Cindy Weinstein shows how descriptions of allegory as a mechanical process correspond to accounts of labor.[31] This study continues the process of reappraising allegory, by identifying a new ground—U.S. race relations—for which the Frankenstein monster's story can serve as a figure and by providing a new way of thinking about his story as, itself, a commentary on the relation between figure and ground.

A major way I consider this relation between figure and ground is through analysis of the structure of parody. Parody is often celebrated in contemporary culture and theory, and *Frankenstein* has frequently been parodied, most famously in Mel Brooks's film *Young Frankenstein* (1974).[32] This study turns attention to the much longer history of parody as a form, analyzing nineteenth-century parodies of *Frankenstein* and the relation of parody to Shelley's novel. At the same time, I explore the role of parody in black cultural practice, particularly as late-nineteenth-century American writers engaged in it. In this project, parody is at once deeply historical and insistently literary, not so much imposed externally on an original text as given proleptic shape by the text that will be its parodic target.

The issue of form most important to this project—without which its analyses of genre, allegory, and parody could not proceed—is that of metaphor. This is a study of a literary metaphor, but one in which metaphor itself has a changing history and a dynamic form. I discuss this history most explicitly in my examination of Crane's *The Monster,* a text hyperbolically attuned to questions of figurative language; in my account of Crane, a specialized form of metaphor—the dead metaphor—has a privileged place. More generally, the making of literary metaphor suffuses the project as a whole. Shelley's Frankenstein monster, I argue, is a metaphor for metaphor itself, and the Frankenstein stories that follow often dramatize the processes whereby metaphors—like monsters—are made. That the Frankenstein stories I analyze raise highly charged racial questions suggests the high stakes involved in taking metaphor seriously as a way of making cultural meaning.

These stories also suggest the importance of taking culture seriously as a way of understanding aesthetic forms. The fields of aesthetics and cultural studies have often been seen as opposed, if not mutually exclusive, with questions of the aesthetic—associated with beauty, taste, artistry, and the figure of the aesthete—fundamentally isolated from cultural, social, and historical issues. This "isolation" of the aesthetic, Raymond Williams suggested a generation ago, "can be damaging," and recently critics have argued for repairing the damage, rethinking the ways in which aesthetic and cultural concerns, in scholarly fields as in objects under study, constitute each other.[33] Insofar as questions of metaphor, parody, and genre usually fall under the domain of aesthetics, and insofar as race and nation are usually taken to be topics grounded in the study of culture, *Black Frankenstein* advances this reparative conversation between fields. Frankenstein metaphors, as I discuss them, have emerged both through cultural frameworks and as aesthetic forms. In turn, the black Frankenstein monster comments on both cultural and aesthetic modes of making metaphor, and on the relations between these modes.

The third goal of this project—intertwined with both cultural and aesthetic questions—is to explore metaphor's politics. As my opening examples from the aftermath of 9/11 suggest, the Frankenstein monster is often invoked in highly politicized situations. The black Frankenstein monster is a key figure in the history of monsters as politically charged forms, as well as in the history of monstrosity as a constitutive feature of the language of politics.[34] The monster overlaps with a variety of politically charged fictional figures, particularly the vampire, the other undead character who was enshrined in nineteenth-century British fiction and who continues to have a robust afterlife.[35] Bram Stoker's *Dracula* (1897) and Mary Shelley's *Frankenstein* (1818) have elicited complementary political interpretations: in an influential Marxist interpretation, for example, Franco Moretti has argued that Dracula exemplifies the bourgeois capitalist and the Frankenstein monster, the alienated proletariat.[36] *Dracula* also has important racial and ethnic connotations, which have been analyzed in connection to Stoker's own Irishness, the eastern European setting of part of the novel, its orientalist and anti-Semitic elements, and its language of blood.[37] The stories under discussion here confirm the political proximity of Frankenstein and vampire images to each other and to U.S. racial narratives. Frederick Douglass and Dick Gregory, for example, use both kinds of images, and their works suggest that the figure of the Frankenstein monster is more productive for a political account of the origins of racial rebellion, whereas that of the vampire works better to depict continuing racial enslavement.

The black Frankenstein monster also converges, at moments, with other politicized monster figures, including the many-headed hydra, the golem, King Kong, and Caliban.[38] Caliban and the Frankenstein monster have consistently been intertwined in U.S. culture, as in an 1833 review of the novel by the *New-York Mirror* that notes that the monster "created by Frankenstein, stands as much alone as Caliban, and, like that, takes a powerful hold on the imagination."[39] More generally, the monster shares with Caliban a history of reappropriation for radical political ends. Caliban has been recast, most famously, by George Lamming, Aimé Césaire, and others writing in Caribbean and Latin American contexts with explicitly anticolonial goals.[40] The political claims of Caliban do diverge from those of the Frankenstein monster, particularly in their relation to origins: Caliban can assert to Prospero, "This island's mine by Sycorax my mother, / Which thou tak'st from me," whereas the Frankenstein monster has neither mother nor mother country.[41] But the reiterations of the monster's story under discussion here, like anticolonial versions of Caliban, similarly exploit the rich political opportunities of the remake. Indeed, since the monster is himself a remade body, his story suggests in particularly self-reflexive terms the political strength of the idea of remaking.

Yet these stories, I suggest, also reveal the political limits of strategies of reappropriation, and of the metaphors on which such strategies rely. Most obviously, the male focus of these stories limits agency for women, and does not do much to enable feminist critique. Even within their own all-male terms, these works suggest the political limits of revisions that invert existing terms rather than creating new ones. Although they undo cultural constructions of monstrous black men and good white fathers, they keep black protagonists constrained within plots that focus on their white antagonists. As racial allegories, they serve better as accounts of the origins of oppression than as outlines for a postrevolutionary future. And as allegories of American identity, these black Frankenstein stories recast, but do not discard, the defining term of nationality, revising rather than undoing the national body of the United States of America. These works remake the metaphors of *Frankenstein* in radical ways, but they also show the difficulty, to paraphrase Audre Lorde, of using the monster's tools to dismantle the monster's house.[42]

A few comments on scope are in order here. The range is wide, across periods, media, and levels of cultural value. Interpreting some canonical works, I also veer consistently toward the noncanonical; many of the works under discussion here are self-consciously lowbrow works about a low-browed monster. Yet while I have loosened boundaries of canonical value, I have tightened standards for what constitutes a usable example. This study is about what is particular to the Frankenstein monster as a metaphor, and what kinds of commentaries those distinctions enable about U.S. culture. Not every monster metaphor in U.S. culture qualifies as a Frankenstein metaphor. Rather, I look for the three elements that I defined earlier as distinctive to the Frankenstein story: amalgamation, reanimation, and revolt against a creator. Every text under discussion here contains at least one of these distinctive elements, most have two, and many have all three.

In writing about black American Frankenstein stories, I have imposed certain limits of medium and chronology to provide focus. The objects of study here are primarily works in print and on film, a focus that leaves many media to be examined. In the genealogy of nineteenth-century American Frankenstein stories, for example, further study awaits on the rich theatrical history of *Frankenstein*. I stop in the early 1990s, leaving others to analyze new media that take the Frankenstein story in fresh directions. Such an analysis might take as foundational Shelley Jackson's hypertext novel *Patchwork Girl* (1995), which interweaves contemporary poststructuralist theory with *Frankenstein* and which imaginatively exploits the congruence between the monster's patchwork body and the disarticulated and recombined elements of hypertext form.[43] Jackson's current project, "Skin," is a short story in which thousands of participants have volunteered, through the Internet, to have a single word of the story tattooed on their bodies. This project suggests the ongoing importance of the Frankenstein story to twenty-first-century media that incorporate extreme forms of embodiment as well as the disembodiments of cyberspace.[44]

Similarly, the national framework of this study is meant to focus inquiry rather than to restrict scope. In analyzing African American themes in these works, I do not claim that racial meanings attach only to American—more specifically, U.S.—Frankensteins; nor do I mean to suggest that race is the only index of Americanization in these texts, as if, for example, the class politics so visible in the novel's British reception are not also a part of the American scene. As H. L. Malchow and Chris Baldick, among others, have shown, racial meanings attach to British versions of the Frankenstein monster, and class politics are intrinsic to American ones.[45] This study aims to complement such works, providing a productive point of departure for rethinking *Frankenstein* in an American Studies context. This context allows us to understand its racial dynamics anew as they are forged in relation to iconographies of the United States, even as these iconographies are themselves forged, in part, in transatlantic conversations.

Although I focus on a black/white axis of representation within U.S. culture, other kinds of racial and ethnic allegories about *Frankenstein* are plentiful and remain open to further study. Orientalism and antiblack racism, for example, intersect in the cultural history of the Frankenstein narrative. One such intersection appears in Ambrose Bierce's short story "Moxon's Master" (1898), a retelling of *Frankenstein* in which the monster—a fez-wearing chess-player with the torso of a gorilla—connotes the putative savagery of both black men and the feminized East.[46] Further inquiry might examine the intersection of black Frankenstein stories with other narratives of race and ethnicity, as these narratives illuminate U.S. culture and as they organize other accounts of national, international, and transnational monstrosity.

Extending beyond works of fiction, further inquiry might also examine the role of the Frankenstein metaphor within contemporary cultural theory. I will cite just two examples. In Donna Haraway's "A Cyborg Manifesto: Science, Technology, and Socialist-Feminism in the Late Twentieth Century" (1985), one of the most influential works of contemporary feminist theory, Shelley's *Frankenstein* is named near the outset. More antagonist than ally, the Frankenstein monster is nonetheless a crucial interlocutor for Haraway as she defines the cyborg: "Unlike the hopes of Frankenstein's monster, the cyborg does not expect its father to save it through a restoration of the garden; that is, through the fabrication of a heterosexual mate, through its completion in a finished whole, a city and cosmos."[47] Less focused on gender but equally attentive to the Frankenstein inheritance is Paul Gilroy's *Postcolonial Melancholia* (2004), an analysis of contemporary multiculturalism in Britain. This work is suffused with Frankenstein references and metaphors, including its opening sentence ("Multicultural society seems to have been abandoned at birth"), its interest in the relation between the "treasure trove of Englishness" and the idea of "frankenfoods," and its analysis of British "shoe bomber" Richard Reid, "who, like Victor Frankenstein's hideous offspring, [chose] a path of destruction as his compensation for exile from kith and kin."[48] That Frankenstein metaphors have such a prominent role in these examples suggests the ongoing importance of Shelley's story as both figure and ground for contemporary theories of culture. If the works under discussion here look backward toward the relation of *Frankenstein* to the black Atlantic, then the highly visible traces of *Frankenstein* in the work of Haraway and Gilroy also suggest looking forward toward new roles for Frankenstein—as metaphor, narrative, and organizing framework—in theorizing race and gender in the future.

The biggest restriction I have imposed on this study is in its focus on male writers. Many women writers have explored the implications of *Frankenstein* for women; I have already noted the importance of Shelley Jackson's hypertext novel *Patchwork Girl*. A fuller account of recent *Frankenstein* fiction by U.S. women writers alone might highlight Katherine Dunn's novel *Geek Love* (1983), which explores the intersection of Frankensteinian monstrosity and the freak show; Rebecca Brown's short story "Dr. Frankenstein, I Presume" (1990), which adapts the plot of the Frankenstein film to narrate the dissolution of a lesbian romance; and Achy Obejas's novel *Memory Mambo* (1996), which uses Frankenstein imagery to condemn a male character who thwarts a romance between women.[49] C. L. Moore's short story "No Woman Born" (1944), which casts a female automaton as a version of the monster, offered an early feminist critique of the novel, one that has become foundational not only to science fiction but also to feminist criticism of the Frankenstein tradition.[50] Women's revisions of *Frankenstein* are confined neither to fiction—they include poetry by Margaret Atwood, Phyllis Gotlieb, and Marge Piercy—nor to North America.[51] Scottish writer Liz Lochhead, for example, has repeatedly returned to *Frankenstein* in several genres, from a play, *Blood and Ice* (1982), which reimagines the scene of *Frankenstein's* creation, to a long poem, "Dreaming Frankenstein" (1984), which captures the monster's ongoing presence in Lochhead's work in its opening lines: "She said she / woke up with him in / her head, in her bed."[52]

These works are related to the questions that I pursue in this project, not least because they involve a variety of issues of racial representation. For example, *Memory Mambo* is centered on a Cuban American protagonist and gives its Frankenstein imagery a Hispanic accent, literally as well as thematically; one character describes the novel's monster as "Jimmy Frankenstein (pronounced Frankhen-ess-tein, since life in Mexico produced a sudden accent in Pauli's English)."[53] Racial issues inflect works by white women that focus on white characters, as in *Geek Love*, whose freak-show setting is inseparable from histories of exoticism, ethnography, and racial display.[54] But these works do not intersect directly with the black Frankenstein genealogy as I trace it here, a genealogy centered on conflicts between and within men in the United States in the aftermath of slavery.

Nor do I focus on the wealth of works that focus explicitly on the construction of female monsters. Such stories, which can be traced back to the Pygmalion myth, are particularly prominent in films since *Bride of Frankenstein*. They range from *Frankenhooker* (dir. Frank Henenlotter, 1990), in which a boy from New Jersey reanimates his dead girlfriend from the body parts of Times Square prostitutes, to *The Silence of the Lambs* (dir. Jonathan Demme, 1991), in which a male serial killer constructs a new female body from his victims—one of many transgender uses of the monster plot—and plays Victor Frankenstein to himself.[55] More generally, the idea of a "Bride of Frankenstein" remains one of the most fecund legacies of the Frankenstein story; the phrase "bride of ——" has become its own self-contained generator of parody. In a *Far Side* cartoon by Gary Larson, for example, the Frankenstein monster is shown sitting behind the wheel of a car, handing money to a policeman; the caption reads, "The Bribe of Frankenstein."[56] That the phrase "bribe of ——" still evokes a female monster despite the absence of even the word "bride" suggests yet another of the formal connections between the body parts of a monster and the body of writing devoted to it. Even and especially in an account of monstrosity between men, the female monster is still the Frankenstein story's phantom limb.

In part because there is now such a wealth of feminist criticism in this field, and in part because I have written elsewhere on feminism and *Frankenstein*, I do not discuss female monstrosity at length until this study's final chapter, when Whale's *Bride of Frankenstein* and its successors intersect directly with the black Frankenstein tradition.[57] A full account of women writers' engagement with the Frankenstein story—and of the "bride of" genealogy, with or without actual female bodies—remains this study's own phantom limb. At the same time, a woman writer remains the foundational body, anterior whole rather than auxiliary part, behind this project. Mary Shelley is foundational to the Franken-American and African American monsters who populate this book. Intersecting with a national narrative already devoted to founding fathers, her work does not so much originate as reshape that narrative. Neither secondary bride nor founding mother, she is, symbolically speaking, stepmother to the American Frankenstein lineage. As we will see, the metaphors that her story has generated—metaphors formally made, remade, and unmade in ways that her monster himself prefigures—are central to U.S. culture of the past two centuries, and they continue to blow forward as well as back.

1

United States of Frankenstein

Slavery is everywhere the pet monster of the American people.
—Frederick Douglass, "Slavery and the Irrepressible Conflict"

I.

In 1831, American newspapers were filled with the story of a "monster in iniquity," a murderer whose violent rampage constituted "a spectacle from which the mind must shrink with horror." The monster was found upon capture to be surprisingly articulate, and his story, published in a popular narrative mediated by several different voices, was considered "eloquently and classically expressed." This murderer sounds very much like the monster of Mary Shelley's novel *Frankenstein*, who kills his creator's brother, bride, and best friend, and who is also a figure of surprising eloquence in the first-person story that he tells at the center of the novel's multiple layers of narration. *Frankenstein*, first published in 1818, had renewed visibility in 1831, when it was republished in Britain in a revised edition. But the "monster" reported in the news in this year was a real person, an African American slave; his crimes, assisted by a dozen others, were the murders of his master and some sixty other white people in Southampton County, Virginia; and his account was the document that came to be known as *The Confessions of Nat Turner*.[1]

   This parallel between Frankenstein and the most famous slave revolt in U.S. history provides an important point of origin for the cultural history of the figure of a black Frankenstein monster in American culture. To begin with, the parallel did not go unremarked at the time. The Turner revolt occasioned extensive debate over emancipation in the Virginia state legislature, and this debate, in turn, prompted proslavery apologist Thomas Dew to write a lengthy defense of slavery. Late in the essay, he quoted from a speech by George Canning, the British foreign secretary:

In dealing with a negro we must remember that we are dealing with a being possessing the form and strength of a man, but the intellect only of a child. To turn him loose in the manhood of his physical passions . . . would be to raise up a creature resembling the splendid fiction of a recent romance; the hero of which constructs a human form with all the physical capabilities of man, and with the thews and sinews of a giant, but being unable to impart to the work of his hands a perception of right and wrong, he finds too late that he has only created a more than mortal power of doing mischief, and himself recoils from the monster which he has made.[2]

Canning's words were from an 1824 parliamentary debate about the emancipation of West Indian slaves; the British slave trade had been formally abolished in 1807, but slavery did not end until the Emancipation Act of 1833. His allusion to the "splendid fiction of a recent romance" was, most likely, to Richard Brinsley Peake's 1823 stage adaptation of *Frankenstein* rather than to Shelley's novel. His comment was one of many nineteenth-century conservative British uses of the Frankenstein story as a cautionary tale of social rebellion. Canning supported the abolition of the slave trade, but he favored a gradualist approach to ending slavery, and, in this speech, he argued against the immediate emancipation of West Indian slaves. He used the imagery of the Frankenstein story to represent the enslaved West Indian man as a mischievous and irrational child, albeit one with the "physical passions" of "adult manhood."[3]

In quoting this passage, Thomas Dew brought together not only the Frankenstein monster with Nat Turner but also West Indian with North American slavery. *Frankenstein*, a British novel set primarily in continental Europe, translated smoothly to an American setting, although this was not so much a translation as a retranslation, since Dew restated the fear of black rebellion in the Americas to which Canning had already given voice; as we will see, this fear is already present in *Frankenstein* itself. Dew's use of Canning is an expression of the reciprocal and mutually defining circulation of racial anxieties in Anglo-America, anxieties shaped here by the white experience and imagination of slavery. As Dew's words suggest, the Frankenstein monster was a figure equally at home on the symbolically related sites, the West Indies and Virginia, in which slavery was practiced, as well as in the complementary political assemblies, the British parliament and the Virginia state legislature, in which the slave's fate was debated.

Yet the relocation of the Frankenstein monster from a British debate about slavery to an American one also changed the monster's meaning. Thomas Dew enlisted the figure of the Frankenstein monster on different political grounds than Canning, arguing unambiguously against abolitionism and in support of slavery. His words also changed the ground of the metaphor in another sense. Canning had spoken to British parliament about slave rebellions that could take place in the distant West Indies, but Dew was writing about rebellions that had already come intimately within the homes of white Virginians. Locating the monster within his home country, Dew made his threat all the more terrifying. As Virginia politician James McDowell noted in 1832, "a Nat Turner might be in every family."[4] Invading the domestic interiors of homes and bedrooms, Nat Turner had menaced the supreme icons of domesticity, white women, and he had penetrated the most volatile white interior of all: the psyche. After the Southampton revolt, Dew notes, "reason was almost banished from the mind, and the imagination was suffered to conjure up the most appalling phantoms."[5] The white slaveowner from whose mind "reason" had been "banished" would henceforth be haunted by the "appalling phantoms" of slave revolt.

The literary genre for representing such phantoms is the gothic, and the writings of the American architect of the genre in this period, Edgar Allan Poe, are haunted by the story of his fellow Virginian, Nat Turner. Images of slave rebellion structure Poe's fiction: the black servant, Jupiter, who threatens to whip his white master in "The Gold-Bug"; the orangutan who murders two white women in "The Murders in the Rue Morgue," in an era when racist anthropology habitually aligned black people and orangutans; the dwarf court jester who costumes his tyrannical employer-king as an orangutan and then murders him in "Hop-Frog"; and, above all, the black inhabitants of a mysterious South Sea Island who first appear to befriend and then rise up violently against the white protagonist of Poe's *Narrative of Arthur Gordon Pym*. Displaced across location to foreign settings, across species to the orangutan, and across bodily norms to the dwarf, these narratives refract white American fears of slave revolt.[6]

Like Poe's fiction, Shelley's *Frankenstein* offers an oblique account of white anxiety in the face of slave rebellion. Like Poe, Shelley presents a white protagonist who is haunted and undone by the rebellious monster whom he has created. In turn, we could see Poe's *Pym* as his version of *Frankenstein*, since its plot features several of the same ingredients as Shelley's novel: ship mutinies, monstrous "savages," episodes in which corpses appear to come back to life, and a setting near the edge of the Earth. *Frankenstein* begins and ends near the North Pole, and *Pym* ends near the South Pole, a setting with white birds and animals and a mysterious gigantic figure of "perfect whiteness."[7] Toni Morrison has argued that these images of whiteness at the conclusion of *Pym* offer a "strong suggestion of paralysis and incoherence; of impasse and non sequitur."[8] *Frankenstein* falls outside the scope of Morrison's study, but as with the South Pole of *Pym*, we can see the North Pole of *Frankenstein* as Shelley's meditation on the "impasse" of whiteness in the face of slave rebellion. The North Pole, where the monster appears at the start of the novel and where Victor Frankenstein dies at its end, signifies not the omnipotence of whiteness but rather its impotence. In Shelley's anxious account, the North Pole is a land of frozen whiteness where the white man can only draw his dying breath.

In bringing *Frankenstein* to America, then, Thomas Dew showed how the figure of the monster could be used to condemn rebellious slaves, but his comment also made visible the gothic specter of the white slaveowner undone by his rebellious creation. Shelley's novel emphasizes this specter, focusing on Victor Frankenstein's decline and censoring him for his treatment of his creation. The monster's violence in the novel is not the consequence of putatively premature emancipation from slavery, as George Canning and Thomas Dew suggested, but the result of abandonment and abuse. The monster does not initially think of himself as monstrous; he must be taught to do so by others. In Shelley's account, monstrosity is socially as well as literally constructed, and this social construction is laid bare for the reader's condemnation. The novel is not so much a conservative fantasy as a radical caution to those in power against creating the conditions that will result in rebellion against them.

Destabilizing the slaveowner, *Frankenstein* also humanized the slave. Like the slave who is forced to take his master's surname, the monster who has come mistakenly to be known only as "Frankenstein" is an eloquent figure whose sufferings, like those of the protagonists of slave narratives, command the reader's sympathy. Formally, too, the structure of *Frankenstein* is not unlike that of a slave narrative. The monster's first-person story is mediated by two white men's voices, Captain Walton and Victor Frankenstein—as, for example, Frederick Douglass's narrative was enfolded within the authenticating frames of Wendell Phillips and William Lloyd Garrison. *The Confessions of Nat Turner* offered an extreme version of the racial hierarchy involved in such framing, since Turner's words were rearranged by Thomas Gray, an impoverished slaveowner hoping to profit from the *Confessions*.[9] *Frankenstein* both imitates and revises the slave narrative's structures of mediation. As in a slave narrative, the monster's story is framed by those of others; his first-person story is retold by Victor to Walton. As the frame recedes, the monster's voice seems to stand alone and undistorted in its relation to the novel's reader.[10]

Nat Turner's words are, however, unlike those of the monster in *Frankenstein*, since Turner's account is dominated by divine portents of millennial violence. In African American literature of this era, a voice closer to that of Shelley's monster appears in the 1829 *Appeal to the Coloured Citizens of the World*, the antislavery manifesto authored by free African American David Walker. At the outset of the *Appeal*, Walker declares that "we Coloured People of these United States, are, the most wretched, degraded and abject set of beings that ever lived."[11] He prophesies the revenge of the abject:

> [W]hat is the use of living, when in fact I am dead. But remember, Americans, that as miserable, wretched, degraded and abject as you have made us in preceding and, in this generation, to support you and your families, that some of you, (whites) on the continent of America, will yet curse the day that you ever were born. (72)

For Walker, slaves are like living corpses, "made" by white oppression and symbolically deadened by slavery, but soon to be brought to life by rebellion. This language resonates with that of Mary Shelley's creation, a self-described "poor, helpless, miserable wretch," who declares, "I will revenge my injuries. . . . I will work at your destruction . . . so that you shall curse the hour of your birth."[12] Although there is no evidence that Walker read Shelley, the substantial rhetorical overlap between these passages suggests the affinity of *Frankenstein* with the vocabulary of racial rebellion. This was a vocabulary to which David Walker gave nonfictional voice but for which Mary Shelley had provided a fictional blueprint: a story about a monster whose body incarnates the political ideas of collectivity and reawakening and whose behavior signals political revolt. "Remember that I have power," declares Shelley's monster, sounding like David Walker: "I can make you so wretched that the light of day will be hateful to you. You are my creator, but I am your master—obey!" (116).

Echoing *Frankenstein*'s account of reversible mastery and enslavement, Walker's *Appeal* also suggests the overlap between *Frankenstein* and spe-

cifically American iconographies of national identity. In the early nineteenth century, dominant narratives of national origins presented the
United States as the patrilineal creation of Founding Fathers. This birth
myth was all-male, with men laboring to make a male baby America, and
all-white, with Founding Fathers who were themselves slaveholders ex-
cluding slaves from American citizenship. Reappropriating this iconography, African American men stayed within its male terms but criticized its
racism. David Walker, for example, uses the Declaration of Independence
against itself: "Compare . . . your Declaration of Independence, with your
cruelties and murders inflicted by your cruel and unmerciful fathers and
yourselves on our fathers and on us" (75). So great is the suffering of
slaves, suggests Walker, that "America is more our country, than it is the
whites—we have enriched it with our *blood and tears*" (65). Walker's *Appeal* exemplifies what Eric Sundquist has outlined as a central irony of
this era: that rebel slaves, excluded from dominant definitions of American identity, were actually its best exemplars of nationhood. As Sundquist
puts it, "The slave, not the master, was the truer American."[13]

Compare *Frankenstein*: it too is an all-male story of origins in which
a Founding Father ignores his son, and it too offers a sympathetic coun-
ternarrative in which a revolutionary son exposes the hypocrisy of that
father and demands rights and recognition from him. In *Frankenstein,* as
in David Walker's *Appeal*, it is the enslaved monster, angrily offering his
own declaration of independence, who is the truer republican citizen. The
closest symbolic descendants of Frankenstein in antebellum America are
illegitimate black sons, debased from and by their white paternal foundations. Yet in real-life antebellum America, the voice of the master trumped
that of the slave: Thomas Dew, a respected member of the Virginia elite,
became president of the College of William and Mary, while Nat Turner
was caught, tried, and executed, and his body probably given to surgeons
for dissection.[14] We can see Mary Shelley's Frankenstein monster, whose
body is assembled from corpses stolen from dissecting rooms, as antici-
pating and avenging Nat Turner's fate. In the end of Nat Turner's body
was the Frankenstein monster's beginning, or to put it another way, the
united states of the body of the Frankenstein monster were, from the
start, not only American but African American.

In this chapter, I explore the consequences of this beginning, analyzing
the meaning of the Frankenstein story in nineteenth-century U.S. literature and culture. Building an archive of nineteenth-century references

to the story, I argue for the importance of this archive to narratives of national self-definition and racial revolt. As the examples of Thomas Dew and David Walker suggest, the works under discussion are uneven in their proximity to *Frankenstein*; Dew makes reference to a theatrical version of the novel, while Walker's imagery is only homologous with it. Both Dew and Walker, however, wrote in a culture in which crisis over slavery prompted a heightened interest in the gothic imagery of rebellion, an imagery for which Mary Shelley had provided an organizing template. Even when Frankenstein is not named as a direct source, traces of this template suffuse U.S. culture throughout the nineteenth century because the novel had so effectively given form to existing vocabularies of rebellion. Politically, these vocabularies are diverse: as the examples of Dew and Walker also suggest, the works under discussion exploit both conservative and radical dimensions of the Frankenstein story. But although the story was used by political conservatives, it was more compatible, I argue, with a radical language of racial rebellion. Across the political spectrum, moreover, these works show the intimacy of the story with questions of national self-definition. They suggest the importance of *Frankenstein* as a story at once transatlantic in origins and specific to questions of national and racial formation in the nineteenth-century U.S. body politic.

I begin with an analysis of *Frankenstein*'s origins. The novel's multivalent sources include British debates over slavery, abolition, and racial mixture, along with those over empire, revolution, and class conflict. Examining *Frankenstein* in its British context highlights the importance of race to its history, but it also suggests the difficulty of keeping a stable frame —political or aesthetic—for consideration of the novel's influence. The political valences of the novel are complicated not only by the multiplicity of sources from which it derives but also from the aesthetic complexities of its recirculation in nineteenth-century British culture.

I then turn to American culture in the wake of the Nat Turner revolt, arguing for the importance of the Frankenstein story to U.S. concerns about national and racial identity. The Frankenstein story resonates with the antebellum rhetoric of national self-making, as suggested in Margaret Fuller's essay "American Literature," which uses an extended Frankenstein metaphor to anchor its discussion of literary nationalism. The racial connotations of the Frankenstein story in this period, which are made explicit in a political caricature by Frank Bellew, inflect proslavery polemics by John Van Evrie and George Fitzhugh. Fiction by Herman Melville and nonfiction by Frederick Douglass, however, suggest the stronger link between the Frankenstein story and antebellum critiques of slavery. These writers draw the monster into two different modes of antislavery thought: Melville's adaptation of *Frankenstein* in "The Bell-Tower" indicts the slave-owner, while Douglass's writing more indirectly suggests how the monster could serve as an oppositional symbol of the African American slave, the American nation, and the conflicted relationship between them.

Turning to Civil War rhetoric, I argue that secession and emancipation recast the imagery of the Frankenstein monster in important ways. In the crisis of the war, the monster does not lose his racial connotations, but he also incarnates the rebellious white South, in political caricature by Henry Louis Stephens and in the writings of Charles Sumner and Frederick Douglass. Finally, I argue that the Frankenstein story shadows racial rhetoric at the turn of the century. Intersecting with that racist rhetoric at its nadir in works by Thomas Dixon and Eleanor Tayleur, the monster is refashioned more complexly in poetry that appeared in an African American publication for the 1893 World's Columbian Exposition. Throughout the century, I argue, the Frankenstein story both reflects and reshapes U.S. narratives of race and nation. "American Frankenstein" is a redundancy rather than an oxymoron, for the intertwined national and racial narratives of nineteenth-century America, I suggest, take their form from *Frankenstein*.

II.

As scholars of British Romanticism have shown, poetry, fiction, and other writing produced in Britain in the early nineteenth century was influenced in many ways by transatlantic accounts of slavery, slave uprising, abolitionism, and other discussions of race.[15] In the case of Mary Shelley, there are numerous biographical connections—outlined most substantially by H. L. Malchow—between *Frankenstein* and contemporary British discussions of race. The child of William Godwin and Mary Wollstonecraft, two of the most radical political intellectuals of the era, Mary Shelley was familiar with antislavery rhetoric from her father; her reading about colonial exploration and black people included Mungo Park's *Travels in the Interior Districts of Africa* (1799) and Bryan Edwards's *History, Civil and Commercial, of the British Colonies in the West Indies* (1793); before writing *Frankenstein*, she lived near Bristol, a center of the British slave trade; and she is likely to have read accounts of the violent revolutionary uprising in Saint-Domingue that led to the establishment of Haiti in 1804.[16] Within *Frankenstein*, the monster's large size, unusual strength, and physical agility are consistent with contemporary stereotypes of Africans and West Indians. His skin, first described as "yellow" ("His yellow skin scarcely covered the work of muscles and arteries beneath; his hair was of a lustrous black" [34]) later becomes "in color . . . like that of a mummy" (152)—literally, either brown or black. More important, the monster's behavior reflects contemporary anxieties about black uprising. Edwards, for example, suggested that "the Negroes . . . when invested with command, give full play to their revengeful passions; and exercise all the wantonness of cruelty without restraint or remorse."[17] As a destructive, vengeful figure, the Frankenstein monster incarnates white fears about black power.

Invoking racial uprising, the Frankenstein monster also suggests contemporary fears about racial mixture. "Amalgamation" was the term used in this era to denote interracial combination, and the monster is its embodiment; he exemplifies what Gobineau called the "horror excited by the possibility of infinite intermixture."[18] Moreover, the child of amalgamation, the mulatto, was considered by some to be a scientific anomaly as well as a social abomination. In the pseudoscience of polygenesis, blacks and whites were thought to be of different species, and their offspring sterile. The monster's inability to reproduce, which prompts his request that Victor Frankenstein construct a female mate for him, echoes the sterility hypothesis of polygenesis.[19]

Finally, the monster's story embodies fears about interracial rape. Images of black men raping white women were already a part of the racial discourse of Shelley's era, and in the assault of the monster on Elizabeth, *Frankenstein* evoked such images. This evocation is enhanced, as Malchow notes, in Shelley's alterations to the 1831 edition of the novel.[20] Changing Elizabeth from Victor's cousin to a foundling, Shelley now made her "a different stock" from other Italian orphans, "very fair. Her hair was the brightest living gold, . . . her blue eyes cloudless."[21] The 1831 *Frankenstein* presented an even whiter Elizabeth than before, and her violation by the monster drew implicitly from the racist discourse of interracial rape, as well as from fears of the monstrously mixed mulatto and the dangerously rebellious slave.

Yet Shelley herself was an abolitionist, who with her husband, Percy, boycotted sugar because of its connection to the slave trade.[22] While *Frankenstein* replicates the anxieties of the slaveowner, it more powerfully echoes contemporary abolitionist defenses of the slave. Articulate and eloquent, the monster is a sympathetic figure, pleading for acceptance in a world that shuns him; like a slave, the monster in the novel is denied even his own surname. This sympathetic characterization echoes white British defenses of the slave's humanity, as well as attacks on slavery in West Indian–authored slave narratives such as that of Mary Prince.[23] Other aspects of *Frankenstein*—its isolated monster, its themes of navigation and travel, its interest in Turkey and the polar regions—evoke the slave narrative of Olaudah Equiano, which circulated widely in Shelley's world.[24] Yet abolitionism had its own biases, and *Frankenstein* also replicated its tendency to depict slaves as pitiable victims, dependent on white beneficence. "Make me happy," pleads the monster to Victor in Shelley's novel, "and I shall again be virtuous" (66). As Malchow suggests, even in the ostensibly more antiracist imagery of abolitionist whites, "the idealized black, although a 'man and a brother,' is inevitably still on his knees as a grateful man and a younger brother."[25] Reflecting the goals and the limitations of contemporary abolitionism, Shelley rescues her monster from the status of frightening brute, but she does so by making him a dependent victim.

Racial questions in *Frankenstein* are intertwined with colonial ones, and the same political ambiguities that structure the novel's relation to race inform its account of empire. As Gayatri Chakravorty Spivak first argued, the novel repeatedly locates its characters in relation to the imageries of orientalism and imperial conquest of this period.[26] Again, there is biographical evidence for these connections: Shelley had read widely in the literature of imperialism and orientalism, and she had close contact with members of the East India Company.[27] Visually, the monster's "yellow" color seems more evidently Asian than African; Anne K. Mellor argues that he represents a "new version of [the] Yellow Man, the image of the Mongol as a giant."[28] The novel is also suffused with orientalist imagery that privileges the civilizing West over the uncivilized East. This imagery is most evident in the character of Safie, whose father is a Muslim Turk and whose mother was "a Christian Arab, seized and made a slave by the Turks"; Safie is "sickened at the prospect of again returning to Asia and being immured within the walls of a haram [*sic*]" (83). Walton, aiming to "tread a land never before imprinted by the foot of man" (7), is engaged in an exploratory project with imperialist overtones: heading over the North Pole, he wants to reach India and the East.[29] Henry Clerval, student of "Persian, Arabic, and Hebrew" and "the works of the orientalists" (43), is the novel's most overt imperialist. In a passage Shelley added to the 1831 edition, she made Clerval's goals explicit: "His design was to visit India, in the belief that he had in his knowledge of its various languages, and in the views he had taken of its society, the means of materially assisting the progress of European colonisation and trade" (153).

As *Frankenstein* opposes the racist discourse from which it draws, so too does the novel criticize an imperialist hierarchy. It is sympathetic toward its colonized subjects, the monster and Safie, and harsh toward the ostensibly civilized world that treats them brutally. Again, however, the novel is uneven as an anticolonial intervention, since it situates its colonized characters as victims and defines them in relation to their colonizers. Qualifying her earlier praise of the novel, Spivak argues that "Shelley's emancipatory vision cannot extend beyond the speculary situation of the colonial enterprise, where the master alone has a history, master and subject locked up in the cracked mirror of the present, and the subject's future, although indefinite, is vectored specifically toward and away from the master."[30] Mary Shelley treats her monster sympathetically, but she positions him within the slaveowning and colonial enterprises, moving him "toward and away from the master" rather than in a direction entirely his own.

The racial and imperial valences of *Frankenstein* are, in turn, inseparable from other vocabularies of political conflict. The most identifiable political source for *Frankenstein* is the conservative reaction against the French Revolution articulated by Edmund Burke. Developing an antirevolutionary rhetoric of monstrosity, Burke employed metaphors with the three signature traits of the Frankenstein story: amalgamation, reanimation, and filial revolt. He combined plural images of monstrosity with composited ones, condemning revolutionary France as not only a "world of Monsters" but also a "monstrous compound."[31] This compound was reanimated, for "out of the tomb of the murdered monarchy in France has arisen a vast, tremendous, unformed spectre."[32] The result, for Burke, was the most extreme version of revolt: parricide. Armed insurrection would "immediately degenerate into . . . a species of political monster, which has always ended by devouring those who have produced it."[33]

Transforming Burke, *Frankenstein* adapted more widespread political rhetorics of the body politic. The Frankenstein monster is a descendant of the "many-headed hydra," another image of unnaturally amalgamated and uncontrollable body parts, which first emerged in seventeenth-century British discussions of social rebellion from below.[34] Similarly, the monster embodies aspects of the working-class rebels of the 1810s known as Luddites, and he anticipates the imagery of Marx in several ways: he is at once a symbol of the alienated proletariat turned rebel and an incarnation of the assembled product of labor made under capitalism.[35] The body of Shelley's fictional monster also incarnates class controversies in more material ways. As Tim Marshall has shown, the novel resonates with contemporary British controversies over the practice of graverobbing, which involved the exploitation of corpses of the poor for scientific research and which culminated in the 1832 Anatomy Act giving anatomists access to unclaimed corpses.[36] The multiple meanings of class in *Frankenstein* extend from the real-life bodies of the poor from which Shelley drew to the way her fictional metaphors prefigure the theoretical foundations of Marxism.

These political allegories about race, empire, revolution, and class are not mutually exclusive; indeed, they are mutually interdependent, in the sources from which Shelley drew as well as in the novel itself. For example, Burke's critique of the excesses of the French Revolution is inextricable from his horror at revolutionary uprising in Haiti and at the "savagery" of Native Americans.[37] Nor are the political valences of these mutually constituted allegories fixed: Shelley's novel expresses radical as well as reactionary responses toward revolt.

The novel's political meanings became less multivalent, however, as it circulated in nineteenth-century Britain and underwent extraordinary transformations in popular culture. Such transformations began with the text of *Frankenstein* itself. The 1831 edition differed substantially from that of 1818: Shelley altered some existing passages, added substantial new ones, and included a new introduction, whose account of the story's genesis in a ghost-story competition became intertwined with the novel.[38] From this unstable novelistic foundation, the story proliferated rapidly in other media. The first theatrical adaptation, Richard Brinsley Peake's *Presumption; or, The Fate of Frankenstein* (1823) was so successful that it inspired fourteen other dramatizations within three years, and these dramatizations of *Frankenstein* were themselves immediately parodied. Theatrical adaptations increasingly displaced Shelley's *Frankenstein*. The novel was not readily available from the 1850s to the 1890s, a limitation that increased the extent to which popular understanding of the story mutated from its literary source.[39] As Chris Baldick suggests, the "myth of Frankenstein" far outstripped *Frankenstein*, so that the "series of adaptations, allusions, accretions, analogues, parodies, and plain misreadings which follows upon

Mary Shelley's novel is not just a supplementary component of the myth; it *is* the myth."[40]

The growth of the "myth of Frankenstein" had conservative political consequences. Shelley's own changes to the 1831 edition seem to have been motivated by her increasing self-presentation as a respectable widow. In altering the character of Elizabeth, for example, from a cousin of Victor's to a foundling, she removed from their romantic relationship any taint of incest. Yet her revisions are elsewhere more ambiguous; for example, the new material on Clerval as a colonizer strengthens the novel's anti-imperialist critique.[41] Whatever the ambiguities of Shelley's changes, however, theatrical adaptations of the novel clearly narrowed its politics. As Steven Forry has shown, dramatizations of *Frankenstein*, moving it into melodrama and burlesque, simplified it. The novel's epistolary frame and multiple narrators were eliminated and its number of characters reduced; the creation scene and the murder of Elizabeth were emphasized; and the comic figure of the laboratory assistant was introduced. Most important, the thematic doubling between Victor and the monster was diminished, with both Victor and the monster flattened into stock characters: Victor became the tragic overreacher, while the monster, dumbed-down and literally mute, was a violent brute.[42]

Insofar as these plays developed the racial implications of Shelley's novel, they did so in ways that flattened its antiracist critique. In some productions, for example, orientalism became only a question of costume; in *Presumption*, for example, Safie is described as wearing a "turban head-dress" and silk trousers "to give an Oriental appearance."[43] Other productions drew from the genre of "Wild Man" dramas, which included plays about runaway slaves, and portrayed the monster as brutish.[44] Even the nominal shift of the term "Frankenstein" to mean monster rather than creator—a shift that was disseminated in plays of the 1830s such as the ambiguously titled *Frankenstein; or, The Monster*—contributed to this effect. In Shelley's novel, the monster had no name because his identity had been systematically denied him, and he gave eloquent voice to that denial. As the novel circulated in nineteenth-century theater, however, the creator's name assigned to him displaced the novel's careful exploration of the political consequences of namelessness. He lost his voice.

In popular allusions to the story as well as these direct revisions of it, "Frankenstein" became a ready political metaphor for condemnations of social rebellion. When George Canning invoked "the splendid fiction of a recent romance" in 1824, he was only one of many conservatives who seized on the imagery of the monster to condemn social rebellion. Numerous English political cartoons, for example, attacked Irish nationalism by representing it as a monster and disparaging it as the "Irish Frankenstein."[45] Such images recapitulated the novel's own intimate relation to conservative political vocabularies, while excising its critique of them. Political cartoons, theatrical productions, and comments like those of George Canning did not so much reinvent the story conservatively as centrifuge from it the conservative vocabularies of race, empire, class, and nation within and against which *Frankenstein* had emerged.

III.

As in Britain, *Frankenstein* in America was a textual hybrid. American readers had access to both the 1818 and 1831 editions, and audiences saw theatrical adaptations of *Frankenstein* as early as 1825.[46] But long before Americans discovered Shelley's monster, her monster had already discovered America. At the center of *Frankenstein*, during the monster's first-person narrative of his wanderings, he eavesdrops outside the De Lacey cottage: "I heard of the discovery of the American hemisphere and wept with Safie over the hapless fate of its original inhabitants" (80). The monster is listening to Felix De Lacey instruct Safie from Volney's *The Ruins; or, Meditation on the Revolutions of Empires* (1793), a politically radical argument for equality and democracy.[47] This moment marks the identification of one of the novel's marginalized figures, its literal monster, with a second, Safie, whose associations with Turkey and Islam position her at the eastern edge of the Christian West; like the monster, Safie is "unacquainted with the language of the country, and utterly ignorant of the customs of the world" (85). Both the monster and Safie identify, in turn, with the margins of empire: the Native Americans decimated by European colonization and expelled outside the boundaries of the United States. This is an anticolonial moment of discovery, in which the novel's own marginalized figures are moved through tears to identify with and through the margins of America.

This moment is, surprisingly, built on a false foundation, for Volney's *Ruins*—which Shelley probably learned about from her husband—does not discuss Native American Indians.[48] Whether deliberate or not, this error in *Frankenstein* has thematic implications. The monster's error has the effect of decentering the pedagogic authority of Felix and Volney—

and, by extension, Percy Shelley—in favor of a more direct bond with the "original inhabitants" of America. As misshapen monster and uneducated half-Turkish girl, the monster and Safie are themselves poor copies of their pedagogic originals. As it comes into view within *Frankenstein*, then, America is aligned with socially marginal figures such as Indians, Turks, and monsters and with culturally marginal forms such as imitations and misreadings. Within Shelley's novel, America represents not only the social margins but also the margin of error.

What did *Frankenstein* represent within the margins of America, particularly the United States?[49] There are many ways to approach this question, including through contemporary developments in social history. As Michael Sappol has shown, for example, there was fierce debate in antebellum America about the dissection of bodies for medical purposes, involving riots against medical schools and the passage of legislation; issues of class fueled this debate, which centered on making the unclaimed bodies of the poor available to doctors for dissection. A widespread fascination with dissection can accordingly be found throughout antebellum American literature. For example, John Hovey Robinson's novel *Marietta; or, The Two Students: A Tale of the Dissecting Room and "Body Snatchers"* (1842) features graverobbing and dissection, and George Lippard's bestselling sensation novel *The Quaker City; or, The Monks of Monk Hall* (1845) includes a scene in which a mad male doctor decapitates a beautiful female patient.[50] These novels seem influenced by *Frankenstein*, but the influence went both ways, since controversy about the dissection of bodies increased interest in *Frankenstein*. The novel circulated rapidly in a culture in which, as Gary Laderman suggests, "Readers were hungry for shocking representations of opening, destroying, and peering inside a corpse."[51] More generally, *Frankenstein* participated in what Russ Castronovo has identified as a cultural obsession with death—in seances, ghost stories, accounts of suicide, and other forms—so great that nineteenth-century America can be characterized as a world of "necro citizenship."[52]

If the historical debate about corpses forms one point of departure for thinking about *Frankenstein* in America, then another is the symbolic linkage between the novel's rhetoric of Prometheus and the iconography of the Founding Fathers.[53] *Frankenstein*'s subtitle is "The Modern Prometheus," and it refers to two stories associated with Prometheus: he is the mortal who steals fire from the gods and is punished by being chained to a rock and having vultures peck out his liver, and he is the "plasticator" of man, who molds him from clay. As Stuart Curran has shown, Prometheus was frequently associated with the imagery of America, the American Revolution, and the Founding Fathers. In Joel Barlow's epic poem *The Columbiad*, for example, Columbus sees America as a land where "Freedom, his new PROMETHEUS, here shall rise." The epic poem *Washington, or Liberty Restored* by Thomas Northmore presented George Washington as "Prometheus-like, / He'd stand unmov'd amid the wreck of worlds."[54]

A different set of connections links Victor Frankenstein to another Founding Father, Benjamin Franklin. Shelley alluded to Franklin's experiments with electricity in Victor's narrative in *Frankenstein*: "I eagerly inquired of my father the nature and origin of thunder and lightning. He replied 'Electricity.' . . . he made also a kite, with a wire and string, which drew down that fluid from the clouds" (23). One popular explanation for the name "Frankenstein" is that Mary Shelley was paying tribute to Benjamin Franklin, who was known as "modern Prometheus" in his era and who was greatly admired by Percy Shelley. This theory is almost certainly apocryphal, shaped by the retroactively created mythologies of both Franklin and Frankenstein as manipulators of electricity, but it is symbolically logical: it installs Victor Frankenstein as a polymath monster-maker experimenting on the newly constituted states of the republic. Franklin himself developed elaborate iconographies of Britannia as a mutilated body, with her dismembered limbs representing her revolting colonies, and of the United States as a body newly amalgamated from those limbs. This imagery suggests at least a symbolic overlap between America and the body of the Frankenstein monster. The rhetorical connections between Frankenstein and Franklin are at once retroactive fictions and anticipatory constructions of a Promethean inventor whose subjects for revivification were the newly rearticulated states of the U.S. body politic.[55]

For writers articulating literary nationalism in the antebellum era, the Frankenstein story was a fitting metaphor to describe the beginnings of the nation. The Frankenstein story of filial revolt paralleled, in dystopian form, the most prominent rhetoric of American self-formation: the revolutionary creation of the American nation through filial rebellion against Britain.[56] So too did the image of the monster as an amalgam serve as the spectral counterpart to the favored rhetoric of the nation as a body united from disparate geographic states. Margaret Fuller explicitly develops this metaphor in "American Literature" (1846), an essay in which she evaluates the contemporary state of American letters. The meaning of the Frankenstein story had long interested Fuller: "Moral of Frankenstein forsooth?" she asked wryly in an 1833 letter to her friend James Clarke.[57] In

"American Literature," she answers this question by using the monster's story as a cautionary tale for national self-formation. Fuller wrote "American Literature" after she had left the New England of Transcendentalism for a journalistic career in New York, and shortly before she moved to Europe and became involved in Italian political struggles; this essay has been interpreted to signal both her cosmopolitan impulses and her interest in American themes.[58] *Frankenstein* is a key part of the essay's nationalist themes, for the Frankenstein metaphor enables her to emphasize the dismemberments and revolts that precede and potentially follow American self-formation. Her essay suggests both the salience and the complexity of the Frankenstein story for antebellum literary accounts of American nationalism.

Fuller begins the essay with the difficulty of gestating American literature in the shadow of Europe: "Books which imitate or represent the thoughts and life of Europe do not constitute an American literature. Before such can exist, an original idea must animate this nation and fresh currents of life must call into life fresh thoughts along its shores."[59] To explain the animation of the new nation, she returns to the origins of the United States in filial rebellion: "[T]here is, often, between child and parent, a reaction from excessive influence having been exerted, and such a one we have experienced in behalf of our country against England" (359). The nation is now a "mixed race continually enriched with new blood from other stocks the most unlike that of our first descent, with . . . abundant opportunity to develop a genius wide and full as our rivers, flowery, luxuriant, and impassioned as our vast prairies, rooted in strength as the rocks on which the Puritan fathers landed" (359). Fuller represents the nation as born twice, once by the "Puritan fathers" and once by the "reaction from excessive influence . . . against England" in the revolutionary moment. The result is an amalgamated body that combines the diversity of topography with the multiplicity of national "stocks."

The new nation, Fuller argues, will not produce important literature until it has matured in several ways:

> That day will not rise till the fusion of races among us is more complete. It will not rise till this nation shall attain sufficient moral and intellectual dignity to prize moral and intellectual no less political freedom, nor till, the physical resources of the country being explored . . . [and] netted together by railways and telegraph lines, talent shall be left at leisure. . . . Nor then shall it be seen till from the leisurely and yearning soul of that

> riper time national ideas shall take birth, ideas craving to be clothed in a
> thousand fresh and original forms. (359)

Fuller's call is for national adulthood, embodied culturally in the "fusion
of races," materially in the transportation and communication systems
"netted together," and ideologically in the full attainment of political freedom. These images suggest the necessary repetition of the Frankensteinian themes of revolt and amalgam in postrevolutionary America. The self-
fathered creation of revolt, the nation must allow "national ideas [to] take
birth"; itself an amalgam, the nation must still generate "a thousand fresh
and original forms."

In the next paragraph, Fuller sharpens this image of redemptive birth by
invoking its negative version, the creation of the Frankenstein monster:

> Without such ideas all attempts to construct a national literature must
> end in abortions like the monster of Frankenstein, things with forms, and
> the instincts of forms, but soulless and therefore revolting. We cannot
> have expression till there is something to be expressed. (360)

The Frankenstein monster functions here as a dystopian symbol of an
American literature born grotesque. The implication in the passage, as Baldick suggests, is that "the United States themselves already form a Frankenstein monster, the federal attempt to make one from many (*e pluribus
unum*) having proved either abortive or, at best, embryonic. America itself
might become a colossal, powerful, but alarmingly uncontrolled creation
running wild."[60] As a fulfillment of the essay's earlier metaphors, the passage also completes the imagery of American revolts that began with the
"Puritan fathers." The double meaning of the word "revolting"—both repulsive and rebellious—captures the ambiguity of the Frankenstein metaphor in the American context, for it calls up the generative promise of
America in its revolt against Britain even as it cautions against the possibility that self-parenting may produce "revolting" monsters.

As the essay nears its end, Fuller expresses greater optimism. Praising contemporary writers, Emerson above all, she ends by warning that
"although by a thousand signs the existence is foreshown of those forces
which are to animate an American literature . . . those hopes are not yet
alive which shall usher it into a homogeneous or fully organized state of
being" (374). Even the most utopian features of these hopes, however,
seem narrowly separated from monstrosity: the "forces which are to ani-

mate" literature suggest the reanimated Frankenstein monster, and the "fully organized state of being" is only slightly more "homogeneous" than the united states of the monster. As Fuller's essay shows, two of the governing features of the Frankenstein monster are also dangerously reversible: a nation that has been amalgamated from disparate parts may easily be dismembered, and a country born in filial revolt may, in turn, rebel against itself.

This essay, then, confirms the generative overlap between the origin stories of the Frankenstein monster and the American nation. It also begins to suggest the gender implications of linking *Frankenstein* to American literary nationalism. As Fuller's essay confirms, the Frankenstein story, with its focus on a male creator and creation, slotted neatly into the male iconography of "Puritan fathers," as well as that of the Founding Fathers. But her very interest in the Frankenstein story also interrupts this all-male American narrative. "American Literature" was published the year after Fuller's *Woman in the Nineteenth Century* (1845), and it reflects her feminism.[61] In the essay, for example, she praises the contemporary women writers Catherine Maria Sedgwick and Caroline Kirkland, and she singles out for commendation a play called *Witchcraft, a Tragedy* for "resting the main interest upon force of character in a woman" (369). Fuller does not write about Mary Shelley; it is characteristic of the asymmetrical reputations of the two Shelleys in the nineteenth century that Fuller elsewhere praised Percy Shelley at length but did not mention Mary.[62] Indeed, despite her earlier reference to "Frankenstein" in her letters, her description of the Frankenstein monster as "soulless" suggests that she had not actually read the novel.

Yet Fuller's own career has important parallels with that of Mary Shelley, since both were women writers working within and against the terms of male Romanticism. Fuller was also linked by her contemporaries to an earlier "revolting" woman in America: Anne Hutchinson, reviled in Puritan New England both for the words of antinomian dissent that issued from her mouth and for the deformed fetuses that allegedly issued from her womb.[63] If the Puritan fathers provide Fuller with one symbolic point of departure for imagining Victor Frankenstein in America, so too do the reputedly monstrous births of Anne Hutchinson constitute an indigenous American *Frankenstein*—a foundational tale of monster-making in which woman's words, like women's bodies, are seen as producing monsters. The symbolic descendant of Hutchinson, Fuller is at once monster-maker and monster. As she aligns the Frankenstein monster and America, so too does her essay bring into view her own affinity with both Mary Shelley and her monster, as a "revolting" woman among the "Puritan fathers," the Founding Fathers, and the self-made men of the American Renaissance.

IV.

Fuller does not write in "American Literature" about slavery, which she adamantly opposed; she most likely uses the phrases "mixed race" and "fusion of races" in this essay to denote the combination of different white ethnicities.[64] But these phrases in her essay return us to possible intersections between the Frankenstein story and discussions of racial slavery. These intersections emerged in many areas, including debates about dissection. I have already mentioned the probable dissection of Nat Turner, an act that Franny Nudelman interprets as a form of "racial violence" that "staged the triumph of science over the insurgent."[65] More generally, corpses seized for medical dissection were disproportionately those of the poor, including many people of color. This issue erupted in an 1882 scandal at the Jefferson Medical College in Philadelphia in which a doctor was accused of taking corpses for medical use from African American burial grounds.[66] This history suggests that the American reception of *Frankenstein* was inseparable from a culture that often linked dead bodies—and stories about them—with questions of race.

Such intersections are overt in an 1852 political cartoon by Frank Bellew, "The Modern Frankenstein," which depicts Horace Greeley, the editor of the *New York Tribune* and a well-known abolitionist. Bellew, a popular illustrator and cartoonist, was drawn to the Frankenstein story throughout his career: in a later cartoon entitled "The American Frankenstein" (1874), he depicts the powerful railroad industry as a Frankenstein monster, holding a cudgel called "Capital," on a violent rampage.[67] In the later cartoon, the monster is physically darkened, but not racially marked; he is bolted together from metal parts, suggesting a mechanical monster like a train. In "The Modern Frankenstein," however, the monster is depicted overtly as a black man. As Sarah Burns, analyzing this cartoon in the context of nineteenth-century painting, suggests, it depicts a "powerful, dreadful, and relentless black giant whose awakening portended disaster for all."[68]

In the context of the black Frankenstein tradition, we can see Bellew's monster as the visual embodiment of the language of George Canning: "a

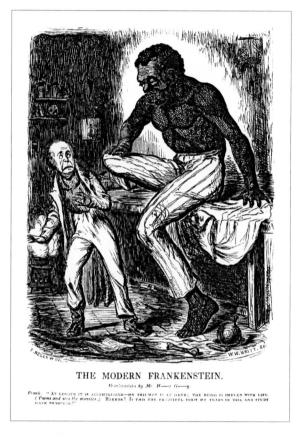

THE MODERN FRANKENSTEIN.

Frankenstein by Mr. H——r G——y.

Frank. "At length it is accomplished—my triumph is at hand; the being is imbued with life. (*Turns and sees the monster.*) Horror! Is this the frightful form my years of toil and study have produced!"

Frank Bellew, "The Modern Frankenstein," *Lantern*, 31 January 1852. (Harvard College Library)

human form with all the physical capabilities of man, and with the thews and sinews of a giant." His body is powerful, if not also eroticized, in its intimate relation to the white man who comes up to his waist. The monster's face, however, is freakish—mouth gaping, teeth protruding, eyes half closed; the Frankenstein monster is here the black man depicted as racist caricature and, more specifically, in the shape of what Leonard Cassuto has analyzed as the "racial grotesque."[69] Depicted in the process of sitting upright, towering over his maker, and perhaps getting ready to leave the room, the monster may also evoke the figure of the runaway slave.[70] The most important element of the monster as Bellew depicts him, however, is his relation to the creator figure. The emphasis here is on Greeley's anxiety at the awakening of his monster, as signaled visually in the image of his grimacing and puny body, and verbally in the caption. Underneath the title is the line "Frankenstein by Mr. H——e G——y," and the caption reads "Frank. At length it is accomplished—my triumph is at hand; the being is imbued with life. (Turns and sees the monster.) Horror! Is this the frightful form my years of toil and study have produced?" These lines suggest a theatrical version of the Frankenstein story, with the spotlight on the setting of the doctor's laboratory and on the moment at which the creator "[t]urns and sees the monster." Staging black monstrosity, the cartoon focuses on the horrified gaze of the white man. The Frankenstein story enables a menacing joke on the white abolitionist.

Other accounts of abolitionism invoked *Frankenstein* with a similar, if less direct, focus on white creator-figures. In *Cannibals All!* (1857), George Fitzhugh defends slavery by comparing it favorably to waged labor in the North. As part of this defense, he attacks "socialists and communists," whose visions of social change are too sweeping: "When they attempt to go further—and having found the present social system to be fatally diseased, propose to originate and build up another in its stead—they are as presumptuous as the anatomist who should attempt to create a man. Social bodies, like human bodies, are the works of God, which man may dissect, and sometimes heals, but which he cannot create."[71] Fitzhugh's image of the "anatomist who should attempt to create a man" strongly suggests Victor Frankenstein; as in "The Modern Frankenstein," the yield of the comparison is in tying the monster to his creator. Fitzhugh's animus in this passage is against the "socialists and communists" who attempt to reengineer a slave society, but his target elsewhere, and throughout his work, is the Northerner who would attempt to re-create the South in its own image. In a letter to William Lloyd Garrison, Fitzhugh writes, "We are satisfied with our institutions, and are not willing to submit them to the *experimentum in vile corpus!*"[72] In Fitzhugh's geography of monstrosity, the axis of conflict is between regions, and the question is whether the North will make a monster out of the South.

If Bellew and Fitzhugh highlight the white monster-maker, other American defenders of slavery focused on a link between monstrosity and racial "amalgamation." This link informs the writings of John Van Evrie, a doctor, editor, and advocate of polygenesis whom George Fredrickson characterizes as "perhaps the first professional racist in American history."[73] Van Evrie's *Negroes and Negro "Slavery,"* a racist polemic first published in 1853, had a widespread Northern readership. In this work, Van Evrie warns that if the American government supports racial equality, the result will be intermarriage and then mulatto sterility:

> When the whole force of government is brought to bear against . . . "prejudice" . . . [then] the hideous affiliation, the monstrous admixture of blood, the vile obscenity that they may term marriage, follows with equal certainty. But the result of this admixture—the wretched progeny—the diseased and sterile offspring—has a determinate limit, and it is solely a question of time when it becomes wholly extinct.[74]

Van Evrie's monster metaphors echo the language of *Frankenstein*, from his condemnation of "monstrous admixture" to his suggestion that mixed-race children represent "wretched progeny." These echoes arise not because Shelley's novel provided him with a direct source but because *Frankenstein* had so effectively formalized conservative vocabularies of repugnance and fear. Like Thomas Dew defending slavery after the Nat Turner revolt, Van Evrie redistributed the conservative impulses already in *Frankenstein* into the terms of contemporary American racism. In these terms, amalgamation—perceived as the corollary and consequence of abolition—threatened to turn America into a nation of self-extinguishing monsters.

These terms linked monstrosity with national as well as racial decline. Van Evrie's greatest fear is that mulattoes will destroy America: "[T]he nation, weighed down by mulattoism, by such an ulcer on the body politic . . . would doubtless fall a conquest to some other nation or variety of the master race, and again become English provinces or dependencies of some other European power!" (156). Identifying England as the site of abolitionism, he warns, "it could not be long before the forms as well as the spirit of republicanism would disappear from the New World, and . . . all that Washington and Jefferson and the glorious spirits of 1776 labored for would be lost to mankind" (323). In Van Evrie's circuit of logic, amalgamation will render sterile not only its "wretched progeny" but the nation as a whole, for the monstrous mulatto will destroy the republic created by the "glorious spirits of 1776." By displacing abolitionist impulses onto Britain, he looks toward a future in which white America will rid itself of the monster of "mulattoism."

These symbolic linkages among monstrosity, race, and nation became more acute in the 1850s, with growing national dissent over slavery. The tension between two foundational narratives of American revolt—an

enshrined national declaration of independence from Britain and a demonized racial nightmare of black independence from white people—became increasingly acute. Russ Castronovo has shown that the literature
of this period is filled with patrilineal narratives fractured by slavery, in
which "the nation's genealogy is inhabited by lost members, dispossessed
bastards, forgotten orphans, and rebellious slaves."[75] The Frankenstein
monster is another such dispossessed bastard, forgotten orphan, and rebellious slave. The figure of a black Frankenstein monster stands at the
convergence of an Anglo-American equation between slavery and monstrosity, an American narrative about the founding of the white nation in
filial revolt, and a consequent American tension between this founding
narrative and the equally foundational presence of slavery.

The politics of this convergence were reversible. John Van Evrie invoked monsters in support of slavery, but the imagery of the Frankenstein story echoed even more strongly in antislavery writing of this era,
which inverted the racist equation of slaves and monsters and focused the
question of amalgamation on the figure of the mixed-race slave denied
recognition by his white father. There are traces of Shelley's *Frankenstein*
throughout the writings of Herman Melville, who acquired a copy of the
novel in London.[76] "The Bell-Tower" (1855), his most concise and direct
adaptation of *Frankenstein*, adapts Shelley's novel for an antislavery racial
allegory, although it also suggests some difficulties involved in making
such an adaptation.

"The Bell-Tower" is set in an unnamed European city where an architect, Bannadonna, obsessively builds a bell-tower and constructs an
automaton to ring the bell; the automaton kills him, and ultimately the
bell-tower, fatally cracked, falls in on itself. This plot combines aspects of
both Shelley's novel and the popular mythology of the Frankenstein story.
Unlike Shelley's Victor Frankenstein, Bannadonna focuses on building a
machine, but this mechanical focus is consistent with popular versions of
the Frankenstein story; although the monster in *Frankenstein* has no mechanical components, popular versions had moved the story in this direction as early as Peake's 1823 play *Presumption*, in which Victor Frankenstein calls his creation "a huge automaton in human form."[77]

An indirect adaptation of *Frankenstein*, "The Bell-Tower" is a similarly
indirect critique of U.S. race relations. Melville published this story just
after *Benito Cereno*, his allegorical novella of slave revolt, and "The Bell-
Tower" offers a complementary racial allegory.[78] Its epigraph begins, "Like

negroes, these powers own man sullenly; mindful of their higher master; while serving, plot revenge."[79] This epigraph, described as "From a Private Ms.," suggests that he who makes "negroes" serve him will become the object of their vengeance. Similarly, the setting of the story in a crumbling city "with dank mould cankering its bloom" (174) evokes the American South decaying under the weight of slavery. The object at the story's center, the flawed bell, suggests a more northern American icon. As Carolyn Karcher has shown, Melville's bell recalls the Liberty Bell in numerous ways: for example, it has a flaw in its casing and it cracks when it is tolled at Bannadonna's funeral, as the Liberty Bell had cracked when tolled for Justice John Marshall and George Washington.[80] Obsessed with creating his own liberty bell through the unfree labor of others, Melville's Bannadonna is another American Prometheus: Victor Frankenstein as slave-owner.

Melville's Frankenstein monster, meanwhile, is a displaced version of an African American slave. As described by the narrator after the murder, the automaton

> had limbs, and seemed clad in a scaly mail, lustrous as a dragon-beetle's. It was manacled, and its clubbed arms were uplifted, as if, with its man-acles, once more to smite its already smitten victim. One advanced foot of it was inserted beneath the dead body, as if in the act of spurning it. (182)

There are no overtly racial elements in this description, but the "mana-cled" arms evoke the chains of slavery, and the "scaly mail" distinguishes the surface, if not the color, of the automaton's skin from those around him. The key element of the description is its emphasis on the act of re-bellion. Melville's interest here is not, as in abolitionist discourse, to hu-manize the slave—indeed, the automaton is both inhuman and inhumane —but to show the arrogance of the master. The end of the story cements its connections to *Frankenstein* and its caution against slavery: "So the blind slave obeyed its blinder lord; but, in obedience, slew him. So the creator was killed by the creature" (186–87).

"The Bell-Tower," then, brings the Frankenstein monster into the orbit of abolitionism, although not simply as a fictional figure placed on the historical ground of slavery. Rather, Melville highlights the process of making the Frankenstein monster and the slave into metaphoric figures for each other. The epigraph simultaneously introduces "negroes" as a topic and relegates them to the status of metaphoric comparison—"like negroes" rather than "negroes" themselves. Similarly, the setting of the story is southern, but it is the "south of Europe," simultaneously displacing as well as evoking the comparison to the United States South. The story's fablelike final sentence, meanwhile, leaves "the creature" open to being both monster and slave. If Melville's writing, as Cindy Weinstein has shown, consistently explores the labor involved in creating allegory, "The Bell-Tower" highlights this labor from the start, in a story that is itself about the labor of creation.[81]

At the same time, "The Bell-Tower" also suggests a fundamental distinction between an adaptation of Shelley's novel and an allegory of slavery. *Frankenstein* does not depict slavery as an ongoing process; abandoned by his creator, Shelley's monster is never forced by his creator into sustained unwaged labor. To adapt *Frankenstein* for antislavery purposes required adding to its creation story a plot of servitude against which the creation could then rebel. An African American Frankenstein allegory, this story implies, requires not only the presence of a monstrous slave but also a way to dramatize ongoing enslavement.

A black Frankenstein story could also invoke the voice of the monster himself. In the era of Nat Turner, I have suggested, David Walker's *Appeal* echoes the voice of the Frankenstein monster. In antebellum slave narratives, the language of monstrosity is frequently used in order to demonize slaveowners—and the institution of slavery—rather than slaves. Harriet Jacobs, for example, remembers that her former master "peopled my young mind with unclean images, such as only a vile monster could think of," and describes her resistance as "struggling alone in the powerful grasp of the demon Slavery; and the monster proved too strong for me."[82] Such passages highlight the connection between monstrosity and the sexual exploitation of black women, as well as a resistant strategy by which, as Cassuto puts it, "the master is renamed 'monster.'"[83]

The most sustained echoes of the Frankenstein monster's voice in African American writing in this era, however, are in the writings of Frederick Douglass. There is no evidence that Douglass read Mary Shelley; his favorite novelists were Dickens and Dumas.[84] But his writing indirectly returns to the imagery of monstrosity organized by *Frankenstein*. Eduardo Cadava, comparing Shelley's *Frankenstein* with Douglass's 1845 *Narrative*, posits a complex "echolalia" between them, identifying resemblances between their accounts of language and reading.[85] This "echolalia" is a sustained one, for throughout his oratory, autobiographies, and journalism, I suggest, Douglass adapted the most radical elements of a black Frankenstein story for political critique.

This critique is centered on the exposure of the father who, like Victor Frankenstein, ignores his illegitimate son. White fathers, Douglass writes in *My Bondage and My Freedom*, will inevitably reject their slave children: "Men do not love those who remind them of their sins . . . and the mulatto's face is a standing accusation against him who is master and father to the child."[86] The mulatto child, he notes, is destined to be rejected by others in addition to his white father, as in the case of a slave named William Wilks, who is so despised by his white half-brother that the latter "gave his father no rest until he did sell him" (115). The Frankenstein monster, rejected not only by his maker but also by another son of the Frankenstein family, William, makes similar claims. What sparks the monster's murder of William is the boy's declaration of his father's power: "Let me go, or I will tell my papa. . . . Hideous monster! let me go; My papa is a Syndic—he is M. Frankenstein—he would punish you. You dare not keep me" (96–97). William is Victor's brother, not his son, but his emphasis on a "papa" named Frankenstein in his retort to the monster suggests that theirs is a conflict between two sons of a father named Frankenstein, the smugly legitimate scion and the despised bastard. William is too young to effect the revenge of the white son on his half-white brother, but as in the fraternal conflict outlined by Douglass, the two sons cannot peacefully coexist. The monster's story of his brother, like his account of his father, provides a template for rebellion that Douglass reshapes in his memoirs. In his filial and fraternal revolt against white hypocrisy, Douglass embodies the claims of both the mixed-race slave and the Frankenstein monster.

Echoing *Frankenstein* in his autobiography, Douglass also evokes it in his journalism and oratory. "The black baby of Negro suffrage," he writes in *Douglass' Monthly* in 1860, "was thought too ugly to exhibit. . . . The negro was stowed away like some people put out of sight their deformed children when company comes."[87] In the speech "Slavery and the Irrepressible Conflict" (1860), Douglass develops this association of slavery and monstrosity more extensively: "Slavery is everywhere the pet monster of the American people. All our political parties, and most of our churches, kneel with humility at its accursed shrine of tears and blood! . . . [T]he human mind . . . fails to overtake and comprehend this huge and manyheaded abomination."[88] The charge that slavery is America's "pet monster" has a double force: "pet" suggests that slavery is both white America's favorite monster and its defining term of domestic identity. Lest "pet" seem too domestic, in the sense of domesticated, Douglass moves to the more violent image, drawn from the many-headed hydra, of slavery as a "huge and manyheaded abomination." Like the Frankenstein monster, slavery is an unnatural amalgam of body parts, coercively maintained as pet by the white "American people."

In condemning slavery as the nation's "pet monster," Douglass revises the rhetoric of filial revolt that customarily organized discussions of America and England. Douglass lectured extensively in England, and his writing frequently invokes the legacy of British abolitionism to support U.S. battles for racial equality; such praise for British abolitionism, along with a broader strain of Anglophilia, was common in African American writing in this period.[89] "Slavery and the Irrepressible Conflict" was delivered at a celebration commemorating the British abolition of West Indian slavery. Douglass notes early in this speech that "[t]he abolition of slavery in the West Indies is now . . . esteemed by every true-hearted Briton as the chief glory of his country. . . . How striking and humiliating is the contrast in respect to slavery, between England and America, the mother and the daughter!"[90] He proposes an American imitation of England—a repetition of its antislavery movement—rather than a new rebellion against it. His rhetoric precisely inverts that of Van Evrie, who also highlighted English abolitionism but who proposed a second American Revolution against it. It also returns to the ground of Mary Shelley, in a transatlantic circuit whereby—like Melville getting a copy of *Frankenstein* in London —Douglass acquires from England a way of seeing revolt.

Finally, Douglass's metaphor of "the mother and the daughter" briefly interrupts the male focus of most allegories of filial revolt, from *The Tempest* to *Frankenstein*. Melville sustains this male focus hyperbolically. His protagonist Bannadonna seeks phallic mastery: "mounting [the tower], he stood erect" (175). Margaret Fuller implicitly challenges this male focus by her own entry into the discourse of literary nationalism; herself an errant daughter of the American Renaissance, Fuller's account of the "revolting nation" raises the possibility of female monster-makers as well as founding mothers. And Douglass offers, in this moment, an account of national identity that inverts the usual masculine imagery of America as a land of Founding Fathers and Sons of Liberty. Instead, he offers an antimonstrous account of America as antislavery daughter.

V.

The antebellum figure of an African American Frankenstein monster, I have argued, originates in the convergence of, and tension between, two ideas: a transatlantic understanding of the black slave as a Frankenstein monster who revolts against his white master and an American model of the United States as a Frankenstein monster who revolted against Britain. In the Civil War, the figure of the black Frankenstein monster takes on important new forms. The war, the central political event of nineteenth-century America, turned on the rhetoric of national dismemberment and reamalgamation. "United States" was a plural noun at the start of the Civil War and a singular noun at its end, reflecting the triumph of the pro-Union belief that the nation was one organic body rather than two legitimate Union and Confederate nations. As John Lothrop Motley explained at the start of the war, "The United States happens to be a plural title, but the commonwealth thus designated is a unit, 'e pluribus unum.'"[91] National dismemberment was both cause and mirror of the experience of individual soldiers, who were riven by amputation, illness, and the psychic traumas—phantom limbs, neurasthenia, and hysteria—that marked men's experiences of fighting the Civil War. Unnaturally dismembered, both soldier and nation needed reamalgamation. As Emma Willard wrote in 1862, the war "[had] so commingled and dissolved the political elements, that they are now in a plastic state, and ready to be moulded for futurity."[92] The "mould[ing]" of this "plastic" state took myriad forms. For example, the rhetoric of the new artificial-limb industry, which was centered in the North, equated prosthetic reconstruction of the soldier's body with national reunion.[93] More generally, the literature of the Civil War and Reconstruction, as Lisa Long has shown, was obsessed with the possibilities of rehabilitation for both individual and national bodies politic.[94]

In its focus on dismemberment and reamalgamation, Northern rhetoric about the Civil War evoked *Frankenstein*. A political caricature by Henry Louis Stephens, a popular illustrator and satirist, envisions "The New Frankenstein: A Glimpse of the Horrible Fate in Store for Jeff Davis at the Hands of the Monster 'Rebellion.'" This cartoon was published in *Vanity Fair* in May 1862, relatively early in the war; it depicts the eruption of black power in wartime before the formal enactments of liberty, such as the Emancipation Proclamation or the acceptance of enslaved men into the army. In the cartoon, a dark-skinned, heavily muscled man, depicted from behind, holds a pale, helpless Jefferson Davis, president of the Confederacy, above his head. The image is an attack on both seces-sion and slavery; as Sarah Burns notes, "Although the wrathful creature nominally stands for rebellion rather than for slavery per se, his dark-ness unmistakably links one with the other."[95] In the context of a black Frankenstein tradition, "The New Frankenstein" advances the narrative of rebellion against a white creator only incipient in Bellew's "The Modern Frankenstein." In the earlier image, the monster has just awakened, in a laboratory-like space; in this image, the monster's rebellion is fully under way, and he is at large on an unbounded mountain-top that recalls the Alpine and North Pole settings of confrontation in Shelley's novel.

Here, as in "The Modern Frankenstein," the emphasis is on the relation between monster and monster-maker, but the threat is now to a national body politic—the Confederacy, headed by Davis—rather than to a single influential man like Greeley. The imagery is of the Confederacy as a royal-ist monarchy, as signaled by the crown, which is now turned topsy-turvy. Adapting the longstanding iconography of the world turned upside down, the image also anticipates another vocabulary of inversion that came to saturate public depictions of Jefferson Davis. Postwar cartoons frequently presented Davis as cross-dressed in defeat; here, his world is turned topsy-turvy by the male monster he has made, both by defending slavery and by seceding from the Union. Already a symbol of the rebellious slave, the Frankenstein monster now underpins the representation of sectional revolt.[96]

These symbolic possibilities are developed in the wartime rhetoric of Massachusetts senator Charles Sumner. A committed abolitionist, Sum-ner condemned secession and advocated for immediate wartime eman-cipation and black military service; chair of the Senate Foreign Relations Committee during the war, he also lobbied Britain to support the Union. Sumner is connected to the cultural history of *Frankenstein* in several ways. He met Mary Shelley in 1838 while in London, as he recounted in a letter to a friend: "I talked a good deal with Mrs. Shelley. She was dressed in pure white, and seemed a nice and agreeable person, with great clever-ness. She said the greatest happiness of a woman was to be the wife or mother of a distinguished man."[97] This anecdote reflects Mary Shelley's self-presentation as conservative conservator of her husband's literary legacy. It draws Sumner and Shelley together in the orbit of the Anglo-American literary elite, while severing the "nice and agreeable" Shelley from the grotesque male monster for whose creation she had become famous.

VANITY FAIR·

THE NEW FRANKENSTEIN.
A GLIMPSE OF THE HORRIBLE FATE IN STORE FOR JEFF DAVIS AT THE HANDS OF THE MONSTER " REBELLION."

Henry Louis Stephens, "The New Frankenstein," *Vanity Fair,* 10 May 1862. (Mortimer Rare Book Room, Smith College)

Conversely, Sumner himself was symbolically aligned with the Frankenstein monster by the *Southern Literary Messenger* in 1854. "A Few Thoughts on Slavery," a defense of slavery, includes a long attack on Sumner, who had just given an antislavery speech in the Senate against the repeal of the Missouri Compromise:

Here is Mr. Sumner's formula. "Slavery is the forcible subjection of one human being in person, in labor, and property, to the will of another—without a father, without a mother, almost without a God—the slave has nothing but a master." We cannot say that we exactly understand what Mr. Sumner means by the declaration that the slave is without father or mother. We are disposed to regard it as a rhetorical bull, for the Senator hardly intends . . . to suggest that his generation is like the wild and awful conception of Frankenstein. Unable to solve the mystery, we pass on with the single remark that it had been better for the peace of the country if the Senator, and each member of his party, "without a father and without a mother," had never been born.[98]

This passage begins with an attack on Sumner's definition of slavery as the erasure of family bonds. The idea of the slave "without a father, without a mother, almost without a God" suggests Harriet Beecher Stowe's character Topsy, the slave child raised without parents: "I spect I grow'd. Don't think nobody never made me."[99] The *Southern Literary Messenger* uses a Frankenstein analogy to turn this account back against Sumner, who "hardly intends" to compare slave's "generation" to "the wild and awful conception of Frankenstein." The conclusion extends the analogy between slave to monster to include Sumner himself, fantasizing that "the Senator . . . had never been born." Elsewhere, the essay condemns the abolition of slavery in Jamaica: "The gift of freedom has converted the fair island of Jamaica into a howling wilderness," for "the negro relapses into barbarism when released from subjection to the white man" (203). This account of Jamaican "barbarism" as the result of emancipation complements George Canning's Frankenstein metaphor in his 1824 speech against West Indian emancipation, and it echoes George Fitzhugh's defense of the South to William Lloyd Garrison. In its condemnation of emancipation, the deepest wish of the *Messenger* is that the white slaveowning South not itself be condemned, for "we are not the monsters our enemies would paint us" (204).

In Sumner's own use of the Frankenstein metaphor, he did precisely that, equating monstrosity with the white slaveowning South. In an 1863 speech called "Our Foreign Relations," he argues against British recognition of the Confederacy. A new nation founded on slavery, he predicts,

will be the soulless monster of Frankenstein, the wretched creation of mortal science without God,—endowed with life and nothing else: forever raging madly, the scandal of humanity; powerful only for evil, whose destruction will be essential to the peace of the world.[100]

Fuller had feared that immature works of American literature were "the monster of Frankenstein, things with forms, and the instincts of forms, but soulless, and therefore revolting"; Sumner similarly condemns the revolting Confederacy as a "soulless monster." As in Fuller's "American Literature," the reference suggests that Sumner has not read the novel, whose monster is not soulless, but is referring to the popular myth. As in the cartoon "The New Frankenstein," the monster combines secession and slavery: the Confederacy, an "embryo" nation, is "nothing else than animate slavery."[101] In an 1861 speech, Sumner specifies the unwelcome behavior of this monstrous "creation": "the Rebellion is slavery itself,—incarnate, living, acting, raging, robbing, murdering, according to the essential law of its being."[102]

Drawing on the Frankenstein story to condemn sectional revolt, Sumner also suggests that story's relevance to national dismemberment. In another 1863 speech, "Our Domestic Relations," he explains that the United States was created as a *Plural Unit,* meant to function as an amalgamated body:

> When the Constitution was proclaimed . . . our career as a Nation began, with all the unity of a nation. The States remained as living parts of the body, important to the national strength, and essential to those currents which maintain national life, but plainly subordinate to the United States, which then and there stood forth a Nation, one and indivisible.[103]

The singular "national life" made by the Founding Fathers has now been dismembered by secession into its own "living parts." For Sumner, the Confederate States of America is not a legitimate nation but a collection of disarticulated limbs, "Rebel States" that "have sacrificed that corporate existence which makes them living, component members of our Union of States."[104] The languages of dismemberment and filial revolt, key inheritances of the Frankenstein story, are inextricable in his condemnation: "Behold the Rebel States in arms against that paternal government to which . . . they owe duty and love."[105] For Sumner, the overarching goal of "the paternal government," its current version of the founding fathers, should be "changing Slavery into Freedom."[106] In his abolitionist version of the nation as monster, he envisions the body parts of the United States as one nation—indivisible, under God, and without slavery.

As the complementary titles "Our Domestic Relations" and "Our Foreign Relations" suggest, Sumner situated his rhetoric of monstrosity in international frameworks. Sumner's goal was to sever the strong affiliation between Britain and the Confederacy, which he did by invoking—as had Frederick Douglass in "Slavery and the Irrepressible Conflict"—a shared Anglo-American history of abolitionism. In "Our Foreign Relations," Sumner notes that "[i]n other days England has valiantly striven against Slavery . . . and now she is willing to surrender, at a moment when more can be done than ever before against the monster, wherever it shows its head,—for Slavery everywhere has its neck in this Rebellion."[107] The rhetoric of monstrosity overlaps with that of the many-headed hydra, a figure whose intrinsic expansionism—"wherever it shows its head"—here serves to highlight the imperialist implications of sectional rebellion. The Confederacy, Sumner writes, is "a monster-empire," and his goal is "the exclusion of such a monster-empire from the family of nations."[108]

In his condemnation of the "monster-empire," Sumner, like Douglass, restores the transatlantic rhetoric of abolitionism from which *Frankenstein* had itself emerged. He also exposes some contradictions of that rhetoric for pro-Union American writers during the Civil War. One contradiction lay in the need to condemn the filial rebellion of the white South against the Union while continuing to celebrate America's original filial revolt against Britain. What Margaret Fuller had encouraged as America's "reaction from excessive influence" against Britain could not, for Northerners, translate into praise for the South's own filial revolt against the North; this was a difficulty that Confederate writers fully exploited, claiming the legacy of the American Revolution for themselves. Another impasse in Sumner's rhetoric inhered in the relation between antislavery and anticolonial politics. Sumner honors the legacy of British abolitionism, yet his monster metaphors do not translate into a corresponding sympathy for anticolonial struggles against the British Empire. Instead, he aligned Confederate secession with the 1857 uprising of Indian soldiers against the British Empire: "I should not be astonished to see the whole rebellion crumble like your Sepoy rebellion, which for a while seemed as menacing to your Indian empire as ours has been to our republic."[109] Sumner's metaphor of the Frankenstein monster as embodying both slavery and secession could itself be disunited into two rebel states. The "paternal government" of the United States, like the "family of nations," was antislavery but proimperial, intent on subduing wayward sons of liberty when they threatened abolitionism but also when they challenged nations and empires.

Expanding outward to transatlantic stories of rebellion, Sumner's monster metaphors resonated with his own internal bodily injuries. Sumner was famously caned on the floor of the Senate in 1856 during a debate over slavery in Kansas, by proslavery South Carolina congressman

Preston Brooks; the beating was so severe that it took Sumner three years to recover.[110] Sumner's supporters analogized the injuries to his body with the internecine conflict over slavery in Kansas: "Bleeding Sumner" and "Bleeding Kansas" were two twinned themes in the presidential campaign of 1856.[111] Less directly, Sumner's psychological trauma prefigured the neurasthenia and hysteria that male soldiers experienced in the Civil War. "I have now nothing but a lack of strength, & a morbid sensibility of the nervous system," he declares in a typical letter during his convalescence.[112] His treatments included the application of extreme heat to his head, about which he writes, as if a soldier, "I am now at close quarters with the enemy."[113] Injured in the divided house of Congress, Sumner's mind and body incarnated the divided state of Kansas and prefigured the state of the soldier fighting for the disunified nation.

These images anticipate the monster stories that Sumner soon told about secession and slavery. In the same letter about his medical treatment putting him "at close quarters with the enemy," Sumner compares himself to "Prometheus with the vulture at his liver."[114] The affinity is with the Prometheus who suffers rather than with Prometheus the maker of man, although Sumner, in this moment, was trying to mold Kansas into a free state; after the war, he worked to reamalgamate the United States in postslavery form. From the perspective of slavery's apologists, Sumner —another Promethean Victor Frankenstein—was making a monster out of the nation. At the same time, Sumner's metaphors of injury also suggest that he, like the nation, is at risk of becoming a monster. The mutiny of his body against him prefigures that of the "rebel states" that he will condemn in wartime, and the "morbid sensibility" colonizing him from within will be writ large in the "monster-empire" he condemns in the world. Back in the Senate during the Civil War, he declares that "the rebel States could not come back, except on the footing of the Decltn. of Indep. & the complete recognition of Human Rights. . . . And then what a regenerated land!"[115] In Sumner's monster metaphors, the Confederacy, like slavery, was a Frankenstein monster that must die; at the same time, in a parallel monster story, he himself—like the nation at war—awaited a less "soulless" form of "regeneration."

Whereas Sumner's metaphors suggest his newly created connection to the imagery of monstrosity, that connection was already in place for African Americans. The writings of Frederick Douglass exemplify how the imagery of monstrosity could be reappropriated from within in relation to the war and how they could be extended in its wake. Douglass admired

Sumner's antislavery politics, praising him in an 1860 editorial with a series of gothic metaphors that presented slavery as monstrosity:

> He has dared to grapple directly with the hell-born monster itself. . . . [He has] left it writhing under the sunlight of truth in all its filth and barbarism. . . . He has torn out its very heart, and shown it to be full of rottenness and uncleanness. . . . [H]e denounces it as a thing not fit to live anywhere, but to slink away out of sight with murder, piracy, and every other revolting and shocking abomination with which this earth is blasted.[116]

Like Sumner, Douglass redirected his rhetoric to condemn the Confederacy along with slavery. In an 1861 editorial, Douglass declares, "We have no tears to shed . . . over the fall of Fort Sumter," for if Confederates had not attacked the fort, "the South might have got the most extravagant concessions to its pet monster, slavery."[117] In an 1862 speech, he condemns secession in the same terms: "I am convinced that this rebellion and slavery are twin monsters, and that they must fall or flourish together." Amnesty toward the Confederacy will encourage the monster: "[J]ust take back the pet monster again into the bosom of the nation, proclaim an amnesty to the slaveholders . . . [and] you will hand down to your children . . . all the horrors through which you are now passing."[118] For Douglass as for Sumner, the "pet monster" has produced a civil war, and any attempt to domesticate the Confederacy—taking it back "into the bosom of the nation"—will only increase the horrors of domestic war.

In another wartime editorial, Douglass situated that monster in a more elaborate national allegory, which turned on the Frankensteinian idea of a creation who rebels against his creator:

> [W]e have as a nation been forging a bolt for our own national destruction, collecting and augmenting the fuel that now threatens to wrap the nation in its malignant and furious flames. We have sown the wind, only to reap the whirlwind. . . . [W]e have gone on like the oppressors of Egypt, hardening our hearts and increasing the burdens of the American slave, and strengthening the arm of his guilty master, till now, in the pride of his giant power, that master is emboldened to lift rebellious arms against the very majesty of the law, and defy the power of the government itself. . . . The Republic has put one end of the chain upon the ankle of the bondman, and the other end about its own neck. They have been planting tyrants, and are now getting a harvest of civil war and anarchy.[119]

This passage sketches a drama of monster-making with three actors: the "we" of the nation, which has forged "a bolt for our own national destruction" by condoning slavery; the slave, not a monster but a victim of monstrous behavior; and the slaveowning South, the true monster of the passage, a "giant power" forged by the national approval of slavery and now emboldened to rebel against its maker. The nation is like Victor Frankenstein injured by his own creation, but with a third actor: the slave. Like Sumner, Douglass argued that the secessionist Confederacy was a monster, but Douglass also focused—from within—on the role of the unmonstrous and heroic "American slave."

Also like Sumner, Douglass forecast a redeemed future for the body politic. In "The Mission of the War," an 1864 speech, he underscores the parental link between slavery and the Confederate army, this time in relation to the ill-treatment of Union soldiers in Confederate prison camps: "In all the most horrid details of torture, starvation and murder, in the treatment of our prisoners, I beheld the features of the monster in whose presence I was born, and that is Slavery."[120] The nation and its male soldiers have been dismembered; there are now "stumps of men" wandering the land (5). But the future will be different: "The issue before us is a living issue. We are not fighting for the dead past, but for the living present and the glorious future" (13–14). And the movement from buried bones to new life is triumphal: "You and I know that the mission of this war is National regeneration" (21). Like Sumner, Douglass predicts that a new national body will be "regenerated" from war, but for Douglass, this future will leave behind "the monster in whose presence" he himself was born.

VI.

The writings of Sumner and Douglass suggest the continuity between antebellum and wartime abolitionist conceptions of black monstrosity, but the Civil War also deepened the racist discourse of monstrosity in new ways. The term "miscegenation" was invented during the war, in an 1864 pamphlet titled *Miscegenation* and written to smear Lincoln's reelection campaign with the suggestion that his Republican Party advocated "the blending of the races." The pamphlet's anonymous authors, David Croly and George Wakeman, argued that the Civil War was "a war looking, as its final fruit, to the blending of white and black."[121] A parody presented as if it were an endorsement of interracial sexuality, particularly of liaisons between black men and white women, the pamphlet failed to affect the campaign, but it had lasting popular influence. As Martha Hodes has shown, liaisons between white women and black men were treated with relative toleration in the antebellum era, but the Civil War prompted harsh new punishments of them.[122] The movement from "amalgamation" to "miscegenation" was not merely a change of vocabulary but also an index of the new demonization of interracial contact as a symbol of black emancipation.

This new demonization strengthened the metaphorical connection between black men and monsters. The word "miscegenation" was a linguistic amalgam; after Croly and Wakeman's pamphlet was exposed as a hoax, the *New York World,* their employer, predicted that "[t]he name will doubtless die out by virtue of its inherent malformation. We have bastard and hump-backed words enough already."[123] The prediction of linguistic sterility echoed older racist claims about mulatto sterility, and Croly and Wakeman's pamphlet also stimulated a reassertion of the theory of polygenesis. Refuting the claims of *Miscegenation* in Congress, Samuel Cox asserted that "the mulatto does not live; he does not recreate his kind; he is a monster."[124]

For defenders of slavery, the "monster" mulatto became a symbol of Union victory. Van Evrie, republishing *Negroes and Negro "Slavery"* after the war as *White Supremacy and Negro Subordination,* lamented in a new preface that Northerners "now rule the South by military force . . . and are striving to 'reconstruct' American society on a Mongrel basis."[125] The reconstruction of a "Mongrel" America, like the invention of the "bastard and hump-backed" word "miscegenation," insistently embodied racial conflict through a vocabulary of monstrosity. "His yellow skin scarcely covered the work of muscles and arteries beneath; his hair was of a lustrous black," exclaims Victor Frankenstein of his creation (34); "We must become a yellow-skinned, black-haired people," declared Croly and Wakeman in *Miscegenation.*[126] The monster with yellow skin and black hair, the "hideous progeny" of Shelley's novel, was symbolically reborn in racist parody as the symbol of the miscegenated nation.

Accompanying the new focus on miscegenation was an obsession with sexual violence. Although the image of the black man sexually assaulting white women had appeared in earlier racist rhetoric, only in the postwar era did that image become symbolically central to American culture and systematically reinforced through lynching. The myth of the black rapist had several targets: functioning most overtly to police black emancipated men, it reinforced white men's control over white women, and it both effaced and disparaged black women. The myth also constituted a sexual projection on the part of white men toward black men, a fantasy of black sexual potency that white men then brutally attacked.[127]

Even more strongly than the antebellum language of amalgamation, the postwar myth of the black rapist relied on monster metaphors. This monster mythology was crystallized in the novels of Thomas Dixon, which depicted a postwar white South politically emasculated by Confederate loss and in search of racial and regional redemption. *The Leopard's Spots* (1902), for example, offers a plot of white male renewal centered on the monstrous specter of the black rapist. This specter appears first in the form of a black Union soldier whose rape of a white woman on her wedding day is narrowly averted; later in the novel, another black man, Dick, rapes and murders the novel's white heroine, Flora. Dick is decried as a "damned black beast" throughout, and his crimes against Flora are described with emphasis on the violation of the white female body: "Flora lay on the ground with her clothes torn to shreds and stained with blood."[128] The blood leads to the clothing of the black man: "Look at the black devil's clothes splotched all over with her blood" (382). As this moment neatly condenses, the novel's vision of white male redemption is based on the sight of the "damned" black devil.

The Leopard's Spots does not cite *Frankenstein*, but it offers a fulfillment of the novel's scene of greatest horror. The violation of the white woman by an inhuman "beast" is anticipated in *Frankenstein*, in the monster's murder of Elizabeth:

> She was there, lifeless and inanimate, thrown across the bed, her head hanging down, and her pale and distorted features half covered by her hair. Every where I turn I see the same figure—her bloodless arms and relaxed form flung by the murderer on its bridal bier. . . . I saw at the open window a figure the most hideous and abhorred. A grin was on the face of the monster; he seemed to jeer, as with his fiendish finger he pointed towards the corpse of my wife. (135–36)

Victor's description of Elizabeth sexualizes her murder; the "bridal bier" setting, disheveled form, and vampiric mark on the neck mark the crime as one of symbolic, if not literal, rape. A work like *The Leopard's Spots* did not so much racialize the Frankenstein story as racialize it anew. Dixon strengthened the conjunction of monstrosity, race, and rape already

present in Anglo-American racism when Shelley wrote and which she refracted in *Frankenstein* through the terms of the gothic. In Shelley's version of interracial rape, monstrosity is explicit, while blackness is only
implicit; in Dixon's ostensibly more realist narrative, blackness is explicit,
while monstrosity is implied metaphorically. In both versions, rape is represented indirectly, as an act beyond the pale of literal representation. In
both texts, it is the white body of the female victim that organizes the
sexual and racial dynamics of the scene.

Yet this discourse of monstrosity was unstable, not least in the very
excess of the rhetoric it generated. The black rapist was considered so inhuman that he incited a corresponding rage on the part of his victims:
"A whole community is frenzied with horror, with the blind and furious
rage for vengeance."[129] In *The Leopard's Spots*, the most elaborate image of
monstrosity is not that of the black rapist but of the white mob assembled
to punish him. From the fire of lynching emerges a new body: "Under the
glare of the light the crowd seemed to melt into a great crawling swaying
creature, half reptile half beast, half dragon half man, with a thousand
legs, and a thousand eyes, and ten thousand gleaming teeth, and with no
ear to hear and no heart to pity!" (384). This "thousand-legged beast," as
the chapter is entitled, is its own Frankenstein amalgam, a figure of violence who has been grotesquely combined from collections of body parts
—excess legs, eyes, and teeth, but insufficient ears and hearts—that are
isolated, if not literally dismembered, from their original sources. This
image of the "crawling swaying creature" complicates Dixon's vision, since
it reverses the vectors of monstrosity that organize the rest of his novel.
By enshrining the lynch mob as the means to eradicate the black "beast,"
Dixon also reveals how white America could become—if it were not already—a monster too.

Turn-of-the-century racist invocations of black monstrosity also en-
compassed female versions of the Frankenstein monster. In a 1904 essay
in *The Outlook* titled "The Negro Woman," Eleanor Tayleur described
African American women as a "dark, helpless, hopeless mass," who are
"leading . . . lawless and purposeless lives": "As she exists in the South today the negro woman is the Frankenstein product of civilization, a being
created out of conditions of sectional hate and revenge, and set in motion
by wild experimentalists who knew not what they did."[130] For Tayleur,
the "negro woman" is a Frankenstein monster both because she is a hybrid being created by "wild experimentalists"—presumably, abolitionists
and the postwar supporters of black freedom—and because she is now

dedicated to revenge: "she is the victim of every injustice of society, and she revenges herself upon it by striking at the very foundations of the political and social structure" (267).

This transfer of the language of the Frankenstein monster to women has several effects. As with the male monster, the image's effect is of a child out of control: "There is something almost sardonically humorous in the thought of this woman, with the brain of a child and the passions of a woman, steeped in centuries of ignorance and savagery, and wrapped about with immemorial vices, playing with the die of fate" (270). The imagery of "the brain of a child and the passions of a woman" echoes that of George Canning—"a being possessing the form and strength of a man, but the intellect only of a child." Unlike Canning, however, this monster is "sardonically humorous," as if the transfer of the Frankenstein metaphor to a female body—a body already infantilized—makes the monster at once more victimized and more laughable. Compared to the rhetoric of the mythic black rapist, Tayleur's image of a female monster poses less of a threat of direct physical violence; the black woman's influence is felt more through her "social and moral decadence," as the essay is subtitled. Finally, the female monster, unlike the male monster, has the capacity to reproduce. The essay closes, "unless we succor these Hagars . . . they will raise up Ishmaels whose hands shall be against our sons forever" (271). This passage turns to the metaphor of Abraham's slave wife, Hagar, and her outcast son, Ishmael, to describe black women and their children. But it also returns to the Frankenstein metaphor, making black women into monster-makers—Hagars who give birth to Ishmaels—as well as monsters themselves.

As with Dixon's "black beast," however, Tayleur's racist metaphor of a black female Frankenstein monster leaves white people in an uncertain, and potentially monstrous, role. For Tayleur, slavery was an ennobling system for black women, because it enabled "the uplift of close personal association with white women" (267); this phrase both mystifies enslavement as "close personal association" and locates the ability to provide "uplift," a word customarily associated with African American reform, with white people. Now, by contrast, "When the black woman imitates the white, she only imitates what is worst in her. . . . she copies her independence in utter abandon of all restraints, she copies her vices and adds to them frills of her own" (268). This is a negative portrait of white women, who already embody the threats of independence, vice, and vulgarity. Tayleur's essay explicitly uses Frankenstein metaphors to condemn black women, but like Dixon's drawing attention to the white "thousand-legged beast," her language of monstrosity brings with it an unflattering focus on the white creator.

In an era of revitalized racism, African American writers also reversed metaphors of black monstrosity in new ways. For example, in a critique of the charge of interracial rape leveled against black men, Frederick Douglass observed in 1893 that "[i]t is an effort to divest the Negro of his friends by giving him a revolting and hateful reputation. Those who do this would make the world believe that freedom has changed the whole character of the Negro, and made of him a moral monster."[131] Organizing his rhetoric through monster metaphors, Douglass condemns the idea that freedom has created a "moral monster"; the truly "revolting" figure is the racist who rebels against the reality of black freedom. Ida B. Wells extended such critiques in her accounts of lynching, as in her description of one "display of almost indescribable barbarism. This time the mob made no attempt to conceal its identity, but reveled in the contemplation of its feast of crime."[132] Such condemnations made a spectacle of the lynch mob as a collective body both viewing and feasting on its crime. In *Frankenstein*, Victor recoils at the monster who "seemed to jeer, as with his fiendish finger he pointed towards the corpse" (135–36). In the reappropriations of monstrosity offered by Wells and Douglass, the voyeuristic and jeering monster is the white lynch mob.

One final example suggests the complexity of the conjunction between blackness and *Frankenstein* at the turn of the century. The Chicago World's Columbian Exposition of 1893 was the premier public event of the era, attended by more than twenty-five million people; it featured exhibitions of American scientific and cultural progress and, by contrast, ethnological displays of peoples from Africa and Asia. African Americans were excluded from the planning of this event and were acknowledged in a "Colored People's Day" that featured watermelon stands. They contested this racist treatment in a variety of ways; the quotations from Douglass and Wells in the preceding paragraph are taken from their coauthored pamphlet *The Reason Why the Colored American Is Not in the World's Columbian Exposition* (1893), which directly condemned the event's racism.

Atlanta University, accorded one of the few display spaces for African American institutions, eschewed such direct protest, exhibiting materials on black achievement in the rhetoric of racial uplift. Among its materials was a special "Exposition Number" of the university's official bulletin, whose stated goal was to "win appreciation for the work which the

Atlanta University *Bulletin,* July 1893, p. 1. (Robert W. Woodruff
Library of the Atlanta University Center)

University is doing, and . . . add to the number of its valued friends." At
the top of the first page was a poem by A. T. Worden called "The Modern Sphinx," which links African Americans and the Frankenstein story.
Interpreted in the contexts of its complex publication venue as well as
the black Frankenstein tradition, "The Modern Sphinx" suggests both
the yields and contradictions of normalizing monstrosity. These changes,
I suggest, return full circle to the contradictions of the transatlantic discourse of abolitionism from which Mary Shelley had originally drawn.[133]

"The Modern Sphinx" uses the term "Frankenstein" in its first stanza, opposite an image of a black woman:

Behold in this calm face
The modern sphinx, with such a thoughtful mien
As bids pause, when like a Frankenstein,
A nation dares create another race.

This stanza combines the imagery of the sphinx—often associated with Africa, blackness, and femininity—with that of the Frankenstein story.[134] The woman in the illustration is a "modern sphinx," whose "thoughtful" demeanor makes pause any nation that, "like a Frankenstein," "dares create another race." The precise reference to the Frankenstein story is unclear, but the suggestion seems to be that white America, by enslaving Africans, has created a new race. In the second stanza, this new race is marked by "pleading":

No longer here the crude
And unformed features of a savage face;
But in those pleading eyes a kindred race
Asks for the highway out of servitude.

This stanza seems to suggest that slavery, the founding of "servitude," was the original act of monstrous creation by white America. The rest of the poem is a plea for tolerance of black women who "Have crooned as foster-mothers / . . . And for their sisters pale have gladly died" and who refrain from violence: "And yet no hand is raised in cruel wrath / And all their wrongs evoke as yet but tears." The poem ends with an invocation to "Study the problem well, / For in this Sphinx a message somewhere lies; / A nation's glory or its shame may rise / From out the reading what these features tell."

In its racist imagery of "pleading," formerly "savage" black women, the poem trades in contemporary racial stereotype. As in Eleanor Tayleur's essay, the black woman seems to be "dark, helpless, hopeless"; here, she combines two types, inscrutable Sphinx and inhuman monster. This poem was written by a white man, A. T. Worden, a white Baptist minister who lived in New York and maintained both a congregation and an active career as a writer. Author of a historical novel, *Napoleon Smith* (1888), Worden published poetry in mainstream venues including *Godey's* and the *Saturday Evening Post*.[135] Worden's poems were generally conservative in their satiric targets; a poem on the "New Woman," for example, warns that "the comin' woman had better / Go slow till the old one is gone."[136] "February Twenty-Second: As Explained by George Washington Smiff to His Descendants" is a poem written in dialect about "How de Fader ob dis country, known as Gawge G. Washington / Coma ter give me his cognomen on de day dat I / was bawn."[137] With its racist stereotypes, "The Modern Sphinx" is the complement rather than the antidote to such minstrel depictions of black men as dialect "Gawge" Washingtons.[138]

But the poem's republication by an African American university in the context of the World's Columbian Exposition changes its context, moving it into the realm of racial uplift. Although Worden was white, for readers viewing the poem in this context, "Atlanta University" seems to be the African American author of the text; against the Exposition's own emphasis on "savage faces" in its ethnological displays, the poem presents "a kindred face" and a plea for tolerance. Robert Rydell, noting the "Frankenstein" image in the poem, suggests that "[f]rom the perspective of many African-Americans, this is precisely what the World's Columbian Exposition signified—a veritable cultural Frankenstein."[139] Under the imprimatur of Atlanta University, the poem registers a challenge to the racist ethnological freakery of the Exposition.

Within this framework, the poem moves the Frankenstein story decisively into the world of women. It is not only that this is a female Frankenstein monster, as in Eleanor Tayleur's writing, but also that the "modern Sphinx" is linked to an actual community of African American women, as signaled in the photograph that fills the bottom half of the page. The picture of the "Senior Normal Class in Atlanta University"—the Normal Department of the university trained teachers—gives specificity to the abstract illustration of the unnamed mythological "Sphinx." The photograph shows thirteen African American women students, positioned in "a winter scene"; its complement is on the back cover of the *Bulletin*, in a slightly smaller photograph of seven African American male students, captioned "The Senior College Class in Atlanta University." The page as a whole situates black women on the front page, literally, of the discourse of African American racial uplift. In the relation between the poem and its visual contexts, the threat of an uncontrollable black monster, implicitly male, has become the triumphant promise of black women, while the objectification of the "savage" black person at the Exposition has been normalized with the image of the "Senior Normal Class."

Yet the poem itself, in reversing monstrosity, also normalizes a narrow version of femininity. The third stanza begins with the simile, "Like as the Amazon / . . . / So do these patient millions still press on"; this is not a reference to the active female Amazonian tradition but a naturalizing comparison that turns black women into a river. In the fourth stanza, even the forward flow of water has constricted, as black women

> Such at the cradle-side
> Have crooned as foster-mothers, sung and wept,
> Across the chamber doors of pain have slept,
>   And for their sisters pale have gladly died.

Black women come into view as "foster-mothers," presumably to white children, and then as willing martyrs to white women, "their sisters pale." Racial-uplift discourse for women was centered on middle-class femininity; an article in the *Bulletin* explained the curriculum of Atlanta University as "instruction in cooking, sewing, dress-making, nursing, and housekeeping to girls."[140] The poem heightens such domesticity by locating women as nonviolent and long-suffering martyrs. By the poem's end, this positioning encompasses even the figure of the Sphinx. The final stanza exhorts readers to "Study the problem well, / For in this Sphinx a message somewhere lies; / A nation's glory or its shame may rise / From out the reading what these features tell." Women remain the symbolic center of the poem, but as a "problem" to be studied.

At stake in this transformation are the normalizing impulses of class as well as gender. Uplift ideology relied on both psychological and social forms of internal repression, with a focus on middle-class respectability often producing feelings of shame and anger that were displaced onto other African Americans.[141] The class norms of this discourse saturate the *Bulletin*. For example, an alumna laments that the majority of tourists to Florida sees "only the illiterate class" of black people: "The writer knows of repeated instances in which many of the tourists pay . . . to attend some public display given at their request by the class of the least progressive colored people. There they see plantation dancing, hear minstrel singing . . . and things in general which show the colored people at a great disadvantage."[142] Such contrasts between educated African Americans and the objects of their gaze also emerge in descriptions of interracial contact, as in an article by an unnamed "young man in the junior class" about his favorite books. He praises Washington Irving for his depiction of Indians because Irving shows "the crude, mean, coarse ways and inclinations of savage life."[143] Interpreted in relation to the Exposition, such displacements seem to replicate the event's own contrast between civilized viewers and the uncivilized "others" on display. Such descriptions also reassured the Exposition's white attendees that Atlanta University—and, by extension, the ethos of racial uplift—was the opposite of the "crude, mean, coarse [and] savage." In the *Bulletin* as a whole, the alumni of racial uplift redefine themselves in contrast to a discourse of monstrosity, but only by displacing monstrosity onto others and condemning it in themselves.

In this context, the emphasis in "The Modern Sphinx" on middle-class African American femininity further reaffirms the potentially accommodationist impulses of racial uplift. The poem valorizes black women, but this valorization serves to emphasize the "pleading," "patient," and "gladly" martyred spirit of uplift as a whole. These are the same traits that define the Frankenstein monster, in his initial confrontation with his maker: "What I ask of you," he pleads to Victor when asking him for a mate, "is reasonable and moderate. . . . the gratification is small, but it is all that I can receive, and it shall content me" (98–99). In divorcing itself from the Frankenstein tradition, the poem paradoxically returns to the same hierarchies of Shelley's novel, wherein, as Spivak characterizes it, the monster's fate "is vectored specifically toward and away from the master."[144]

The limits of a plea for normalization are illustrated on the penultimate page of the *Bulletin* in "Atlanta University Boys at the Exposition," a report on the African American students employed there "to wheel rolling chairs"—a task that metaphorically encapsulates the role of black people as essential yet subservient laborers propelling white America forward.[145] The report asserts that these men had been given "the most fair, liberal, and courteous treatment, which they have highly appreciated," and it features a wholly positive letter from one worker, "J. W. Johnson"—James Weldon Johnson, then a student. "No one . . . can form any idea of the immensity and grandeur of the Exposition," Johnson enthused; "there are many wonderful exhibitions here, but to my mind the most wonderful is that of the skill and genius which has in so short a time created this, the most beautiful spot on the face of the earth."[146] Johnson went on to write *The Autobiography of an Ex-Colored Man* and to play a leading role in African American letters and racial struggles over the following forty years. In this early moment, he seems to write unironically and uncritically about the Exposition as "the most beautiful spot on the face of the earth," even though this "beautiful spot" offered almost no place for African Americans.

In *Frankenstein*, by contrast, the monster refuses to accept his place-lessness. Rebelling violently against Victor's broken promises, he disrupts Victor's world far more fully than through the language of moderation and martyrdom. "The Modern Sphinx" and its surrounding uplift documents recast the language of black monstrosity, but they also give up the monster's open expression of anger. Wells and Douglass are further than A. T. Worden from a direct citation of *Frankenstein*, but they are closer to the novel's most radical implications for political protest. The Exposition, Douglass declared sharply, was not a White City but a "whited sepulcher," and "when it is asked why we are excluded from the World's Columbian Exposition, the answer is Slavery."[147]

In its citation of the Frankenstein story, then, "The Modern Sphinx" offers one fulfillment of the legacies of Shelley's novel. In the rhetoric of nineteenth-century America, I have argued, the figure of the Franken-stein monster is embedded and embodied in racist descriptions of Afri-can American men, from the antebellum image of Nat Turner as Frank-enstein to the midcentury rhetoric of Van Evrie to Civil War accounts of the Confederacy and postwar mythologies of the black rapist. Throughout this archive, these descriptions are, in turn, inseparable from nineteenth-century iconographies of the American nation, a duality that informs postwar depictions of the black rapist as much as it does antebellum ac-counts of the rebellious slave. Yet Shelley's monster could only be used for racist rhetoric by severing the Frankenstein monster from his own sym-pathetic first-person voice, from the critique of injustice that accompanies his radical turn to violence, and from the narrative of doubling between monster and maker that implicates Victor Frankenstein in the monster's crimes at every turn. The monster could become a racist metaphor only, in other words, by dismembering the image of "Frankenstein" from the novel *Frankenstein*.

By contrast, the congruence of the Frankenstein story with white aboli-tionist and African American writing suggests that the story could be ap-propriated for antiracist purposes more easily than it could be used to en-ergize racist metaphors of blackness and nationhood. For antiracist writ-ers, the process of "remembering" the monster—in both senses—restored his more literary antecedents in Shelley's novel and his more liberal and radical political legacies as well. As the example of the Atlanta University

Bulletin shows, however, this process of remembrance had its own internal divisions and limitations. The tensions within the novel between a liberal plea for tolerance and a more militant expression of violence return in the interstitial fractures of turn-of-the-century racial-uplift discourse. African American cultural critique, like the rhetoric of the white nation, was an amalgam of disunited states. Embodying both white and black Americas, the Frankenstein monster incarnated a body politic that was, like the nineteenth-century United States, not only tenuously joined at its edges but also revolting from within.

2

Black Monsters, Dead Metaphors

Symbol, n. Something that is supposed to typify or stand for
something else. Many symbols are mere "survivals"—things which
having no longer any utility continue to exist because we have
inherited the tendency to make them; as funereal urns carved on
memorial monuments. They were once real urns holding the ashes
of the dead. We cannot stop making them, but we can give them a
name that conceals our helplessness.

—Ambrose Bierce, *The Devil's Dictionary*

I.

Throughout nineteenth-century American culture, I have argued, the figure of the Frankenstein monster served as an evocative political metaphor
for the American nation, the African American man, and the conflicted
relationship between them. In building an archive of nineteenth-century
black Frankenstein stories, I have argued that the Frankenstein monster
functions metaphorically, but I have not yet examined what it means,
aesthetically as well as politically, for a metaphor to be aligned with a
monster. In this chapter, I explore the metaphoric equation between the
Frankenstein monster and the African American man, as that equation
appeared in fictional form in the turn-of-the-century writing of Stephen
Crane. Crane's novella *The Monster* (1898), I argue, is important not only
because it provides a sustained and self-conscious literary narrative of a
black Frankenstein monster but also because it explores a self-reflexive
conjunction between the making of monsters and the making of metaphors. The conjunction between these terms illuminates the political figure of the black Frankenstein monster, the complex literary surfaces of
Crane's writing, and the meaning of metaphor itself.

To make these claims, I begin by identifying an intrinsic connection between the fictional figure of the Frankenstein monster and the literary figure of the dead metaphor, outlining this connection generally and then in historical relation to late-nineteenth-century American accounts of metaphor. Turning to *The Monster*, I interpret it, first, as an antiracist allegory strengthened by its allusions to *Frankenstein* and then, second, as an exploration of metaphor, made on the grounds of aesthetics rather than politics and focused on the "dead metaphor" of black monstrosity. I then bring together the novella's political and aesthetic registers, showing that although these registers are, at times, mutually reinforced, Crane's interest in metaphor subsumes his examination of race. By the end of *The Monster*, I argue, Crane brings even his aesthetic project to a halt, making his monster metaphors, so extravagantly revivified, dead again.

II.

If Mary Shelley set a metaphoric equation between monsters and texts when she declared, "I bid my hideous progeny go forth and prosper," then what are the terms of this equation? We may begin to answer this question by looking at some of the literary properties of metaphor. Like the Frankenstein monster, metaphor emerges through amalgamation. In the most influential twentieth-century model of metaphor, I. A. Richards defined it as the "interaction" of two parts, the "tenor" (the thing or idea being described) and the "vehicle" (the image to which it is compared).[1] The interaction between tenor and vehicle is a forcible amalgamation, especially in the case of the bad metaphor, in which tenor and vehicle seem strangely joined, or that of the mixed metaphor, in which disparate metaphors compose a mismatched whole; as Dale Pesmen has shown, mixed metaphors are commonly reviled as "repulsive, nauseous, disgustful, spoiled, [and] repugnant."[2] The signs of amalgamation are visible in a different way in the simile, with its raised join between tenor and vehicle in the words "like" or "as."[3] The simile, like the mixed metaphor, suggests the seams on the body of the Frankenstein monster, particularly as he is represented, in his most famous visual form, by Boris Karloff, with neck bolts and head sutures. These bolts and sutures enact the "like" and "as" of the simile, while the monster's grotesque body as a whole suggests the "repulsive" and "repugnant" effects of mixing metaphors together.

So too does the birth of the Frankenstein monster through a process of reanimation embody metaphoric properties. Metaphor, etymologically from the Greek *meta* (over) and *pherein* (to carry), often transgresses the boundary between animate and inanimate. Classical writing on metaphor emphasizes this trait: Aristotle, for example, privileged the "practice of attributing life to inanimate things by metaphor," and Quintilian, assessing different categories of metaphor, highlighted the "wonderfully sublime effect" produced when inanimate things are made animate.[4] The Frankenstein monster is particularly close to the rhetorical process of personification, which turns inanimate objects into people; the monster is the personification of personification. Animation is also central to the literary figure of synecdoche, in which the part stands for the whole. Many synecdoches animate body parts as if they were whole bodies ("All hands on deck," "We need some new blood," "I'm glad to see some new faces here today"). The Frankenstein monster has been popularized through his neck bolts and suture marks, two types of synecdoche. But he also exemplifies the very principle of synecdoche: he transforms the idea that animated parts might stand for a whole into the idea that a whole monster might be assembled from animated parts.

The Frankenstein monster is not only animated but reanimated, and, as such, his closest resemblance is not to the simile, the mixed metaphor, or the synecdoche but to another literary figure: the dead metaphor. Dead metaphors are metaphors that have ceased to register as metaphors, such as "the leg of a table." Some linguists and philosophers define this category broadly, suggesting that all idioms are dead metaphors, since they are phrases whose original metaphoric content has now ceased to register.[5] "To throw down the gauntlet," meaning to challenge, once referred to the practice of throwing down a glove to issue a challenge; "three sheets to the wind," meaning drunk, originally referred to the ropes or "sheets" that controlled the direction of a boat's sails, whose looseness in the wind signaled that the vessel was out of control.[6] Whether the category is construed narrowly or broadly, dead metaphors can be reanimated. "The leg of a table" is a dead metaphor, no longer evoking a human leg, but the image of "an unshaven leg of a table" would be a live metaphor, since the adjective "unshaven" first restores the literal idea of a human leg and then brings back to life the metaphor made from comparing the long thin rod that supports a table (the tenor of the metaphor) to a human or animal leg (its vehicle). A description of a leg of a table as something that "looks hip but is knee-deep in lacquer and has a flat-footed design" would reanimate the dead metaphor through puns, which call attention to the body parts—hips, knees, and feet—associated with a literal leg and, in so doing, make possible a live metaphor that draws together tenor (table part) and vehicle (leg). Considered as dead metaphors, idioms, too, may be reanimated. For example, idioms may be literalized to make their metaphoric meanings stand out afresh. When asked "Are you a man or a mouse?" Groucho Marx replied, "Throw me a piece of cheese and you'll find out."[7]

A more sustained example of the reanimation of dead metaphors is provided by Ambrose Bierce in his late-nineteenth-century compendium of satiric word definitions, *The Devil's Dictionary* (1881–1906). Bierce has no entry for "metaphor," but his definition of "symbol" takes dead metaphors as both its theme and its literary figure. In his definition, symbols are, if not dying, then barely alive "survivals," "things which having no longer any utility continue to exist because we have inherited the tendency to make them."[8] His metaphor for this deadened status of symbols is that of funereal urns carved on memorial monuments, which were "once real urns holding the ashes of the dead" but have now been flattened into mere images. These urns, then, are dead metaphors for representing ashes, which themselves are the synecdochal remains of entire corpses. The definition emphasizes death, both in the example of the funereal urns and in the fatalistic "helplessness" of symbol-makers. Yet by invoking urns in this context, Bierce also reanimates them: he first names the literal significance of urns and then uses them as a vehicle for describing symbols as dying. The urns may be dead metaphoric vehicles to describe corpses, but they become live metaphoric vehicles to characterize symbols themselves. This is a transformation of a live metaphor into a dead one, and of a dead metaphor—the funereal urn—into a live one.

Like Bierce's urn, Shelley's monster is a literary elaboration of the dead metaphor. The very category of this literary figure implies a corpse: as the poet Donald Hall puts it, "The phrase 'dead metaphor' . . . implies that the metaphor was once a living organism, like a human being, but died and became a corpse"; the philosopher Max Black, distinguishing between dead and live metaphors, suggests that the former are "beyond resuscitation," whereas the latter need "no artificial respiration."[9] The Frankenstein monster can be seen as the "corpse" of the dead metaphor brought back artificially to life. This reanimating process is also one of amalgamation, given that so many dead metaphors involve a body part: the neck of a bottle, the spine of a book, the arm of a chair, the lip of a cup, the foot of the mountain, the roof of the mouth, the limb of a tree, or the face and hands of a clock. The Frankenstein monster is both a reanimation and an amalgamation of the severed body parts that customarily populate the category of dead metaphor. Indeed, it is not only that the reanimation of the monster resembles the reanimation of the dead metaphor; it is also that the monster literally embodies this process of reanimation.

At the same time, *Frankenstein* as a whole also recapitulates the more customary movement of metaphor from the literal to the figurative, since the novel's plot progresses from the literal making of the monster by Victor Frankenstein to his figurative "making" by society into a monster. As George Lakoff and Mark Johnson note, the concept of "making" is itself metaphoric, involving conceptual transformations as well as literal ones.[10] *Frankenstein* takes the difference between forms of "making" as one of its major topics. As its narrative turns from a literal monster toward a figuratively made one, *Frankenstein* restores metaphoric meaning to monstrosity. There are, then, not one but two ways in which *Frankenstein* comments on the dead metaphor. Both in its initial reanimation of the monster's body and in its narrative as a whole, *Frankenstein* recapitulates the process of bringing dead metaphors back to life. In so doing, the monster functions as a metaphor for metaphor by literalizing the operations of metaphor itself.

I have outlined this claim ahistorically, but metaphor has its own history, in which both Shelley's *Frankenstein* and late-nineteenth-century American writing can be situated. Frankenstein's monster is often interpreted as a gothic response to Enlightenment rationalism; the monster can be seen, similarly, as a response to Enlightenment approaches to metaphor. Eighteenth-century writers often attempted to systematize the study of metaphor and to quarantine its usage as an inessential ornament to plain language. In Samuel Johnson's definition of the term, for example, metaphor is a distortion of language: "The application of a word to an use to which, in its original import, it cannot be put."[11] By contrast, Shelley's novel embraces metaphor, with its densely metaphoric language, characters, and plots. Her novel is contemporary with, but more dystopian than, the privileging of metaphor by Romantic poets, as in Percy Bysshe Shelley's praise of the "vitally metaphorical" language of poetry.[12] With its metaphor-like monster, *Frankenstein* qualifies the Romantic enthusiasm for metaphor of Mary Shelley's contemporaries, including her husband, while also rejecting the rationalist approach to metaphor of her Enlightenment predecessors. Written in an era of revolutions, the Frankenstein monster literalizes metaphor's revolutionary potential—as threat as well as promise.[13]

Late-nineteenth-century America constituted another site of concentrated interest in metaphor, particularly metaphor seen as threat. In the same era in which Bierce produced his *Devil's Dictionary*, numerous writers published popular guidebooks, school textbooks, dictionaries, and academic monographs that attempted to explain and systematize the use of literary figures. These works included Brainerd Kellogg's *A Text-Book on Rhetoric*, which went through eighteen editions between 1880 and 1904, and Adams Sherman Hill's *The Principles of Rhetoric and Their Application* (1888), which was influential in academia.[14] The profusion of rhetoric guides in this era reflected the expansion of education to a growing population that included new immigrants and emancipated slaves, people who could benefit from the immediate "application" of rhetoric. At the same time, these books codified rhetoric as an academic field in America. In both democratic and elite registers, these books were part of the project of what Dennis Baron characterizes as "schoolmastering the language" and what Michel Foucault, in *Discipline and Punish*, more broadly terms the "humble modalities" of power.[15] Rhetoric disciplined people socially as well as linguistically. For example, in an invocation against mixed metaphor, Adams Sherman Hill cautioned that disparate figures "should not be brought close together, for the more forcible they are, the more detrimental they must be to each other," a warning that echoes the era's prohibition on miscegenation.[16] The mixed metaphor was sometimes condemned as a "monstrous union," imagery central to the condemnation of mulattoes. Mixed literary figures were like mixed-race literal bodies, or even interspecies bodies, as in Brainerd Kellogg's caution that the mixed metaphor was "like the mythical mermaid—what begins as a human being ends as a fish."[17]

Such codifications of metaphor were, in turn, congruent with the classificatory impulses of the era, from the formation of anthropology, sociology, psychology, statistics, and other academic disciplines that organized human history and behavior into social science to the development of criminology, eugenics, and other pseudoscientific modes for codifying social norms. These new disciplinary forms simultaneously rationalized new bodies of knowledge and policed the boundaries of deviance. Machines were central to such processes, from the typewriters and assembly lines that exploited human labor to cameras that captured motion and railroads that speeded the flow of capital. Mark Seltzer, following Foucault, suggests that the constant focus in this era on "the intimacy between the natural and the technological" constitutes a "body-machine complex," which emerged in social theory like that of Thorstein Veblen, visual forms like the composite photograph, and fiction by naturalist writers Stephen Crane, Theodore Dreiser, Jack London, and Frank Norris.[18]

Rhetoric guidebooks employed related vocabularies of mechanization and discipline. Simon Kerl suggested in his 1869 *Elements of Composition and Rhetoric* that rhetoric was like a train that needed strong control: "The steam-engine, when not hitched to any thing, is but an ingenious and interesting curiosity; but when it is attached to the multifarious industry of mankind, it moves the whole world. So it is with language, in regard to thought."[19] Metaphors, like steam engines, could escape attempts at their control. Kellogg urged eternal vigilance for the teacher of metaphor:

> The *teacher* should *prune* closely here. Let him see to it that the image is choice and apt and not far-fetched, that there is no mixing of incongruous things in it, that, so far as may be, it is the pupil's own, and that he does not use it solely for ornament, varnishing or veneering his style with it, but that he lays it under tribute to his thought—thinks in it, and expresses himself by it, and through it.[20]

This passage warned against the far-fetched metaphor, the mixed metaphor, the cliched metaphor, and the purely ornamental metaphor—a catalogue of excesses that overwhelms the closing exhortation of metaphor as an underlying "tribute" to thought. But the passage also illustrates the difficulty of avoiding these excesses, since its own metaphors —the need to "prune" imagery, as if it were a plant, but then the student "varnishing or veneering his style," as if it were a piece of furniture—are "incongruous[ly]" mixed.

Other discussions suggest concern about the relation of metaphor to national identity. David Jayne Hill concluded his discussion of metaphor with the assertion that "[w]hen America's Milton and Shakespeare come, they will not go . . . to Homer and Virgil for their imagery, but to the hidden quarries of nature, and from their interminable depths they will bring materials for castles of diction as grand as the old-time structures from which others steal the moss-grown stones."[21] Metaphor, in this formulation, is a key feature of American literary nationalism; the "hidden quarries" of the American landscape are both Hill's own metaphor and the literal ground to which American writers will turn.

National questions were, in turn, inseparable from racial ones. In Theodore Hunt's discussion of literary figures, the point of departure is the "savage":

> Most abundant among the Southern and Eastern nations, [examples of figurative language] are numerous everywhere. Largely used by children and by savage peoples, they are modified by age and culture. They decrease in number and increase in purity and power as civilization goes on.[22]

This racist account of figurative language assumes a developmental narrative from savagery to civilization, from childhood to adulthood, and from impurity to purity, with all of these negative terms mapped geographically onto "Southern and Eastern nations." At the same time, in the orientalizing discourse of the era, the "East" was also seen as an overcivilized, decadent realm, known for the overuse of literary figures. James De Mille, in *The Elements of Rhetoric* (1878), cautions, "The metaphor should not be carried too far, nor should too many be introduced. The effect of this is to overload the style with ornament, and to render it weak and tedious. This is a fault which pervades Oriental writing."[23]

Like the era's simultaneous embrace and recoil from the machine, such ambivalent invocations of "civilization" were central to the culture of late-nineteenth-century America. As Gail Bederman has shown, a discourse of white "civilization," defined in contrast to nonwhite "savagery," pervades the culture of the period.[24] Hunt's introduction of a "savage" element into a history of metaphor relies on a similar trajectory, in which savagery is an origin from which civilized metaphor emerges in adult triumph but is also a threat against which it must always maintain its distance. Conversely, De Mille's caution against "Oriental" overuse of metaphor polices the boundaries of "civilization" from the other end, warning against the dangers of overcivilization. The prohibitions on figurative imagery that saturate these guidebooks testify to the political pressures on metaphor against falling into either the infantilized impurity of the "savage" or the decadent excess of the "overcivilized."

Hunt's identification of metaphor with "children and savages" also intersects with issues of gender, in an era when the concern about "overcivilization" was inextricable from anxieties about imperiled masculinity. As Bederman shows, a variety of men in this period, from G. Stanley Hall to

Theodore Roosevelt, reasserted their superior access to white male "civilization"; they tempered new anxieties about their possible "overcivilization" —with its threat of male effeminacy—by promoting the restorative value of a temporary immersion in ostensibly savage forms of masculinity.25 This was also the era in which homosexuality was codified as such by the new fields of psychoanalysis and sexology. The threat of failed masculinity was not only of becoming feminized but of being homosexual—a threat linked not to hypermasculine "savagery" but to feminized "overcivilization."[26]

In Hunt's discussion of metaphor, the affiliation of "savages" with children suggests their feminization. At the same time, Hunt implies that those civilized Westerners who use metaphor excessively are not infantilized but emasculated. He ends his section on figurative language with a quotation: "'Embellishment,' says Quintilian, 'should be manly.' Even the best of [literary figures] are to be used with discretion. As they are liable to abuse in the line of the fanciful or absurd, special care should be taken."[27] Hunt stops short of identifying the opposite of "manly" embellishment, but Quintilian had already named it:

> Healthy bodies . . . are tanned, slim, and muscular. . . . [I]f one feminizes them by plucking the hair and using cosmetics, the very striving for beauty makes them disgusting. . . . [D]ecent and impressive apparel lends men authority . . . but a womanish and luxurious dress, instead of adorning the body, exposes the mind within. In the same way, the translucent and many-coloured style of some speakers emasculates subjects which are clothed in this kind of verbal dress.[28]

Quintilian's analogy between the bodies of men and texts aligns literary embellishment with cosmetics and costume; its consequences are both femininity and feminization, as the body is made "womanish" and "emasculate[d]." Hunt develops the same ideas more obliquely: the unmanly male writer would be feminized by his "fanciful" overuse of literary figures into a domain of "abuse"—potentially either homosexuality or the self-abuse of masturbation. In Hunt's nineteenth-century version of these longstanding cautions, the man whose metaphors escape his control faces the prospect of a decline into "mechanical artifice," a regression to "savage[ry]," and the prospect of his own emasculation.

These concerns lead back to *Frankenstein*, since fears of the mechanical and the savage were long associated with the Frankenstein monster. I have already noted that the monster's affinity with "mechanical artifice" goes back at least to Peake's 1823 play *Presumption*, in which the monster is called "a huge automaton in human form," and I have argued that his savage connotations were developed, in nineteenth-century America, in representations of African American men. The connection of the Frankenstein story to emasculation is twofold. Within *Frankenstein*, the uncontrollable monster threatens to unman Victor, while the novel itself, as an uncontrollable monster made by a woman writer, presented monstrous femininity run amok; together, the novel's male monster and female author threaten to emasculate male characters within the narrative and male readers without. If the outlines of the Frankenstein monster are discernible in the nineteenth-century American textbooks on metaphor, it is because the anxieties that these books associate with metaphoric excess—the machine, the savage, and the emasculating feminine—are both acute in American culture in this period and embodied in the Frankenstein monster himself.

Whereas such accounts are anxious in tone, there were also more sympathetic approaches to metaphor in this era. In a section called "Mixed Metaphors Are Not Always Objectionable," for example, De Mille notes that Shakespeare himself "shows a lordly disregard of convention" in this area.[29] Another text from this period more fully recuperates metaphor in ways that suggestively overlap with *Frankenstein*. Gertrude Buck's *The Metaphor: A Study in the Psychology of Rhetoric* (1899) is an academic monograph on the unconscious psychological processes involved in the creation and perception of metaphor. Buck, a professor at Vassar, was the author of plays, poetry, and fiction as well as several important works of rhetoric.[30]

The Metaphor seems, at first, to use the same governing negative terms as metaphor textbooks. Like Hunt, Buck outlines a model of metaphor as "mechanical," and she proposes instead a biological model:

> The [usual] explanation conceives of metaphor as a mechanical product, like a box, whose parts, gathered from different sources are put together to make a whole. The other [explanation] regards it as the result of a vital process, more like a plant or an animal. . . . [Metaphor] is no artificial, manufactured product, but a real organism, growing and dying.[31]

Buck, too, defines metaphor in relation to childlike savagery: "The sophisticated modern, when he gives utterance to perception, is making a radical metaphor just as truly as does the savage or the child" (33). And

Buck, too, identifies metaphor with the threat of femininity: "the practical man is straightaway seized with a distrust of the figure [metaphor], amounting almost to fear. He regards metaphors much as the old saints regarded women—as charming snares, in which he may too easily be entangled" (30). In the age of the "sophisticated modern," metaphor is identified through the negative terms of the mechanical, the savage, and the "entangl[ing]" feminine.

Yet Buck alters these terms significantly. Her argument is not that metaphors become "mechanical artifice" when they are used badly but that metaphors are mistakenly condemned as such by those who fail to understand how they function. Misreaders of metaphor see it mistakenly as a writer's deliberate artifice, intended to snare the reader, whereas in Buck's psychological model, metaphor emerges organically from an unconscious initial perception of two images simultaneously. The completed verbal metaphor elaborates "this primitive perception in the act of differentiation, two or more images appearing side by side" (35). The reader of metaphor then recapitulates this process, understanding metaphor by developing in the mind a "composite photograph made by the rapid alternate presentation of the two images" (54). This explanation, which draws from the form of the "composite photograph" as well as theories of psychology, does not undo the racism of Buck's account. She recasts one racist model of development, in which history progresses from childlike savagery to adult civilization, into another, in which the psyche moves from "primitive perception" to sophisticated "differentiation." However, Buck refutes the misogynist equation of metaphor with femininity. She offers the anecdote of the "practical man" in order to criticize him as a prime example of what she terms "metaphorophobia" (30)—an unfounded fear of metaphor. Hers is a celebratory account, in which deviance is not intrinsic to metaphor but is instead a social construction created by its audience. To return to *Frankenstein*, this is the monster's story as he himself would tell it: an account not of innate monstrosity but of being made monstrous by the views of others.

An even stronger overlap with the monster's story emerges elsewhere in Buck's monograph. Her recuperation of both metaphors and monstrosity is clearest in her final chapter, "Pathological Forms of Metaphor." Such forms are of two kinds: "frigid metaphors," which are either "artificial throughout" or are "perverted . . . into conceit," and mixed metaphors (60). Like her account of "metaphorophobia," this diagnosis of frigidity and perversion uses the new vocabularies of psychology and sexology to understand the world of metaphor. But Buck uses these normalizing discourses against themselves. In the case of mixed metaphors, her argument is that metaphors are not mixed in the mind of the writer, for the writer perceives his first metaphor as passing immediately from figurative to literal status: "The second figure does not jar with the first, for the first has ceased to be figurative" (64). The writer understands his metaphors only as dead; the reader, however, restores them to figurative status and thus sees them as mixed. She summarizes: "Mixed metaphor . . . is not mixed from the writer's point of view. . . . It is always the reader who makes the mixed metaphor, not the writer. This statement is not intended as a defense but only as an explanation of the essential nature of this phenomenon" (67). In other words, Buck argues that mixed metaphors are created when the reader reanimates dead metaphors, bringing them back to life as a grotesquely mixed whole.

This is, I have been arguing, what happens in *Frankenstein*, not once but twice. The creation of the monster enacts the process by which dead metaphors are brought back to life and reassembled into an amalgamated whole; this process of revivification—the making of a monster—is then recapitulated in the plot of the narrative, as the monster develops from a literal monster into a socially constructed one. Buck's claim that "[i]t is always the reader who makes the mixed metaphor, not the writer" closely resembles this second reanimation in *Frankenstein*, when the monster's "readers," from the De Laceys to Victor to William, make him into a metaphorical monster. Buck concludes with the assertion that metaphor "is not . . . an isolated phenomenon, a 'freak' in literature . . . but a genuine expression of the normal process of thought at a certain stage in its development" (69). Buck depathologizes metaphor, turning it from monstrous "freak" into "normal process," while also condemning "metaphorophobia." Writing from within the limits of a discourse of "savagery," but against the misogyny of conventional rhetoric, Buck suggests the flexibility of both metaphor and monstrosity in late-nineteenth-century America. In a culture organized by the policing of boundaries, metaphors were often seen, like the Frankenstein monster, as figures of monstrous excess. But as Buck's monograph shows, metaphors—like monsters—could also be reanimated from within.

Writing at the same time as Gertrude Buck, Stephen Crane, I suggest, took up the same antimetaphorophobic project, choosing to reanimate both dead metaphors and the monster who signified them. To understand this project, I begin by situating Crane in relation to contemporary discourses of monstrosity—including lynching, freak shows, and medical research—that suggest his aesthetic as well as political interest in the metaphor of the black man as Frankenstein monster. Turning to *The Monster*, I interpret it first as a political allegory, showing how *Frankenstein* provides Crane with a fictional template through which to expose the racism that turns black men into monsters. Yet Crane also undermines this allegory, particularly in the sustained pejorative equation that he develops between the Frankenstein monster and the black dandy. Politically ambiguous in relation to *Frankenstein*, Crane's novella is more consistent, I suggest, in a second inheritance from Shelley's novel. Crane implicitly draws from the Frankenstein tradition its self-reflexive alignment between monsters and metaphors, and he pursues this alignment in the profusion of strained similes, mixed metaphors, and many other extravagant literary figures that are the distinguishing stylistic trait of this novella.

Looking at *The Monster* through the lens of *Frankenstein*, then, provides a way of understanding its extraordinary figurative surface. As if in defiant response to "metaphorophobia," Crane's prose strains, mixes, and otherwise revivifies metaphor, including the metaphor of black men as monsters. Crane, like Gertrude Buck, revalues the "freak" of metaphor. His interest in a black Frankenstein monster, from this perspective, is less a critique of racism than a self-reflexive exploration, on the grounds of aesthetics rather than politics, of the ways in which metaphors, like monsters, are made.

III.

First published in *Harper's* in 1898, Stephen Crane's *The Monster* is a novella in twenty-four sections focusing on Dr. Trescott, a respected small-town white doctor, and Henry Johnson, the doctor's black coachman. The first quarter charts Johnson's friendship with Trescott's son, Jimmie, and his place in the town's black community. When a fire breaks out at the Trescott house, Johnson saves Jimmie but is horribly injured: his face is burned away, and he apparently becomes insane. Trescott alone nurses Johnson. The last quarter of *The Monster* charts the revulsion of the townspeople against Johnson and their ostracism of Trescott for his continued support of Johnson.[32]

The Monster firmly links the figure of the Frankenstein monster with that of the black man, and it is concerned throughout with the relationship between them—although this relationship remains surprisingly un-deranalyzed in the substantial body of criticism now devoted to this text.[33] We can begin to evaluate the relation of *The Monster* to *Frankenstein* by assessing the variety of discourses of monstrosity pressing on Crane's text. Critics have suggested several sources for the character of Henry Johnson, including a man from Crane's hometown of Port Jervis, New York, whose face was "eaten by cancer," and John Merrick, the "Elephant Man," who was rescued by a sympathetic doctor and whose story Crane would have encountered while living in England.[34] The "Elephant Man" was initially exhibited in a freak show, and as Bill Brown has shown, Crane's novella is inseparable from the elaborate world of turn-of-the-century amusements —not only freak shows and dime museums but also circuses, vaudeville, photography, and world's fairs—that turned ostensible monstrosity into marketable spectacle.[35] *The Monster* draws repeatedly from this world, as when Jimmie Trescott organizes an exhibition of Henry Johnson to his friends.

More specifically, Henry Johnson may be a reference to the real-life William Henry Johnson, a black man who was known as a "pinhead" because of his foreshortened forehead and apparent mental retardation. Marketed under the names "What Is It?" "Monkey-Man," and "Zip"— an adaptation of the minstrel-show character known as the "Zip Coon" —Johnson had a long and successful career in freak shows from 1860 to 1926. The similarity of names may be coincidence, but Crane's Henry Johnson indisputably draws from the world of William Henry Johnson, whose various stage names suggest three racist stereotypes of ostensible black monstrosity: the inhuman animal linked to the monkey, the black performer made grotesque by minstrelsy, and the freak so reduced to ob-jectified spectacle that his name is "What Is It?"[36]

So too does *The Monster* suggest the most violent exhibition of a black "monster" for white audiences in this era: the spectacle of lynching. Elaine Marshall has shown the strong correspondences between *The Monster* and the eyewitness account written by Crane's brother William of the lynching of a black man named Robert Lewis in Port Jervis in 1892. Lewis, who was accused of raping a white woman, was hanged by a crowd of two thousand white people. William Crane interrupted the hanging and tem-porarily saved Lewis, a moment he described as follows: "I could see that he was alive. . . . His face was covered with blood and I did not recognize him. . . . At this point Raymond Carr struck a match and held it down to the negro's face, and said 'you have got the right man boys, that is Bob

Lewis.'" Despite Crane's efforts, Lewis was hanged again. As Marshall outlines, this episode shares with *The Monster* a number of narrative elements, including a black man whose face is disfigured in proximity to fire and a white man who seems to bring him back from the dead but cannot prevent further disaster. The resonances of Crane's novella with lynching and freak shows underscores the continuity between these forms, as complementary public spectacles of racism and monstrosity.[37]

If the black protagonist of *The Monster* is shaped by political discourses that linked monsters to black men, then the novella's white doctor suggests a different set of associations among monster-making, writing, and art-making. We can begin to identify these connections through a story involving another of Crane's brothers. As a medical student in New Jersey in 1883, Wilbur Crane brought home a dismembered female corpse, with plans "to boil the subject" and then to mount the resulting skeleton. The corpse froze while stored in a barrel on his roof and was then discovered by horrified neighbors and seized by the police.[38] This macabre story suggests the myriad power relations involved in the medical dissection of bodies in this era. These power relations, as I noted in chapter 1, included racial ones, as in the scandal in 1882 at the Jefferson Medical College regarding corpses allegedly taken from African American burial grounds.[39] The story of Wilbur Crane, a medical student at the same moment, suggests gender hierarchies rather than racial ones; his project enhances the power of the would-be doctor with the gender hierarchy of a man boiling a dismembered female corpse. The story of Crane's brother William bespoke the most public of monster stories in nineteenth-century America, the lynching of black men; the story of his brother Wilbur situated dead bodies within the more clandestine realm of the doctor's home laboratory. In relation to *Frankenstein*, Wilbur's story evokes the project of Victor Frankenstein to build both the monster and his female mate. The anecdote offers fraternal, if not also thematic, connections among the doctor who wants "to boil the subject," the artist who wants to exhibit a completed work, and the writer who wants to construct a story of a monster.

Stephen Crane elsewhere made such connections explicitly. Michael Fried has shown that Crane's writings and the paintings of his contemporary, Thomas Eakins, offer parallel meditations on the act of writing, with Eakins's *The Gross Clinic*, for example, aligning the scalpel of the surgeon with the pen of both writer and artist.[40] In at least one moment in Crane's oeuvre, however, he brings the work of doctor and artist together more directly. In an unpublished sketch from the early 1890s about the New York City Art Students' League Building, he includes this anecdote about art classes:

> Once when the woman's life class bought a new skeleton for the study of anatomy, they held a very swagger function in their class room and christened it "Mr Jolton Bones" with great pomp and ceremony. Up in the boy's life class the news of the ceremony created great excitement. They were obliged to hold a rival function without delay. And the series of great pageants, ceremonials, celebrations and fetes which followed [was] replete with vivid color and gorgeous action.[41]

Relocating the skeleton from the world of the doctor to that of the artist, this anecdote turns it into an artwork mounted for exhibition. It presents men reacting competitively, if not also anxiously, to the prior creations of women; the "great pageants, ceremonials, celebrations and fetes" of the male students are compensatory productions in the face of the "woman's life" class. The male students who bring their skeleton to life through pageantry reprise the project of Victor Frankenstein, but they work belatedly in the shadow of women who have already brought monsters to life— from Mary Shelley to the students who make "Mr. Jolton Bones."

Explicitly narrating gender anxieties, this anecdote may have racial connotations as well. "Mr. Bones"—sometimes "Bones" or "Brother Bones" —was the name given to one of the stock figures of the minstrel show, an unsophisticated and hapless character who moved constantly while singing.[42] Crane's "Mr. Jolton Bones" suggests a version of this stock figure, with an emphasis on his dependent relation to his presumably white audience: he moves only when others manipulate him, and he exists as a character only for their entertainment. A latter-day Frankenstein monster, Mr. Bones also suggests a present-day minstrel.

In turning to *Frankenstein* in his fiction, then, Crane was inclined as much toward the aesthetic legacy of the novel—its self-reflexive equation of monsters and texts—as toward the racially grounded discourses of monstrosity that had informed it from the start. But as the anecdote of "Mr. Bones" suggests, the political implications of monstrosity were not separate from its aesthetic ones. Race rattled the bones of monstrosity throughout Crane's world.

IV.

How, then, does *The Monster* adapt *Frankenstein*? Most visibly, Crane borrows from *Frankenstein* the narrative of a male body hideously transformed in a scientist's laboratory and brought back by the scientist from the dead. Crane disaggregates these components of the Frankenstein story —body, laboratory, scientist—and recombines them. Johnson's disfigurement in the fire occurs in the doctor's laboratory, an apartment adjoining his home where Trescott spends "hours when he might have been sleeping, in devoting himself to experiments which came in the way of his study and interest" (405). This setting of nighttime experimentation positions the doctor as a version of Victor Frankenstein, and during the fire, the laboratory itself turns Johnson into a monster, when his face is scarred by chemicals from an exploding jar. After this disfigurement, Johnson's rescue is represented as the emergence of a new form from the laboratory: "a young man . . . had gone into the laboratory and brought forth a thing which he laid on the grass" (408). The bringing forth of Johnson as dehumanized "thing" constitutes a moment of monstrous birth, for which the midwife is less the nameless rescuer than the chemicals of the laboratory itself. These Frankensteinian elements of the fire scene are underscored in one of the original *Harper's* illustrations for *The Monster* by Peter Newell. This image depicts Johnson, hulking and hunched, amid a swirl of fire; it is entitled "In the Laboratory."[43]

The fire scene is followed by a second depiction of reanimation, one even more overtly linked to *Frankenstein*. Immediately after the fire, a rumor spreads that Johnson has died, and "[t]he morning paper announced the death of Henry Johnson. . . . There was also an editorial built from all the best words in the vocabulary of the staff" (412). The news that Johnson lives is treated by the townspeople as an unwelcome return from the dead, a return for which Trescott is held responsible. Using language that directly echoes Shelley's novel, Trescott's friend Judge Hagenthorpe warns him that "you are performing a questionable charity in preserving this negro's life. . . . he will hereafter be a monster, a perfect monster, and probably with an affected brain" (413). By "preserving" Johnson, Hagenthorpe warns, Trescott is revivifying a corpse: "He will be your creation, you understand. He is purely your creation. Nature has very evidently given him up. He is dead. You are restoring him to life. You are making him, and he will be a monster, and with no mind" (414).

IN THE LABORATORY.

Peter Newell, "In the Laboratory," illustration for Stephen
Crane's *The Monster*, *Harper's New Monthly Magazine*, August
1898.

The fire scene and its aftermath can be read allegorically, as a condemnation of the way racism turns black men into "things."[44] Even before the
fire, Johnson is treated as monstrous; as he walks through town to visit
his girlfriend, one man cries, "you ought to see the coon that's coming!"
(396). In a world that already considers the black man a "coon," the fire
replicates rather than creates Johnson's monstrosity. In Crane's literary refraction of this world, fire is both a literal reminder of and a literary symbol for the searing power of racism. The consequences of the fire—"he

now had no face. His face had simply been burned away" (411)—deepens this allegorical play between literal and symbolic injury. "I wonder how it feels to be without any face?" (424) asks the town's barber, whose question suggests a symbolic query about racial identity. As Ralph Ellison's protagonist literalizes the racism that made black people symbolically invisible, so Henry Johnson literalizes the ongoing cultural effacement of black men by racism.[45]

The *Frankenstein* allusions of the fire scene strengthen this racial allegory, or rather, they translate the racial politics already implicit in *Frankenstein* into more explicit racial critique. Crane condenses the all-over deformity of Shelley's monster to the face, and further condenses the possibilities for facial distortion into the horror of facial absence. Contracting Shelley's monster, Crane also expands Shelley's monster-maker. There is no single Victor Frankenstein in *The Monster*, but the laboratory central to *Frankenstein* becomes a metaphor for the environment in which racism is forged, as well as a metonymic reference to the role of medicine in eugenics and other forms of racist pseudoscience. The fire scene presents the black man as a Frankenstein monster seared into being in the laboratory of American racism.

The second episode of Frankensteinian reanimation, in the aftermath of the fire, deepens this racial allegory. The mistaken sanctification that follows upon the rumor of Johnson's death shifts the charge of monstrosity from Johnson to the townspeople, for it suggests that the town prefers a dead black man to a live one. This possibility is then realized in the conversation between the doctor and the judge. Although Trescott is accused of monster-making, he is the one white man who refuses to demonize Johnson; it is, rather, the judge who would abandon Johnson who sets the term "monster" in motion. In animating the word "monster," the judge relocates the agency of monster-making, previously dispersed to the realm of fire, back to the realms of human speech and action. As voiced by the town's exemplar of official law, the judge's words bring to fruition the monster-making already signaled by the white men who call Johnson "coon."[46] After this moment of borrowing from *Frankenstein*, *The Monster* seems to swerve away from it: unlike the increasingly murderous monster of *Frankenstein*, Johnson remains an entirely blameless figure, and unlike the increasingly craven Victor Frankenstein, Crane's Dr. Trescott refuses to abandon his creation. However, these divergences from *Frankenstein*'s plot are faithful to the novel's themes. As in Shelley's novel, both monster and doctor become outcasts. As in the novel, Crane greatest indictment is of a society that makes and shuns monsters.

Yet this first interpretation of the role of *Frankenstein* in *The Monster* —as an intertext that strengthens Crane's antiracist allegory—is insufficient to account for either the political or the aesthetic complexities of the novella. Crane was not noticeably interested in contemporary political struggles for black equality, and there is ample evidence throughout *The Monster* of racist stereotypes. For example, Johnson's girlfriend, Bella Farragut, lives with her family on "Watermelon Alley," and in one home "[t]he pickaninnies [are] strewn upon the floor of the living-room" (425). More systematically, Crane, unlike Mary Shelley, gives his monster no articulate voice or extended first-person story. He is first introduced in the context of his friendship with Jimmie: "These two were pals. In regard to almost everything in life they seemed to have minds precisely alike" (392). This description infantilizes Johnson, presenting the adult black man as the white boy's ideal companion—another version of Twain's Jim and Huck.[47] These words might be meant ironically, as an exposure of this stereotype rather than an enactment of it, but it is difficult to be certain. The project of assessing Crane's politics is linked to the problem of assessing his tone, or what Michael Warner terms the "difficulty of judication" in *The Monster*, whereby Crane "persists in signaling valuations even as he disables our mechanism of valuation."[48]

These interpretive difficulties are particularly acute in relation to Johnson's role, before the fire, as a dandy. "Dandy" became a popular term in early-nineteenth-century Britain, used to characterize, pejoratively, an aristocratic man with an excessive interest in fashion; the figure of the American dandy—originally, "Yankee Doodle Dandy"—was characterized by class pretensions as well.[49] In gender terms, the Anglo-American dandy's interest in feminine display rendered him effeminate, possibly homosexual, although the dandy was also sometimes seen as a ladies' man. As Shane White and Graham White have shown, the figure of the black dandy, which first emerged in the early-nineteenth-century urban North, capitalized on the radical potential of theatrical self-display. In their public promenades, the black dandy and black "dandizette"—the term for the female version, for which there is no equivalent in the white dandy tradition—engaged in important rituals of freedom, both claiming urban public space and expressing control over the display of their bodies. For many white people, the black dandy represented a threatening traversal of boundaries, and white commentaries on the black dandy were "usually set in a framework of failed imitation, of a clumsy, inept and inappropriate black translation of whites' mores into blacks' own lowly situation."[50] Later in the century, the black dandy became an openly ridiculed character in the minstrel show in the character of the "Zip Coon," an urban man whose grotesque imitations of white men were a source of humor to white audiences. The minstrel Zip Coon was a kind of freak—as exemplified by William Henry Johnson, the freak known as "Zip." Yet this character could also be double-edged. Since the Zip Coon was usually portrayed by a white man in blackface, he presented white audiences with the image of a white man imitating a black man imitating a white man. As an imitation of an imitation, the Zip Coon dandy of the minstrel show was a racist stereotype, but the African American dandy also staged white fantasies of self-satire, as projected onto and deflected through the bodies of black men.[51]

In *The Monster*, Crane similarly positions the black dandy in a double-edged relation to the minstrel tradition, simultaneously ridiculing him and using him to satirize his white audience. Here is Johnson on his way to visit Bella:

> No belle of a court circle could bestow more mind on a toilet than did Johnson. On second thought, he was more like a priest arraying himself for some parade of the church. As he emerged from his room and sauntered down the carriage drive, no one would have suspected him of ever having washed a buggy.
>
> It was not altogether a matter of the lavender trousers, nor yet the straw hat with its bright silk band. The change was somewhere far in the interior of Henry. But there was no cake-walk hyperbole in it. He was simply a quiet, well-bred gentleman of position, wealth, and other necessary achievements out for an evening stroll, and he had never washed a wagon in his life. (395)

This passage works within the pejorative tradition of ridiculing the dandy for his effeminacy. The mark of femininity is the lavender trousers, whose color was already coded as effeminate, if not also homosexual, in this era. Crane's reference to the "cake-walk" deepens the connection to minstrelsy. The cakewalk was a form of black performance that involved strutting and dancing and the rewarding of cakes as prizes; originating in African dance forms and adapted by American slaves, the cakewalk was closely associated in the postwar period with minstrelsy. One black newspaper in 1898 summarized its pejorative associations: "The whites go to these exhibitions of buffoonery to laugh at and ridicule the monkefied contortions of the principal actors."[52] Although Crane's narrator asserts that Johnson had "no cake-walk hyperbole," when he walks through the town, his white audience treats his promenade as a cakewalk: "'Hello, Henry! Going to walk for a cake to-night?' . . . 'Why, you've got that cake right in your pocket, Henry!' . . . Henry was not ruffled in any way by these quiet admonitions and compliments. In reply he laughed a supremely good-natured, chuckling laugh" (396). Henry's eager embrace of the cakewalk, and his enthusiasm for performing for white audiences, redoubles the racist effect of these stereotypes. Crane does not simply have Johnson perform this minstrel role; he also has him internalize its effects: "Henry was not at all oblivious of the wake of wondering ejaculation that streamed out behind him. . . . With a face beaming with happiness he turned away from the scene of his victories into a narrow side street" (397).

Yet there is, again, the possibility of a different interpretation. The cakewalk, like the dandy and Zip Coon roles, was also reappropriated by African Americans. Cakewalk performances by antebellum slaves included imitations of strutting whites, and when white audiences later in the century laughed at the cakewalk, they were applauding a version of blackness that was itself a satiric imitation of whiteness.[53] Perhaps Crane's depiction of the Zip Coon figure is intended to suggest Johnson's power to renegotiate stereotypes or to criticize the white male audiences for minstrelsy for projecting their own fantasies onto black men. The latter interpretation is supported by other elements of this scene. For example, one white man observing Johnson says, "Didn't I give him those lavender trousers?" (397); the revelation that the trousers are actually his suggests that the black dandy is literally clothed in the fantasies of the white man and, thus, that the effeminacy associated with the trousers may be his own. Moreover, a consistent strain of phallic imagery runs throughout *The Monster*, and it is difficult not to interpret "the wake of wondering ejaculation" that follows Johnson—as well as the teasing reference to "that cake right in your pocket"—in sexual terms.[54] Beneath the dandy's feminized clothing is phallic hypersexuality, and the "ejaculation" that Johnson elicits is the homoerotic pleasure that the sight of the black man brings to the white man.

Yet again this interpretation cannot be sustained. Once Johnson arrives at the home of the Farraguts, it is difficult to interpret Crane's description of his behavior there with Bella and her mother as anything but a reinscription of racist norms: "They bowed and smiled and ignored and imitated until a late hour, and if they had been the occupants of the most gorgeous salon in the world they could not have been more like three monkeys" (398). In this description, black characters have so internalized the humiliating terms of minstrelsy that they perform them for one another. The comparison of black people to monkeys deepens the terms of this humiliation, since it implicitly puns on the grotesquerie that occurs when black people act "monkefied" and "ape" white norms—unless that pun is meant ironically. Such ambiguities complicate Crane's use of the language of monstrosity in the service of political critique. On one reading, then, *The Monster*, drawing directly from *Frankenstein*, condemns the way the white world makes black men into rebellious monsters; on another reading, the novella presents Johnson as a monster—at once lavender "belle" and trained "monkey"—of his own making.

But if Crane's racial attitudes seem unclear, his aesthetic project in *The Monster* is more legible. It is to that project that I turn for a second interpretation of the novella. Crane's style throughout his career has been termed realist, naturalist, impressionist, and protomodernist, but whatever its overall designation, its signature trait in *The Monster* is unmistakable: profuse and extravagant figurative imagery, particularly metaphor.[55] From its first sentence onward, the novella is distinguished by such imagery: "Little Jim was, for the time, engine Number 36, and he was making the run between Syracuse and Rochester" (391). This opening returns us to the imagery of the machine so central to the era; the permeable boundary between human and machine is here reprised in a boy's fantasy that he has become an engine.[56] Diminishing the machine to the level of child's play, this image also highlights the machinery by which metaphors themselves are made. For the opening sentence of *The Monster* not only forges a strained likeness between boy and engine, but forges that likeness in an unusual way: it is marked only with "was," as if Jimmie has actually transformed himself into an engine. A few paragraphs later, Jimmie's father is introduced with another literary figure: "The doctor was shaving this lawn as if it were a priest's chin" (391). In contrast to the metaphor of the engine, this comparison is explicitly rendered as a simile. But this likeness between a lawn and a priest's chin is so unlikely that it remains a hypothetical "as if it were" rather than moving into the status of "was." In both cases, Crane highlights the making of metaphor by emphasizing the strained and jarring alignments between terms.

Similarly, Crane's description of Johnson as a dandy turns on questions of figurative comparison. The dandy passage begins with two comparisons, a metaphoric likeness between Johnson and a "belle of a court circle," followed by a simile comparing him to a priest. The priest simile signals the affinity between this moment and Crane's opening description of Trescott shaving the "priest's chin," and as the dandy passage continues, Crane similarly develops the likeness between Johnson and a gentleman in ways that recall the opening comparison between Jimmie and the engine. Like the boy who feels so much like an engine that he "was" one, Johnson feels as well as looks so gentlemanly that he "was simply a quiet, well-bred gentleman of position." The rest of this scene is also structured in terms of literary figures. Crane's reference to the cakewalk functions as a hinge between two forms of figurative likeness, the internal metaphor (engine) and the external simile (priest's chin). In asserting that Johnson's appearance "had no cake-walk hyperbole in it," Crane's narrator suggests that Johnson has so successfully likened himself to white norms that he has internalized the persona of a gentleman; but when Johnson's white viewers then joke about his promenade's resemblance to a cakewalk, they return this likeness to the external, theatrical realm of the minstrel show. By the time Johnson arrives at the home of the Farraguts, the question of likeness has become entirely externalized into the realm of unconvincing "imitat[ion]," and he and the Farraguts imitate so poorly that they are metaphorically likened to monkeys. Read in this context, Crane's comparisons of black people to monkeys are no less racist, but they are more coherent with the ongoing aesthetic project of *The Monster*. These metaphors are not so much discontinuous with the novella's political interest in the making of monsters as they are continuous with its aesthetic interest in the making of metaphors.

We can also position the ambiguities of irony in these passages as part of this aesthetic project. Late-nineteenth-century style guidebooks repeatedly emphasized the need to police irony. "Irony," warned John Genung in *The Practical Elements of Rhetoric* (1887), "is an edge-tool of which the writer needs to be very careful. Not only may the satirical spirit become very enslaving, and lead him to look upon everything with captious and cynical eyes; but it almost inevitably gives his writing an element of offense to simple and straight-forward minds."[57] The difficulty of deciding whether there is ironic intent to statements like "In regard to almost everything in life they seemed to have minds precisely alike" (392) suggests Crane's deliberate play with the "edge-tool" of irony. As with his extravagant metaphors, this is another deliberate experiment with figuration, one that shows his mastery over an "enslaving" form.

So too is the framework for Crane's metaphors—their role in allegory —an arena for aesthetic play. I have already suggested that Melville, in "The Bell-Tower," foregrounds the process of constructing a racial allegory from *Frankenstein*. Crane's relation to allegory is even more stylized. In allegory, Alexander Bain warned, "there is a double meaning, the obvious and the implied, or allegorical. There must often be a great deal of straining to sustain the parallelism throughout a long composition."[58] The fire scene in *The Monster* is so extravagant that it seems to be a deliberate exercise in straining. For this scene is not simply available for interpretation in terms of allegory: in both the quantity and quality of the allegorical possibilities that it elicits, it is overly available.

The scene does use a central metaphor to describe the injury to Johnson: "Suddenly the glass splintered, and a ruby-red snakelike thing poured its thick length out upon the top of the old desk. . . . the red snake flowed directly down into Johnson's upturned face" (406). Michael Fried has interpreted the image of the "ruby-red snakelike thing" pictorially, as a visual symbol for the act of writing or, more specifically, as the inscription of ink on a page. This interpretation directs us to the self-reflexive dimensions of Crane's imagery, but it is insufficient: the fire is a verbal rather than a pictorial inscription, and it is only one of many self-consciously literary metaphors in the scene.[59] Crane surrounds it with a dizzying array of metaphors, including likening the fire to "bloody spectres at the apertures of a haunted house" and "a troop of dim and silent gray monkeys . . . climbing a grape-vine into the clouds" (402). There are symbols within symbols in this scene, as when the fire, "well planned, as if by professional revolutionists" (402), destroys an engraving depicting the signing of the Declaration of Independence: "In the hall a lick of flame had found the cord that supported 'Signing the Declaration.' The engraving slumped down suddenly at one end, and then dropped to the floor, where it burst with the sound of a bomb" (403). Like the image of Johnson's facelessness, this last image may be read allegorically: the symbolic "bomb[ing]" of the engraving may represent the destruction of the legacy of the American Revolution by the forces of racism; the bombers could be the Confederacy or their postwar defenders, the Ku Klux Klan, who used the legacy of the Revolution as inspiration for their own declarations of violence.[60] Similarly, the image of the "troop of dim and silent gray monkeys" shifts the earlier comparison of black people with monkeys into a more allegorical mode. Again, what is significant about these allegorical possibilities is less their precise meaning than their sheer excess, in both quality and quantity. The figurative imagery of the fire scene seems to demand allegorical interpretation, but it makes any individual interpretation difficult, if not impossible. In so doing, it foregrounds the making of allegory as its very theme.

Choosing the allegorical "straining" that writers like Bain cautioned against, Crane also flouts the usual goals to which allegory aspired. Allegory, Bain specified, is a didactic project: "When, with a view to some moral or instruction, subjects remote from one another are brought into a comparison sustained throughout the details, the result is an Allegory."[61] Crane's instructive project is unclear, and in this scene's profusion of imagery, he seems to block even "a view to" morality. At stake in the legibility of allegory, moreover, was religious truth, as Theodore Hunt outlined:

> There is a kind of obscurity essentially involved in this figure [allegory], in that the main idea is concealed under the terms used. This obscurity, however, is not in the line of deception. It is understood both by writer and reader, is temporary only, and has reference to the final revelation of the truth. . . . The final purpose or use of this figure is, to make clear. It is so used in Scripture.[62]

Crane's fire scene violates these terms: the scene's obscurity is ongoing rather than temporary, and its reader is, if not deliberately deceived, then certainly confused. As for the scriptural foundations of allegory, Crane seems to offer a sly joke about them, in the passage about "Signing the Declaration." The Declaration of Independence has often functioned as a form of American scripture, and its enactment has been enshrined as a sacred rite in American culture; Crane's reference may be to one of the most famous of its enshrinements, the painting by John Trumbull commonly known as *Signing of the Declaration of Independence* (1817–18).[63] In this scene, the description of the engraving—"slumped down suddenly at one end, and then dropped to the floor, where it burst with the sound of a bomb"—seems literally to explode the scriptural text of the Declaration, its engraved representation, and the moment of national birth for which it stands.

Interpreting this scene as a self-reflexive commentary on allegory also returns us to its relation to *Frankenstein*. Only partially legible as a racial allegory about monsters, the scene more coherently constitutes Crane's exploration of the equation between writing and monster-making. His similes, like the comparison of both the lawn and Johnson to priests, are deliberately grotesque figures; his preference for mixed metaphors, like the combination of "belle of the court" and "priest" in the passage about Johnson, are monstrous amalgams. The many metaphors of the fire scene, so promiscuously mixed, are monsters run amok. Similarly, the image begging to be read allegorically, the destruction of "Signing the Declaration," is an example of a preexisting symbol—the Declaration of Independence—reanimated in new form. As made in the laboratory of language, all metaphors are monsters, from the ancillary images of monkeys and specters to the governing image of the scene, the "ruby-red snakelike thing." The phrase "ruby-red snakelike thing" is a concentrated example of a monstrous form, for it combines an animal simile (snakelike) with a color adjective that is linked alliteratively to a jewel metaphor (ruby-red), and it uses the resulting amalgam to animate the otherwise inanimate fire. Whether or not Crane is referencing the novel *Frankenstein*, his project both pays homage to its author and usurps her. Like the male art students remaking their own skeleton, Crane outdoes Shelley by turning his metaphors into monsters.

On one view, then, *The Monster* is an antiracist political allegory; on a second view, it is an allegory about allegory. What is the relationship between these interpretations? Crane's interest in demonstrating his mastery over metaphor is inextricable from his choice of the black man as metaphoric topic. For as we have seen, the image of the black man as monster was, by Crane's era, so common as to saturate popular and political culture. This saturation made it a deadened metaphor. It was not deadened in the sense of no longer having material consequences, which were very real in lynching and other acts of racist violence, but, rather, deadened in the sense of overuse, overfamiliarity, and overdetermination. Crane's alternative to this deadening is to reanimate the metaphor of the black monster, by literalizing it and by juxtaposing it with new metaphors. Mastering the metaphor of the black monster becomes, for him, a concentrated example of mastering metaphor itself.

The politics of this mastery are, on one level, conservative: here is another white man mastering a black man, now on the terrain of metaphor. As Joseph Church, interpreting *The Monster* psychoanalytically, suggests, Crane uses "the black man as a signifier he can re-mark," so that Johnson "ultimately becomes a sign of Crane's power as artist."[64] On another level, however, Crane effects a more radical political critique, along with an aesthetic critique, of a culture that deadens blackness into monstrosity. The metaphors of the fire scene direct us to his interweaving of political and aesthetic critiques. Like the "ruby-red snakelike thing," the image of the faceless "thing" depends on color, but in opposite ways. Crane animates the fire by naming it as "ruby-red," but he makes defacement a metaphor for Johnson's black skin; color is the vehicle for the snake image, and the tenor for Johnson's face. Together, these two "thing" images suggest a critique of racial norms, albeit on the grounds of aesthetics rather than politics. Crane condemns Johnson's transformation into "thing" because such a designation narrowly fixes the meaning of blackness rather than allowing a much larger field of figurative possibility. For Crane, Johnson's upturned face represents not a blank page awaiting inscription, as Fried argues, but a page already overwritten, aesthetically and politically, by racial stereotypes.

Crane's critique of this overwriting emerges more fully in another passage in the fire scene. Placed just before the image of the "ruby-red snakelike thing," this is a passage of extreme figurative density:

> At the entrance to the laboratory [Johnson] confronted a strange spectacle. The room was like a garden in the region where might be burning flowers. Flames of violet, crimson, green, blue, orange, and purple were blooming everywhere. There was one blaze that was precisely the hue of a delicate coral. In another place was a mass that lay merely in phosphorescent inaction like a pile of emeralds. But all these marvels were to be seen dimly through clouds of heaving, turning, deadly smoke.
>
> Johnson halted for a moment on the threshold. He cried out again in the negro wail that had in it the sadness of the swamps. Then he rushed across the room. An orange-colored flame leaped like a panther at the lavender trousers. This animal bit deeply into Johnson. There was an explosion at one side, and suddenly before him there reared a delicate, trembling sapphire shape like a fairy lady. With a quiet smile she blocked his path and doomed him and Jimmie. Johnson shrieked, and then ducked in the manner of his race in fights. He aimed to pass under the left guard of the sapphire lady. But she was swifter than eagles, and her talons caught in him as he plunged past her. (405–6)

This passage offers a dizzying mixture of figurative imagery: the fire is likened through similes to a garden, a delicate coral, a pile of emeralds, a panther, and a fairy lady, and embedded within these figures are additional figures, with the fairy lady likened first to a sapphire, then to a boxer, and finally to swooping eagles. "Mixed metaphor" seems inadequate to describe this frenetic accretion of wildly disparate figurative comparisons into one composite whole. This is a monster of a metaphor —a metaphor conceived of, and as, a monster.

Within this monstrous metaphor, two forms of color imagery collide, comparable to the contrast between the "ruby-red snakelike thing" and Johnson as faceless "thing." The imagery of violet, crimson, green, blue, orange, and purple suggests color used in free metaphoric play, as the figurative vehicle for characterizing fire. By contrast, several images rely on the essentialist fixity of blackness as racial stereotype: "the negro wail that had in it the sadness of the swamps" and Johnson ducking "in the manner of his race in fights." Johnson's lavender trousers stand at the junction of these two color systems, linked to both the free play of bright color and the racial stereotype of the dandy; the intersection of these systems is signaled violently through the image of the orange flame "bit[ing] deeply" at the trousers. As with the earlier depiction of the trousers, it is possible to read the imagery of the "negro wail" as Crane's uncritical reiteration of racist stereotype. But the combination of stereotype with the imagery of color in this passage also suggests a more directed critique of racial norms. In the juxtaposition between the unfettered colors of the fire and the fettered designations of race, the former overwhelms the latter. Recontextualizing racial stereotype within an extravagant field of color possibility, Crane makes the dying metaphor of the monstrous black man come back to life.

This conjoining of racial and aesthetic registers continues throughout the novella. When Johnson is mistakenly thought after the fire to be dead, Crane emphasizes that the sanctification of him that follows is a verbal construction, "built from all the best words in the vocabulary of the staff." When the living Johnson is then demonized as a monster, Crane focuses on the role that language, specifically figurative language, plays in this demonization. Significantly, *The Monster*'s most direct allusion to *Frankenstein* comes in the form of a character's speech, when Hagenthorpe says to Trescott, "You are making him, and he will be a monster." This line is at once a warning and a command: the sentence takes an implicit simile, the claim that the revived Johnson will be like a monster, and moves that simile to the status of fact. At this moment, Crane offers a critique of how white men turn black men into metaphoric monsters, by highlighting the making of metaphors themselves.

As the novella continues, Crane expands both his political critique of racial monstrosity and his aesthetic investigation of metaphor. To represent the growing ostracism of Johnson and Trescott, Crane repeatedly uses figurative imagery that calls attention to its status as figuration. Throughout this inquiry, Crane remains uninterested in providing interior depth to Johnson. This is not—or not only—because he is unable to imagine full subjectivity for a black person, but because his primary interest is in exploring the metaphoric relation between surfaces—words, images, characters—rather than depth within them. He exposes the dependence of the white townspeople on monster metaphors, and, in so doing, asserts his own superior expertise in reanimating dead metaphors with new life.

This exposure emerges most clearly in Crane's version of interracial rape. The fear of the black rapist hovers at the margins of a section depicting a children's birthday party:

> Hearing a noise behind her at the window, one little girl turned to face it. Instantly she screamed and sprang away, covering her face with her hands. "What was it? What was it?" cried every one in a roar. Some slight movement of the eyes of the weeping and shuddering child informed the company that she had been frightened by an appearance at the window. At once they all faced the imperturbable window, and for a moment there was a silence. . . .
>
> None [of the boys] wished particularly to encounter a dragon in the darkness of the garden, but there could be no faltering when the fair ones in the dining-room were present. Calling to each other in stern voices they went dragooning over the lawn, attacking the shadows with ferocity, but still with the caution of reasonable beings. They found, however, nothing new to the peace of the night. Of course there was a lad who told a great lie. He described a grim figure, bending low and slinking off along the fence. He gave a number of details, rendering his lie more splendid by a repetition of certain forms which he recalled from romances. For instance, he insisted that he had heard the creature emit a hollow laugh.
>
> Inside the house the little girl who had raised the alarm was still shuddering and weeping. . . .
>
> She was not coherent even to her mother. Was it a man? She didn't know. It was simply a thing, a dreadful thing. (428–29)

This scene offers a critique of racism centered on its creation of the metaphor of black monstrosity. In its menace to domesticity, Johnson's apparent "appearance at the window" recalls Victor's horror in *Frankenstein*: "I saw at the open window a figure the most hideous and abhorred. A grin was on the face of the monster; he seemed to jeer, as with his fiendish finger he pointed towards the corpse of my wife."[65] Unlike the monster's appearance in *Frankenstein*, the appearance of the figure in *The Monster* is not verified by the narrator; he is the creation of a girl's psyche, as imagined first behind her covered eyes and then made visible to others through the "slight fluttering" on the eyes themselves. The girl's screaming, shuddering, and weeping, which suggest bodily as well as psychic violation, further bring this monster into being. As the invented source of violation, Johnson—the "thing" from the fire, here "simply a thing, a dreadful thing"—is positioned within the overdetermined cultural vocabulary of black men as monsters who threaten white women. We can measure Crane's critique of this vocabulary by contrasting him with Thomas Dixon. In Dixon's *Leopard's Spots*, the white Flora is raped by the monstrous Dick; in Crane's critique of such plots, a white girl shudders from the wholly imaginary specter of the metaphorically monstrous Johnson.[66]

In making this critique, Crane indicts white women and men differently. For him, white women are the most culpable makers of the metaphor of black monstrosity, from the girls at the birthday party to the adult women whom Crane satirizes later in the novella. For example, Crane focuses on a woman who viciously condemns Trescott: "'Serves him right if he was to lose all his patients,' she said suddenly, in blood-thirsty tones. She snipped her words out as if her lips were scissors" (434). The pejorative metaphor of female speech as castrating scissors reverses but also complements the earlier description of the little girls idealized as "the fair ones" at the birthday party. In both cases, women are associated with aggression, whether as "blood-thirsty" proponents of male failure or as incitements for boys to attack shadows.

As with the male art students who want their own reanimated skeleton, these boys respond proprietorially with their own monster story. Their display of masculinity is belated, fearful, and imitative of adult norms that are themselves ridiculed in the chivalric metaphors of the passage, which position little boys as mock-knights protecting fair ladies. Once again, Crane makes clear that there is no actual monster in the garden, only an imaginary dragon. The result is a boy's "great lie," made "more splendid by a repetition of certain forms which he recalled from romances. For instance, he insisted that he had heard the creature emit a hollow laugh." The boy's invented narrative is performed for the female audience whose fear brought it into being. The addition of the "hollow laugh"—the "for instance" of the paragraph—builds "the creature" into the specifications demanded at the outset by the girl who thinks she hears a noise behind her. In Crane's account of racist myth-making, women are both generative and castrating, and the frightening force of white femininity prompts the white boy's creation of narratives centered on metaphoric black monsters.[67]

From here it is only a short distance to the castrating powers of the lynch mob. Two sections later, it is the day after the birthday party, and the chief of police visits Trescott at home to inform him that Johnson is now in jail. Three important passages in this section align monstrosity, race, and metaphor. The section begins with a description of Trescott's rebuilt home:

> The black mass in the middle of Trescott's property was hardly allowed to cool before the builders were at work on another house. It had sprung upward at a fabulous rate. It was like a magical composition born of the ashes. The doctor's office was the first part to be completed, and he had already moved in his new books and instruments and medicines. (430)

This passage may be read several ways. It offers another trace of the Frankenstein story, with the doctor's laboratory, the setting for scientific creation, constituted as a kind of reanimated monster, "a magical composition born of the ashes." As with the destruction of "Signing the Declaration," the passage is also available for racial allegory, with the reconstructed house providing a symbolic model for the Reconstructed nation (the "house divided" by slavery); the "black mass" signifies the residue of slavery, now rebuilt into the "ashes" of a still-racist culture devoted to lynching. Characteristically, however, this allegory is so hyperbolic that it calls attention to itself. The house "sprung upward at a fabulous rate" suggests a metaphor for the fabulous construction of metaphor itself. Crane situates the police chief on the terrain of both monster-making and metaphor-making, each a "magical composition" in the overlapping laboratories of doctor and writer.

With this setting in place, Crane develops his version of another metaphoric monster: the lynch mob. Describing the birthday party to Trescott, the police chief codifies rumor as fact, declaring, "First thing he did was to break up a children's party." Later, this broken-up party becomes reconstituted as a crowd of adults. Johnson, he narrates to Trescott, "went right out on the main street, and an Irish girl threw a fit, and there was a sort of a riot. He began to run, and a big crowd chased after him, firing rocks. But he gave them the slip somehow. . . . We looked for him all night, but couldn't find him. . . . Of course nobody really wanted to hit him, but you know how a crowd gets. It's like—it's like—" (431)

These words describe the making of a lynch mob, again incited by a girl's "fit" and assembled from a crowd, which is now united in the desire to inflict collective injury. The boys hunting in the garden have become a lynch mob, a transformation prefigured earlier in *The Monster* in the image of Jimmie Trescott in the burning house: "upon his little white-robed figure played caressingly the light from the fire" (404). The "little white-robed figure" suggests a Klansman at a lynching; more specifically, the illumination of this figure in the light of fire recalls the case of the Robert Lewis lynching which Crane's brother William tried to prevent. Within *The Monster*, this image of the hooded boy prefigures the larger collectivity of the adult lynch mob, the truly monstrous body of his narrative. Crane condemns the monstrous quest of an adult crowd that grows out of the hunt of little boys for imaginary dragons.

Once again, Crane's attack centers on the making as well as the meaning of monster metaphors. This passage concludes with a simile whose completion is unspeakable: "It's like—it's like—." Although Crane leaves this sentence unfinished, the implication is that the word that the chief cannot bring himself to speak is that which is spoken constantly about Johnson: "monster." As with Judge Hagenthorpe's earlier warning to Trescott that "[y]ou are making him, and he will be a monster," Crane puts these crucial words of monster-making in the mouth of an official figure of authority. But whereas the judge's words confidently turn from "making a monster" into being one, the police chief cannot complete a metaphor that would indict himself and his own world. The arrested simile thus stands as Crane's critique of the officer of the law, who will not complete a sentence—either linguistic or legal—that serves as evidence of his own monstrosity.

A third passage further extends the politics and aesthetics of its monster metaphors. The section closes with the chief's warning to Trescott, "If I were you, I'd come to the jail pretty late at night, because there is likely to be a crowd around the door, and I'd bring a—er—mask, or some kind of a veil, anyhow" (432). Crane ends this conversation without the doctor's reply, and does not return to it. But the veil is connected to other scenes both earlier and later in the novella. Earlier, when Johnson is recovering from the fire, he is swathed in bandages that mask his face: "The bandages on the negro's head allowed only one thing to appear, an eye, which unwinkingly stared at the judge" (413). Later, after Johnson has healed and has become an object of horror, he is described as "seated on a box behind the stable basking in the rays of the afternoon sun. A heavy crêpe veil was swathed about its head" (435). Together, this imagery of bandages, masks, and veils constitutes a metaphor for Johnson's status as a black man, at once made invisible by the racist world he inhabits and rendered hypervisible, as in a freak show.

This imagery prefigures the more famous representation of the veil outlined by W. E. B. Du Bois five years later: "the Negro is . . . born with a veil, and gifted with second-sight in this American world,—a world which yields him no true self-consciousness, but only lets him see himself through the revelation of the other world."[68] Like Du Bois, Crane links the veil to the effects of racism on African American identity; Crane's monster is positioned both beneath a veil and atop a box, recalling the lineage of platforms—the auction block, the minstrel stage, the freak show—on which black bodies were consistently exhibited to punitive effect. The connection Crane draws between veil and bandage emphasizes the injurious nature of these forms of scrutiny. In Crane's account, Johnson is not only veiled from self-consciousness but bandaged against it. Conversely, Crane also offers an avenue for resistance to this injury, in the image of the unwinking eye. Although the eye is another form of freakishness and the object of white scrutiny, it also has the power to unnerve the judge from speaking: "he evidently had something further to say, but he seemed to be kept from it by the scrutiny of the unwinking eye, at which he furtively glanced from time to time" (413).[69] Linked to blackness, the veil also moves across race, in the police chief's recommendation that Trescott himself find "some kind of a veil." Within Crane's political allegory, the passage marks the recognition that the veil may cover not only the defaced black man but also the white man who is symbolically effaced, if not also blackened, by association with him.

A mobile political symbol, the veil bears a complicated relation to Crane's aesthetic exploration of metaphor. Calling attention to what lies beneath it, the veil is a metaphor for Johnson's absent face; contiguous with his absent face, it is also metonymic of it. But since the face is itself a metaphor, a symbol of the cultural effacement of the black man, the veil is also a metaphor of a metaphor. As a metaphor for metaphor, the veil calls attention to the difficulty of finding literal ground "beneath" figurative language. Once again, Crane's approach is to foreground the importance of a metaphor by placing it in spoken dialogue. Like the crowd passage, the veil appears in relation to a vocal interruption, here not the police chief's unspeakable simile but a stammer ("a—er—"). Like the thwarted simile, the stammer highlights the police chief's difficulty in acknowledging that the process of monster-making has again boomeranged back on a member of the white world. The metaphor of monstrosity, set in motion by one white authority figure, the judge, has been turned back by another, the police chief, against a third, the doctor. This filial revolt of metaphor against its makers returns to the Frankenstein imagery that suffuses the opening passage of this section. The image of the "magical composition born of the ashes," initially a figure for the doctor's rebuilt house, has come, by the end of this section, to stand for the reconstruction of the doctor himself into a symbolic monster.

Yet even this third interpretation of *The Monster*—as a rewriting of *Frankenstein* that situates racial critique within an exploration of metaphor—is incomplete. As the novella progresses, black people, too, participate in the demonization of Johnson. Just before the birthday party, Alek Williams, the man hired to house Johnson, goes to Hagenthorpe to recount how frightening he finds Johnson. "Folks go round sayin' . . . he's er devil!" Williams tells Hagenthorpe, and although he acknowledges that "T'ain't no devil," he still insists that "he *looks* like er devil" (419). Here is another highlighted simile about monstrosity, in which one black man likens another to the devil. Crane then provides Williams with an ulterior motive for such metaphor-making: he asks for more money from the judge in a scene that presents him as a greedy buffoon. While Crane's racist characterization of Williams undermines the novella's political project, it strengthens its aesthetic one. As with his earlier presentation of Johnson as a dandy, his interest in Williams lies in his relation to the making of metaphors.

In this case, black characters who liken Johnson to a monster see that likeness rebound on themselves. When Williams returns home, for example, he finds that "[h]is wife was regarding him with wide eyes and parted lips as if he were a spectre" (425). When he and his wife look toward the room containing Johnson, "They continually pointed their speech and their looks at the inner door, paying it the homage due to a corpse or a phantom" (426). This description again positions the Williamses as makers of figurative imagery, with "pointed" speech and looks. The object of their gaze, the blank inner door, is another example of metonymy, for it is aligned with the defaced body they imagine to be just behind it. Paying the door "the homage due to a corpse or a phantom," they make their lodger into a monster who is both corpse and phantom.

Yet this image turns back on Williams as the scene progresses. He fearfully unlocks the door, "and as it swung portentously open he sprang nimbly to one side like the fearful slave liberating the lion" (426). But Johnson is not there, prompting Williams to run wildly in fear:

> Then he tumbled headlong into the night. He was yelling: "Docteh Trescott! Docteh Trescott!" He ran wildly through the fields, and galloped in the direction of town. He continued to call to Trescott, as if the latter was within easy hearing. It was as if Trescott was poised in the contemplative sky over the running negro, and could heed this reaching voice —"Docteh Trescott!" (427)

This scene positions a black man running in fear toward an all-powerful white man; the galloping implicitly compares him to a horse, and the simile "like the fearful slave" suggests that he is a kind of "fearful slave." Again, such descriptions are racist caricatures. As such, they contradict the antiracist elements of the novella, but they are continuous with Crane's aesthetic interest in metaphor. Crane presents black people as participants in the project of metaphor-making, but he suggests that this project threatens to turn them into monstrous specters in their own eyes as well.

As with Crane's portrayal of white monster-making, his sharpest critique of black monster-making is effected through a misogynist focus on women. In between the sections with the birthday party and the police chief is one in which Johnson visits Bella Farragut, who is so frightened by him that she crawls away in fear:

> There appeared suddenly before the Farraguts a monster making a low and sweeping bow. . . . Bella, blubbering . . . was crawling on her hands and knees fearsomely up the steps. . . .
>
> She shielded her eyes with her arms and tried to crawl past it, but the genial monster blocked the way. "I jes drap in ter ax you 'bout er daince, Miss Fa'gut. I ax you if I kin have the magnifercent gratitude of you' company on that 'casion, Miss Fa'gut."
>
> In a last outbreak of despair, the girl, shuddering and wailing, threw herself face downward on the floor, while the monster sat on the edge of

the chair gabbling courteous invitations, and holding the old hat daintily
to its stomach. (429–30)

Reprising the courtship scene from earlier in the novella, Johnson speaks
and acts in uncomprehending repetition of his dandy manners. The repetition functions both to underscore the monstrosity inherent within the
black dandy figure and to position Johnson's monstrosity in proximity to
disordered femininity. As in the birthday-party scene, Crane offers the
tableau of a woman so undone by the sight of the monster that her own
vision must be blocked; like the white girl "covering her face with her
hands," Bella "shield[s] her eyes with her arms." However, in contrast to
the white girl, who is actually a child, Bella is infantilized through the imagery of blubbering and crawling. And in contrast to the hypersexuality
implicitly attributed to him in the party scene, Johnson is here returned
to the feminized realm of the dandy who sits "daintily" holding his hat.
While Crane's white women are sources of anxiety to white men, he situates both men and women in the novella's black community in degraded
proximity to femininity. In Crane's asymmetrical account of monster-
making, black people, like white people, make Johnson into a monster,
but this project serves less to distance them from monstrosity than to
highlight their own feminized proximity to it.

Crane's exploration of metaphor, then, often supports but in the end
overwhelms his antiracist allegory. The two strands of the novella, the
political and the aesthetic, intertwine throughout the narrative, but they
ultimately diverge. Crane's primary interest is in his aesthetic project, and
that project is—for him—finally at odds with his political one. The last
glimpse of Johnson in the story is in relation to the white boys who stare
at him:

> The monster on the box had turned its black crêpe countenance toward
> the sky, and was waving its arms in time to a religious chant. "Look at
> him now," cried a little boy. They turned, and were transfixed by the so-
> lemnity and mystery of the indefinable gestures. The wail of the melody
> was mournful and slow. They drew back. It seemed to spellbind them
> with the power of a funeral. (438)

Under the veil, Johnson is both entirely objectified and completely "in-
definable," in his speech and gestures as well as in his countenance. In
Crane's exhumation of *Frankenstein*, the monster has been emptied out

of political content as well as of an interior literary self. Without interiority, he is an entirely opaque surface; in the terms of metaphor, he is all vehicle, no tenor. Described by one critic as "an almost inanimate object" in this scene, he is now deanimated—a deadened metaphor who, once brought back to life, is now dead again.[70] It is no surprise that this passage is filled with funereal imagery, depicting Johnson as a veiled and wailing mourner. Taken metaphorically, this funeral marks the symbolic murder of the black man by the world that has made him a monster. Taken metametaphorically, as a comment on metaphor, this funeral marks the death of the reanimated metaphor of the black man as monster.

This deadening of metaphor is complemented by the novella's actual ending, five sections later. Crane concludes with Trescott and his wife. Trescott comes home from an argument with other men over Johnson to find his wife sobbing because no women have come to the tea party she prepared:

> Glancing down at the cups, Trescott mechanically counted them. There were fifteen of them. "There, there," he said. "Don't cry, Grace. Don't cry."
>
> The wind was whining around the house and the snow beat aslant upon the windows. Sometimes the coal in the stove settled with a crumbling sound and the four panes of mica flushed a sudden new crimson. As he sat holding her head on his shoulder, Trescott found himself occasionally trying to count the cups. There were fifteen of them. (447–48)

This passage registers the transformation of both Trescotts into social pariahs. In keeping with the novella's gender dynamics, Crane presents women as both victims and villains in this drama. Trescott is impotent against both his wife's sobbing and the cruelty of the town's women, and he is finally reduced to a mute counting of the empty cups. The conclusion is pessimistic, emphasizing the determinist crush of social forces against the possibility of individual agency.

What is most important about this conclusion, however, is not its content but its form. The adjective "mechanically" recalls the engine metaphor of the novella's first line ("Little Jim was, for the time, engine Number 36"), but with a difference. In contrast to the rest of *The Monster*, this conclusion is almost devoid of figurative language. There is the possibility of personification in Crane's references to the mica panes of the stove that "flushed a sudden new crimson" and to the "whining" of the wind; the empty cups hint at a metonymic association between the open mouths of cups and the mouths of the women who drink from them; and this hint of metonymy, in turn, suggests a dead metaphor—the "lip of the cup"— waiting to be brought back to life. Yet Crane does not revive this dead metaphor; nor does he develop any of the figurative possibilities of this final paragraph. The absence of figurative language in the novella's conclusion is even more striking when contrasted with the last passage about Johnson. As "the monster on the box," Johnson is transformed entirely into an opaque surface for the metaphoric projections of others, whereas the description of Trescott refuses any translation into metaphor. In the terms of metaphor, Johnson is all vehicle, and Trescott is all tenor.

This dismemberment of metaphor into its component parts concludes Crane's engagement with metaphor and monstrosity. As an aesthetic project, the novella's ending is a form of triumph, since it showcases, one final time, Crane's own mastery of metaphor. That mastery includes taking metaphors apart as well as putting them together, deanimating as well as reanimating them, and, above all, exaggerating rather than running from their potential monstrosity. In its aesthetic register, this conclusion decisively confirms Crane's extravagant transformation of what Gertrude Buck called "metaphoraphobia." *The Monster* not only revalues the "freak" of metaphor, as Buck suggests. The novella is a testament to metaphorophilia.

Politically, however, the novella ends in defeat: no respite looms for either the black man made monstrous or the white man who comes to his aid. In the novella's most pointed alteration of *Frankenstein*, the monster never finds a voice. The divergence of the novella's aesthetic and political registers may reflect Crane's lack of interest in politics; at this moment, the tenuous connections between the novella's antiracism and its exploration of metaphor rupture entirely. Or it may testify, conversely, to the intractability of a turn-of-the-century political culture that so insistently conceived of black people as monsters. In the realm of the literary, Crane could remake monstrous metaphors as he pleased; dead metaphors could live again. But in the realm of the literal, black people were constantly reanimated as vehicles for monstrosity, and it was not metaphors but men who were killed again and again.

3

The Signifying Monster

Any attempt [of the black man] at engaging in pursuits where
his mind is employed is met by an attitude that stigmatizes his
effort as presumption. Then if the daring one succeeds, he is
looked upon as a monster. He is put into the same category with
the "two-headed boy" and the "bearded lady." There has not, in the
history of the country, risen a single intellectual black man whose
pretensions have not been sneered at, laughed at, and then lamely
wondered at.   —Paul Laurence Dunbar, "Our New Madness"

I.

In turn-of-the-century American fiction, I have argued, the Frankenstein
monster operates not only as a metaphor for the African American man
but also as a metaphor for metaphor itself. Stephen Crane's *The Monster*
adapts the Frankenstein story in two ways, developing both its implicit
racial politics of monstrosity and its aesthetic equation between monsters and metaphors. In this chapter, I analyze the sustained presence of
Frankenstein imagery in the writings of Crane's African American contemporary, Paul Laurence Dunbar. Dunbar (1872–1906) and Crane (1871–
1900) were both writers of extraordinary promise, concentrated ambition,
and prolific output who died young. In Dunbar's last novel, *The Sport of
the Gods* (1902), the protagonist, an alcoholic and dissolute black man,
brutally murders his lover; the chapter depicting the murder is entitled
"Frankenstein." This novel was published three years after *The Monster*,
and although there is no direct evidence that Dunbar read Crane, it seems
likely: *The Monster* was published in *Harper's*, and Dunbar followed the
contemporary literary scene closely; Dunbar and Crane shared the same
agent, Paul Revere Reynolds.[1] *The Monster* and *The Sport of the Gods* have
thematic similarities as well: both adapt *Frankenstein*; both mobilize a

contemporary set of associations for black monstrosity that include the minstrel and freak shows; and both represent a black monster in direct proximity to a dandy tradition and in antagonistic relation to women. Like Crane, too, Dunbar focuses on the making of monster metaphors. The name "Frankenstein," for example, appears in *The Sport of the Gods* only in a chapter title: to understand its meaning, the reader must make the metaphor afresh, connecting vehicle ("Frankenstein") to tenor (the murderous black man). Yet for all these similarities, Dunbar constructs a very different Frankenstein monster from Crane's. Unlike Crane's Henry Johnson, Dunbar's Joe Hamilton is an actual murderer, and his behavior could legitimately be condemned. Conversely, unlike Crane, Dunbar was an active participant in struggles for racial equality. Paradoxically, in *The Sport of the Gods*, a more clearly antiracist writer constructs a more truly monstrous black monster.

The key to understanding this apparent paradox inheres, I argue, in Dunbar's relation to parody. In this chapter, I trace a network of connections among Mary Shelley, Paul Laurence Dunbar, race, and parody, beginning with the role of parody in *Frankenstein* itself. As with metaphor, I suggest that we can understand Shelley's novel not only as a target for parody but also as a self-reflexive enactment of it. I first analyze the role of parody within *Frankenstein*, reading the novel backward through one of its 1820s stage parodies and forward through the animal-fable tradition that makes a brief appearance within it. Enacting the formal properties of parody, Shelley's novel suggests its oppositional possibilities in two distinct modes: the overt mockery of a figure of authority and the covert imitation of a servant role.

These possibilities, I suggest, structure the writing of Paul Laurence Dunbar. Reassessing Dunbar's career, I identify parody as a governing mode throughout his writing, a mode that he employs across genres, signals through irony, and directs at the targets of white mastery and black subservience. Reversing Dunbar's own status as self-described black "monster" in a white literary world, his writing embodies the possibilities of parody outlined within *Frankenstein*. At the same time, his parodies draw from the African American history of signifying and the folk traditions of the animal trickster and the human "badman." Bringing together the themes of *Frankenstein* with black cultural practice, his writing, I suggest, offers a model of parody that situates the parodist as a signifying monster.

Turning to Dunbar's fiction, I begin with the antilynching short story entitled "The Lynching of Jube Benson." This story, I suggest, combines a hostile parody of racist nostalgia with a more sympathetic parody of *Frankenstein*. Through this double parody, Dunbar exposes the most demonized figure of the era, the mythic black rapist, as a monster performed by white men themselves. I then analyze *The Sport of the Gods* as a complementary but more complex interweaving of *Frankenstein* and parody. The opening chapters of the novel, as in "The Lynching of Jube Benson," parody a Southern white justice system that makes black men into metaphorical monsters. However, *The Sport of the Gods* shifts focus by turning to the black dandy, a figure whose parody of white norms eventually results in his transformation into a monstrous murderer. This transformation is accompanied by a transfer of the role of monster-maker to a black woman character, against whom Dunbar's monster wreaks his murderous revenge. In the aftermath of this murder, *The Sport of the Gods* adapts *Frankenstein* once more, to relocate the source of monster-making in racism. But the novel's multiple parodies, I argue, are undercut by a nihilism that leaves its signifying monster with nowhere to go.

At the same time as Dunbar exhausts his monster plot, however, he uses *Frankenstein* to effect one further political attack. In "The Lynching of Jube Benson" as well as *The Sport of the Gods*, I suggest, Dunbar employs narratives of monstrosity to engage in a veiled—and venomous—parody of *Uncle Tom's Cabin*. Working interstitially between Shelley and Stowe, Dunbar uses the undomesticated monsters of one white woman writer to forge his own space of resistance against the domesticated monsters of another. In this as in other ways, the Frankenstein monster provided Paul Laurence Dunbar with forms through which to parody the racist construction of black masculinity in turn-of-the-century America.

II.

Parody and its affiliated terms are notoriously difficult to define. Parody, from the Greek *parodia*, "counter-song," originally denoted the comic imitation of works through song. Although such imitation is often assumed to be hostile, Linda Hutcheon notes that *para* can mean "beside" as well as "counter" and that rather than registering contempt for an original, parody may function more neutrally as "a method of inscribing continuity while permitting critical distance."[2] The term "pastiche" has a more overtly neutral origin: supplanting the Italian *pasticcio*, the term first denoted a mixture of foods, and *pasticcio* was adapted in the Renaissance to describe a mixture of texts combined without any ridiculing intent. "Pastiche" is now often seen negatively, in two ways. It is usually defined either as a clumsy combination of parts or as a lesser version of parody—unmotivated or "blank" parody, in Fredric Jameson's influential formulation, "amputated of the satiric impulse."[3] By contrast, "travesty," another term linked to parody, has always implied the impulse to ridicule. From the Italian *travestire*, "to disguise," travesty characterizes the degradation of high into low, a process originally linked to the use of theatrical costume.[4]

These terms overlapped in the era of *Frankenstein*, as an account contemporary with the novel suggests. Isaac D'Israeli, man of letters and father of Benjamin D'Israeli, included an essay titled "Parodies" in the 1823 edition of *Curiosities of Literature*, his popular essay collection. D'Israeli defines parody as "a work grafted on another work, but which turned on a different subject by a slight change of the expressions."[5] This model of parody as "grafting" also suggests the combination of parts inherent to pastiche, although D'Israeli does not use the term. He distinguishes parody from mimicry, which it "strongly resembles," because the latter involves merely "the pleasure of repeating attitudes and intonations" (213). By contrast, parody is an intentional transformation of an original, though its intentions may vary: "It might be a sport or fancy, the innocent child of mirth . . . [or] that malignant art which only studies to make the original of the parody, however beautiful, contemptible and ridiculous" (214). D'Israeli is particularly interested in stage parodies, such as Greek comedies in which "the same actors who had appeared in magnificent dresses [in tragedies], now returned on the stage in grotesque habiliments, with odd postures and gestures, while the story, though the same, was incongruous and ludicrous" (217). The idea of making the "magnificent" into the "ridiculous" also connotes travesty, and D'Israeli discusses the "travesty of great personages" in French stage parodies: "out of the stuff of which they made their emperors, their heroes, and their princesses, they cut out a pompous country justice, a hectoring tailor, or an impudent mantua-maker" (218). Costume, the defining tool of travesty, returns not once but twice in this example, in the metaphor of new roles "cut out" of old ones and in the resulting figures of the tailor and mantua-maker. As D'Israeli's essay suggests, parody was a capacious and shifting term in the era of *Frankenstein*, multivalent in intent, continuous with pastiche, and encompassing the aims and methods of travesty.[6]

D'Israeli wrote this essay at the moment when *Frankenstein* was becoming the object of parody. The first stage melodramas of the novel, in the early 1820s, were immediately parodied. Richard Brinsley Peake, for example, parodied his own melodrama, *Presumption*, with *Another Piece of Presumption* (1824), in which a tailor named Frankinstitch builds a monster, Hobgoblin, from the body parts of other tailors.[7] Other theatrical parodies proliferated: as William St. Clair summarizes this history, "Parodies parodied parodies, moving in any direction that the moment made promising. . . . *Frankenstein* survived in a free-floating popular oral and visual culture, with only the central episode of the scientist making the Creature holding it tenuously to its original."[8]

Yet *Frankenstein* not only served as an object of parody from the 1820s onward; the novel's depiction of the monster, I suggest, already enacted the operations of parody, along with those of pastiche and travesty. A hint of this enactment emerges in Joyce Carol Oates's description of the monster: "though he is meant to be Frankenstein's ideal . . . he is only a fragment of that ideal—which is to say, a mockery, a parody, a joke."[9] Oates's account of the monster as "a parody" echoes Ebenezer Cobham Brewer's definition of the Frankenstein monster, in his 1870 *Dictionary of Phrase and Fable*, as "only animal life, a parody on the creature man."[10] We can explore this formulation of the monster as a parody more systematically, using Peake's 1824 self-parody, *Another Piece of Presumption*. Peake's play exemplifies the operations of parody, but in so doing, I suggest, it also highlights the ways that parody is thematized within *Frankenstein*.

First, what D'Israeli calls the "grafted" combination of parody and original is everywhere in *Another Piece*, including the name of the tailor, Frankinstitch, which grafts "Frankenstein" onto "stitch"; the title of the play, which grafts "another piece" onto Peake's own *Presumption*; and its plot, which grafts *Presumption* onto *Frankenstein*. But grafting is already enacted in *Frankenstein*, since the monster is grafted from multiple originals. What D'Israeli outlines as the "odd postures and gestures" of parody, its "incongruous and ludicrous" dimensions, is embodied in *Frankenstein* in the monster's body. Similarly, both the parody and the novel exemplify pastiche. In *Another Piece*, this idea is anatomized in Frankinstitch's account of the creation of Hobgoblin:

What a wretch have I form'd—There's Jemmy Wilson's hair—Billy Boroughs's head—Bobby Bluethread's arms—Old Nicholas's neck—Christopher Cabbage's back—Ben Baste's one leg, and Patrick Longmeasure's tother—Dreadful incorporation of nine Tailors—but my man is made! (167)

This speech exaggerates pastiche, comically naming persons as well as body parts. In a kind of comic version of the Renaissance blazon, which anatomized the beloved's body parts, here the "wretch" is formed by a "Dreadful incorporation" of bodies whose very names signal the processes—measuring, threading, basting—of sartorial incorporation.[11] But the speech also highlights the presence of pastiche within *Frankenstein*. *Frankenstein*'s plot of how a "man is made" from different parts supplies not only an original text to be parodied but a model of how to go about making parody and pastiche.

The play is also a model of travesty. D'Israeli's emphasis on the "grotesque habiliments" of parody, and his example of the emperor travestied as a "hectoring tailor," are redoubled in Peake's plot of a tailor who makes a grotesque body from other tailors. *Another Piece* travesties *Frankenstein*, which had never been considered a "high" work but could still be lowered significantly. In Peake's *Presumption*, for example, the character of the servant, Fritz—who becomes the laboratory assistant, Igor, of twentieth-century *Frankenstein* films—lowers the novel into comedy. But *Presumption*'s Victor Frankenstein still has lofty goals: "Like Prometheus of old, have I daringly attempted the formation—the animation of a Being!" (139). In *Another Piece*, however, Frankinstitch has become a wholly comic figure, his godlike declaration now reduced comically to its everyday tools: "I have animated him with the parlour bellows" (167). Lowering Frankenstein into Frankinstitch, *Another Piece* makes visible the operations of travesty already in the novel. Victor's project is a religious travesty in which he debases God's role as Creator, and it is also a social travesty in which Victor descends from his own elite upbringing as a syndic's son into the disreputable spheres of the "dissecting room and the slaughterhouse."[12] The result of this lowering, the Frankenstein monster, is another travesty: a graceful original become grotesque imitation. Before Peake's Frankinstitch and Hobgoblin, Shelley's monster-maker and monster already travesty God and man.

Both Peake's play and Shelley's novel, moreover, exemplify the workings of self-directed parody. These workings are already present within *Frankenstein*, since Victor intends for the monster to be a new version of himself. He explicitly describes the monster as a self-imitation: "I doubted at first whether I should attempt the creation of a being like myself . . . but my imagination was too much exalted . . . to permit me to doubt of my ability to give life to an animal as complex and wonderful as man" (31). Like Peake, Victor signals his own status as the parody's original: "A new species would bless me as its creator and source; many happy and excellent natures would owe their being to me" (32). Both self-aware and self-interested, Victor intends himself to be the "source" text for new ones. The relation between monster and creator is customarily seen as one of doubling, but we could also see the monster as Victor's unintentional self-parody.

Yet their relationship is more complicated still, for the monster becomes an agent as well as an object of parody. Once the monster learns to read, he avidly consumes four texts: Milton's *Paradise Lost*, Plutarch's *Lives*, Goethe's *Sorrows of Werther*, and Victor Frankenstein's journal. His molding of his mind through the first three of these—"I now continually studied and exercised my mind upon these histories" (86)—constitutes a pastiche in both senses, a combination of originals and a project without ridiculing intent. After reading Victor's journal, however, the monster intentionally seizes angry control of parody. His efforts at revenge constitute his active self-transformation from parody to parodist. He first makes himself into a parody of Milton's Satan—"I, like the arch fiend, bore a hell within me" (92)—but his primary original for parody is Victor. When Victor rejects him, for example, he parodies his authority: "I can make you so wretched that the light of day will be hateful to you. . . . I am your master" (116). His murder of Elizabeth is a parody of Victor's destruction of his bride, rendered with a malignant grin: "A grin was on the face of the monster; he seemed to jeer, as with his fiendish finger he pointed towards the corpse of my wife" (136). And in recalling her murder to Walton, the monster precisely parodies Victor's own quest: "The completion of my demoniacal design became an insatiable passion" (154).

The monster's role as parodist complicates the dynamics of parody earlier established in the novel. If Victor functions as a parodist—the corpses he works from are his originals, and the monster is their parody—then the monster's rampage suggests that a parody may escape its creator's control. The monster's rebellion against Victor, in this model, suggests the instability of a parody in relation to its creator. But since the monster is also a version of Victor, he suggests the debased relationship of a parody to its original. Despite Victor's goal of creating a "beautiful" version of himself, he creates a self-parody who is, to use D'Israeli's term, "malignant." In a familial model of textual relationships in which originals give birth to parodies, the Frankenstein monster exemplifies parody's status as an illegitimate form. The monster's revenge on Victor accordingly enacts the debasing effect of a bastardized parody on its original. "[S]ometimes I was furious, and burnt with rage; sometimes low and despondent. I neither spoke or looked, but sat motionless, bewildered by the multitude of miseries that overcame me" (132). This is Victor speaking, but his terms—rage, despondency, isolation, bewilderment, misery—are similar to those with which the monster earlier describes himself. As both parodist and parody, the monster travesties his original, bringing him "low" to his own level of abjection. As a parody of Victor, the monster is not only bastardized but parricidal.

These operations, too, have their later counterparts in *Another Piece*. Hobgoblin hits Frankinstitch, who says to him, "Oh Monster—what strike your father!—I'm down—(trips) Oh you bastard!" (175). The combination of literal downward movement and the charge of "bastard" neatly condenses the effect of a parody in knocking a paternal original off a secure base. Yet *Another Piece* restores its original foundations. At the end of the parody, Hobgoblin and Frankinstitch kill each other, but the ghosts of the nine tailors appear, demand their lost body parts, and retrieve them. This comic ending allows for the restoration of pastiched and parodied parts to their originals, just as *Another Piece* itself allows for, and indeed encourages, another viewing of Peake's *Presumption*. In *Frankenstein*, conversely, Victor dies, an ending that suggests the inability of originals to survive the assault of parodies on them. Whereas *Another Piece* allows for a mutually reinforcing relationship between parody and original, *Frankenstein* enacts a model of parody that is not only self-reflexive but self-consuming.

The Frankenstein monster, then, enacts many of the operations of parody, for both are grafted, lowering, self-reflexive, self-parodic, mimicking, bastardized, parricidal, debased, and debasing forms. These operations have no intrinsic political meaning. Although contemporary cultural theory has often emphasized the radicalism of parody, parody has often been intended conservatively, to police perceived political or aesthetic excess. Eighteenth-century British literature, for example, includes many parodies intended to mock literary innovation, such as Fielding's *Shamela*, Swift's *Tale of a Tub*, and Pope's *Dunciad*. Politically as well as aesthetically, the historical moment for parody just prior to *Frankenstein* was largely conservative, and indeed, the cultural history of *Frankenstein* intersects with the conservative history of parody in the person of George Canning, the British foreign secretary whose allusion to *Frankenstein* in an 1824 parliamentary speech against West Indian slave emancipation I discussed in chapter 1: "To turn [the negro] loose . . . would be to raise up a creature resembling the splendid fiction of a recent romance."[13] Long before making this speech, Canning was associated with what Simon Dentith characterizes as "perhaps the most visible example in English literary history of the conservative function of parody."[14] Canning was a founder and principal contributor to the literary journal *The Anti-Jacobin* (1797–98), which attacked the French Revolution and its English sympathizers. *The Anti-Jacobin* offered parodies of poems by English authors sympathetic to the French Revolution, printed alongside their originals. "We reverence LAW," wrote Canning in the journal's prospectus, and "of JACOBINISM in all its shapes, . . . whether as it openly threatens the subversion of States, or gradually saps the foundations of domestic happiness, We are the avowed, determined, and irreconcileable enemies."[15] Canning's *Anti-Jacobin* writings and his speech alluding to the Frankenstein monster are more than a quarter century apart, but they are politically continuous: the condemnation of the revolutionary who "openly threatens the subversion of States" becomes a critique of the rebellious slave. Parodies of *Frankenstein* continued this conservative impulse. Works like *Another Piece* realize the potential of parody to discipline an original, circumscribing the pathos of the monster and turning him into a joke.

Yet Canning's parliamentary allusion to the Frankenstein monster is also a clue to the stresses within the conservative use of parody. His reference to "the splendid fiction of a recent romance" was not to the novel but to Peake's theatrical version, *Presumption*; the reference reflects the uncontrolled circulation of works about *Frankenstein* as well as that of the monster within them. A greater instability informs D'Israeli's essay on parody. Like Canning, D'Israeli was a political conservative; his first novel, *Vaurien* (1797), was an attack on William Godwin and other English supporters of the French Revolution. In his essay on parody, D'Israeli favors parody as a policing mechanism, "a refined instructor for the public" (218); he concludes his essay favoring its "legitimate use" (220). Yet his writing also reveals the less "legitimate" potential of parody, in the example he gives of mimicry:

> The African boy, who amused the whole kafle [coffle] he journeyed with, by mimicking the gestures and the voice of the auctioneer who had sold him at the slavemarket a few days before, could have no sense of scorn, of superiority, or of malignity; the boy experienced merely the pleasure

of repeating attitudes and intonations which had so forcibly excited his interest. (213)

D'Israeli here denies any political content to mimicry, but the example works against his declared purpose, for it outlines a politically radical scenario. Even if the "African boy" does not intend his mimicry politically, it may certainly be received as such by others in the slave "kafle." The example provides a blueprint for the radical use of mimicry, as well as for parody.[16] What is to be dreaded about parody is not only, as D'Israeli states, the public's ability "to laugh at what at another time they would shed tears" (220). It is also the possibility—which he raises only to disavow—that that laughter may function to unseat the political hierarchies on which conservatism depends.

From this perspective, while *Another Piece* is conservative in the way that it mutes the monster, it also has more radical political dimensions. *Another Piece* travesties anything resembling a social elite, starting with the transformation of Dr. Frankenstein into Mr. Frankinstitch. More generally, what I have characterized as the bastardized, parricidal, debased, and debasing elements of parody have a political meaning in this play and in *Frankenstein*, for they translate politically into the "subversion of States." This subversion links *Another Piece* to the practices of inversion, misrule, and excess theorized by Mikhail Bakhtin as the carnivalesque. Parody and travesty are central to Bakhtin's discussion of the practices of carnival. The carnivalesque is a low and lowering world of travesty, located in the lower social orders, enacted through "downward movement" toward the earth and into the body: "Down, inside out, vice versa, upside down."[17] When Hobgoblin throws Frankinstitch to the ground, his gesture suggests a comic and carnivalesque world in which political foundations, like paternal ones, are turned topsy-turvy.

But it is Shelley's tragic vision, not Peale's comic one, that most closely approaches the terms of Bakhtin. The monster is the embodiment of Bakhtin's model of parodies, which "degrade, bring down to earth, turn their subject into flesh."[18] The monster's fleshiness also suggests Bakhtin's notion of the grotesque body, in which irregularities and openings dominate. The grotesque body "ignores the closed, smooth, and impenetrable surface of the body and retains only its excrescences . . . and orifices, only that which leads beyond the body's limited space or into the body's depths."[19] With his "yellow skin scarcely cover[ing] the work of muscles and arteries beneath" (34), the Frankenstein monster's body is an unsmooth surface leading directly into his depths. His skin is an open orifice; his actual open orifice—his mouth—travesties Victor; and the open orifice of the book's conclusion refuses to snap shut.

The Frankenstein monster's violent rebellion against Victor, then, suggests one form of radical politics for parody: the openly carnivalesque subversion of what Canning terms the "reverence [for] LAW." A second, more covert form of subversion emerges from another moment in the novel, the monster's mimicry of the De Laceys:

> My organs were indeed harsh, but supple; and although my voice was very unlike the soft music of their tones, yet I pronounced such words as I understood with tolerable ease. It was as the ass and the lap-dog; yet surely the gentle ass, whose intentions were affectionate, although his manners were rude, deserved better treatment than blows and execration. (77)

Imitating the De Laceys, the monster intentionally acts only as a mimic, but in transforming their "soft music" with his "harsh" organs, he effects an unintentional parody of them. As Victor, through self-parody, becomes an object of parody as well as a parodist, so too the monster, through mimicry, becomes a parodist as well as a parody.

The image of "the ass and the lap-dog" deepens the significance of this parody. This reference is to the animal fable known as "The Ass and the Lap-Dog," and the animal fable as a genre is relevant to *Frankenstein* in several ways. I have been interpreting the novel allegorically, and fables are closely linked to allegories, while animals are closely linked to fables; Thomas Harvey, defining a fable in 1887 as "a short allegory," specifies that "[m]ost fables are short stories about certain animals that are regarded as representatives of particular qualities; as, the fox, of cunning; the lion, of strength."[20] *Frankenstein* can be seen as a kind of animal fable, one in which the animal acting allegorically—the monster—represents the quality of monstrosity; indeed, he both embodies and enacts monstrosity, whereas the fox or the lion must have the qualities of cunning or strength imputed to it. With its cautionary tale of a monstrous animal, *Frankenstein* seems a fable extended and exaggerated, as in the grotesque, and a fable imitated with a difference, as in a parody. The place of "The Ass and the Lap-Dog" in *Frankenstein* is thus not only that of a small fable within a big one; it is also that of a short original contained within a long parody.[21]

This particular fable also takes parody as its theme. In "The Ass and the Lap-Dog," the ass, observing that the lap-dog is praised for his affectionate behavior, tries clumsily to imitate him, only to be punished by the master. The fable offers a precise analogue to the monster's efforts at speech, which begin as mimicry and emerge as parody. "The Ass and the Lap-Dog" first appeared in Aesop, and it was adapted by La Fontaine, who is customarily cited as the source for this passage in *Frankenstein*.[22] But it seems more likely that Mary Shelley knew of this fable through its inclusion in her father's *Fables Ancient and Modern*, in which Godwin retold Aesop's fables in his own prose; he published this two-volume collection under a pseudonym in 1805, and she read it as a child.[23] The familial connection deepens the relevance of this fable to *Frankenstein*, since it suggests a symbolic parallel between the monster and Mary Shelley. As the monster repeats and revises the speech of others, so too does the daughter retell her father's story. Both risk becoming unintentional parodists of their originals—and thereby appearing, literally or metaphorically, as asses.

Within the novel, this fable takes on additional significance after Safie arrives. Safie also engages in mimicry, but for the purpose of learning a language rather than just imitating its sounds:

> Presently I found, by the frequent recurrence of one sound which the stranger repeated after them, that she was endeavouring to learn their language; and the idea instantly occurred to me, that I should make use of the same instructions to the same end. The stranger learned about twenty words at the first lesson, most of them indeed were those which I had before understood, but I profited by the others. (78–79)

The monster is mimicking Safie's mimicry of the De Laceys, two activities that proceed unevenly: "I may boast that I improved more rapidly than the Arabian, who understood very little, and conversed in broken accents, whilst I comprehended and could imitate almost every word that was spoken" (79). This description marks a contrast between the monster and Safie, but it also establishes a parallel between them, whereby the monster's very form—an imperfect imitation of the human—is the embodiment of Safie's "broken accents." Neither character intends to engage in parody, but their mimicry does so unintentionally. In the monster's case, this is a parody of a parody: when the monster and Safie together imitate the De Laceys, he is primarily imitating her imitation. To return to the terms of the fable, he wishes only to occupy her favored role as metaphorical lap-dog of the De Laceys.

The political effects of this project seem conservative, for the monster in the novel as for the ass in the fable. The ass is not mimicking the powerful master; rather, he is imitating the lap-dog, a small, physically weak animal with no function except to symbolize fidelity to the master. The lap-dog is a symbol of cooptation, used to characterize someone who ingratiates himself with elites. The lap-dog is both domesticated and feminized, and it may symbolize erotic desire, particularly when seen as the pet of the mistress; even if the mistress's lap-dog does not actually pleasure the lap on which he lies, he is, as one critic puts it, "privy to the woman's most prized anatomical area."[24] In pretending to be the lap-dog, then, the ass is mimicking a position of subservience to authority rather than authority itself. This is a model of mimicry not as a direct protest against those in power, as in D'Israeli's example of the "African boy" imitating his auctioneer, but rather as a more indirect critique within hierarchies of the disempowered. It is as if, for example, the field slave in the antebellum American South mimicked the house slave or Shakespeare's Caliban mimicked Ariel. In each case, the master still prospers.[25]

The potential conservatism of this mimicry is reinforced in the fable's moral, which in La Fontaine is "Let's not force our talent. . . . / Never can a clod, however he grimace, / Pass himself off as a gallant."[26] There are some dozen fables involving the ass in La Fontaine, and they emphasize the folly of his efforts to escape his subservient role. In "The Ass Wearing the Lion's Skin," the ass wears a lion's skin and appears fierce but then is exposed and humiliated for his efforts. This story, which turns on the direct mimicry of those in power—the lion is "the king of beasts"—functions similarly as a cautionary tale. As in "The Ass and the Lap-Dog," the ass is discovered and beaten, and the moral in La Fontaine is that people should not try to rise above their station: "The lordly outfits they own / Don't quite make up for their being a joke."[27] "The Ass and the Lap-Dog," then, seems to belong to a conservative fable tradition that operates in what Gillian Brown terms a "paradigmatic state of caution."[28] As cited self-punishingly by the Frankenstein monster, this fable seems to function as an admonition against the impulse to mimic anything, even the posture of subservience.

But such fables also have the potential to function less conservatively. The morals to Aesop's *Fables* were added later; Aesop's versions are brutal allegories of power relations, in which the ass has the lowest role. He echoes, if not also alludes to, the human ass, as orifice and bottom body part in what Bakhtin calls the "material bodily lower stratum."[29] Aesop's ass fables shift attention to this bottom of the body politic, and the ass's speech approaches the carnivalesque in the very idea of expulsions—vocal if not also fecal—from an ass. Godwin's versions of the fables do not go this far, but they reflect his own political radicalism as well as a general Enlightenment interest in fables as instruments of democratic education. His version of "The Ass in the Lion's Skin," for example, begins with a defense: "An ass is a very useful and a very patient animal; one would have expected therefore that every body would have thought of him with respect."[30] Because the ass is treated badly, his wearing of the lion's skin is, for Godwin, a reasonable effort to claim the respect due him. Godwin ends the fable not with the punishment of the ass but with his friendship with his former tormenters:

> [The boys] resolved not to teaze him any more. . . . they did not disturb him when he was feeding. And now, instead of running away the moment they came in sight, he would trot to meet them, would rub his head against them to tell them how much he loved them, and would eat the thistles and the oats out of their hand: was not that pretty?[31]

This fable's moral is no longer a caution against ambition but a plea to be kind to animals: this is a vindication of the rights of the ass. It is, however, a program for liberal reform rather than class revolution. Loving his master, the ass now has no more desire to rebel; literally eating out of the master's hand, he has been so fully domesticated that he approaches the status of a lap-dog.

In "The Ass and the Lap-Dog," the ass challenges hierarchy more indirectly, by destabilizing a triangular relation among the three terms—ass, lap-dog, master—that constitute its system of class relations. Godwin's version of the fable begins with the ass's anger at inequality. The ass laments that the lap-dog "is fed out of his own plate, and sleeps all night upon a cushion. . . . I on the contrary am obliged to carry heavy loads, get nothing in return but blows, and am forced to sleep . . . in the fields."[32] His first mimicry, practiced in private, elevates his position in his own eyes at least: "he would steal behind the barndoor, and practice his airs and graces. . . . he thought he was quite perfect."[33] Although the ass's public mimicry is ultimately unsuccessful, his efforts nonetheless highlight both the legitimacy of his anger and the vulnerability of the lap-dog to parody. In such a parody, the mimicry of subservience does not overtly dislodge the power of the master. Nonetheless, in a rigid system of class relations, not available for total upheaval, such mimicry at least distances the parodist from total subservience.

Exploited for its radical potential, then, "The Ass in the Lion's Skin" confirms the overt radicalism of a parody of power, whereas "The Ass and the Lap-Dog" suggests the interstitial value involved in a parody of powerlessness. The animal fable of the ass outlines at least two potentially radical ways for those condemned as monstrous to use parody: the open destruction, parricidal and debasing, of powerful originals through overt parodies of them; and the covert destabilization of those originals through parodies of disempowerment itself.

These political possibilities for parody return us to *Frankenstein*, in which the monster imitates powerless Safie as well as powerful Victor, and they also return us to turn-of-the-century American fiction about a black Frankenstein monster. Paul Laurence Dunbar's writing parodies *Frankenstein*, and he too enacts the processes of parody within *Frankenstein*. Dunbar's writing, I suggest, offers a parody of black subservience as well as white power. To return to the language of the animal fable—a language adopted by Dunbar as well as by Shelley—his parodies inhabit the roles of the ass, the lap-dog, and the lion.

III.

Paul Laurence Dunbar was the most famous black writer of his era, known primarily for his poetry but also for the fiction, essays, and plays he produced before his early death at age thirty-three. Raised in Dayton, Ohio, the son of former slaves, Dunbar was befriended by the elderly Frederick Douglass, dubbed by Booker T. Washington the "Poet Laureate of the Negro race," and praised by W. E. B. Du Bois. Throughout his short life—which included a troubled marriage to writer Alice Dunbar-Nelson —he considered himself a committed participant in the struggle for black equality. This commitment emerges most forcefully in his essays for black newspapers, in which he condemned lynching, segregation, and other forms of racism in the urban North and the rural South.[34]

Yet Dunbar's essays reached only a small audience, and he was much more famous for a very different and politically more ambiguous kind of writing: his dialect poetry. This poetry adopts the folk speech of Southern black people and often seems to commemorate slavery nostalgically. In "Chrismus on the Plantation," for example, the narrator remembers a holiday after the Civil War, when free slaves rallied around their impoverished ex-master:

> you wants us to fu'git dat you's been kin',
> An' ez soon ez you is he'pless, we's to leave you hyeah behin'.
> Well, ef dat's de way dis freedom ac's on people, white en black,
> You kin jes' tell Mistah Lincum
> fu' to tek his freedom back.[35]

This image of black people so loyal to their white masters that they "tell Mistah Lincum / fu' to tek his freedom back" seems to validate the racist nostalgia for slavery common to Dunbar's era, a sentiment that fed directly into the rise of Jim Crow segregation and the resurgence of the Ku Klux Klan. Although many of Dunbar's contemporary black readers supported him, he was later repudiated by writers in the Harlem Renaissance and, still later, the Black Arts movement, for his apparent capitulation to stereotype. More recent discussions of Dunbar have moved outside this dichotomy of appreciation or dismissal. Yet in contrast to the large-scale recovery of other black writers of the era, such as Charles Chesnutt, Pauline Hopkins, and Frances Harper, Dunbar remains an anomalous and understudied figure in African American and American literary studies.[36]

We can begin to make sense of the apparent disjunctures in Dunbar's writing by identifying the extreme constraints within which he wrote. Dunbar became a celebrity when William Dean Howells, the premier critic and arbiter of literary value in the era, championed his dialect poetry. These were the terms of Howells's praise:

> Paul Dunbar [is] the only man of pure African blood and of American civilization to feel the negro life aesthetically and express it lyrically. . . . [His dialect poems] describe the range between appetite and emotion . . . which is the range of the race. . . . These are divinations and reports of what passes in the hearts and minds of a lowly people whose poetry had hitherto been inarticulately expressed in music, but now finds, for the first time in our tongue, literary interpretation of a very artistic completeness.[37]

Howells situates black culture as a limited sphere devoted, like minstrelsy, to a narrow range "between appetite and emotion," and he names Dunbar as the voice of "a lowly people." This praise combined the racial hierarchies inherited from slavery with the professional hierarchies of a young writer transformed into a "hot property" by an established older one. From the start, Dunbar was abjectly positioned by a white literary elite as a commodity, between minstrel and slave.[38]

His position was also that of the freak. This imagery emerges, for example, in an 1898 essay entitled "Our New Madness," in which Dunbar discusses the new interest among African Americans for vocational education, such as the Tuskegee Institute. Although he praises such initiatives, he focuses on the continuing plight of the black intellectual:

> Any attempt at engaging in pursuits where his mind is employed is met by an attitude that stigmatizes his effort as presumption. Then if the daring one succeeds, he is looked upon as a monster. He is put into the same category with the "two-headed boy" and the "bearded lady." There has not, in the history of the country, risen a single intellectual black man whose pretensions have not been sneered at, laughed at, and then lamely wondered at. If he was fair of complexion, they said that he derived his powers from his white blood. If he was convincingly black, they felt of his bumps, measured his head, and said that it was not negro in conformation. It is his intellectuality that needs substantiating.[39]

This critique of the racism confronting the "intellectual black man" invokes two well-known freak-show figures. The "bearded lady" is an image of gender inversion; the "two-headed boy" signals infantilization, while also connoting that a black man's intellect—his ability to use one head—is as freakish as having two heads.[40] The image of head measurement, a reference to the popular pseudoscience of phrenology, further aligns the measurement of the outside of the black man's head with the condemnation of its inside. The passage reflects Dunbar's own experience as a black man emasculated and infantilized by a literary culture to which he did not "conform" and as a dark-skinned man whose intellectuality was considered at odds with his "convincingly black" skin.

This passage, a critique of the racism confronting the black intellectual, revised a general association in this era of writers with freaks. As Rachel Adams notes, an 1896 *Life* magazine cartoon presented Howells,

Twain, and other contemporary writers as a set of freak show exhibits, their images advertised on posters hung outside a tent whose entryway reads "Curiosities of American Literature."[41] This title—presumably an allusion to D'Israeli's *Curiosities of Literature*—underscores the affinity of literary culture with the freak show; the cartoon's humor depends on the incongruity of juxtaposing a "high" writer like Howells with the "low" freak-show world. For the black writer, however, there was little incongruity, since a racist culture already positioned him as a freak. In Dunbar's case, this problem was compounded by the difficulty of presenting himself as an intellectual after he had become famous as the unintellectual voice of a "lowly people." To the extent that he was even credited with his own self-making, Dunbar could not escape the voyeuristic exhibition spaces of the auction block and the minstrel stage. The freak show, for him, had no exit.

Dunbar's role as performer, reading his poetry for white audiences, exacerbated these constraints. J. Saunders Redding, reflecting on the internal contradictions of Dunbar's celebrity, recalled a story told to him by Alice Dunbar-Nelson. At the end of one of Dunbar's poetry readings, "an aristocratic white lady" rose to praise him:

> "Paul"—she had never seen him before much less met him—"Paul," she said, in a most complimentary and gratified tone, "I shall never again wax impatient and cross at the childish antics of my servants, members of your race. Tonight, you have made me understand and love them." Following this remark, the applause was resumed more enthusiastically than before. Paul Dunbar fled through a side door to an anteroom where his wife waited. There he dropped to his knees before her, buried his head in her lap, and wept convulsively.[42]

The language of this anecdote registers the pain of Dunbar's forced minstrel role; the woman who praises the "childish antics" of her servants reprises the terms of Howells's praise. This is another scene of abjection, in which Dunbar is first brought low by the woman's servantlike use of his first name and then, by the end, is literally on the ground. It is also another tableau of gender inversion, in which a white woman so emasculates a black man that he is brought to his knees. "I see now very clearly that Mr. Howells has done me irrevocable harm in the dictum he laid down regarding my dialect verse," Dunbar wrote regretfully to a friend in 1897.[43] Dunbar's celebrity came at terrible cost, and a recent biographer,

Eleanor Alexander, argues for the central role of self-hatred in his life, as fuel for his depression, alcoholism, and the physical abuse he apparently inflicted on his wife.[44] If this anecdote leaves Dunbar with his head in his wife's lap, his career testifies more generally to the pain of the black writer positioned, metaphorically, as a lap-dog to white audiences.

The lap-dog was also a symbolic monster. Dunbar offers his own monster metaphor—"if the daring one succeeds, he is looked upon as a monster"—in the context of the freak show, but the terms of his career also correspond metaphorically to monstrosity as shaped by the Frankenstein tradition. As a black writer "made" by a white one, Dunbar emerged into literary celebrity as a kind of Frankenstein monster. His ongoing effort to re-create himself as an intellectual constituted a second monster story. This was one in which he attempted to be creator to his own creation, but his efforts were condemned as "presumption"—the same single-word lesson extracted from *Frankenstein* in the title of Peake's stage melodrama. Dunbar's career suggests a particularly acute enactment of the terms of parody as they initially appear in *Frankenstein*. White audiences praised him as an authentic "original" for his dialect poetry, but when he attempted to present himself as an intellectual, he was seen as a grotesque parody of white norms.

Yet if Dunbar could not escape these terms of monstrosity, he could mock them: like the Frankenstein monster, he could transform himself from the role of debased parody into that of debasing parodist. We may, I suggest, understand his writing as a series of tightly controlled and intermittently visible parodies necessitated by the extreme constraints imposed on his career. His parodies operate across many different genres, through the mechanism of irony, and against several targets, including Dunbar himself. Interpreted as both parody and self-parody, his writing takes aim at two targets: white mastery and black subservience. For a black writer allowed no more authority by his white audience than that of literary lap-dog, a parody of subservience provided a measure of resistance from the indignities of this role. Dunbar's writing, in short, enacts the political possibilities of the ass who parodies both lap-dog and lion.

These parodies, I suggest, have hybrid origins. In interpreting a turn-of-the-century African American writer through the frameworks provided by both *Frankenstein* and the European fable tradition, I take my cue from Dunbar himself. In his novel *The Sport of the Gods*, Dunbar explicitly cites "Frankenstein," and at least once in his writing, he describes himself as the ass from the animal fable. Yet Dunbar's parodies are also firmly rooted in the black cultural tradition of signifying and in a moment in African American culture when the longstanding traditions of the animal and human trickster coexisted with the emerging folk outlaw hero of the black "badman." Before turning to Dunbar's fiction about the Frankenstein monster, I interpret his literary voice, developed across genres, as the meeting point between the strategies of parody outlined within *Frankenstein* and those developed in black cultural practice. In a variation on the "Signifying Monkey" tradition, Dunbar's hybridized version of parody constitutes, I suggest, the revenge of a signifying monster.

IV.

"[U]nless the prototype is familiar to us," D'Israeli cautions, "a parody is nothing!" (215). Among the prototypes for Dunbar were works by white authors that represented black as well as white people as nostalgic for slavery. In Thomas Nelson Page's story "Marse Chan" (1887), for example, an ex-slave, Sam, describes to a white narrator his attachment to his former owner, a dead Confederate soldier, and to the days of slavery: "Dem wuz good old times, marster—de bes' Sam ever see! . . . Niggers didn't hed nothin' 't all to do. . . . Dyar warn' no trouble nor nothin'." Sam's only expression of dissent comes at the beginning at the story, when the narrator sees him talking to an old dog: "Yo' so sp'ilt yo' kyahn hardly walk. . . . Jes' like white folks—think 'cuz you's white and I's black, I got to wait on yo' all de time. Ne'm mine, I ain' gwi' do it!" But his outrage is comic: this is his former master's dog, who knows "I don't mean nothin' by what I sez" and whom Sam is happy to serve. The voice of the black man in this story is so naturalized into servitude that he is not only doglike but servant to a dog. Sam's words are most sincere only when they are most abject.[45]

By contrast, I suggest, Paul Laurence Dunbar's literary voice is least sincere when it seems to be most abject. Dunbar's most famous poem in standard English, "We Wear the Mask," provides a sustained metaphor of parody: "We wear the mask that grins and lies, / It hides our cheeks and shades our eyes."[46] This poem presents grinning—a signature trait of minstrelsy—as a necessary strategy of self-preservation in a racist world. The mask in the poem has cheeks and eyes beneath, but in the case of Dunbar's dialect poems, it is not clear that there is a stable original beneath the parodies of minstrelsy. Dunbar was an Ohioan with no direct experience of Southern life; his favorite authors as a youth were

Shakespeare, Tennyson, and Wordsworth; and he wrote several kinds of dialect, including poetry mimicking the speech of poor whites, which he modeled on similar works by white Indiana writer James Whitcomb Riley.[47] His poems in black dialect were thus one mimicry among many, and he invented them from a variety of mediated sources, including Joel Chandler Harris's Uncle Remus tales, which were themselves a Southern white journalist's redaction of black folk dialect. In an interview, Dunbar praised Harris as a white writer who "shows the most intimate sympathy" with black people, but he also prefaced this comment by noting, "Why, the white people of the south talk like us—they have imported many of our words into the language—and you know they act like us."[48] In drawing from Harris, Dunbar imitated an imitation; he "imported" what was already an import. Rather than expressing an authentic voice, Dunbar's dialect poems are, aesthetically, a black writer's mimicry of a white mimicry of black speech—a parody that destabilizes an already unstable original.

Politically, too, Dunbar's dialect poetry mimics the racist nostalgia of his white contemporaries, but with crucial differences that suggest deliberate parody. In "The Old Cabin," for example, a former slave reminisces about slave days with pleasure: "You could see de dahkies dancin' / Pigeon wing an' heel an' toe— / Joyous times I tell you people / Roun' dat same ol' cabin do." This sounds like Sam of Page's "Marse Chan," but Dunbar's narrator prefaces these reminiscences with a more painful memory: "my min' fu'gits de whuppins / Draps de feah o' block an' lash / An' flies straight to somep'n' joyful / In a secon's lightnin' flash."[49] These lines reveal the violence that must be repressed—the auction block and the lash—in order to present a nostalgic account of slavery. Not all of the dialect poems will sustain such an interpretation, but in this poem at least, Dunbar offers a parody of racist nostalgia that exposes its false foundations.

The possibility of parody emerges in more overt form in Dunbar's writing for the stage. His best-known dramatic pieces were his lyrics for black vaudeville shows, comic musical entertainments staged by black actors for white audiences.[50] These entertainments were pejoratively known as "coon shows," and in songs with titles like "The Hottest Coon in Dixie," Dunbar seemed to reproduce the minstrelsy implied within his dialect poems directly on the stage. Yet as with the dialect poems, these songs were only one form of mimicry among many; his recently recovered play *Herrick*, for example, is a full-scale imitation of an eighteenth-century English comedy of manners. And although his plays use minstrelsy, they use it to effect multiple parodies. *Jes Lak White Fo'ks*, for example, makes fun of pretentious black people, along the lines of the Zip Coon dandy figure in the minstrel show. But Dunbar also parodies white people who long to be British aristocrats: "All de yankees is dissatisfied / Wid a deir untitled station. / Dey is huntin' after title."[51] Repositioning white Americans as inadequate imitations of British originals, such lines show that it is not only black people who desire to be "jes lak white fo'ks." Such layered theatrical parodies also reposition the dandy. Across race, the dandy and the parodist have always been closely intertwined roles. The black dandy always involved a strong element of racial parody; as Shane White and Graham White note, "even as they borrowed from whites, there was a conscious undercurrent of satirizing . . . that which they were appropriating."[52] Works like Dunbar's *Jes Lak White Fo'ks* draw from the radical possibilities of the dandy role—that of a parodist who exposes the parodies of others.

Dunbar's fiction takes parody in more covert directions. *The Fanatics* (1901), Dunbar's Civil War novel, centers on the divided loyalties of the white wartime residents of an Ohio border town; its only black character is a man known as "Nigger Ed," introduced as a grotesque figure, both "town crier and town drunkard."[53] Ed is transformed by his experience assisting white men in a Union regiment, after which "he capered no more in the public square for the delectation of the crowd that despised him" (77). But Ed's Civil War experience does not propel him toward black community or political protest—the results of such experience in other African American Civil War novels of the era, like Frances Harper's *Iola Leroy* (1892). Rather, Dunbar concludes the novel with Ed in another subordinate role: "And so they give him a place for life and everything he wanted, and from being despised he was much petted and spoiled, for they were all fanatics" (196). This conclusion leaves Ed in the role of a domesticated pet, "petted and spoiled." Ed's story as a whole seems to capitulate to the desire of white audiences to see black men safely contained in the postwar world—as lap-dogs.

Yet in contrast to Thomas Nelson Page's character Sam, who is both doglike and slave to a dog, the character of "Nigger Ed" functions not to naturalize black subservience but to denaturalize white mastery. At a town meeting, for example, "Both sides hated him and his people. He was like a shuttlecock. He was a reproach to one and an insult to the other" (115). Highlighting Ed's status as "shuttlecock" for white men, Dunbar shows how he functions as a catalyst for white men to restore their own masculinity. The novel's concluding sentence, as Lisa Long argues, may be read as political critique: "Whether Ed is bullied or 'petted,' he is still enslaved."[54] Dunbar's writing functions to expose the continuity between despising black people and petting them. "Nigger Ed" is not a lap-dog but a parody of one.

However, in each of these genres—poetry, drama, fiction—it is difficult to confirm that Dunbar's writing is parodic, since he does not overtly signal it as such. In contrast to a work like Peake's *Another Piece of Presumption*, which names itself as a parody, or to Canning's *Anti-Jacobin*, which printed parodies alongside originals, Dunbar's parodies are hard to distinguish as parodies. To receive Dunbar's work as parodic, we have to rely on an external signal, the antiracist politics he expressed in his journalism, and on an internal signal, the presence of irony in his style. For example, in the context of Dunbar's essay expressing rage at the freak-show treatment of black men, the conclusion of *The Fanatics*—"from being despised, he was much petted and spoiled"—seems to be meant ironically, as a critique of the black man in the role of the lap-dog.

The question of parody in Dunbar's writing, then, is inseparable from that of irony. Irony and parody are structurally related: irony, Linda Hutcheon notes, is parody's "rhetorical miniature."[55] Both may be intentional or derived through reception. For example, Peake's *Another Piece of Presumption* has the ironic effect of exposing the elements of parody already present within *Frankenstein*, although Peake does not seem to intend this irony: it is ironic, in other words, that Peake parodies *Frankenstein*, since *Frankenstein* is already a parody, but Peake himself is not being ironic. Irony is, accordingly, central to Hutcheon's redefinition of parody as "a form of imitation . . . characterized by ironic inversion, not always at the expense of the parodied text."[56]

Dunbar's writing exemplifies this model of parody as an ironic inversion of an original. He wrote within the extremely constrained space of literary representation accorded legitimacy by whites, and his writing suggests that for him, the inversions of irony may have seemed the only inversions possible. The happy slaves, grinning dandies, and symbolic lap-dogs of his writing are ironic inversions of these roles—inversions that do not expand to the capacious world of the carnivalesque but that nonetheless do not leave their confined spaces unchanged. What Hutcheon terms "irony's edge" cuts, in Dunbar's writing, against the white people who force black people to assume roles of abjection, at the same time that it cuts against the black people who assume them.

The latter group includes Dunbar himself: a black man ostensibly "petted and spoiled" by a white audience; a man whose black friends "looked upon him," James Weldon Johnson remembered, "as a spoiled child"; and a man well-known for his interest in dress and fashion, whom biographers characterize as a dandy.[57] Dunbar's parodies of abjection can be seen as self-parodies, and his ironies as self-directed. This combination of parody and self-parody is, at times, barely perceptible: "Now from the bottom of my heart I want to thank you," Dunbar wrote to Howells after his rave review. "I feel much as a poor, insignificant, helpless boy would feel to suddenly find himself knighted."[58] In this letter, Dunbar pays appropriate homage to his benefactor. But the hyperbole of the knight metaphor—another image of Dunbar brought to his knees by a white person—also hints at a parody of both his own abjection and the white man's largesse.

This parodic possibility comes more clearly into view in another letter from Dunbar to Howells, in which he invoked the animal fable "The Ass in the Lion's Skin." After an evening in which he had borrowed Howells's coat, Dunbar wrote to thank him: "Let me thank you for your kindness, although the circumstances brought to my mind the old fable of the ass in the lion's skin. Not withstanding all of my precautions, I have taken a cold."[59] Dunbar presents himself as so abject that even borrowing the great man's coat cannot keep him from falling ill. But the hyperbole of his abjection suggests parody, particularly when juxtaposed with Dunbar's private letters to his wife, in which he had no trouble assuming the role of literary lion. "It is very tiresome," he wrote Alice Dunbar after a reception in Washington, "playing lion and having people exclaim over your youth and ask for your autograph."[60] Here Dunbar mocks his own celebrity, but not his ease at "playing lion." In another letter to Alice from the same Washington trip, he embraces the symbolic roles of both ass and lion: "Darling, I don't care if you do say I am a conceited donkey. . . . The fact is I am tired of being bored and lionized! behold the conceit, but it's plain fact."[61] Dunbar's comfort with being "lionized" results in his "conceit" in two senses of the term, both his imagery and his egotism. These private letters offer a confidently self-mocking performance of the roles of both ass and lion, and they suggest that Dunbar's self-description as "the ass in the lion's skin" to Howells may be a similarly controlled performance. Drawing directly from the animal-fable tradition, Dunbar uses it to mock both white mastery and black abjection. The joke is on both Howells and Dunbar.

Elsewhere in his letters, such dual parody emerges more overtly. Dunbar met Frederick Douglass at the 1893 World's Columbian Exposition, and after Douglass invited him to meet some wealthy white people, he wrote his mother:

> I am invited to attend a reception at this Mrs. Jones' house, given to five distinguished Englishmen who want to see some of the representative colored people in this country and think mamma, your poor little ugly black boy has been chosen as one of the representative colored people after being in Chicago only 5 weeks.[62]

This letter includes the same painful elements as the anecdote about Dunbar's performances retold by J. Saunders Redding: white condescension, black powerlessness, and a scene of gender inversion in which a white woman diminishes a black man. The racial hierarchies involved in that anecdote are redoubled here by national ones, with "distinguished Englishmen" gazing voyeuristically at black Americans. However, in this more private literary context, Dunbar subjects such hierarchies to parody. His account mocks the voyeurism of the white people who are his ostensible benefactors, along with his own abject role as "poor little ugly black boy." The letter may register self-hatred, but as a literary text, it also treats self-hatred ironically.

So pervasive are irony and parody in Dunbar's work that it is difficult not to see them in even his most straightforward writing: his journalism for black newspapers. In an essay entitled "Representative American Negroes," for example, Dunbar opens with a critique of his topic: "The street corner politician, who through questionable methods or even through skillful manipulation, succeeds in securing the janitorship of the Court House, may be written up in the local papers as 'representative,' but is he?" This critique of corrupt politicians turns on an obvious irony: the man whose job is to represent people politically fails to represent them morally. Dunbar then abandons this critique to offer a respectful enumeration of the achievements of Washington, Du Bois, and other prominent African Americans of the era. But irony seems to enter in again at the end of his essay, when he concludes, "In looking over the field for such an article as this, one just begins to realize how many Negroes are representative of something."[63] It is hard not to read "representative of something" as ironic in tone, suggesting Dunbar's covert critique of the whole category of "representative American negroes."[64] Once again, this parody is self-directed, since Dunbar was acutely aware of his own status as "representative." Like the corrupt "street corner politician" who disrupts a system of political representation, Dunbar the ironist disrupts a system of literary representation. The essay suggests that it would be a mistake to assume that Dunbar's writings are ironic and parodic only when he is speaking to a white audience and straightforward when speaking to an African American one. Rather, irony so thoroughly suffuses his writing that almost all of it can be located along a continuum of parodic modes.

Dunbar's corrosive use of irony, parody, and self-parody has affinities with that of an author he devoured in his youth, Mark Twain, especially Twain's *Huck Finn*. Twain has some of the same parodic targets as Dunbar: as *Jes Lak White Fo'ks* parodies the white fascination with "huntin' after title," *Huck Finn* parodies similar pretensions in its depictions of the false King and Dolphin. The character of Jim bears some resemblance to Dunbar's Ed; both are figures whose names ironize rather than reinforce the racism of the term "nigger." At his most radical, Twain exposes the racism of a culture that wants to turn "Jim," as he is called throughout the novel, into "Nigger Jim," as he has come mistakenly to be known in the twentieth century; and at his most radical, Dunbar extends this critique. The cross-racial lineage from Twain to Dunbar accords with Arnold Rampersad's assertion that the value of *Huck Finn* for African American writers has been second only to that of *The Souls of Black Folk*.[65]

Dunbar's work—like Twain's—is also inextricable from black cultural traditions.[66] His parodies bear a close relationship to the tradition of the animal-trickster tale, in which, typically, a small or otherwise weak animal, like a rabbit, outwits a powerful and strong one, like a fox, through cunning, wit, and guile. African in origin, these stories were adapted by African Americans as protests against slavery. We can see Dunbar's parodies of black abjection as trickster tales, acts of resistance to racism arrived at through cunning reversals. His parodies take their place among the rich multiethnic array of trickster figures who saturate American literature at the turn of the century.[67]

At the same time, Dunbar's version of the trickster tale underscores the tale's transatlantic hybridity. When Dunbar called himself "the ass in the lion's skin," he explicitly drew the European fable tradition into African American culture.[68] This project was less an adaptation of European fables than a restoration of their connection to African culture, since an African context had been present in the European fable tradition all along. Aesop drew some of his fables from Egypt and Libya; Godwin, in his version of "The Ass in the Lion's Skin," pauses to specify that it takes place "in a country where lions live; I suppose in Africa."[69] Conversely, the most famous versions of the African trickster in Dunbar's era were a white American's version of the form. Joel Chandler Harris's Uncle Remus tales enclosed the animal stories of Br'er Rabbit in the constraining frame tale of the former slave, Uncle Remus, who narrates them to a white boy. As the European fable tradition had always been linked to Africa, the African trickster folktale of Dunbar's era was inseparable from its white Euro-American redactions. Working within the animal-trickster tradition, Dunbar highlights the hybridity intrinsic to both the European fable and African American folktale.[70]

Dunbar's parodies draw, in particular, from the folklore figure of the Signifying Monkey. Signifying is a form of verbal play, closely related to playing the dozens, testifying, rapping, and other African American verbal forms; originating in African trickster tales, the Signifying Monkey outwits more powerful animals through indirection and wit. As Henry Louis Gates, Jr., has influentially theorized this figure, the work of the Signifying Monkey is the revision of language: "The ironic reversal of a received racist image of the black as simianlike, the Signifying Monkey, . . . ever embodying the ambiguities of language, is our trope for repetition and revision." In a literary context, the Signifying Monkey represents the process by which black writers revise previous texts, whether by black or white predecessors; signifying offers "repetition with a signal difference."[71] This is close to the idea of parody as repetition with ironic inversion, and parody is central to signifying as Gates characterizes it. We can see Dunbar's parodies as signifying on racist literary traditions, as well as on the discourses of minstrelsy and freakery that shaped his reception. In emphasizing the role of animal fables within *Frankenstein*, I have already moved this English gothic novel toward an African American animal-trickster tradition. Dunbar's writing, in turn, suggests that writing rooted in African American trickster traditions could also move toward, and exploit its affinity with, the English gothic novel. His parodies offer a sustained example of the symbolic congruence between the figure of the Signifying Monkey and that of the Frankenstein monster.

The historical moment of this convergence points us, as well, toward another figure in African American folklore. Tricksters like Br'er Rabbit had originated in the antebellum era, but a new folk hero was emerging in African American popular culture in the 1890s. Many songs and tales featured the exploits of the black "badman," a bandit figure whose most famous real-life exemplar was Lee Shelton, a man who shot another man in an 1895 St. Louis barroom brawl and who became known in legend as Stagolee. Badmen like Stagolee were physically powerful, sexually voracious, violent, merciless, and remorseless. Politically, the badman symbolized absolute fearlessness in the face of white law, although his nihilism could also turn against black people; an affiliated figure, the "bad nigger," was even more nihilistic and was feared by blacks themselves. The human badman was a more assertive outlaw figure than the animal trickster, although the trickster, too, had antisocial dimensions. The movement from trickster to badman involved not so much a rejection of the earlier role as a recasting of it, in the translation from a small figure who was forced to engage in indirect subversion against the white master to a larger-than-life figure who could openly wreak revenge against all those who crossed him, black or white.[72]

The Frankenstein monster has much in common with the outlaw hero of the badman. Although the monster's parodies resemble those of the trickster, his violence and nihilism are more congruent with the badman. In his sexualized murder of Elizabeth, for example, the monster is less the trickster, a relatively asexual figure, than the badman, a figure of outsized sexual appetites and prowess. Even the monster's composite body has some affinities with the badman; in one version of the badman story, for example, Stagolee boasts, "I got three sets of jawbone teeth and an extra layer of hair."[73] Although such parallels do not add up to a precise correspondence, they suggest that in turn-of-the-century African American culture, the role of the monster was already being reinvented from within. What I have been characterizing as the revenge of a signifying Frankenstein monster was a revenge elsewhere performed in the African American culture of Dunbar's era by the badman.

When Paul Laurence Dunbar turned to the figure of the Frankenstein monster in his fiction, then, a space had already been created for that monster in African American folk culture—a liminal space, both celebratory and apprehensive—between trickster and badman. Meanwhile, Dunbar's career already testified to the subversive possibilities of the black writer as a signifying monster. In his parodies of black subservience and white mastery, Dunbar had implicitly appropriated that role for himself. In his fiction that draws explicitly from *Frankenstein*, I argue, this project becomes even more complex. This is fiction by a signifying monster about a signifying monster, a domain of multiple parodies, directed outward and inward, and of sharp and self-cutting ironies.

V.

I turn now to Dunbar's use of *Frankenstein* in his fiction, beginning with
the short story "The Lynching of Jube Benson." Although this story was
published after *The Sport of the Gods*, Dunbar's literary career was highly
compressed, and these works can be seen as contemporary and complementary meditations on the fictional possibilities of *Frankenstein*. "The
Lynching of Jube Benson" is the shorter and simpler meditation, employ-
ing strategies that *The Sport of the Gods* complicates. "The Lynching of
Jube Benson" reveals the value to Dunbar of both the figure of the Frankenstein monster and the monster's strategies of parody.

"The Lynching of Jube Benson," published in a 1904 collection of
Dunbar's short fiction entitled *The Heart of Happy Hollow*, opens with
three white men discussing a magazine account of a lynching. When one,
a journalist, declares "rather callously" that "I should like to see a real
lynching," another, a doctor named Melville, narrates his own involvement in a lynching seven years earlier.[74] In this earlier story, Jube Benson,
the black handyman for Melville's white landlord, is lynched for the rape
and murder of his landlord's daughter, Annie Daly, before the real murderer is discovered, too late, to be a white man who had blackened his
face in disguise. "The Lynching of Jube Benson" closes with the doctor,
who now regrets his support for the lynching, declaring to his friends,
"Gentlemen, that was my last lynching" (119). As this summary suggests,
"The Lynching of Jube Benson" is one of Dunbar's most explicitly antiracist works, exploding the myth of the black rapist central to turn-of-
the-century lynching.

Within this antiracist framework, "The Lynching of Jube Benson" parodies the literary representation of white racist nostalgia. Melville—whose
name I will return to later—opens his retrospective narration with descriptions of Jube Benson that liken him to both a dog and a slave. Jube,
Melville remembers fondly, was "an apparently steady-going, grinning
sort," so devoted to Annie that he "would fetch and carry for her like a
faithful dog" (112–13); when Jube protects Annie from other suitors, Melville praises him as "a perfect Cerberus" (113). Melville's dog metaphors
naturalize Jube's subservience, a combination of slave fidelity and minstrel
"grinning." This process of abjection is condensed in the issue of naming,
with Melville patronizingly calling the black man "Jube" throughout the
story. We could interpret Jube as a racist stereotype akin to Sam in Page's
"Marse Chan." But images of black abjection often function parodically

in Dunbar's writing, and here there is a strong internal signal that this is parody: Jube is being described by a white man to other white men. Melville does not recognize the parody—he narrates unironically—but his narration functions ironically to readers who can recognize his condescension.

As the story continues, Dunbar suggests that Jube may be exploiting the possibilities of parody. Jube, Melville remembers, was "devoted to the point of abjectness" (114), and "[h]e manufactured duties for the joy of performing them. He pretended to see desires in me that I never had, because he liked to pander to them" (114–15). Melville's racist nostalgia is here exaggerated beyond its usual conventions, since he remembers Jube as not only "pander[ing]" to his desires but inventing the very desires to which he can then pander. The hyperbole of this invention suggests a form of parody, a trickster role wherein Jube exaggerates his abjectness in order to signify on it. When Jube was Melville's "Cerberus," Melville recalls, he was "a most admirable liar" to Annie's other suitors; perhaps he lies to Melville too.

Jube's role as panderer raises the question of Dunbar's self-presentation in *The Heart of Happy Hollow*. The collection opens with a foreword by the author, which asks readers, "Happy Hollow; are you wondering where it is?" and concludes, "Wherever laughter and tears rub elbows day by day, and the spirit of labour and laziness shake hands, there—there—is Happy Hollow."[75] The phrases "laughter and tears" and "labour and laziness" suggest the stereotypes of racist nostalgia and minstrelsy. The voice of the foreword and that of Jube Benson seem to be coordinated racist examples of black abjection rendered comic.

Yet the phrase "happy hollow" also suggests a false presentation of happiness, a possibility deepened by its Shakespearean resonances. Dunbar was an avid reader of Shakespeare, and this phrase, I suggest, is an allusion to *King Lear*. Early in that play, Edgar narrates his escape from unjust persecution by hiding in a tree: "I heard myself proclaimed, / And by the happy hollow of a tree / Escaped the hunt" (II.iii.1–3). It is at this moment that he decides to disguise himself as a madman, Tom o' Bedlam, assuming "the basest and more poorest shape / That ever penury . . . / Brought near to beast" (II.iii.7–9). The "happy hollow of a tree," for Edgar, is both a literal place—"happy" here denotes fortunate—and a symbolic site; an empty space provides a launching point for the impersonation of abjection. The allusion highlights the possibility that Dunbar engages in a similar impersonation in this volume as a whole. "Brought near to beast" by the imperatives of minstrelsy, Dunbar—like Jube Benson—may be merely "Happy Hollow."[76]

As Melville continues, his narration transforms the metaphor of the loyal dog into that of the violent demon. When he fell ill with fever, he remembers, he was nursed by both Jube and Annie: "To my chimerical vision there was only a black but gentle demon that came and went, alternating with a white fairy, who would insist on coming in on her head, growing larger and larger and then dissolving" (114). The metaphor of the "white fairy" is asymmetrical with that of the "black but gentle demon." "White fairy" is an idealization of white womanhood, albeit one whose imagery of inversion, enlargement, and dissolution suggests anxiety about the power of femininity. "Black but gentle demon," however, shifts between praise and an image of the "black demon" only barely restrained, syntactically and culturally, by "gentle[ness]." Once Annie is found "bruised and bleeding, her face and dress torn from struggling" (115), the imagery of black demonization becomes more explicit. Just before Annie dies, "Her eyes half opened," and she says, 'That black—'" (116). This interrupted phrase, which sends Melville and others in search of Jube, calls attention to its missing noun, with the dash functioning as a redundancy; a racist culture that requires the phrase "but gentle" to moderate "black" also needs no noun to repeat the demonization already implicit in "That black—." When Melville finds Jube, he calls him "you hound." The syntactic gap between "black" and its nouns has now closed: the image of the black man as loyal dog has become its inverse, the black beast.

At this point, however, Melville's narration changes, as he retrospectively confesses that racism shaped his pursuit of Jube:

> I saw his black face glooming there in the half light, and I could only think of him as a monster. It's tradition. At first I was told that the black man would catch me, and when I got over that, they taught me that the devil was black, and when I had recovered from the sickness of that belief, here were Jube and his fellows with faces of menacing blackness. There was only one conclusion: This black man stood for all the powers of evil, the result of whose machinations had been gathering in my mind from childhood up. (117–18)

This passage interrupts both the doctor's racist narration and Dunbar's ironized rendering of that narration. At this moment, Dunbar unironically uses Melville's voice to offer an account of the origins of racism that turns on the metaphoric equation of black men with monsters. The fury of the lynch mob emerges from a lifetime of white acculturation in this metaphoric equation, which makes all black men's faces into figures of "menacing blackness." In naming the origins of his racism, Melville claims responsibility for it. The Shakespearean allusion here is not to *King Lear* but to *The Tempest*, in Prospero's famous recognition of Caliban: "[T]his thing of darkness I / Acknowledge mine."[77]

Melville's confession is also an echo of one of *The Tempest*'s descendants: there is no named reference to *Frankenstein* in "The Lynching of Jube Benson," but a story in which a doctor confesses to making a violent monster suggests an intentional reference to the Frankenstein story. Like Victor Frankenstein, Dr. Melville conjures up a man, a result "whose machinations had been gathering in my mind from childhood up." In *Frankenstein*, Victor glimpses the metaphorically darkened face of the monster over the violated body of his white bride. As Melville confronts "the black face glooming . . . in the half-light," Dunbar stages a similar scene, but he makes his monster innocent, and he highlights white responsibility for his making. Intertwined in "Jube Benson," then, are two different but complementary parodies: a sympathetic parody of *Frankenstein* that adds force to a hostile parody of white racist nostalgia.

Neither parody can save Jube Benson, since Melville's insight into monstrosity comes too late: Jube is lynched, with Melville "the first to pull upon the rope" (118). But the denouement to the lynching launches a new monster story. After Jube is lynched, the true culprit appears: "we saw in the full light the scratched face of Tom Skinner—the worst white ruffian in town—but the face we saw was not as we were accustomed to see it, merely smeared with dirt. It was blackened to imitate a Negro's" (119). "That black—" described by the dying Annie is not a black man but a white man in blackface. Melville's earlier descriptions of Jube suggested that the image of the black man "performing" abjection may only register what the white man wants to see; this climax shows that the image of the black man as monster is so fully a projection of white fantasy that it turns out to be performed by a white man himself.

This closing revelation prompts another sympathetic parody of the Frankenstein story. Finding "little curled pieces of skin" under Annie's fingernail, the doctor takes the skin to his microscope to confirm Skinner's guilt: "There, determinedly, I examined it under a powerful glass, and read my own doom. It was the skin of a white man, and in it were embedded strands of short, brown hair or beard" (119). In this moment, a focus on white skin—shredded, curled, blackened, hairy, pathologized as a laboratory specimen, confirmed as evidence of guilt, and personified in the very name of "Skinner"—parodies white America's obsession with black skin. The doctor has gone into his laboratory and emerged with a true monster: the white man. Melville is, himself, another of these white monsters. The image of the doctor reading "his own doom" through a "powerful glass" suggests that he is looking into a mirror as well as a microscope.

Characteristically, however, Dunbar does not conclude "The Lynching of Jube Benson" with this redemptive moment of white self-scrutiny. The last line of the story returns to its contemporary frame, as Melville comments to his companions, "Gentlemen, that was my last lynching." This moment is ironic, since Dunbar has already exposed these companions as anything but gentlemanly. The journalist who longed to "see a real lynching" has surreptitiously been taking notes on Melville's story from the start: "'Tell us about it,' said the reporter, feeling for his pencil and notebook, which he was, nevertheless, careful to hide from the speaker" (112). Despite its exposure of racism, Melville's story still makes for good copy, which the journalist will eagerly market. With this conclusion, Dunbar condemns the voyeurism of Melville's listeners, of the readers of the journalist's future story, and, by implication, of the audience for "The Lynching of Jube Benson." This condemnation cuts against Dunbar too, since he is writing this story for public consumption. To the extent that "Jube Benson" parodies Dunbar's own role as "monster," it bitterly forecasts both his own destruction at the hands of his white audience and the voyeuristic pleasure that his demise will provide them.

Dunbar's self-directed irony at the story's conclusion coincides with another, perhaps less intentional irony of "Jube Benson": its exclusion of women, both from the clubby world of the "gentlemen" and from the lynching story itself. There are no black women in the story, and its white woman is violently evacuated from it. As if mirroring Melville's metaphor of the "white fairy" who gets larger but finally dissolves, the body of Annie looms larger as it is magnified under the doctor's microscope but then is eclipsed by the story's dramas among men. This might be Dunbar's intentional exposure of the ways that white women, along with black men, suffer from the myth of the black rapist. But if so, there is little in the story to recuperate the silencing of Annie's voice, parallel to the suggestion that Jube parodies his abjection. Dunbar condemns even the possibility of Annie's speech, since by gasping out the phrase "that black—" before she dies, she incites mob violence. "The Lynching of Jube Benson" is a brilliantly controlled double parody, at once a hostile mimicry of the white man's voice and a sympathetic parody of *Frankenstein*. But in giving self-reflexive voice to a signifying monster, this story also silences. Its murdered white woman and its absent black women speak not at all.

VI.

The Sport of the Gods (1902) focuses on the downfall of a black family, the Hamiltons, in the late-nineteenth-century rural South and urban North. As the novel begins, the family—Berry and Fannie and their children, Joe and Kitty—is living happily in the South, where Berry and Fannie work as butler and housekeeper for a white family, the Oakleys. Everything changes when Frank Oakley, brother of the family patriarch, Maurice, steals money from his brother and blames the theft on Berry, who is imprisoned. Fannie, Joe, and Kitty move to New York City, where they all succumb to urban temptations: Fannie remarries a gambler, Kitty becomes a dissolute showgirl, and Joe, who falls into a life of drunken idleness, murders his lover, Hattie Sterling, in an alcoholic rage and is imprisoned. Justice of sorts is effected when a white journalist, Skaggs, revisits the story of Berry Hamilton's crime and finds evidence that he was falsely accused. Released from prison, Berry reunites with his wife, and at novel's end, they return to the South, but Kitty remains a fallen showgirl and Joe is still imprisoned for murder.[78]

The Sport of the Gods is a grim and complicated novel, difficult to situate in relation to Dunbar's own writing—it is the only one of his four novels centered on black characters—as well as to the writing of other writers in his era. Its clearest affinities are with the naturalism employed by Dunbar's white contemporaries, although studies of naturalism have ignored it.[79] The novel's naturalism is signaled from the outset by its title, another allusion to *King Lear*. Here it is Gloucester's famous lament, "As flies to wanton boys are we to th' gods; / They kill us for their sport."[80] The "gods" in Dunbar's world are not detached Olympians killing men for sport but the emblem of socially constructed forces; as Kevin Gaines argues, the title is "a profoundly ironic euphemism for a network of exploitative social relations."[81] For example, the intervention of Skaggs is the novel's *deus ex machina*, but Skaggs is not godlike. Like the white journalist in "Jube Benson," Skaggs is a shifty opportunist, so untrustworthy that his own account of his origins is a lie. Skaggs claims that he was brought up on a Southern plantation with "little darkies," but "It was the same old story that the white who associates with negroes from volition usually tells to explain his taste. The truth about the young reporter was that he was born and reared on a Vermont farm" (69). This revelation ironizes what is already a white fantasy about interracial intimacy by exposing it as a lie about a fantasy. Similar moments of ironic destabilization saturate the novel, and they undercut any fixed notion of naturalism. Dunbar's is a denaturalized naturalism, an ironic inversion of naturalism—in short, a parody of naturalism.

It is within this context of parodied naturalism that we can understand Dunbar's use of *Frankenstein*. The influence of the Frankenstein story on *The Sport of the Gods*, I suggest, begins long before the chapter explicitly named "Frankenstein," and it saturates the novel as a whole. Traces of the Frankenstein story organize the novel's opening depiction of race relations in the South, its critique of the figures of the black dandy and actress, its climactic murder, and its account of the murder's aftermath. In each case, Dunbar borrows from *Frankenstein* its strategies of parody as well as its monster plot. As in "Jube Benson," the parody is sympathetic, although here it is even more sharply undercut by its own ironies. *The Sport of the Gods* leaves its characters, particularly its women, adrift in a world of monsters.

As in "Jube Benson," the opening chapters of *The Sport of the Gods* expose the racism of the metaphors used by Southern white men. When Berry Hamilton is accused of theft, Maurice Oakley—his ostensibly benevolent employer—quickly condemns him: "To think of that black hound's treachery! I'll give him all that the law sets down for him" (18). Aligned with a dog, Berry is further dehumanized by a group of three white men who debate his crime in a bar; this chapter is ironically entitled "The Justice of Men." Horace Talbot, "noted for his kindliness towards people of colour" (29), suggests that Berry should not be condemned: "that man took that money with the same innocence of purpose with which one of our servants a few years ago would have appropriated a stray ham" (30). "Servants" is a euphemism for slaves; the passage aligns the free black man with the slave, and both with the commodities they steal. As with Melville's voice in "Jube Benson," Dunbar uses these white men to connect antebellum slavery with postwar racism.

Here, too, Dunbar exposes the continuity between metaphors of black docility and those of black monstrosity. Another participant in the conversation, Beachfield Davis, tells a story about a black man who took his prize dog out hunting without his permission: "When a nigger and a dog go out together at night, one draws certain conclusions. . . . He'd been possum huntin' with my hound—with the finest hound in the State, sir. Now, I appeal to you all, gentlemen, if that ain't total depravity, what is total depravity?" (31). The racist story of "a nigger and a dog" reprises the "black hound" metaphor, separating out its vehicle and tenor and annexing it to "total depravity." When a third man, Colonel Saunders, dares to ask if there is any doubt about Hamilton's guilt, "They turned on him as if he had been some strange, unnatural animal" (31). Saunders quickly capitulates, and Dunbar's narrator leaves this scene with the ironic observation that "as far as the opinion of the gentlemen assembled in the Continental bar went, Berry was already proven guilty" (32). As in "Jube Benson," the "gentlemen" are anything but gentlemanly; the "justice" ostensibly guaranteed by a judge and jury is only a fixed arrangement in which black men are "already proven guilty" by racism. As in "Jube Benson," moreover, this hostile travesty of the white world is intertwined with a more sympathetic parody of *Frankenstein*. There are no overt *Frankenstein* references in this scene, but the conversation centers on the making of an innocent black man into a metaphorical monster. By the end of this scene, Berry Hamilton has become a figure of "total depravity"—a monster made by white men.

By contrast, the novel introduces Berry Hamilton's son, Joe, as a symbolic monster more ambiguously. The distinguishing trait of Joe Hamilton is that he is, like Stephen Crane's Henry Johnson, "a dandy" (3). This is Dunbar's first description of Joe, a barber for white men:

> [He] was of a cheerful disposition, but from scraping the chins of aristocrats came to imbibe some of their ideas, and rather too early in life bid fair to be a dandy. But his father encouraged him, for, said he, "It's de p'opah thing fu' a man what waits on quality to have quality mannahs an' to waih quality clothes." (3)

The first sentence of this description metonymically aligns the chins of white men with the ideas inside their heads and suggests that it is Joe's "imbib[ing]" of these ideas that prompts him to become a dandy. Joe's identity is organized by this ingestion of white norms, as when, after a party at the Oakleys', he "contented himself with devouring the good things and aping the manners of the young men whom he knew had been among last night's guests" (20). As in Crane's portrait of Henry Johnson, these descriptions raise the question of metaphoric resemblance: Joe, like Henry, attempts to liken himself metaphorically to white gentlemen. As in *The Monster*, Dunbar's narrator depicts this metaphor as a strained or false one: as Henry ends up "like . . . monkeys" rather than white gentleman, Joe is merely "aping" the manners of Southern white men, who themselves imitate British aristocrats. In Dunbar's opening descriptions of Joe, the black dandy is both a strained metaphor for the white gentleman and a failed imitation of him. The black dandy's ingestion of white norms is intended as mimicry, but it emerges as parody.

Yet Dunbar's representation of the black dandy differs sharply from that of Crane. It is, for one thing, self-directed: for Dunbar, himself a dandy, the critique of internalizing white norms is an internal one. Conversely, more clearly than in Crane's novella, the black dandy functions to parody an external target: the dandy's white "originals." Dunbar's narrator criticizes Joe Hamilton for his mimicry of white norms, but since the novel is simultaneously developing the theft plot, it is also exposing those norms. While Joe is "devouring the good things" of white people, his father's paternalist employer is likening him to "servants who . . . would have appropriated a stray ham." The simultaneity of these narratives cuts both ways, deepening the critique of Joe for his deluded parody of white gentlemen but also turning against the white men who are themselves parodies of true gentlemen.

This critique of white men intensifies in Dunbar's characterization of Frank Oakley, the thief for whose crimes Joe Hamilton is framed. Frank, a "great favorite both with men and women, . . . a handsome man, tall, slender, and graceful" (6), is an aesthete drawn to Paris, "where he could find just the atmosphere that suited his delicate, artistic nature" (6). He offers another version of the dandy, that of the white Southern aristocrat, who is linked, in turn, to the sexual decadence of Europe, where there were "temptations which must assail any man of Francis's looks and talents" (7). Although Frank is described as a former suitor to his sister-in-law, the implication is of effeminacy, if not homosexuality; when he steals from his brother, his deviance from the law is continuous with his deviation from conventional masculinity. Frank Oakley is the cautionary tale for the reader of the decline of the dandy, a clear sign of the downfall of Joe Hamilton to come.[82]

Dunbar's initial portrait of Joe Hamilton, then, already begins to establish him as a monster, but one whose symbolic monstrosity is more complicated than that of his father. Berry Hamilton, entirely innocent, is made monstrous by the white men at the Continental Bar, but Joe willingly makes himself grotesque by internalizing white norms. This process is still, indirectly, a consequence of racism, since racism establishes the hierarchy by which a black man might feel that he has to imitate a white one. But the origins of Joe's monstrosity inhere nonetheless in voluntary behavior. As Dunbar introduces a second Frankenstein story, he establishes that the dandy—by implication, Dunbar himself—is a metaphorical monster of his own making.

Once Berry Hamilton is jailed, Joe's descent into monstrosity accelerates:

> Dandy as he was, he was loyal, and when he saw his mother's tears and his sister's shame, something rose within him that had it been given play might have made a man of him, but, being crushed, died and rotted, and in the compost it made all the evil of his nature flourished. . . . Joe went seldom to see his father. He was not heartless, but the citadel of his long desired and much vaunted manhood trembled before the sight of his father's abject misery. . . . in the hothouse of pain he only grew an acrid, unripe cynic. (34)

The mixed metaphors of this passage align Joe with, respectively, a crushed, rotted, and composted plant; a trembling citadel; and an unripe plant nurtured in a hothouse of pain. The opening phrase "Dandy as he was" implies a disengaged passivity, if not also the feminization associated with the dandy. This passivity becomes an image of detumescence, as the "something that rose in him" is then crushed. In the last sentence, "acrid" and "unripe" would seem logically to modify "fruit," a word associated in twentieth-century slang with male homosexuality.[83] Although Dunbar may not have intended this connotation, the passage as a whole highlights failed masculinity as a key dimension of Joe's transformation into a monster. The dandy's rage further lowers him to impotence, if not also to the state of an unspeakably rotten "fruit."

When the Hamiltons move to New York, the black men of the urban North are both incitement to and mirror for Joe's decline into monstrosity. Entranced by "the young fellows passing by dressed in their spruce clothes," Joe imagines that "[s]ome day some greenhorn from the South should stand at a window and look out envying him, as he passed, red-cravated, patent-leathered, intent on some goal" (49). In this moment, Joe turns himself into a feminized, "patent-leathered" object of the gaze, although the men he admires are also hypermasculine: "He looked with a new feeling at the swaggering, sporty young negroes. . . . [He] felt that he might, that he would, be like them" (57). Joe now mimics "sporty young negroes" rather than white gentlemen, but this mimicry leads to further disaster. His favorite place is a bar called the Banner Club, "a social cesspool, generating a poisonous miasma and reeking with the stench of decayed and rotten moralities" (67). These metaphors of decay position the Banner Club as the perfect environment, "reeking" and "rotten," in which Joe's already "rotten" identity will wither further.

This new setting also changes the novel's account of monstrosity, since it relocates the laboratory for monster-making from the white Continental Bar to the black Banner Club. Failed masculinity is once again the index of monstrosity, as suggested in Dunbar's account of one singer at the Banner Club, "a little, brown-skinned fellow with an immature Vandyke beard and a lisp. He sung his own composition and was funny; how much funnier than he himself knew or intended, may not even be hinted at" (70). With the lisp, "immature" beard, and performance that "may not even be hinted at," this description connotes homosexuality, extending the sexual implications of Frank Oakley's European decadence into the black urban North. This man is not mentioned again, but the moment is significant, both as possible historical evidence for a gay presence in turn-of-the-century black New York and, within the novel, as a homophobic commentary on masculinity. Even before Joe brings his dandy persona into the Banner Club, this setting is already undercut from within by a feminization it both mocks and applauds. The black men of Dunbar's New York —hypermasculine yet feminized—are already making metaphoric monsters of themselves.

In this new laboratory for monstrosity, the internal degradation represented as feminization becomes inseparable from the grotesquerie represented by women themselves. The novel's female equivalent to the "sporty young negroes" of New York is the black showgirl. As Joe becomes entranced by the men of the Banner Club, Kitty is charmed by the showgirl: "the glare of the footlights succeeds in deceiving so many people who are able to see through other delusions. The cheap dresses on the street had not fooled Kitty for an instant, but take the same cheese-cloth . . . and put it on the stage, and she could see only chiffon" (58–59). This description positions the cheap costume of the showgirl as a parody of pure chiffon, a parody that Kitty embraces when she becomes a showgirl. As black men in New York become "hard with dissipation," Kitty is coarsened by her showgirl life, and by the novel's end, "She had had experiences, and her voice was not as good as it used to be, and her beauty had to be aided by cosmetics" (124). Although Dunbar does not detail these presumably sexual "experiences," Kitty is a fallen woman: a female version of a monster. The debasing femininity that Dunbar locates within the dandy and the "lisp[ing]" man as effeminacy—if not also homosexuality—is externalized, and made monstrous, in the debased femininity of the showgirl. In Dunbar's account of urban temptation, the black woman seduced by theatrical glamour ends by becoming a female grotesque.[84]

As Joe's story unfolds, the black actress is revealed not only as a monster but also as the novel's truest monster-maker. Joe falls in love with a showgirl named Hattie Sterling, introduced as a "yellow-skinned divinity" (71). Hattie's status as "divinity" derives both from her yellow skin, which functions within the novel's African American world as a form of privilege, and by her beauty, which entrances Joe despite its imperfections: "nothing could keep her from being glorious in his eyes,—not even the grease-paint which adhered in unneat patches to her face, nor her taste for whiskey in its unreformed state" (71). Hattie's taste for whiskey is a metaphor for her own "unreformed state," and her patchy makeup signals her inability even to maintain the illusions of the showgirl. Like Kitty, Hattie is a version of the fallen woman as female grotesque, but she also has the power to ruin others, like a Hollywood femme fatale. As the woman who will drive Joe to violence, Hattie is positioned from the start as his "divinity." Within the novel's emerging Frankenstein story, she will be god to his monster.

It is in this context that the chapter entitled "Frankenstein" begins. Four years have passed, and Joe's decline is intertwined with Hattie: "Hattie Sterling had given him both his greatest impulse for evil and for good. She had at first given him his gentle push, but when she saw that his collapse would lose her a faithful and useful slave she had sought to check his course" (113–14). This description positions Joe as "faithful and useful slave" to Hattie's master, and in a continuous cycle of mastery and enslavement, "he soon tired of being separated from Hattie, and straightened up again. After some demur she received him upon his former footing. It was only for a few months. He fell again. For four years this had happened intermittently" (114). This is, most evidently, a temperance narrative that implicates Dunbar, whose own alcoholism was apparently advanced by this point in his life. But the temperance narrative is enfolded within two other narrative frames. First, this is a master-slave story in which the dynamics of racial slavery, earlier invoked by the white men of the Continental Bar, reemerge within the sphere of black heterosexual romance. Second, this is a Frankenstein story in which the agency of monster-making has shifted from the white men of the Continental Bar to the black men of the Banner Club and now to the single figure of the black femme fatale.

As their relationship heads toward violence, Dunbar highlights Hattie's combined roles as both slavemaster and monster-maker. When Joe returns after a three-day binge, "battered, unkempt, and thick of speech" (114), she again rejects him: "'Well, you're a beauty,' she said finally with cutting scorn. 'You ought to be put under a glass case and placed on exhibition'" (114). Hattie's "cutting" comment metaphorically castrates Joe, and her image of him as something "under a case and placed on exhibition" suggests both the scientific entombment of the museum and the voyeurism of the freak show. Declaring that she will find a new lover, Hattie insults him again:

> There was an expression of a whipped dog on his face.
> "Do'—Ha'ie, do'—" he pleaded, stretching out his hands to her.
> Her eyes blazed back at him, but she sang on insolently, tauntingly.
> The very inanity of the man disgusted her, and on a sudden impulse she sprang up and struck him full in the face with the flat of her hand. He was too weak to resist the blow. . . . he lay at her feet, alternately weeping aloud and quivering with drunken, hiccoughing sobs.
> "Get up!" she cried. . . . "Now, go, you drunken dog, and never put your foot inside this house again." (115)

This passage charts Joe's abjection before Hattie, as he sprawls, sobs, and quivers before her. Already feminized, Joe is now so emasculated that he lacks even the ability to enunciate "Don't, Hattie, Don't," let alone the power to stand erect. The dog metaphors of the passage—from "an expression of a whipped dog" to "you drunken dog"—illuminate this shift, for they revise the imagery associated with racism earlier in the novel. The innocent black man unjustly condemned as a metaphoric "hound" by white men has become the ruined figure justly vilified as a "drunken dog" by a black woman.

Accordingly, later that night, Joe returns and murders Hattie, bringing to a climax the novel's use of *Frankenstein*:

"You put me out—you—you, and you made me what I am." The realisation of what he was, of his foulness and degradation, seemed just to have come to him fully. "You made me what I am, and now you sent me away. You let me come back, and now you put me out."

She gazed at him fascinated. She tried to scream and she could not. This was not Joe. This was not the boy that she had turned and twisted about her little finger. This was a terrible, terrible man or a monster.

He moved a step nearer her. His eyes fell to her throat. For an instant she lost their steady glare and then she found her voice. The scream was checked as it began. His fingers had closed over her throat just where the gown had left it temptingly bare. They gave it the caress of death. She struggled. They held her. Her eyes prayed to his. But his were the fire of hell. She fell back upon her pillow in silence. He had not uttered a word. He held her. Finally he flung her from him like a rag, and sank into a chair. And there the officers found him when Hattie Sterling's disappearance had become a strange thing. (119–20)

Joe's charge to Hattie at the start of this passage, "you made me what I am," unmistakably alludes to the monster's fury at Victor Frankenstein. In the next paragraph, the sentence "This was a terrible, terrible man or a monster" cements Joe's role as metaphorical Frankenstein monster. Dunbar's description of Hattie both positions her as a mute victim and confirms that she is responsible, through her "twist[ing]" and "turn[ing]" of Joe, for making him into a monster. The final paragraph plays out the Frankenstein story of monstrous revolt, as Joe turns against his maker. The femme fatale's ability to make the man her "slave" becomes the ability of the man to silence her "cutting" voice and to effect a "caress of death."

This moment confirms the place of *Frankenstein* in *The Sport of the Gods*, but that place is a perplexing one. Why does Dunbar recast Victor Frankenstein as Hattie Sterling? In the Berry Hamilton plot, the master-slave dynamics of *Frankenstein* precisely parallel relationships between white and black men; the white men in the Continental Bar, like Dr. Melville in "Jube Benson," are versions of both Victor Frankenstein and slavemasters. But in the Hattie Sterling plot, Dunbar displaces authority across both race and gender, from the white slaveowner to the black actress. It is significant that Hattie is "yellow-skinned," since that designation partially identifies her with white femininity. Yet Hattie is a light-skinned black woman, not a white woman. As a black woman, and as an actress of fading glamour, whatever authority she has over men is declining rapidly.

The murder scene similarly reanimates *Frankenstein* in unexpected ways. In "Jube Benson," Dunbar translates the triangle of Victor, monster, and the murdered Elizabeth into the triangle of Melville, Jube, and the murdered Annie. But in *The Sport of the Gods*, Dunbar conflates the monster's rage against his maker with his murder of Elizabeth. The imagery of this paragraph—Hattie's choked scream, open robe, and praying eyes—recalls the monster's sexualized violation of Elizabeth, but here these traits are associated with the monster's maker. This adaptation undercuts the most prominent legacy of *Frankenstein* for antiracist critique: sympathy for the monster. In "Jube Benson" and in the Berry Hamilton plot, Dunbar exploits this legacy, since Jube and Berry are innocent. Here, however, Joe is guilty of murder, and his crime seems to reinforce the stereotype that Beachfield Davis, earlier in the novel, terms "total depravity." Paradoxically, then, Dunbar's *Frankenstein* plot assigns the role of Victor Frankenstein to its least powerful character and deepens rather than undercuts the monstrosity of his black male protagonist.

There are several possible explanations for these changes. Dunbar's marriage was apparently riven by conflict over his wife's higher class position and her lighter skin. According to biographer Eleanor Alexander, Dunbar was physically abusive to his wife: he raped her during their courtship and beat her throughout their marriage, which ended after a particularly severe beating one night when Dunbar was drunk. In his letters to Alice, Dunbar expressed self-lacerating remorse for his behavior: "I was a drunken brute," he wrote after the rape, "who let his passion obscure his love."[85] Written well into their marriage, *The Sport of the Gods* —an account of a black man who sinks into alcoholic ruin and gives the "caress of death" to his lover—may register Dunbar's lacerating indictment of his own behavior. In this context, Dunbar's parody of the Frankenstein story furthers his self-punishment. Using the frame of *Frankenstein*, Dunbar condemns his fulfillment of the terms of monstrosity as they had been imposed on him by a racist world and as he reproduced them in his abuse of his wife.

A less biographical explanation for Dunbar's distortion of *Frankenstein* lies in his relation to naturalism. Scenes of animalistic violence against women were well established in white naturalist fiction by this time. In Frank Norris's *McTeague* (1899), for example, the ruined dentist, McTeague, murders his wife, Trina, in an alcoholic rage:

Usually the dentist was slow in his movements, but now the alcohol had awakened in him an ape-like agility. . . . all at once [he] sent his fist into the middle of her face with the suddenness of a relaxed spring.

Beside herself with terror, Trina turned and fought him back; fought for her miserable life with the exasperation and strength of a harassed cat. . . . But her resistance was the one thing to drive him to the top of his fury.[86]

This scene's animal metaphors are typical of the naturalist project of showing that men are like animals, in their brutishness, their dynamics of dominance and submission, and their enslavement to environmental forces. Norris here names apes and cats, and his novel is also saturated with dogs; the opening chapter, for example, introduces "a stone pug dog" in McTeague's office and features a scene of McTeague delivering a wounded dog to a veterinary hospital. Dogs are even more central to the writings of Jack London, whose *The Call of the Wild* shows how a domestic dog recovers his inner "dominant primordial beast" in the wild, and whose *White Fang* charts the domestication of a wild dog in thrall to his ideal "Love-Master."[87] Stories like these metaphorically used dogs to symbolize the atavism of white men, and Norris's *McTeague* makes the white murderer into an "apelike" murderer as well.

There are strong echoes of McTeague's murder scene in *The Sport of the Gods*: both murderers are men roused from alcoholic torpor into sudden frenzy, and both victims are women whose taunting of men leads to their intimately hands-on murder. But Dunbar shifts the racial context and meaning of this scene. In the white naturalist world, white men could be aligned with animals as a fresh expression of determinism, but in Dunbar's world, black men had long been condemned as apes and dogs. When Dunbar depicts a black protagonist as a "whipped" and "drunken" dog, he does so not to show that all men are essentially animals but to underscore how his black protagonist is socially constructed as a dog, initially by white people and then by his own internalization of racist norms. Dunbar wants not to naturalize animal metaphors but to denaturalize them. Similarly, Dunbar's Frankenstein monster is a figure whose monstrosity, like his body, has been socially rather than naturally constructed. If the novel redoubles rather than undercuts the idea of black men as monsters, then it does so in the service of exposing the artificial construction of that monstrosity. Dunbar's monsters, like his dogs, are not a variant on the naturalist impulse to determinism but a parody of naturalism itself.

Yet the gender politics of this parody, as with "Jube Benson," generate their own set of ironies. It is ironic that Joe feels enslaved to Hattie, since she has none of the social authority of the white men in the novel. It is possible that Dunbar intends this irony, deliberately displacing authority to the novel's least authoritative character to reinforce his critique of naturalism. Yet even if this irony is intended as such, it functions at the expense of women themselves. Throughout *The Sport of the Gods*, femininity is a debased and debasing term, condemned both when it appears within men as the mark of their emasculation and when it appears outside them, in the form of actual women. As in "Jube Benson," *The Sport of the Gods* leaves women voiceless and dead, and both black and white female corpses function in these works as metaphoric vehicles for renegotiating relations between men. As a version of Victor Frankenstein, Hattie Sterling remains grotesque, more monster than monster-maker. Dunbar may intend the murder of Hattie as irony, but it registers as misogyny.

In the aftermath of the murder, Dunbar brings the novel's *Frankenstein* imagery to two different conclusions. Joe, the novel's monster, is reduced to "one whose soul is dead," his only interest Hattie's dog: "The only thing which he noticed or seemed to have any affection for was a little pet dog which had been hers. . . . He would sit for hours with the little animal in his lap, caressing it dumbly" (121–22). In an ironic fulfillment of the novel's dog metaphors, Hattie's pet has become Joe's lap-dog, reversing his own abject status as lap-dog to Hattie while also aligning him forever with her mute dog. This abjection mirrors Dunbar's autobiography: among the many self-lacerating letters Dunbar wrote Alice was one in which he characterized his heart as a "dead, dumb-self lying there—white and cold—a corpse which no spark can make into life."[88] This passage both evokes and displaces the Frankenstein story, refusing Dunbar the possibility of Frankensteinian reanimation as his novel also distances this imagery from Joe.

Yet as the novel reduces its monster to a deadened dog, it also reactivates the imagery of the Frankensteinian monster-maker one final time. When Berry and Fannie return to their former home in the South, they find that the Oakley patriarch has gone insane from the revelation of his brother's crime. This is the end of the novel:

[Berry and Fannie] sat together with clasped hands listening to the shrieks of the madman across the yard and thinking of what he had brought to them and to himself.

It was not a happy life, but it was all that was left to them, and they took it up without complaint, for they knew they were powerless against some Will infinitely stronger than their own. (148)

The mad white patriarch, obsessed with "what he had brought to them and to himself," has become a version of the ruined Victor Frankenstein. This conclusion does not absolve Joe of his monstrosity, but it relocates the responsibility for making monsters with the white patriarch who initiated Joe's ruin. Returning to the Southern grounds of the novel's beginning, Dunbar leaves the reader not with the black monster but with the white monster-maker forever haunted by his creation. This focus on the "madman" also ironizes the final sentence. The Hamiltons seem to be "powerless against some Will infinitely stronger than their own," but this sentence is undercut by the previous one, which firmly identifies the agency of their family's destruction with the insane white patriarch. The "Will" that is stronger than the Hamilton's does not belong to God or the gods but to Oakley. As in "Jube Benson," *The Sport of the Gods* ends with a focus on the white men who set black monstrosity in motion.

Yet this conclusion also leaves its black characters with no way out. *The Sport of the Gods*, I have argued, offers a sympathetic parody of *Frankenstein* that radiates outward from the chapter entitled "Frankenstein" to encompass its opening scenario of monster-making in the rural South, its cautionary tale of the dandy in urban New York, and its climactic murder and aftermath. In each case, Dunbar signifies on *Frankenstein* by using the novel's strategies of parody as well as its monster plot. There is no resolution to this account of monstrosity, since there is no escape from the conditions that generate it. *The Sport of the Gods* leaves its monster imprisoned, its women murdered, and its ironies with no edge to cut against except themselves. Faithful to *Frankenstein* to the last, this novel ends, like Shelley's, in nihilism, and its parodies, like those within *Frankenstein*, are ultimately not only self-reflexive but also self-consuming.

VII.

Across the writings of Paul Laurence Dunbar, I have argued, a signifying monster takes revenge through parody. In Dunbar's fiction alluding to *Frankenstein*, a signifying monster writes about a signifying monster, and the result is an incisive but self-cutting critique of racism. To understand the full force of Dunbar's versions of monstrosity, it is important to identify one further target of parody encoded within them. We can, I suggest, read both *The Sport of the Gods* and "Jube Benson" as veiled and hostile parodies of *Uncle Tom's Cabin*. This hostile coding is inseparable from Dunbar's more sympathetic parodies of *Frankenstein*. Understanding these intertwined parodies illuminates the violence against women that suffuses Dunbar's writing, while confirming the importance of both Shelley and Stowe as influences, interlocutors, and antagonists in his fiction.

The reception of *The Sport of the Gods* was mixed. Some readers praised it, including Du Bois, who approved of its depiction of urban vice: "One has but to read Dunbar's *Sport of the Gods* to get an idea of the temptations that surround the young immigrant."[89] More typical, however, were reviews that condemned the Joe Hamilton plot, as in the *Athenaeum*'s prediction that "the vivid portrayal of these objectionable, ham-twitching young men of colour is apt to have unpleasant associations."[90] This reviewer coyly heightened the presumably sexual "unpleasant associations" of "ham-twitching young men of colour" by leaving them unspecified, thereby both reinforcing racist stereotype and misreading Dunbar's own critique of Joe Hamilton as an endorsement of him. More negative still was Philadelphia's *North American*: "the writing is altogether lacking in any kind of distinction. It is crude, slangy and vulgar. There is absolutely nothing in the book upon which might be based a solitary excuse for its being."[91]

But some reviewers liked *The Sport of the Gods*, and those who did invariably compared it to *Uncle Tom's Cabin*, the most famous abolitionist novel and the touchstone of all subsequent protest fiction: "Since *Uncle Tom's Cabin* no stronger arraignment of the conditions which limit the blacks in this country has been penned; and like Harriet Beecher Stow's [sic] great novel, Dunbar's is as picturesque a work of art as it is an irresistable plea."[92] Like Stowe, Dunbar is both "picturesque" and "irresist[i]ble," a connection elaborated in another review:

[*The Sport of the Gods*] takes up the Negro where Harriet Beecher Stowe left him in slavery and transports him to darker New York. . . . he is just as picturesque a figure as he was in "*Uncle Tom's Cabin*"—only now he serves a cafe or carries luggage instead of picking cotton. He is even a more vital part of American life.[93]

Praising Dunbar's black characters for their resemblance to Uncle Tom, this reviewer identifies the New York café as the geographical extension of Uncle Tom's Southern cabin. So powerful is the legacy of Stowe's novel that, as a third reviewer suggested, it provides a model for the way Dunbar's novel enslaves its readers: "As *Uncle Tom's Cabin* in its day held the reader captive, so does this novel of the new negro, enfranchised but still a charge upon our consciences."[94]

With such praise, these reviewers also suggest the extreme constraints that Stowe's legacy imposed on Dunbar. As numerous critics have shown, *Uncle Tom's Cabin* contributed to racist representations even as it supported abolition: the novel privileges light-skinned black characters over dark-skinned ones; it largely excludes black women from its ethos of feminization; and it circumscribes the agency of black men, leaving them either dead or exiled by novel's end.[95] In the reviews of Dunbar's novel, the ability of *Uncle Tom's Cabin* to "hold its reader captive" is yet another form of enslavement for black readers and writers; the way that black people have been "penned" by Stowe is as much a form of penned-in incarceration as emancipation. The terms of the "picturesque" are those of a colonizing white gaze; as *Uncle Tom's Cabin* allowed white readers a glimpse into the slave, so *The Sport of the Gods* provides a new view of the "untrodden land" of "darker New York." The black man, moving north from cotton field to café, still comes into view in a position of servitude to whites, and the black male writer is acknowledged only when he appears on feminized white ground.

Dunbar's overt relation to this legacy was not to bury Stowe but to praise her, as in his tribute poem written after her death in 1896. The sonnet "Harriet Beecher Stowe" begins, "She told the story, and the whole world wept / At wrongs and cruelties it had not known," and ends, "blest be she who in our weakness came— / Prophet and priestess! At one stroke she gave / A race to freedom and herself to fame."[96] This language is typical of the many encomia to Stowe by black and white writers in this era. This praise had strategic political value in an era of violent retrenchment for black people, since it kept alive the legacy of abolitionism and used Stowe to authorize continuing battles against racism. Yet black writers at the turn of the century also offered critiques of Stowe. In *A Voice from the South* (1892), for example, Anna Julia Cooper noted that "an authentic portrait . . . presenting the black man as a free American citizen, not the humble slave of *Uncle Tom's Cabin*—but the *man*, divinely struggling and aspiring yet tragically warped and distorted by the adverse winds of circumstance, has not yet been painted. It is my opinion that the canvas awaits the brush of the colored man himself."[97] Cooper's critique of Stowe is sympathetic and overt; Dunbar, I suggest, used "the brush of the colored man" against Stowe in ways that were both less sympathetic and less overt. Dunbar's sonnet "Harriet Beecher Stowe" may be read ironically, as Dunbar's covert expression of weariness with the hierarchical story of a white woman rescuing an entire people from "our weakness" with "one stroke" of her pen, while simultaneously securing her own celebrity as "prophet and priestess." Dunbar's extravagance, here as in his other writing, calls attention to itself. This is a tribute poem so hyperbolic that we may also read it as its opposite: a parody of a tribute.

In *The Sport of the Gods* and "The Lynching of Jube Benson," Dunbar engages in an even more heavily encoded attack on Stowe. When Joe Hamilton murders Hattie Sterling, he violates the laws of "picturesque" representation established, in their liberal abolitionist version, by Stowe. Turning his black protagonist into a monster, Dunbar leaves the legacy of Uncle Tom irretrievably behind. The name of Joe Hamilton's victim is suggestive in this context. "Hattie" is a diminutive of Harriet; Stowe's daughter, also named Harriet, was known as Hattie. The surname "Sterling" offers a more indirect nominal clue. In this era, Stowe remained the "sterling" emblem of American racial representation, its literary gold standard. In strangling Hattie, Joe debases this gold standard, destroying the "sterling" embodiment of the most famous "Hattie" in American culture.[98]

"The Lynching of Jube Benson" extends this attack, for we can see this story as a critique not only of white conservatives but also of white liberals and, above all, of Stowe. Names are significant in this story as well. The name "Dr. Melville" invites a connection to Herman Melville. It is possible, for example, to interpret Dunbar's Dr. Melville as a version of Melville's Captain Ahab: Dunbar's Melville is, like Ahab, a figure undone by the monomaniacal pursuit of a creature who turns out to be overwhelmingly and definingly white. But Dunbar is unlikely to have read *Moby-Dick*, or to have seen Melville as a touchstone for racial representation, whereas he clearly read Stowe, and her racial representations remained an overwhelming presence in his era.[99] The name "Tom Skinner" suggests a covert critique of Stowe. The story flays the tradition of racial representation created by Stowe, "skinning Uncle Tom." In his coded attack on Stowe, Dunbar is himself a "Tom Skinner."

This coded strategy of critique—an extremely hostile parody—becomes clearer when we see Dunbar as a progenitor of a more famous African American critique of *Uncle Tom's Cabin*: Richard Wright's *Native Son*. In his first book of fiction, the collection of short stories entitled *Uncle Tom's Children* (1938), Wright explicitly set out to combat what he perceived as the passive black men of *Uncle Tom's Cabin* with angry, violent, and politically aware black characters.[100] Two years later, in "How Bigger Was Born," Wright's introduction to *Native Son* (1940), he described his own horror at the results: "I found that I had written a book which even bankers' daughters could read and weep over and feel good about. I swore to myself that if I ever wrote another book, no one would weep over it."[101] His response to the reception of *Uncle Tom's Children* was to create an anti–Uncle Tom named Bigger Thomas. Directing his fury at both Stowe and the white "bankers' daughters" who might "feel good about" his work, Wright revenged himself on them in *Native Son*. At the start of the novel, Bigger Thomas suffocates, decapitates, and burns the body of a white woman, and then he rapes and kills his black lover and throws her corpse down an air shaft. These acts of extreme violence against white and black women are meant to signal Bigger Thomas's break from dehumanized passivity, but the novel's misogyny exceeds its naturalist frame.[102]

Writing forty years earlier, Dunbar similarly invented, in Joe Hamilton, his own "bigger Thomas," a black protagonist who would decisively interrupt an Uncle Tom tradition. In the character "Tom Skinner" in "Jube Benson," he laid that tradition to rest in a different way, by exposing black men as the literal embodiments of white fantasy. The vehicle for racial critique, for both writers, was violence against women. Although Dunbar's tone seems more parodic than Wright's, and his relation to naturalism seems more ironic, his misogyny is similar. Both writers leave their female characters violated and dead. For both writers, moreover, the target of misogynist violence is not only the dead Stowe but the live white women who shaped the reception of their work. Like Wright, Dunbar participated in a literary culture whose elite institutions were controlled by white men but whose popular audience was often dominated by white women. In silencing Annie, Dunbar silences his version of the white "bankers' daughters": the white women patrons whose racism literally and metaphorically brought him to his knees. Similarly, Joe Hamilton's murder of Hattie Sterling in *The Sport of the Gods* removes the most powerful and disapproving audience for his actions. That Hattie Sterling is a light-skinned black woman rather than a white woman seems, in this context, a displacement from necessity; it would have been impossible for Dunbar to represent an interracial murder openly, as Wright did forty years later at the start of *Native Son*. In the revenge that Dunbar's writing effects on Stowe, then, it anticipates Wright's more open critique of her. Conversely, Dunbar's use of the Frankenstein story is more overt than that of Wright, although both men worked versions of the story into their writing. *Native Son,* as James Smethurst has shown, strongly echoes the imagery of James Whale's 1931 film *Frankenstein.*[103]

Ironically, however, Wright criticized Dunbar as a writer tragically defined by his dialect poetry, rather than identifying him as a precursor in the project of skinning Uncle Tom.[104] It is a further irony that Dunbar himself came to be so closely associated with the pejorative idea of the "Uncle Tom." Wright began *Uncle Tom's Children* with a denunciation of this figure, "the cringing type who knew his place before white folk."[105] According to Thomas Gossett, the idea of the "Uncle Tom" emerged in full force after World War II, when he "became a symbol of the black who commands no respect from others and demands no rights. . . . [He] was capable of betraying the rights of other blacks in order to curry favor with the whites."[106] Ironically, the symbol was not only detached from but at odds with Stowe's character, who does command some respect and demand some rights; Stowe's Uncle Tom is himself no "Uncle Tom." By the 1970s, Dunbar was frequently cast in this role; one biography, for example, concluded, "Are Dunbar's writings 'black' or do they qualify him as a chief 'Uncle Tom' writer of his race, or both? Dunbar cannot be exonerated from all charges of 'Uncle Tomism.'"[107] This judgment, I have argued, was a profound misreading of Dunbar, not only because of Dunbar's critique, throughout his writing, of an "Uncle Tom" position but also because of his own covert critique of Stowe's Uncle Tom. That Dunbar should been condemned as an "Uncle Tom"—another version of the lap-dog—seems a profound irony of literary history.

Yet if Dunbar could not exonerate himself from the charge of being an "Uncle Tom," he could at least set that role in tension with another one. In *Sport of the Gods* and "Jube Benson," Dunbar wages an assault on *Uncle Tom's Cabin* concealed within his more visible and sympathetic inversion of *Frankenstein*. If Hattie is, metaphorically, both Victor Frankenstein and Harriet Beecher Stowe, so too is Joe both a Frankenstein monster and an inversion of Uncle Tom; in "Jube Benson," the character of Tom Skinner is similarly both the novel's ultimate monster and its anti–Uncle Tom. The parody of Shelley fuels the parody of Stowe: when Dunbar locates the murder of Hattie Sterling under the chapter title "Frankenstein," he symbolically positions Harriet Beecher Stowe as an author of black characters so grotesque that they constitute literary monsters for the black writers working in her wake. Through this double parody, Dunbar employs the foundational monster story of one white woman writer to combat the foundational racial narrative—itself another kind of monster story —of another. In Dunbar's writing, Harriet Beecher Stowe becomes the symbolic cousin of Mary Wollstonecraft Shelley—if not also, in the mixed legacy that she created for subsequent African American writers, the bride of Frankenstein.

4

Souls on Ice

I remember coming home from the movie theatre one day in
tears. I had just seen *Frankenstein*. My momma asked me what
was wrong. Still crying, I told Momma, "I just saw *Frankenstein*
and the monster didn't scare me." Momma couldn't explain it and
I couldn't understand it. I was afraid I wasn't normal. But now
that I look back, I realize why I wasn't frightened. Somehow I
unconsciously realized that the Frankenstein monster was chasing
what was chasing me. Here was a monster, created by a white man,
turning upon his creator. The horror movie was merely a parable
of life in the ghetto. The monstrous life of the ghetto has been
created by the white man. Only now in the city of chaos are we
seeing the monster created by oppression turn upon its creator.

—Dick Gregory, *The Shadow That Scares Me*

I.

In turn-of-the-century American fiction, I have argued, the figure of a
black Frankenstein monster structures the extravagant metaphors of Stephen Crane and the ironized parodies of Paul Laurence Dunbar. These
are literary examples, but in the works of both writers, verbal depictions
of monstrosity edge consistently toward visual ones. Dunbar wrote for the
visual medium of the stage; he often performed his own poetry; and his
writing includes many moments of visual revelation, as when Dr. Melville
looks into the microscope in "The Lynching of Jube Benson." Crane's metaphors are so visually evocative that one of the earliest reviewers of *The
Monster* compared its chapters to a set of paintings: "when the last block
is put in place the whole design flashes into an orderly picture—like the
landscape painted on six separate boards by a variety artist, and suddenly
clapped into a gilt frame."[1] For this reviewer, the novella's fragmented

structure became coherent within the frame of the composite painting, an image that echoes the Frankenstein plot of combining body parts into a corporeal whole.

While the Frankenstein stories of Crane and Dunbar move toward visual media, *Frankenstein* was already an inherently visual novel. The word "monster" derives from the Latin *monstrare*, to show or display, and as numerous critics have suggested, *Frankenstein* frequently focuses on vision, in its emphasis on face-to-face confrontations, like those between the monster and Victor; its secret moments of surveillance, like the monster's scrutiny of William; its moments of visual blockage, like the inability of the blind De Lacey father to see the monster; and its interest in visual forms of evidence, like the miniature portrait of Victor's mother.[2] Stage adaptations of *Frankenstein* enhanced its visuality, since they gave specificity to episodes that the novel had left undetailed, like the scene of the monster's creation. They also heightened the importance of the monster's appearance by making him mute. Deprived of his eloquent voice, he could speak to audiences through his visual presentation alone.

From the start, moreover, *Frankenstein* was not only highly visual but also protocinematic. Written seventy-five years before the invention of film, the novel prefigures the vocabulary of cinema. For example, Shelley's focus on faces and portraits constitutes a protocinematic use of the closeup.[3] More generally, as William Nestrick first argued, the narrative of *Frankenstein* parallels the operations of film. The projection of films involves bringing still images to life, and editing is "a mechanical stitchwork, a piecing together that becomes another cinematic equivalent of the Frankenstein Monster."[4] Amalgamated and reanimated, the monster's story enacts both the combination and projection of film images.

In this chapter, I focus on the visual dimensions of the black Frankenstein metaphor, tracking this metaphor through twentieth-century U.S. culture. Two films provide the foundation for this analysis. One is the first film version of *Frankenstein* (dir. J. Searle Dawley, 1910), which was also the first horror film; the other is the foundational film of American racism, *The Birth of a Nation*. Subsequent black Frankenstein stories, I suggest, take up the conjunction of monstrosity, blackness, and sexuality together established by these films. I pursue these conjunctions in the most famous Frankenstein films, James Whale's *Frankenstein* (1931) and *Bride of Frankenstein* (1935), interpreting them as racial allegories in which the monster takes form through contemporary iconographies of race, rape, and lynching. These films affirmatively extend the homosocial possibilities of the 1910 *Frankenstein* film, while revising the racist imagery of *Birth of a Nation*. Forty years later, the racial connotations of the Whale films—although not their homoeroticism—find explicit fulfillment in the blaxploitation film *Blackenstein* (dir. William Levey, 1973). *Blackenstein* makes the figure of a black monster overt within the parodic aesthetics of blaxploitation. In so doing, I suggest, it both extends and sabotages the political potential of a visibly black Frankenstein monster.

After looking at black Frankenstein monsters in film, I then turn to nonfiction writing and performance by black men, which highlight the visual dimensions of monstrosity. I first identify traces of the Frankenstein story in nonfiction essays by James Baldwin and Eldridge Cleaver. In the eras of civil rights and Black Power, both Baldwin and Cleaver highlight the figure of a black monster as seen on, and against, a ground of white ice, though they use this figure in very different ways. I then focus on activist and comedian Dick Gregory, whose autobiographies, nonfiction essays, and concert performances of the 1960s and 1970s include a half-dozen explicit, self-conscious, and sustained parables of a black Frankenstein monster. Moving gothic horror into comic satire, Gregory brings to fruition the black Frankenstein story as I have been tracing it in nineteenth- and twentieth-century American culture, elaborating—yet also finally leaving behind—the role of a signifying monster.

In moving across the twentieth century, I interpret a range of cinematic, theatrical, and literary texts, but visuality remains the fundamental register here. Almost all twentieth-century versions of *Frankenstein* are shaped by its cinematic adaptations, and particularly by the image of Boris Karloff as the monster. The performances of Dick Gregory are important as visual events; even the literary works under discussion highlight issues of visuality. Across cinematic, theatrical, and literary registers, these twentieth-century texts illuminate the theme of visibility, in two senses: the literal visibility entailed in the visual medium of cinema and the symbolic visibility attained by open rather than connotative strategies of representation.

I also shift, in this chapter, from horror to comedy, including the camp sensibility of the Whale films, the semicomic parody of *Blackenstein,* and the stand-up comedy routines of Dick Gregory. This movement from horror to comedy is less a rupture than a readjustment. From the stage parodies of *Frankenstein* of the 1820s onward, the book's reception was never far from comedy. Some twentieth-century black Frankenstein stories, exploiting the intrinsic comic potential of the Frankenstein story, conjoin that potential with antiracist critique. This is "black comedy," I suggest, which develops both the psychological and racial senses of the term.

Finally, the texts in this chapter open out into a more capacious set of sexual possibilities. The narrative of homosexual panic in the 1910 *Frankenstein* film takes more affirmative form in works by the gay artists Whale and Baldwin. A full twentieth-century genealogy of gay male Frankenstein stories would include, at minimum, the films *Flesh for Frankenstein* (dir. Paul Morrissey, 1973) and *Frankenstein: The True Story* (dir. Jack Smight, 1973), which are associated, respectively, with Andy Warhol and Christopher Isherwood, two major twentieth-century gay icons.[5] Such a genealogy would highlight the novel *Father of Frankenstein* (Christopher Bram, 1995) and the film adapted from it, *Gods and Monsters* (dir. Bill Condon, 1998), which imaginatively re-create James Whale's life through his relation to *Bride of Frankenstein*.[6]

Some of the works under discussion in this chapter anchor the story's focus on relations between men; others begin to suggest new places for women in the black Frankenstein story. In the racial ambiguities of Whale's female monster and the secondary characters of Dick Gregory's parables, black women—occluded from most black Frankenstein stories—begin to appear. In their use of visual vocabularies, their movement toward humor, and their political reach, the works under discussion in this chapter reveal the importance of the Frankenstein monster to twentieth-century black cultural practice, as well as the importance of racial frameworks for understanding representations of *Frankenstein* in a cinematic era. The black Frankenstein monster testifies to the cultural opportunities, aesthetic and political, afforded by strategies of visual reappropriation. He also, I argue, testifies to the limits of those strategies.

II.

The first film version of *Frankenstein*—the one-reel 1910 work directed by J. Searle Dawley, made under the aegis of the Edison studios and known as the "Edison *Frankenstein*"—was considered lost for many years and has only recently become available for public viewing.[7] The name "Edison *Frankenstein*" already suggests a particular cultural anchor for this film: Thomas Alva Edison, like Benjamin Franklin, was an American icon with symbolic affinities to Victor Frankenstein. As the inventor of the light bulb and phonograph, developer of early film technologies, and founder of the first movie studio, Edison was aligned, in public mythology, with extravagant inventiveness. As Thomas Elsaesser notes, "A direct line can be drawn from Prometheus, Faust and Dr Frankenstein to Thomas A. Edison—all obsessed with the integral (re)production of life, which in turn needs to be juxtaposed to the desire for a new script, a new mode of writing with images, associated with a scientific urge to analyse movement and break it down into constituent parts."[8]

Breaking down Shelley's novel to twenty-five single-shot "scenes," the film begins with "Frankenstein" (no first name is given) leaving his father and his fiancée, called only "Sweetheart," for college. There, he creates a monster in a vat of chemicals; horrified, he flees home and prepares to marry but is haunted by the reappearance of the monster. Finally, on his wedding night, he banishes the monster, who turns out—in the film's most significant alteration of the novel—to be only a projection of his psyche. As the film's promotional material puts it, "the creation of the monster was only possible because Frankenstein had allowed his normal mind to be overcome by evil and unnatural thoughts."[9] These "unnatural thoughts" are unmistakably represented, in the Edison *Frankenstein*, as homosexual ones, for the film, I suggest, highlights the productive relation between visibility and male homosociality—both homoerotic and homophobic—in the Frankenstein story.

As I have already noted, Eve Kosofsky Sedgwick first identified the organizing tableau of Shelley's *Frankenstein* as that of "two men chasing one another across a landscape. It is importantly undecidable in this tableau . . . whether the two men represent two consciousnesses or only one; and it is importantly undecidable whether their bond . . . is murderous or amorous."[10] For Sedgwick, who characterizes nineteenth-century British literature as an "age of Frankenstein," the murderous-amorous bond between Victor and the monster exemplifies the operations of "homosexual panic," the result of a culture in which "intense male homosocial desire [is] at once the most compulsory and the most prohibited of social bonds."[11] More affirmatively, male homosocial desire also pervades Shelley's *Frankenstein*, from Victor's intimacy with Clerval, who "call[s] forth the better feelings of my heart," to his bond with Walton, who "desire[s] the company of a man . . . whose eyes would reply to mine."[12] A foundational text for gay and lesbian studies, *Frankenstein* highlights complex patterns of homoerotic longing and homophobic recoil between men.[13]

Paring Shelley's novel down to precisely this plot of longing and recoil, the Edison *Frankenstein* depicts a man who is haunted by his illicit relationship to another man and who expels him from his life and psyche by marrying a woman. The film was made at the turn-of-the-century moment when the category of "the homosexual" was being codified in the clinical discourses of sexology and psychoanalysis and when more self-defining gay subcultures in the United States formed and thrived.[14] Emerging at a foundational moment for both cinema and sexuality, the Edison *Frankenstein* brings together the making of monsters, homosexuals, and films. The film, I suggest, illuminates the importance of cinema for envisioning a homosocial Frankenstein story, as well as the importance of the Frankenstein story for envisioning the operations of film.

The film's creation sequence exemplifies these self-reflexive connections. The setting for the creation is a vat situated behind huge wooden doors at the back of Frankenstein's college quarters. As the creation sequence begins, Frankenstein closes and bars the doors, behind which he has hidden the makings of an illicit male body; this is a literal closet, if not also a sexual one.[15] The sequence then cuts between shots of the vat in which the monster forms and shots of Frankenstein viewing the vat through a

Edison *Frankenstein,* 1910

Edison *Frankenstein,* 1910

small hole in the closet door; the hole has a covering that swings to the side. This viewing hole is typical of the interest in early cinema in depicting acts and apparatuses of looking, with a consequent alternation of shots, as Tom Gunning notes, from "a curious character who uses some sort of looking device (reading glass, microscope, keyhole, telescope, transom window . . .) to the scenes which these devices make visible."[16] Like many such objects, the viewing hole in Frankenstein's closet acts as a self-reflexive symbol of cinematic production and projection. It simultaneously symbolizes the lens of a camera and the hole through which such images, after the development of projection technology in the 1910s, were projected onto a screen; in early viewing technologies such as Edison's own Kinetoscope, the peephole was also the aperture through which the individual viewer viewed the film. Bringing together movie-making and monster-making, the film's creation sequence also connects the peephole—often associated with pornography—to voyeurism between men.[17] This is both an encounter between men and one within Frankenstein's psyche; the intertitle for this moment reads, "The evil in Frankenstein's mind creates a monster," as if his desires have created, rather than simply responded to, this moment. A metaphor for cinematic viewing, the viewing hole is also a two-way aperture into Frankenstein—a window into his psyche as well as an orifice through which he himself peers.

Once the monster comes to life, he sexualizes these viewing scenarios. At the end of the creation sequence, a long shot shows his hand reaching out through the door, while Frankenstein retreats to the side in horror; coming out of the closet, groping in the air above the viewing hole, the monster's hand reaches into the space where Frankenstein's body has just been. Frankenstein's recoil from this bodily contact is also an invitation, since he flees to his bed and throws himself on it, apparently fainting and then sleeping on his back, legs splayed. The invitation is answered when the monster emerges through a gap at the back of the bed curtains, reaches over Frankenstein, and gropes above his torso with his hands. This scene of one male body approaching another in his bed has strong erotic connotations; it is, again, an encounter both between men and within Frankenstein. The parted curtains of the bed form another in the

Edison *Frankenstein*, 1910

Edison *Frankenstein,* 1910

film's series of viewing apertures, and they again imply an opening into Frankenstein's psyche. In this overtly erotic moment, the open curtains also suggest other physical orifices, as if the monster could penetrate any open zone of the other man's body—eyes, mouth, anus—along with his mind.

A scene of homoerotic invitation, this is equally one of homophobic recoil. Asleep, Frankenstein remains literally curtained and symbolically closeted; when he awakens and sees the monster, he throws himself to the floor in horror. The bed scene reinforces the psychological dynamics of attraction and repulsion between men, if not also more explicit connotations of anal penetration. For the remainder of the film, Frankenstein resists the monster. In the film's penultimate shot, he looks in the mirror and sees the monster, and then the monster's image vanishes; the final shot is of Frankenstein and his wife embracing, an embrace that the audience sees reflected in the mirror. These shots suggest the restoration of both the heterosexual couple and the dynamics of heterosexual voyeurism, as Frankenstein becomes a spectator to himself as a heterosexual man. Yet these shots do not dispel the force of the homosocial imagery that precedes them. Rather, with their mirror imagery, they reveal the dependence of Frankenstein on mechanisms of psychological as well as cinematic projection to sustain his heterosexual self-image. The film's conclusion suggests not the disappearance of the monster but his suppression: its mirror is another closet door.

Here and throughout, the film's visual reflexivity contributes to its lack of sexual closure. The film's viewing hole, its symbol of cinema, requires the closed space of the closet to give it a defined shape; the closet operates, in Foucault's famous formulation, as an institutional "incitement" for the telling of a sexual story, like the closed space of the confessional.[18] Within this film, the cinematic aperture and the sexual closet create each other, a reciprocity that suggests, in turn, the privileged place of cinema for telling *Frankenstein* stories that center on a homosexual closet. The creation sequence, for example, requires not only a self-reflexive agent of voyeurism, the viewing hole, but also the emerging cinematic tool of editing, as it cuts between monster in the closet and the scientist looking at him, to establish the monster as the object of Frankenstein's gaze. Editing sutures the monster and his maker together, and the peephole is the aperture by which both a sexual closet and a cinema are made possible.

If Thomas Edison introduces the links between the Frankenstein monster and the operations of cinema, then D. W. Griffith supplies what will henceforth be that monster's cinematic racial ground.[19] Griffith's *The Birth of a Nation* (1915) has no apparent relation to Shelley's *Frankenstein*, but it provides, I suggest, a second point of origin for what happens to the Frankenstein story on film. Earlier, I discussed how the novels of Thomas Dixon crystallized the racist language of black monstrosity in late-nineteenth-century America. Adapting Dixon's novels, Griffith brought this monster to cinema, centering his epic of the Civil War and Reconstruction on the alleged menace posed by the black rapist to the white world around him, and on the opportunity that figure provided for the revival of white masculinity in the form of the Ku Klux Klan. Both Edison and Griffith represent the birth of a monster; both link their stories of monstrosity to sexual obsessions; and both animate their monsters through, and reflexively about, the emerging vocabulary of cinema.

Birth of a Nation is a monster movie, although it is not usually classified as such.[20] Its mise-en-scène of claustrophobic interiors and menacingly empty exteriors is that of horror, its organizing emotion is fear, and its narrative is propelled forward by the imagery of monstrosity. First among the film's monsters is a former slave named Gus, who attempts to rape a white woman, Flora; she throws herself over a cliff to escape him. Its second black monster is Silas Lynch, "mulatto leader of the blacks," who has risen to political power after the Civil War and who wants to marry another white woman, Elsie, the daughter of his white mentor.[21] A third black monster is collectively rendered: the black crowd that attempts, late in the film, to break into a cabin filled with white people. The film ultimately exorcises its monsters—Gus is murdered by the Klan, Lynch is seized, and the black crowd is dispersed—and concludes with the double wedding of four white protagonists. As James Snead suggests, "The film's movement from order to chaos and back to restored order resembles the structure typically found in horror or disaster movies, and by all measures, one must call blackness, in all its shades, the dark nightmare at the center of this disaster fantasy."[22] For the white audiences who flocked to the film, *Birth of a Nation* provided the visual foundation for horror against which they would define subsequent representations of both monstrosity and blackness.

The monsters of the film come to life through the emerging vocabulary of cinema. The sequence in which Gus menaces Flora in the woods, for example, enlists two of the many techniques significantly developed by Griffith—the closeup shot and cross-cutting—to mark Gus as a rapist. Closeups of Gus focalize his menace to Flora, as when he approaches her early in the sequence, after staring at her from afar, "his eyes wide in appeal" (120), and then again after she has begun to flee, and he "comes forward, foaming at the mouth" (122). Voyeurism doubly organizes these closeups, as the audience that has been watching Gus look at Flora now sees Gus in detail; the shot with Gus's wide eyes is a circle vignette, in which the image appears as an irislike circle ringed by black, creating a visual peephole. The editing of the scene enhances Gus's monstrosity, cutting between Gus advancing and Flora wandering and then between Gus advancing and Flora fleeing. That Flora does not see Gus at first only serves to equate him further, as Manthia Diawara notes, with "the unseen danger that stalks the innocent in many thrillers and horror movies."[23]

In giving cinematic form to black monstrosity, *Birth of a Nation* evokes several features of the Frankenstein story. In the sequence in the woods, Gus echoes the sexual menace of the Frankenstein monster, and the parallel between the edited film text and the monstrously amalgamated Frankensteinian body is here developed to its most pejorative extreme. As in *Frankenstein*, the film's monsters are dehumanized; as in *Frankenstein*, they are creatures who escape their creators' control. Gus is introduced as "the renegade, a product of the vicious doctrines spread by the carpetbaggers" (112), an explanation that casts him as the creation of white Northerners. When he chases Flora through the woods, he is, like the Frankenstein monster, an outsized, physically grotesque figure who lurks in the unpatrolled spaces of nature. Meanwhile, Silas Lynch is another kind of Frankenstein monster, a mulatto body. Like Gus, Lynch is the creation of white people, especially his mentor, the abolitionist Northern senator Stoneman; first introduced as "Stoneman's protegé" (94), Lynch too becomes a "traitor to his patron" (102) when he tries to seize Stoneman's daughter Elsie. The summary of the film submitted to the U.S. copyright office directly stated the Frankensteinian implications of Lynch's betrayal: "Lynch tells [Stoneman] he is to marry Elsie. Stoneman now realizes the Frankenstein he has himself created."[24] With Silas and Gus, *Birth of a Nation* updates to the terrain of cinema the most conservative racial allegories of the Frankenstein story: its condemnations of racial amalgamation and black revolt.

Yet the echoes of *Frankenstein* in *Birth of a Nation* also highlight the political instabilities of Griffith's film. *Birth of a Nation* unabashedly endorses white supremacy, but the very hyperbole with which the film focuses on whiteness—from its exaggerated lighting of white characters to its emphasis on the white sheets of the Klan—also makes white supremacy visible as an identity needing constant maintenance; the "invisible Empire" of the Klan requires constant visibility.[25] The Frankenstein story highlights such paradoxes, since it shifts emphasis from monsters to their creators. The first monster-makers represented in *Birth of a Nation* are white Southerners: in a scene meant to convey the origins of the Klan, two white children cover themselves in a sheet and frighten black children ("the sheet begins to move. . . . The black children become frightened, turn, and flee back down the path" [114]). Here, as white people make the Klan into a fear-inspiring creation, they are both monster-makers and monsters.

Later, the Klansmen assembled en masse present another such beast. At the moment when Gus is surrounded by white people in sheets, for example, he seems one monster among many; he is as much a frightened spectator of the faceless white-clad men who hover around him as he is the object of their gaze. Since the Ku Klux Klan is forged from the legacy of the Confederate dead, it is, like the Frankenstein monster, an entity reanimated from corpses; as in Thomas Dixon's novel *The Leopard's*

The Birth of a Nation, 1915

Spots, in which the Klan is "a great crawling swaying creature, half reptile half beast," the white and black "beast" are doubles. Similarly, the Reconstructed white nation symbolized by the double marriages at the end of the film is an amalgamated body, made from the union of white Northerners and Southerners. Although *Birth of a Nation* recognizes only one site of horror—the free black person—its overlap with *Frankenstein* emphasizes that is also shows white people making monsters of themselves.

This overlap also highlights the sexual dynamics of *Birth of a Nation.* The film is hyperbolically focused on a monster's threat to women, but the Frankenstein story, especially in the version offered in the Edison film, insistently draws attention to the same-sex dimensions—both homoerotic and homophobic—of men engaged in monster-making. Juxtaposing *Birth of a Nation* with the Edison *Frankenstein* underscores the anxious same-sex dynamics of the Griffith film, as well as the way the vocabulary of cinema brings these dynamics into view. In the sequence in the woods, for example, cross-cutting brings Gus's body into proximity not only with that of Flora but also with her brother Ben, the "Little Colonel," who is edited into the sequence in shots that show him in pursuit of Gus. Flora's body becomes the conduit for a narrative between men: in one shot, Ben finds and touches Gus's cap; in another, he finds Flora, and she mouths the name "Gus" before she dies; in a third, he seizes Gus's body with other Klansmen; and when the Klansmen conduct a hasty trial, he points to Gus, who is then taken away and killed. Gus's initial pursuit of Flora echoes the Frankenstein monster's pursuit of the bride; in this case, Flora is not Ben's bride but his sibling and, hence, an even more direct metonymic extension of him. Ben's subsequent pursuit of the monster completes this homosocial circuit: his gesture to Gus in the Klan courtroom is a psychological consummation of their bonds, if not also a literal "fingering" of him. The murderous-amorous bond between men so central to the Edison *Frankenstein* returns, in *Birth of a Nation*, as the foundational myth of the monstrous black rapist and the catalyst for the rebirth of the monstrous white nation as a whole.

III.

James Whale's films *Frankenstein* (1931) and *Bride of Frankenstein* (1935) transformed the Frankenstein story in popular understanding. Whale's *Frankenstein* focuses on the moment of the monster's creation and shows his murder of a child, his attack on the scientist's bride, Elizabeth, and his death in a fire at a mill; in contrast to the novel, both the scientist and the bride emerge unscathed. The film's sequel, *Bride of Frankenstein*, expands on the episode of the novel in which Victor begins to create a female mate for the monster and then aborts the project. *Bride of Frankenstein* opens with a framing device, a discussion among Lord Byron, Percy Bysshe Shelley, and Mary Shelley about the Frankenstein story. Mary Shelley summarizes the plot of the first film, but with an important revision: the monster is still alive. The film segues into its new story, in which the monster wanders the countryside. Pursued by a group of angry townspeople, he is caught and imprisoned. Escaping, he finds solace with a blind hermit who plays music and teaches him to speak, but he is again discovered and must flee for his life. Meanwhile, Dr. Frankenstein (Colin Clive), happily reunited with Elizabeth (Valerie Hobson), falls under the spell of his former teacher, Dr. Praetorius (Ernest Thesiger), who wants to create a female mate for the monster but needs the expertise of Frankenstein (whose name in these films is Henry). The two stories intersect when Dr.

Praetorius encounters the monster in a crypt, where the doctor is grave-robbing for his experiments and the monster is hiding from the crowd. Praetorius instructs the monster to abduct Elizabeth, after which Henry, fearing for her safety, lends his skills to the scientific project. The climax of the film is the creation scene in which the two men bring a female monster to life. Afterward, the bride (Elsa Lanchester) recoils from the monster's advances; he, in rage and despair, blows up the castle, himself, Dr. Praetorius, and the bride. Alone among the film's characters, Henry and Elizabeth escape, and they look tearfully back on the exploding castle in the film's final moment.

These films were so successful that their imagery—the large, lumbering, square-headed male monster with suture marks and neck bolts and the female monster in a long white dress with a white-streaked Nefertiti hairdo and wild, glazed eyes—became the standard currency for popular understanding of the Frankenstein story. The 1931 *Frankenstein* helped to secure Universal Studios, which had produced *Dracula* (dir. Tod Browning) earlier that year, as the leading Hollywood studio for horror. The 1935 *Bride of Frankenstein* was so popular that it played eleven times a day in a three-thousand-seat Los Angeles theater. Both films were praised by critics, particularly *Bride of Frankenstein*: the *New York Times* called it "a first-rate horror film," and subsequent critics have termed it "a masterpiece," "a nearly perfect feature," and "the last word in monster movies: glittering and intelligent, frightening and humorous, with the right touches of both whimsy and the Gothic macabre."[26]

Poised between horror and humor, the Whale *Frankenstein* films both reflected and transformed U.S. cultural politics of the 1930s. In a 1931 book called *Frankenstein, Incorporated*, for example, I. Maurice Wormser condemned corporations as Frankenstein monsters:

We are all familiar with Mrs. Shelley's thrilling tale of Frankenstein, the modern Prometheus, who artificially created and vitalized a monster. . . . The fable is not without its application to the corporate business organizations of to-day. Corporations are not natural living persons, but artificial beings, *corpora ficta*. They are created by the nation or state, which endows them with distinct personality . . . and comprehensive powers. Frankenstein's creature developed into a deadly menace to his creator. The nation and the state must curb certain grave and vicious abuses in their corporate offspring."[27]

Writing in the same year as Whale's *Frankenstein*, Wormser, a legal scholar, uses the scale, artifice, and power of the monster to criticize the *corpora ficta* of capitalism. Responsibility for this monster lies with the "nation and the state," whose individual citizens must now act: "thoughtful people are wondering how we are to act toward these business giants of undreamed-of size and uncontrolled power. Modern American society is a Frankenstein which has created these new and mighty monsters."[28] In a 1933 Supreme Court decision, Justice Brandeis reiterated this comparison, explicitly linking the Frankenstein monster to corporations that required regulatory control.[29] Wormser and Brandeis connected the monster directly to the excesses of capital; more recent commentators have suggested that the Whale films offer an allegorical gloss on the class disruptions of Depression-era America. David Skal suggests, for example, that Whale's monster represented a "battered hood ornament for a wrecked economy."[30] Similarly, in an analysis linking class relations in Shelley's era to those of the 1930s, Paul O'Flinn argues that the 1931 Whale *Frankenstein* "concerns above all mass activity in times of crisis. . . . where that activity is violent and insurrectionary (the monster's story) it is systematically denigrated; and where it is traditional and reactionary (the millburning), it is ambiguously endorsed."[31] The direct references of Wormser and Brandeis, and the allegorical interpretations of Skal and O'Flinn, draw attention to the Whale *Frankenstein*'s relevance to the operations of capital in an era of economic flux. In so doing, they update the class allegories already present in Shelley's novel.[32]

Complementary with these interpretations focused on class and capital, I suggest, we can understand the Whale films, and particularly *Bride of Frankenstein*, as oblique commentaries on race relations in the United States. This is a film whose setting is an unspecified Mitteleuropa and whose director and monsters—James Whale, Boris Karloff (born William Henry Pratt), and Elsa Lanchester—are all English, but whose narrative reflects American iconographies of race, rape, and lynching. Responding to the cinematic vocabulary of monstrosity instantiated by *Birth of a Nation*, *Bride of Frankenstein* presents a monster who is, symbolically, a black man in flight from a lynch mob. The film's sympathy for the monster in racial terms is complementary with its interest in him as a sexually heterodox figure, an interest that updates the Edison *Frankenstein* as well as Shelley's novel. But the film's racial and sexual narratives are, in turn, complicated by the figure of the bride, whose actions seem to imply either a white woman's horror at black men or the suicidal impulses of the "tragic mulatta." Racial dynamics are, to be sure, far less visible here than in the black Frankenstein stories of Crane and Dunbar. But the apparent invisibility of race in the Whale films, I suggest, allows them to express racial narratives whose sympathy for the monster is far stronger than in other black Frankenstein stories and whose politics are more radical than those of ostensibly more realist films of the decade.

Although the 1930s were a decade of political progress for African Americans on some fronts, they were dominated by retrenchment. The Scottsboro case (1931), in which an all-white jury sentenced nine young black men to death for allegedly raping two white women, offered a legally sanctioned version of the tradition in which black men were brutally murdered for their supposed sexual crimes. The lynching of black men increased in the first half of the decade; antilynching activist Jessie Daniel Ames suggested that it was distinguished in this era not only by its frequency but also by the "bestial excesses which characterized the mobs." Protests against such crimes by black and white activists were often thwarted. In 1934, the NAACP renewed its long-term lobbying effort for a national antilynching bill, but the bill was defeated in the following year, 1935—the year of *Bride of Frankenstein*'s release.[33]

At some remove from these political struggles but not unrelated to them, Hollywood was itself a contested arena for black representation throughout the 1930s. The decade was framed by the release of films that featured black characters in demeaning stereotypes, from *Hearts in Dixie* (dir. Paul Sloan, 1929), which introduced the character of Stepin Fetchit, to *Gone with the Wind* (dir. Victor Fleming, 1939), whose black characters recycled the imagery of happy slaves in the antebellum South. For black actors, the period was dominated by domestic-servant roles. As Donald Bogle summarizes, "No other period in motion-picture history could boast of more black faces carrying mops and pails or lifting pots and pans than the Depression years."[34] Black activists consistently fought against such representations. In the case of *Gone with the Wind*, for example, the NAACP worked during production to temper the racist content of the story; black actors won desegregation of set facilities; black activists protested the film upon its release; and Hattie McDaniel, working against the constraints of the role of "Mammy," became the first black actor to receive an Academy Award. As the example of this film suggests, the apparent uniformity of black servant roles on screen in this era served as an ideological screen for the contestations of both race relations and racial representations.[35]

In this context, we can see the male monster of *Bride of Frankenstein* as a creature marked not by an undifferentiated monstrosity but by behavioral and visual codes associated with blackness. In a 1944 article, Lawrence Reddick listed nineteen stereotypes assigned to black men in film, among them those of irresponsible citizen, social delinquent, vicious criminal, and "mental inferior."[36] These options catalogue the Frankenstein monster's behavior; he is the "mental inferior" turned delinquent and criminal, so irresponsible that he is denied even the status of citizen. The monster's large, awkward form also embodies the racist association of blackness with subhumanity. So too does his facial appearance, which makeup artist Jack Pierce apparently designed "to give the monster a primitive, Neanderthal appearance" by sloping "the brow of the eyes in a pronounced ape-like ridge of bone."[37] The monster's skin color was not black, but neither was it white:

> The color of the skin was particularly difficult to get just right. Something that would screen like the pallor of a dead man. Grey-white . . . did not give the right effect. . . . Neither did the yellowish tones. A dead, greenish-grey finally passed the test—the seventh one. The impression of "dead" finger tips was given by the use of black make-up.[38]

The abandonment of "grey-white" and "yellowish tones" for "greenish-grey" makeup literalizes the extent to which the monster is, if not black, then dramatically off-white. Although Pierce may not have intended for the makeup to be interpreted racially, the monster's appearance was the muted symbolic inheritance of *Birth of a Nation*. The "foaming at the mouth" of Griffith's monster Gus could no longer be openly displayed, but the outsized, off-white monster on the rampage as he appeared in the Whale films reflected Gus's legacy.

The muted expression of racist stereotypes appears elsewhere in the horror films of this era. Jungle-horror films of the decade, as Rhona Berenstein has shown, conflate black Africans, the ostensible primitivism of the jungle, and gorillas.[39] More specifically, we might think of the Frankenstein monster as sibling to that 1930s movie protagonist who not only appears "ape-like" but in the form of an ape: King Kong, who became, as Thomas Cripps puts it, "an enduring mythic figure, part 'bad nigger' and part universal victim of exploitation."[40] I have suggested that the bad-man folklore tradition, which emerged in the 1890s, was a space within African American culture in which a Frankenstein-like figure of outsized and monstrous violence could flourish. If *King Kong* (dir. Cooper and Schoedsack, 1933) offers one 1930s Hollywood version of the badman, then the Frankenstein monster of the Whale films is another. Like King Kong, Whale's Frankenstein monster is as much sympathetic victim as he is source of horror. King Kong becomes a figure of pathos when he is captured, bound, and brought from "Skull Island" to be exhibited in New York City, as freak-show spectacle and ethnographic specimen. The Whale *Frankenstein* films have no such distinct geographical trajectory from the exotic to the domestic; their setting remains European throughout. But this consistency of setting also means that the Whale films are more uniformly local than *King Kong* in the racial narratives they express: the horror of the Frankenstein monster is that, unlike King Kong, he is not imported from without but created from within.

Within the home territory of 1930s America, Whale's films resonate with contemporary accounts of lynching. The 1931 *Frankenstein* concludes with a sequence depicting the monster's flight from a crowd of angry townspeople, whose pursuit of him is represented with the visual markers—barking dogs, fiery torches, angry shouts—of a lynch mob. *Bride of Frankenstein* extends the force of this imagery, presenting the monster in a condition of continual flight from a murderous mob. Captured partway into the film, he is strung up on a tree as an angry cluster of white people surrounds him. This moment is so reminiscent of the imagery of lynching that, as with the monster's symbolic blackness, the film redraws the boundaries between ostensibly fantastic and realist cinematic genres. Hollywood films overtly about lynching in this era were timid to the point of incoherence: for example, *Fury* (dir. Fritz Lang, 1936) displaced the antiracism of a lynching plot by focusing on a white victim.[41] Conversely, *Bride of Frankenstein* is able to engage contemporary racism not despite its fantasy elements but because of them. In contrast to films like *Fury*, whose topicality set sharp limits on their content, *Bride of Frankenstein* could articulate a sympathetic antilynching narrative without restraint.

Bride of Frankenstein reinforces this stance in the sequence with the blind hermit. Unlike the lynch mob that pursues the monster, the hermit teaches him language; the hermit's actions suggest a literal enactment of "color-blind" liberalism. Such sympathy emerges further in the iconography of Christian martyrdom that surrounds this scene: when the old

Bride of Frankenstein, 1935

man comforts the monster to sleep, a closeup shot lingers on a brightly lit crucifix. The crucifix only confirms the monster's Christlike position, arms spread, in the scene when he is strung up on a tree. With the monster already coded as a black fugitive, such religious symbolism evokes a Christian abolitionist narrative of slave humanity, misery, and martyrdom, as enshrined in American culture by Stowe's *Uncle Tom's Cabin.* If Paul Laurence Dunbar's writing covertly rejects the legacy of Stowe, the Whale *Frankenstein* films embrace and extend it. Enslaved and sympathetic, Whale's Frankenstein monster offers another version of Stowe's Uncle Tom.

As the monster's behavior redefines black monstrosity, so too does his body offer a redemptive reworking of the U.S. iconography of lynching. The origins of the Frankenstein monster's body in the dismemberment of corpses prefigures the violation of black men's bodies in white America. In the lynchings of the 1930s, as in those of earlier eras, victims' bodies were dismembered; for example, in 1933 a newspaper reported that George Armwood "was mauled and mutilated before he was lynched . . . and [his] body was then burned and further desecrated." Continuing with the news that "whatever fragments of his corpse remained in his coffin may have been dug up,"[42] this newspaper story offers a plot whose ending —dismemberment—is the precondition for the Frankenstein monster's beginning. In this context, the iconic moment in the 1931 *Frankenstein* when Dr. Frankenstein says "It's alive" inaugurates one racial plot of a black monster's martyrdom, but it also revises others. The reanimation of the monster as a Christian martyr gives new life to men who, like George Armwood, had no chance to reverse their desecration.

Although it is difficult to know whether the racial resonances of the Whale films were visible to their actual spectators, at least one newspaper report of lynching from this era suggests the proximity between horror films and lynchings as visual spectacles: "The lynching site was located across the street from a picture show where a horror film was playing. A number of women emerging from the theater saw the Negro hanging from the tree and fainted."[43] This account literalizes the close connection between the movie theater and the lynching site, which physically neighbor each other as they offer similar sights of terror. Lynching was already an established topic for photographic spectacle, in the many postcards and cartes-de-visites that featured photographs of murdered black men and the white crowds gathered to observe them.[44] In the anecdote of the fainting woman, the connection of lynching to visual spectacle is both less direct and more sustained. The horror film becomes both a metonymic neighbor to and a metaphoric version of the lynching.

More generally, in its evocation of a black Frankenstein monster, *Bride of Frankenstein* revises the intimacy between racial and cinematic forms of horror. At the end of the 1930s, in his introduction to *Native Son*, Richard Wright wrote that "if Poe were alive, he would not have to invent horror; horror would invent him."[45] The Whale *Frankenstein* films are similarly "invented" by lynching and other contemporary racial horrors. As Poe recast the racial anxieties of the era of Nat Turner into the literary gothic, so too do the Whale films offer a reworking of the racial spectacles that might literally be taking place across the street.

This convergence of gothic horror with racial drama is reflected in Whale's own career. Shortly after completing *Bride of Frankenstein*, Whale directed a remake of the musical *Show Boat* (1936), whose story included a major black character, Joe, played by Paul Robeson. During filming, Whale and Robeson apparently became friends. Whale called Robeson one of the "most magnificent actors I have ever been privileged to direct" and planned to work with him on *Black Majesty*, a project written by C. L. R.

James; Robeson apparently was impressed by both Whale's directing and his knowledge of American history.[46] In his version of *Show Boat*, Whale gave Robeson's role and racial themes more prominence.[47] For example, he restored the song "Ol' Man River" and filmed Robeson's performance of it with an emphasis on Joe's struggles, as in a high-angle shot of him in jail, arms spread, straining against the bars in misery. Juxtaposed with the *Frankenstein* films, this shot echoes those of the monster imprisoned by angry townspeople. As directed by Whale, both Joe and the Frankenstein monster are sympathetic figures persecuted as monstrous by the hostile world around them.

Conversely, the film that Whale directed shortly before he made *Bride of Frankenstein* was a horror film with no manifest racial content but with even greater implications for racial metaphor. *Invisible Man* (1933) depicted a scientist who makes himself invisible with a secret formula and then uses his invisibility to go on a homicidal rampage; based on a story by H. G. Wells, the film went through many directors before it was completed by Whale. Although the film made the scientist into an evil lunatic, Wells insisted that the key to the story was that "the condition of invisibility itself should be the factor which drives the man insane."[48] Nearly twenty years later, Ralph Ellison took the "condition of invisibility" as the basis for his novel *Invisible Man* (1952), which begins, "I am an invisible man. No, I am not a spook like those who haunted Edgar Allan Poe; nor am I one of your Hollywood-movie ectoplasms. . . . I am invisible, understand, simply because people refuse to see me."[49] Like Wright's comment about horror "inventing" Poe, this comment reveals the racial significance of apparently nonracial gothic traditions. Ellison's narrator opposes his project to those of Poe and Hollywood, but the "Hollywood-movie ectoplasm" is his point of departure; the horror theme of an "invisible man" provides the gothic figure to which he then gives realist ground. *Frankenstein*, positioned in Whale's career between *Invisible Man* and *Show Boat*, is a meeting point between the racially suggestive metaphors of the earlier film and the overt representation of blackness in the later one. In *Frankenstein* and *Bride of Frankenstein*, Whale's representation of the monster brought together two modes: gothic horror that awaited its racial exfoliation and racial drama that was already suffused with horror.

James Whale's background strongly shaped his authorial signature in these films. Born into a large working-class family in the English Midlands in 1889, Whale began art school, served in World War I, became a successful actor and director, and came to Hollywood in 1929. By the time he made *Frankenstein* in 1931, he was also openly gay: known as the "Queen of Hollywood," he had begun living openly with producer David Lewis in 1930, just before making *Frankenstein*.[50] Whale rejected interpretations of his films as influenced by his sexuality, but so fully do connotations of homosexuality saturate his films, particularly *Bride of Frankenstein*, that they have become a touchstone in gay and lesbian film studies. As Richard Barrios puts it, "Whale's misfit outsiders pitted against hostile mobs, his unholy same-sex friendships, and his amused skewing of heterosexual norms all form a base camp for queer theory."[51]

We can understand the intertwined racial and sexual effects of *Bride of Frankenstein* by reviewing the film's depiction of relationships between men. The opening tableau of *Bride of Frankenstein* frames Mary Shelley in a homosocial triangle with Percy Shelley and Lord Byron; at times, the homoeroticism in the exchange comes to the visual surface, as she is separated off to the side while Byron leans against Shelley, his arm draped over the other man's shoulder. The film quickly falls away from such semiconcealed homoeroticism to more overt connotations of homosexuality. The arrival of Dr. Praetorius activates a story of homoerotic pursuit. Praetorius entices Henry away from his marital bed and invites him to his own apartment; Henry's rival as scientist, Praetorius is also Elizabeth's rival as Henry's lover. Praetorius's behavior strongly connotes homosexuality, as in a scene in which he is shown dining alone in a crypt with a skull set before him, a bottle of wine next to him, a long cigarette in his hand, and an insouciant expression on his face; he is the homosexual as decadent aristocrat.

Most important, the monster stands outside normative male heterosexuality. When he learns to speak, he indiscriminately links the word "friend"—his own term for an affective bond—with the hermit who first befriends him, with Dr. Praetorius, and finally with his female mate. He has no innate understanding that the male-female bond he is to forge with the bride is assumed to be primary or that it carries a different valence from his relationships with the two men. In the film's strongest challenge to normative sexual bonds, it suggests that all affective relationships, with women and men, are as easily "friendships" as "marriages." A more elaborate and sympathetic version of the "murderous-amorous" plot between men in Shelley's novel than that of the Edison film, *Bride of Frankenstein* multiplies bonds between men with a second male doctor and increases the number of women who serve as conduits for homoerotic exchange.

Although the queerness of this narrative does not depend on biography, the film's production history is notable for the number of gay men involved, including James Whale, David Lewis, who consulted on the film, and Ernest Thesiger, who played Praetorius. These men, in turn, circulated in the large world of gay Hollywood of this time; on the semiclosed edges of this world was Charles Laughton, who had sexual liaisons with men but was married to Elsa Lanchester, who plays both Mary Shelley and the monster's bride in the film.[52] In this context, *Bride of Frankenstein*, the work of a gay director, is also collectively authored by the gay Hollywood of its era—and even, ironically, by the antigay Hollywood of its era. The film was made just as the Hollywood Production Code went into full effect; one of the Code's goals, as *Variety* wrote, was "to keep the dual-sex boys and lesbos out of films."[53] Yet the censors who drastically cut *Bride of Frankenstein* inadvertently heightened the film's homoeroticism, as when they substituted the word "friend" for the word "mate," thinking the latter too explicit; the effect was to increase the erotic reach of the term "friendship" in the film.[54] Appropriately for a Frankenstein story, the censors who dismembered *Bride of Frankenstein* also reanimated it, and the film's queerness testifies to the productive results of its censorship as well as to those of its collaborative gay authorship.

The film's sexual dynamics intertwine with its racial ones. Whale's biographers have suggested that his homosexuality inclined him to sympathize with racial outsiders. Gore Vidal summarizes, "Someone who feels excluded from the life of the world because of prejudice—sex, race, religion, nationality . . . might indeed come up with Frankenstein's monster."[55] Yet the racial and sexual narratives of the Whale *Frankenstein* films do not seamlessly combine, and their lines of sympathy ultimately diverge. For if the films depict the monster sympathetically as a black fugitive, they also depict him as a black man who menaces white women.

By the 1930s, the myth of the black rapist had so permeated Hollywood film that the representation of rape was not required in order for its ideological threat to register. *King Kong* provides one fantasy version of this overdetermined cultural fantasy, in the film's imagery of the fair, blonde Fay Wray dangling helplessly in the brutish paw of the dark male gorilla.[56] In films set closer to home, the imagery of interracial rape emerged more indirectly. In *Gone with the Wind*, for example, the scene in which an ex-slave attempts to rob Scarlett depends for its effect on the imagery of rape.[57] In Margaret Mitchell's novel, this imagery is far more explicit; the dictates of the Production Code, along with the declared liberal intentions of the film's producers, muted the sexual content of the scene in the film. By contrast, in *King Kong*, the film's distance from realism enables the explicitness of its rape imagery. The gorilla who dangles the blonde in his paw is at once an unreal creature of fantasy and the direct descendant of the black monsters of the Reconstruction South.

Bridging the ideologically explicit images of *King Kong* and the more muted ones of *Gone with the Wind*, both *Frankenstein* and *Bride of Frankenstein* reflect the racist connection between race and rape. In one sequence in *Frankenstein*, the monster enters Elizabeth's room on her wedding night and corners her behind the locked door; the camera cuts to others hearing her screams, and when they break into her room, her white dress is disheveled and she lies across one corner of the rumpled bed moaning desperately, "Don't let it come here." Although the monster's crime is officially the penetration of the room, his actions are framed precisely according to the imagery of interracial rape. The next scene metaphorically realizes the disastrous consequences of such a rape, when an angry young father displays to the crowd the body of his little girl, whom the monster has accidentally drowned. The imagery of this moment was already set in place by *Birth of a Nation*, in the shot in which Ben carries the body of his dead little sister, Flora, into his home. Updating Griffith, the two scenes together suggest that the body of the girl symbolizes the fatal effects for adult white women of contact with black men. By the end of this sequence, the black man has become the archetypal rapist, and the white woman, if not actually dead, has assumed the role, as Jacqueline Dowd Hall puts it, of "the quintessential Woman as Victim: polluted, 'ruined for life,' the object of fantasy and secret contempt."[58]

Bride of Frankenstein develops the imagery of interracial rape even more fully. The monster's resuscitation of a drowning girl appears, to the men who come upon him, as an imminent sexual violation, as does his abduction of Elizabeth while she is resting in her bedroom. The scenes do not require explicit sexual context for the overdetermined imagery of interracial rape to take hold; as Valerie Smith notes, "The fiction of a black male perpetrator automatically sexualize[s] a nonsexual crime."[59] But the perpetrator, in this case, is also a victim, in an overlay of iconographic forms—rapist and martyr—that sets the film in conflict with itself. In both films, the monster embodies a paradox, the sympathetic lynch-mob target who is also, possibly, a demonic rapist. Because the monster's status as innocent victim is transformed if he seems to pose a sexual threat to white women, the force of this second persona—the black rapist—is so explosive that it overrides the first. The imagery of interracial rape also affects the film's symbolic depiction of homosexuality. Since cultural stereotypes of interracial rape presumed female victims and male attackers, the film's insistence on the monster as a would-be rapist serves to highlight his heterosexuality. As a man, the monster is allowed into some of the homoerotic bonds that are determined, in the film, through the exclusion of women. As a symbolic black man, however, the monster is also defined against these same men, as a figure of monstrous heterosexuality.

The film's concluding sequence confirms the literally explosive consequences of these contradictions. This is the only sequence in which the female monster appears. The bride seems very white: her skin is fair, and she is dressed in a long white gown similar to those worn by both Mary Shelley and Elizabeth earlier in the film. When she first comes to life, she stands neatly between Drs. Frankenstein and Praetorius, but as soon as the monster approaches her, she recoils from his advances, shrieking repeatedly. At her second shriek, she actually falls out of the left-hand side of the frame, as if her dread of the monster is so great as to destabilize the camera. These physical gestures echo visually the repulsion felt by Elizabeth in both films' symbolic rape scenes; once again, a white woman is horrified by the prospect of the black man's sexual advances. The death of the bride concludes the sequence in the first Whale *Frankenstein* film in which the monster's attack on Elizabeth is followed by the death of the little girl. The monster's mate, like the little girl, pointedly signals the fatal consequences for a white woman of being sullied—beneath the white dress, "blackened"—by contact with the black man. In *Birth of a Nation*, Flora jumps off a cliff when Gus approaches. In *Bride of Frankenstein*, the monster's mate does not kill herself, but here too, the prospect of being touched by a black man is a degradation so great that it must lead to death. At the same time, the death of the monster restabilizes its sexual plot. Having incarnated two contradictory sexual threats—the excessively homoerotic white man and the excessively heterosexual black man—the monster cannot survive. His insistence that he and Praetorius die together marks the recognition that at least two of the male identities in the film cannot be reconstituted for normative heterosexuality. The monster's suicide thus enacts the self-canceling effects of embodying sexual and racial contradictions.

This interpretation does not, however, account for the racial ambiguities of the monster's mate. Whale wanted Lanchester to look like an "Egyptian mummy," and her resulting Nefertiti hairdo is an Afrocentric nod to that

Bride of Frankenstein, 1935

image, if not an Afro itself.[60] In Whale's film, the monster's mate resembles the woman whose status between races dooms her to tragedy: the "tragic mulatta." This figure has a long and complicated genealogy in U.S. culture, but the 1930s were a moment of particular visibility for the "tragic mulatta" in popular culture, particularly in plots of racial passing. A year before *Bride of Frankenstein*, for example, *Imitation of Life* (dir. John Stahl, 1934) featured a light-skinned African American girl who passes as white to disastrous effect, rejecting her dark-skinned mother until it is too late. In Whale's own *Show Boat*, the light-skinned woman passing as white is exposed with tragic results: exiled from the world of the show boat, she later resurfaces as a lonely alcoholic in New York.[61]

Flanked by films like *Imitation of Life* and *Show Boat*, the last sequence of *Bride of Frankenstein* suggests both the presence of a mixed-race female character and her involvement in a passing plot. The iconography of the "tragic mulatta" suffuses that of the white-skinned, Nefertiti-haired woman who refuses to acknowledge her kinship with the darker monster and who would rather condemn herself to death than join forces with him. This possibility complicates the film's political allegories yet again, since its sympathies are with the monster in the face of his rejection. As in Dunbar's *Sport of the Gods*, the mixed-race black woman is a barrier rather than an ally to the black man, and the film's antiracist interests rest narrowly with him. The demise of both of the symbolically black figures in the film also reinforces the sexual conservatism of its conclusion. If interpreting the bride as a white woman imposes a limit on the film's identification with the black monster, then seeing her as a "tragic mulatta" narrows its orbit of sympathy still further. All of the film's black and mixed-race figures, as well as its sexually heterodox ones, must die; only the white heterosexual couple survives.

Yet this film's sympathy for its monsters overflows its abrupt attempt at closure, an overflow powered by its comic tone. Whereas comic theatrical adaptations of *Frankenstein* customarily had conservative political effects in their muting of the monster, the Whale films use comedy very differently. Barrios's description of *Bride of Frankenstein* as a "base camp for queer theory" has a second resonance: the film's status as what one critic calls "one of the film world's first camp classics."[62] Queer theory has posited a variety of relationships between camp and homosexuality, from the particular claim that camp "embodies a specifically queer cultural critique" to the more diffuse counterclaim, as Fabio Cleto summarizes, that "camp is not the direct and legitimate offspring of a homosexual selfhood active with the *properties* of 'biological paternity.' . . . through a cultural process . . . of adoption, camp has been brought to its supposed or reclaimed 'homosexual paternity.'"[63]

Bride of Frankenstein both exemplifies and comments on these competing accounts of the gay authorship of camp. The film's campiness is inextricable from the gay men who collectively author it. Anecdotes about the relationship between Ernest Thesiger and James Whale, for example, exemplify one version of high-camp sensibility between gay men. Thesiger came from a more upper-class English background than Whale and adopted a haughty, aristocratic tone; on the set of the *Frankenstein* films, he wore pearls and did needlepoint, and he called himself the "stitchin' bitch." David Lewis recalled Whale acerbically commenting on Thesiger's service in World War I: "He was actually in the trenches—knitting, said Jimmy."[64] Valerie Hobson, who played Elizabeth, remembered Thesiger as "one of the very first people to make 'almost camp' fun. He did it as a serious thing, you know—oooh, the sort of arched eyebrow and arched nos-

tril . . . was what we would call nowadays 'camp.'"[65] Thesiger's portrayal of
Dr. Praetorius, here recalled as an archness of both eyebrow and attitude,
anchors the camp sensibility of the film; he is the "stitchin' bitch" who
organizes Whale's affectionate comic portrait of a stitched-together monster. At the same time, the film's campiness extends to the performances
of actors not identified as gay, such as Boris Karloff and Elsa Lanchester.
As both the monster's intended mate and the wife of Charles Laughton,
Lanchester is, symbolically, the bride of camp in the film. Her role in
Bride of Frankenstein reaffirms that camp in this film has an intimately
familial but not exclusively biological relation to the film's gay authorship.
Cleto's metaphors for the status of camp as the "adopted" child of homosexuality are the very terms of the film's plot, about a monster who is "not
the direct and legitimate offspring" of his two male makers.

The film's camp sensibility intersects, in turn, with its narrative of racial sympathy.[66] Critics often describe the film as a "black comedy," a term
that, like "film noir," customarily refers to a sensibility rather than to a
racial theme.[67] But both "black comedy" and "film noir" have racial implications. The "blackness" of Hollywood film noir is shaped materially
by the presence of black people in small but defining roles, and the genre,
as Eric Lott has argued, provides an ongoing commentary on the construction of whiteness.[68] Black comedy is even more intimately connected
with black cultural history. As Mel Watkins points out, "black comedy" is
closely linked to both the theatrical emergence of African American comedians and their thematic emphasis on the absurdities of racism.[69] *Bride
of Frankenstein*'s humor is not authored by African Americans, but its humor is sympathetically intertwined with its allegorical depiction of black
experience. If this is camp as a queer sensibility, it is also "black comedy"
in a racially marked sense. The comedy that Whale's *Frankenstein* films
generate is laughter not at but with the symbolically monstrous African
American man, and their horror is the horror of American racism.

IV.

The fulfillment of the "black comedy" of Whale's films came more than
three decades later. In the early 1970s, political allegories of the Frankenstein monster proliferated. For example, the cartoonist Jules Feiffer, at-
tacking the Vietnam War, caricatured Richard Nixon as a Frankenstein
monster made by Henry Kissinger; another cartoonist presented Nixon as

Victor Frankenstein making a monster of Haldeman, Ehrlichman, Dean, and other figures in the Watergate scandal.[70] Such caricatures used Karloff's monster as a brisk comic shorthand for indicting a presidential administration seen as out of control both at home and abroad. A more extravagant effort to enlist the Frankenstein story for political allegory was the Living Theatre's production of *Frankenstein*, first staged in 1965. The Living Theatre *Frankenstein* offered a three-hour combination of spectacle, dance, mime, and ritual with numerous targets, including the capitalist exploitation of workers, the brutality of capital punishment, and the violations of state surveillance.[71] It did not focus on racial issues, although in at least one production, a black character played a key role: when Dr. Frankenstein demands that his assistants obtain genitalia for his monster, they turn to a black man, hanging on a cross, to obtain one.[72] The Christian martyr of the Whale film was now the crucified black penis, in a Frankenstein monster forged from 1960s political earnestness and theatrical excess.

The black comedy of Whale's film came to less earnest but even more excessive fruition in the blaxploitation movie *Blackenstein* (dir. William Levey, 1973). "Blaxploitation" is the name given to the action films, marketed to black audiences, that appeared in the first half of the 1970s and that featured cool, fearless, sexually confident black outlaw heroes. The first and best-known of these films were *Sweet Sweetback's Baadasssss Song* (dir. Melvin van Peebles, 1971), *Shaft* (dir. Gordon Parks, Sr., 1971) and *Super Fly* (dir. Gordon Parks, Jr., 1972). Written and directed by African Americans, these films represented a reaction against both the ongoing erasure of black protagonists from Hollywood films and the timidity of white liberal films that did include black people, such as *Guess Who's Coming to Dinner* (dir. Stanley Kramer, 1967), which featured a saintly protagonist played by Sidney Poitier. Blaxploitation protagonists like Youngblood Priest, the drug dealer of *Super Fly*, were the anti-Poitier, or as James Baldwin dryly remarked of *Guess Who's Coming to Dinner*, "A black person can make nothing of this film—except, perhaps, *Superfly*."[73]

Politically, blaxploitation reflected the shift in racial politics in the late 1960s from the largely nonviolent ethos of the civil rights movement to the more militant, separatist, and nationalist claims of the Black Power movement.[74] The fearless male heroes—and several powerful heroines —of blaxploitation reflected Black Power militancy. Black Panther Huey Newton, for example, praised *Sweet Sweetback* as "the first truly revolutionary Black film."[75] Blaxploitation films seldom featured overt political statements; their relation to Black Power inhered, more indirectly, in the confidence of their heroes and in the aesthetics of cool they presented in costume, settings, and music. The moment of this movement was brief: blaxploitation films were quickly coopted by Hollywood studios and were written and directed by white men, and by the mid-1970s, the genre was over.[76]

About a dozen of the original films in the genre combined blaxploitation with horror, a combination that generated its own form of "black comedy." In his tongue-in-cheek history of blaxploitation, Darius James remembers his childhood interest in both Black Power and classic horror: "until the Revolution came, I was forced to wait in the basement of my father's house on a . . . sofa under posters of Angela Davis and H. Rap Brown. . . . I'd watch Universal's old monster movies . . . hallucinating the Famous Monsters of Filmland terrorizing whyte suburboid populations with Huey Newton's helium-squeak voice."[77] James's memory literally juxtaposes the iconic images of Black Power and H. Rap Brown with "old monster movies" to create a new hybrid—a hallucination of Huey Newtons monstrously on the loose, "terrorizing whyte suburboid populations." Modern horror films customarily operate, as William Paul has shown, in an interstitial zone of "laughing screaming."[78] James's memories suggest that blaxploitation horror could operate in this same interstitial zone, but with more overtly political references. In James's memories of laughing screaming, Huey Newton's rampage of terror is made comic by his "helium-squeak voice," while James positions himself in the comically deflating posture of the male revolutionary on a sofa, "forced to wait in the basement of [his] father's house."

Situated between horror and humor, blaxploitation generated its own "Famous Monsters of Filmland." Some were new figures, as in *Sugar Hill* (dir. Paul Maslansky, 1974), in which seventeenth-century slaves rise from the dead; some were fresh versions of old monsters, as in two films made by an African American director, William Crain, and set in contemporary Los Angeles. In *Dr. Black and Mr. Hyde* (1976), a black doctor becomes a monstrous Mr. Hyde, and in *Blacula* (1972), an eighteenth-century African prince, made into a vampire by a slave trader, comes back to life in contemporary Los Angeles as an elegant killer whose victims include white policemen. *Blacula* showed the freedom for political fantasy that horror films could afford. As Leerom Medovoi notes, "precisely because [Blacula] is a monster, [he] can be shown throttling and killing white police officers who have come to Watts, something that would simply be impermissible for any other sort of black character in a Hollywood film."[79]

Designed to capitalize on *Blacula's* success, *Blackenstein* was a product of white Hollywood, made by a white director, William Levey, and a white writer, Frank Saletri, in 1972 and released in 1973 by American International Pictures, a major producer of low-budget Hollywood films. *Blackenstein* has received no scholarly commentary, and viewers generally see it as crude and sloppy, a failure even by low-budget standards.[80] But *Blackenstein* is an important development in the black Frankenstein tradition. Unlike *Blacula*, which invented a racial framework for an existing monster, *Blackenstein* confirmed the existing visual genealogy of black Frankenstein stories, wherein the Whale *Frankenstein* films—the most famous of "Universal's old monster movies"—had already developed the racial implications of the story. Fulfilling the connotations of the Whale films, *Blackenstein* makes the black Frankenstein metaphor into a visible monster, from its comically grafted title onward.[81] Yet *Blackenstein* does not sustain Whale's overt language of sympathy for its covertly black monster, nor does it develop the most overtly political possibilities of racial critique—Huey Newton running amok—intrinsic to blaxploitation horror. The film makes the black monster visible, but it also undermines visibility's radical potential.

Set in Los Angeles, *Blackenstein* begins when a young black woman physicist named Dr. Winifred Walker (Ivory Stone) arrives in L.A. to visit her former mentor, the white Dr. Stein (John Hart), to ask for his help in treating her fiancé, a soldier who has lost his arms and legs in a landmine explosion in Vietnam. The film then introduces the soldier, Eddie Turner (Joe De Sue), in a VA hospital, in a scene in which he lies limbless and immobilized in a hospital bed while an unnamed white orderly (Bob Brophy), large and beefy, looms over him. The orderly is seething with hostility:

Turner: Can I have some ice cream?

Orderly: What the hell'd you say?

T: Can I have some ice cream?

O: Ice cream! Like hell. This ain't no damned hotel.

T: But my throat's dry.

O: Tough. (Pause.) Hey, why don't you reach over there and have a nice, cool drink of water, huh? (Laughs.) The hell with you. You think I got time to be running upstairs and around and all over, just because one of you guys wants special attention? What the hell's so special about you, just cause you're laying there, huh? The hell with you.

This exchange dramatizes racial hierarchy in the tableau of the large white man who towers over the injured black man. Their racial hierarchy is inseparable from the setting of a VA hospital during the Vietnam War. Black Power and other activists frequently criticized the Vietnam War as a conflict run by white men but disproportionately fought by black men, and as an imperialist intervention by a colonizing power. Eldridge Cleaver, for example, declared, "As a colonized people, we consider it absurd to fight the wars of the mother country against other colonized peoples, as in Vietnam right now."[82] In this scene in *Blackenstein*, the white man adds insult to injury to a black man who has been injured while fighting the white nation's war. The camera's sympathy is with Turner throughout the scene, as in several low-angle shots that emphasize the grotesquerie of the orderly's face. Long before Turner turns into "Blackenstein," the film

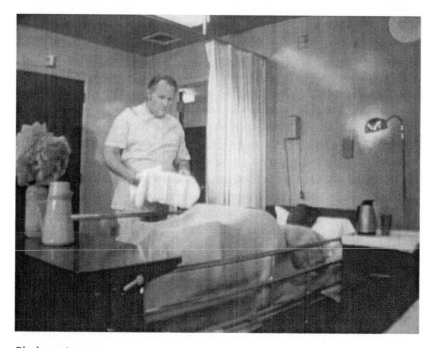

Blackenstein, 1973

sympathetically establishes the conditions for his monstrosity, as a black man victimized first by the American war machine and then by a sadistic captor.

The scene continues with a long monologue by the orderly, which reveals his own insecurities:

> You know, they called me—the service—too. I went down there. I was 45 inches, 17 1/4, 28 inch waist. I walked down there like this and . . . Night before, I was going down for induction, and my gang, they all throwed me a party and they gave me some great gifts—you know those little shaving things and little portable type of radios and stuff like that. And I said, "Hey, gang, I love you. Thanks a lot, I really love you." I'm going to be one of those marching soldiers. And I get down there and I . . . I . . . get rejected. You know, they don't take me. The old ticker there—weight-lifting and athletics—just gave my heart a little murmur. So I had to go back to all these people I said goodbye to the other night.

This monologue charts the horror at his failed masculinity; his apparent physical prowess—he gestures to his chest, arms, and waist as he names their sizes—turns out to conceal a heart murmur that disqualifies him for military service. The shame of this failure takes its shape from its homosocial context. It is the orderly's male friends who allow him to see himself as a soldier, and his reappearance before them is the true sign of his rejection. This story of individual failure is also an allegory of America in Vietnam. As Susan Jeffords has shown, symbolic accounts of impotence pervade white men's novels, memoirs, films, and other narratives about Vietnam.[83] In this case, the orderly's story suggests the experience of a nation that, for all its apparent size and strength, is failing to win the war. Although he does not go to Vietnam, the trajectory of his monologue—anticipation of wartime prowess, return home to group humiliation—encapsulates that of the nation as a whole.

As the scene concludes, the orderly turns back to Turner, connecting his own sense of impotence to his rage against the black veteran:

> Oh what the hell am I even telling you this for? Big deal—you laying there. You know, it's my taxes and my friends' taxes are gonna keep you there. We gotta take care of you. Big deal. What the hell'd you go for? You didn't have to go. You know, that old scam, patriotism, huh? I can see it now. The bands are playing, and the drums are rolling and them blowing

the bugle . . . oh, blow it out your . . . What the hell'd you—why don't you take a look at yourself, huh? You look like a creep, laying there and looking up at me with those stupid eyes of yours. The hell do you know? Close those eyes. It's time for your shot, buddy. Nice big needle. Just relax.

In the orderly's rant, he suggests that Turner is perpetrating "that old scam, patriotism" in order to become a drain on white people. His projection of these ideas onto Turner allows him to disavow his own impotence as a soldier; this is a variation on the process common to Vietnam stories whereby, as Jeffords notes, "American manhood is revived, regenerated principally by a rejection of the feminine."[84] Here, the axis of revivification is race as well as gender: the white soldier-manqué rejects the black one, reestablishing his masculinity as he does so. The monologue ends with the white man's sense of hierarchy apparently restored: he condemns Turner as monstrous "creep" and prepares to penetrate him, in a moment of phallic potency, with his "nice big needle." Yet his self-restoration is incomplete. As the orderly speaks, Turner stares at him, and the camera

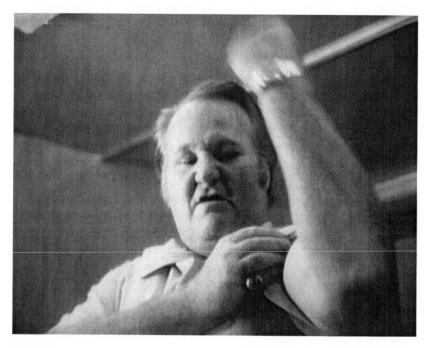

Blackenstein, 1973

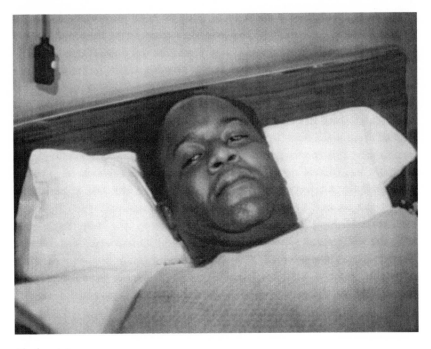

Blackenstein, 1973

cuts between closeups of the speaking orderly and the silent Turner. The orderly is so unnerved at "those stupid eyes" that he cannot overcome his discomfort at the possibility of Turner's suspicion and judgment. The anxious command, "Close your eyes," confirms the destabilizing power of the gaze, not only that of Turner but also that of the audience watching the scene. Even as the white man turns the black man into a symbolic monster, he is haunted by the monster looking back.

When Eddie Turner is physically transformed into Blackenstein, this haunting becomes violent. After Dr. Stein reamalgamates Turner's limbs in an operation back at his mysterious laboratory, Turner emerges as a figure whose large form, lumbering gait, and inarticulate groaning are an affectionate parody of Boris Karloff's Frankenstein monster; his flat-topped hair recalls that of both Karloff and Elsa Lanchester.[85] Blackenstein's Afro is also a takeoff of the imagery of blaxploitation, a genre with an intrinsic affinity with parody. The performances of hair, clothing, and style that infuse the original blaxploitation films are so highly exaggerated that they already seem self-parodying. Even the Black Power movement on which blaxploitation drew seems so stylized that it is on the edge of parody. For example, Angela Davis has lamented the mainstream media's relentless focus on her Afro, which reduced "a politics of liberation to a politics of fashion": "I am remembered as a hairdo."[86] Within the black popular culture of the era, Black Power style could also verge on self-parody. For example, so great was the pressure for Afros that a market developed in wigs that would mimic the "natural" Afro look.[87] Blackenstein, a character in a Hollywood film made by white people, has only an attenuated relation to the Black Power movement. But his square-topped Afro highlights the potential for self-parody in both the Frankenstein and blaxploitation traditions—as well as within Black Power itself.

Blackenstein poster (detail), 1973

Blackenstein initially uses its parodic protagonist in ways that effect a critique of racism. Blackenstein's first act is to murder the orderly, and a closeup of the nameplate VETERANS HOSPITAL as he opens the door makes explicit that the nation at war in Vietnam is the film's foundational house of horrors. As Blackenstein lumbers down the dark hospital corridor, the camera cuts repeatedly to shots of the orderly's earlier monologue. The camera is identified with Blackenstein, and we see his angry view of the space and, as he approaches, the orderly's increasing terror. The actual murder is depicted only in silhouette through a hospital curtain, and it features Turner ripping off the orderly's arm; the final shot is of the orderly's armless body, in a precise reversal of Turner's own original limblessness. As with the orderly's earlier monologue, this individual act of murder is also a national allegory. Blackenstein's murder of the orderly effects his revenge against the white nation that destroyed him while making him fight its unwinnable war.

These two scenes with the hospital orderly, then, suggest *Blackenstein's* force in depicting a black Frankenstein monster in the context of both Black Power and Vietnam. Yet *Blackenstein* dilutes its own political potential. Turner is not, in fact, turned into a monster by the white Dr. Stein. Although the doctor does reattach his limbs, Turner becomes violent only because his medication was tampered with by the doctor's black butler, Malcomb (Roosevelt Jackson), who is in love with Winifred Walker. In separating out the source of *Blackenstein's* violence from his attack on white men, the film vitiates one of the main political contributions of the Frankenstein story: its focus on the origins of violence in abandonment and abuse. So too does *Blackenstein* diffuse the targets of its monster's anger. After killing the white hospital orderly, Blackenstein murders a series of white women in sexually suggestive ways. In the first of these, for example, Blackenstein witnesses a white couple having sex in their house. When the woman, a sexy blonde in a diaphanous nightgown, ventures outside to investigate a noise, he strangles her, disembowels her, and fondles her entrails. As the film progresses, Blackenstein's violence also turns against black people. He murders a black woman behind a nightclub, although not before the camera lingers on her exposed breasts. He does save Winifred Walker—also, by now, topless and helpless—from rape by Malcomb, but his days as an avenging outlaw are over. He is finally disemboweled by vicious dogs.

The film's focus on disembowelment provides an apt metaphor for its relation to *Frankenstein*, since *Blackenstein* guts the Frankenstein story of its political content while eviscerating the meaning of black rebellion in a more contemporary era. The self-consciously political development of the opening plot with the hospital orderly gives way to its manifestly apolitical —albeit misogynist—depiction of grotesque violence. Blackenstein himself remains mute throughout, in stark contrast to his suave and articulate predecessor, Blacula. In making explicit the figure of a black Frankenstein monster, *Blackenstein* goes beyond the Whale films, but it also falls short of them; it silences rather than articulates their political critiques. So too does it squander the satiric opportunities of comedy, black or otherwise. *Blackenstein* may be funny, but its humor is at its own expense.

Yet *Blackenstein* does not, like Blackenstein himself, go entirely to the dogs. For viewers like Darius James, the pleasure of a film like *Blackenstein* extends beyond its serious development of political themes. James delights in what he calls the film's "square-headed brutha" as a figure of pleasurable fantasy, the complement to his childhood memories of "hallucinating the Famous Monsters of Filmland terrorizing whyte suburboid populations."[88] The square head remains *Blackenstein*'s iconic image, and it neatly condenses the film's status as an affectionate parody of both the Frankenstein tradition and the blaxploitation genre. But well before Eddie Turner emerges with his monster Afro, *Blackenstein* makes its impact, in the scene with the hospital orderly. Even when he lies immobilized in the hospital, the black man's gaze already has the power to make the white man come undone.

V.

The shortcomings of *Blackenstein* are not the inevitable result of its being a low-budget production, nor of its being written, directed, and produced by white people. The most trenchantly antiracist horror film of this era, with its own allusion to *Frankenstein*, was the low-budget effort of a white filmmaker. In George Romero's *Night of the Living Dead* (1968), cannibal zombies terrorize an isolated group of white people whose leader is a black man; as Richard Dyer argues, the film's racial significance inheres not only in its representation of a heroic black protagonist but also in its sustained negative depiction of white people and its depiction of whiteness itself as a kind of death.[89] *Night of the Living Dead* unmistakably alludes to Whale's *Frankenstein* films in its opening scene, when the first of the zombies, a tall, mute, pale man, chases a woman across a graveyard with the posture and gait of Boris Karloff's Frankenstein monster.[90] This moment uses the iconography of Karloff to establish the film's governing equation: the monsters in this film are white, not black. If *Bride of Frankenstein* and *Blackenstein* attempt, with uneven success, to humanize the black man made monstrous by a white world, Romero engages in a complementary project of turning the cinematic gaze back against the world of white people. Using the imagery of *Frankenstein* to deepen white self-critique, *Night of the Living Dead* suggests that white people make themselves into their own monsters: self-sustaining and self-replenishing but ultimately self-consuming.

For black writers, I suggest, the Frankenstein story became a complementary touchstone for representing both white anxiety and black revolt. Autobiographical essays by James Baldwin and Eldridge Cleaver echo the Frankenstein story, both situating a hyperbolically visible monster-figure on a blindingly white terrain of ice. James Baldwin's essay "Stranger in the Village" is his meditation on his experience as the only black person in a tiny, all-white Swiss village in the winter of 1951–52; the essay was first published in *Harper's* in 1953, contemporary with Ralph Ellison's *Invisible Man*, and was reprinted in his first nonfiction collection, *Notes of a Native Son*, in 1955, when the civil rights movement had emerged in full force. This essay anchors a long tradition of African American commentary on Europe.[91] It is also, I suggest, a gothic horror story with a muted but evocative relation to *Frankenstein*.

There are no direct citations of *Frankenstein* in "Stranger in the Village," but it is suffused with Frankensteinian traces, beginning with its setting, an "absolutely forbidding" landscape of "ice and snow as far as the eye can reach."[92] Shelley's Victor Frankenstein is Swiss, and Baldwin's setting, a "white wilderness" (118), takes us both to the terrain of Frankenstein's homeland and to the icy white North Pole with which *Frankenstein* begins and ends. In this world of white ice and white people, Baldwin becomes a dehumanized object of constant scrutiny: "there was no suggestion that I was human: I was simply a living wonder" (119). He is both a freak-show exhibit and its close correlate, a gothic demon, especially to the local children who, "having been taught that the devil is a black man, scream in genuine anguish as I approach" (123). Describing himself as a kind of monster, Baldwin identifies his monster-makers as the white people of the Swiss village, "whose culture controls me, has even, in a sense, created me" (120). The village that has "created" Baldwin as a monster is his synecdoche for the white West, onto which, he writes in a Franken-steinian turn of phrase, "I have been so strangely grafted" (121).

Baldwin's rebellion against his "grafted" monstrosity inheres, like that of the Frankenstein monster, in his claim to humanity. Like *Frankenstein*, his essay consistently links monstrosity and visuality, and his claim for humanity accordingly repudiates visual objectification in favor of recognition: "The black man insists . . . that the white man cease to regard him as an exotic rarity and recognize him as a human being" (122). What follows this claim is not an overt turn toward violent revenge but another strategy elucidated in Shelley's novel: dismantling the psyche of the white monster-maker. "it is one of the ironies of black-white relations," Baldwin notes, "that, by means of what the white man imagines the black man to be, the black man is enabled to know who the white man is" (123). The white man, projecting his own insecurities onto the black man, imagines him to be a monster. As in Shelley's *Frankenstein*, this process threatens to destroy its creator: "At the root of the American Negro problem is the necessity of the American white man to find a way of living with the Negro in order to be able to live with himself" (127).

Baldwin concludes his narrative of grafted monsters and tortured monster-makers in two ways. The first is to assert the full rights of the monster, in the form of declaring his own claim to the medieval cathedral at Chartres:

> The cathedral at Chartres . . . says something to the people of this village which it cannot say to me; but it is important to understand that this cathedral says something to me which it cannot say to them. . . . I am terrified by the slippery bottomless well to be found in the crypt, down which heretics were hurled to death, and by the obscene, inescapable gargoyles jutting out of the stone and seeming to say that God and the devil can never be divorced. I doubt that the villagers think of the devil when they face a cathedral because they have never been identified with the devil. But I must accept the status which myth, if nothing else, gives me in the West before I can hope to change the myth. (128)

What Baldwin emphasizes about the cathedral—its bottomless crypt and frightening gargoyles—are those features of medieval Gothic architecture that are also its most gothic in the literary sense; the passage relocates the Anglo-American gothic back to the medieval Europe whence its imagery was initially drawn. This is Chartres cathedral as the setting for a horror story. The passage marks Baldwin's defiant assertion that as a black American already "identified with the devil," his affinity with Chartres is greater than that of white Europeans or Americans.[93] Writing twenty years later about the horror film *The Exorcist* (dir. William Friedkin, 1976), Baldwin made a similar claim about black viewers' greater knowledge of the devil: "he who has been treated *as* the devil recognizes the devil when they meet."[94] From the medieval cathedral to the modern horror film, Baldwin's revisions of the gothic afford black men a defining role, as viewers as well as objects of monstrosity.

At the same time, Baldwin forecasts the ruin of the white monster-maker. Of white indifference to racism, he notes, "anyone who insists on remaining in a state of innocence long after that innocence is dead turns himself into a monster" (129). Like Victor Frankenstein, the white Westerner who refuses to acknowledge his complicity in making a monster himself becomes one. And as in *Frankenstein*, the icy white wilderness of Baldwin's village signals not the triumph of white power but its impending exhaustion. The Swiss village is the last frontier of homogeneous whiteness. In the closing words of his essay, "This world is white no longer, and it will never be white again" (129).

Baldwin's writing resonates with that of other black writers at this moment. Frantz Fanon's *Black Skin, White Masks* (1952), published a year earlier, articulates similar conjunctions among blackness, monstrosity, and visibility. Fanon wrote *Black Skin, White Masks* in response to the racism that he endured while training as a doctor in France, en route to his career as psychiatrist, writer, intellectual, and activist in anticolonial struggles. Like Baldwin, Fanon articulates a critique of European antiblack racism from a position of the black man violated by the scrutiny of others in a white wintry environment: "My body was given back to me sprawled out, distorted, recolored, clad in mourning on that white winter day." Like Baldwin, Fanon echoes the Frankenstein monster in describing this experience. His body is fragmented and monstrous and his desire for connection rebuffed: "While I was forgetting, forgiving, and wanting only to love, my message was flung back in my face like a slap. The white world, the only honorable one, barred me from all participation." More than Baldwin, however, Fanon turns toward a language of violent protest, echoing the monster's revenge: "They would see, then! I had warned them, anyway. . . . I had incisors to test. I was sure they were strong. . . . I resolved . . . to assert myself as a BLACK MAN. Since the other hesitated to recognize me, there remained only one solution: to make myself known."[95] Both Baldwin and Fanon work with the narrative template of *Frankenstein,* but Fanon rewrites the figures of monster and monster-maker as characters in a changing narrative of race relations that will result in the potential overthrow—as well as the global exhaustion—of wintry whiteness.[96]

Fifteen years later, the violent possibilities of the black soul on white ice emerged within African American culture from Eldridge Cleaver, Black Panther minister of information and a leader of the Black Power movement. *Soul on Ice* (1968) is the collection of nonfiction essays he wrote while serving time in a California prison, "on ice." In this volume, Cleaver echoes the terms of the Frankenstein story, beginning in the opening essay, which outlines the symbolic monstrosity through which he was defined by white people. As he remembers, his growing fury at racism became focused on white women, whose ostensible untouchability had historically been the alibi for the lynching of black men: "I flew into a rage at myself, at America, at white women, at the history that had placed those tensions of lust and desire in my chest."[97] In response, he raped white women: "Rape was an insurrectionary act. It delighted me that I was defying and trampling upon the white man's law . . . and that I was defiling his women. . . . I felt I was getting revenge" (14). Cleaver goes on to assert that he has now repudiated rape, and elsewhere he underscored that repudiation.[98] Yet the bulk of *Soul on Ice* is continuous with this opening essay in its central argument: the need for black men to undo their position of symbolic castration. Cleaver's ongoing lament is that "I, the Black Eunuch, divested of my Balls, walked the earth with my mind locked in Cold Storage" (209)—another image of a soul on ice—but now "I have Returned from the dead" (205). The goal of this reanimation is to reclaim black masculinity by any means necessary, including violence. In the future, he declares, "We shall have our manhood. We shall have it or the earth will be leveled by our attempts to gain it" (61).

The figure of the Frankenstein monster shadows Cleaver's self-representation as a man whose sexual desire was created in him by others, who has been reanimated from the dead and reunited with his severed body parts, and who now plans to level the earth in revenge. This narrative is that of *Frankenstein,* as at least two critics have noted in passing. David L. Dudley suggests that "Cleaver, like Mary Shelley . . . shows what happens when a person is not allowed to be self-created. . . . like the monster who kills Frankenstein's wife, the black man also . . . rises to claim the forbidden fruit."[99] Michele Wallace locates the resemblance to *Frankenstein* not in the white man's power but in his impotence: "The white man's culture rendered the white [man] impotent, but the black man a super stud. . . . the white man was a victim of his own Frankenstein monster."[100] Dudley and Wallace briefly cite *Frankenstein* as a fictional analogy for Cleaver, but we could see the Frankenstein story more fundamentally as an organizing template for his position. In *Soul on Ice*, a black man's revolutionary violence is the consequence of a racist society that has already created him as a monster, and his sexual violence is his most directed revenge against white men whose wives symbolize both their authority and their vulnerability.

Like Baldwin, then, Cleaver implicitly echoes *Frankenstein* in condemning a racist world of icy whiteness that turns black men into monsters. Unlike Baldwin, Cleaver focuses on the monster's violence, a difference that partly reflects the perceived political contrast between the militant Cleaver and the more moderate Baldwin.[101] The difference between them is equally over questions of sexuality. In *Soul on Ice*, Cleaver viciously excoriates Baldwin for his "grueling, agonizing, total hatred of the blacks, particularly of himself, and the most shameful, fanatical, fawning, sycophantic love of the whites" (94). His attack is fueled by homophobia— "Homosexuality is a sickness, just as are baby-rape or wanting to become the head of General Motors" (110)—and, in particular, by his horror of black men with white male lovers. For Cleaver, interracial homosexuality means black men being penetrated anally by white men, and it is both metaphor for and evidence of black men's self-hatred: "The cross [Negro homosexuals] have to bear is that, already bending over and touching their toes for the white man, the fruit of their miscegenation is not the little half-white offspring of their dreams but an increase in the unwinding of their nerves" (102). It is this vision of black gay men creating "little half-white offspring," as much as the image of white men turning black men into rapists, that is Cleaver's deepest nightmare of monster-making.

The sexual politics of this homophobic vision are at once consistent with those of Cleaver's contemporaries and continuous with one strand of *Frankenstein*. Cleaver's homophobia extends that of writers like Amiri Baraka, whose 1965 essay (as Leroi Jones) entitled "American Sexual Reference: Black Male" begins, "Most American white men are trained to be fags."[102] *Soul on Ice* also complements the essay that Cleaver claims as one of his models, Norman Mailer's "The White Negro" (1957), which outlined the white "hipster" obsession with black men. To Mailer's account of the white man's interest in the black man, Cleaver adds a condemnation of the black man's desire for the white man. For Cleaver as for Mailer and

Jones, American race relations operate along a male continuum of both homoerotic pursuit and homosexual panic.

This is the same continuum, with different emphases, that organizes Shelley's *Frankenstein* and the Edison *Frankenstein*. The Whale films offer the most sympathetic version of this continuum; *Soul on Ice*, the most homophobic. What Shelley traces as the monster's pursuit of his maker reappears, in Cleaver, as the black man's self-hating pursuit of a white lover. Yet Cleaver's is not the only possible update of *Frankenstein*: Baldwin sees American race relations from an equally homosocial but far less homophobic perspective. "One might," he writes in an essay entitled "History as Nightmare," "over-simplify our racial heritage sufficiently to observe . . . that its essentials would seem to be contained in the tableau of a black and white man facing each other and that the root of our trouble is between their legs."[103] This tableau is not, for Baldwin, disabling: "Stranger in the Village" does not discuss sexuality, but Baldwin was in the Swiss village of Loèche-les-Bains because his white lover, Lucien Happersberger, brought him there from Paris to help him recover from a severe depression.[104] Their relationship was what made possible Baldwin's presence in this setting and, hence, "Stranger in the Village"; it is the absent but structuring center for the essay as a whole. Baldwin, like Cleaver, situates his account of American race relations on a homosocial continuum, but he, like Whale, moves toward expanding rather than condemning the erotic possibilities of the homosocial. In their contrasting versions of *Frankenstein* in black America, Cleaver ends up with more monsters, whereas Baldwin looks toward a world with less. Making their way through icy landscapes, Cleaver aims to freeze the gothic, and Baldwin aims to melt it.

VI.

For another African American commentator, the figure of a black Frankenstein monster was the explicit foundation for political comedy. Writer, activist, and comedian Dick Gregory was born in 1932 in St. Louis, grew up in poverty, became a track star in high school and college, and got his major break as a stand-up comedian in 1961, when he was invited to perform at Hugh Hefner's Playboy Club in Chicago. There, he was a success before a conservative white Southern audience of frozen-food executives: another symbolic version of a black soul on white ice. Within months, he had become a national celebrity, and soon after, he became heavily involved in the civil rights movement, participating in rallies, marches, protests, and other political initiatives throughout the decade. He remains politically active; in more recent years, his interests have turned to health and diet initiatives. He has made many concert recordings and written or co-written more than a dozen books, including essays, histories, and three autobiographies.

In Gregory's work of the 1960s and 1970s, *Frankenstein* is a surprisingly dominant theme. He explicitly names and develops a parable of a black Frankenstein monster in at least half a dozen works of autobiography, essays, and performance. These works cross genres, but they return insistently to questions of visuality, both in the visual presence of Gregory on stage and in his reliance, in his writing, on cinematic versions of *Frankenstein*. Throughout them, he uses the monster both as an organizing framework for a sustained critique of white America and as an intimate symbol through which to narrate his own coming of age. Working with the Whale films, Gregory makes explicit their racial implications, including their significance for his own persona; like Paul Laurence Dunbar, Gregory signifies both on and as the Frankenstein monster. In so doing, he moves the Frankenstein story from Europe to America via Africa and Vietnam, from cinematic image to stand-up theatrical performance, and from gothic horror to black comedy. His version of the black Frankenstein metaphor fully exploits both its comic and political potential—although Gregory, as we will see, intentionally turns from the metaphor as well, and in so doing suggests its limitations.

We can situate Gregory's usof the Frankenstein story on a continuum of strategies of reappropriation that he began to develop from the start of his career. As a black comedian working in front of white audiences in the early 1960s, Gregory developed what Mel Watkins characterizes as "a stand-up persona that cast him as a patient, self-assured ironist, capable of dispensing witticisms about racial relationships with cool detachment."[105] To construct this persona of "cool detachment," Gregory often parodied existing images. For example, in a photograph in his first book, *From the Back of the Bus* (1962), he is costumed as a black Uncle Sam, sitting coolly atop the United States section of a globe, smoking, and gazing at the camera.[106] Similarly, when he ran for president in 1968 on the Peace and Freedom Party ticket, he made a campaign flyer in the form of a facsimile of the dollar bill, with his own face in place of George Washington's. The text on this facsimile parodied the original: "This note is legal

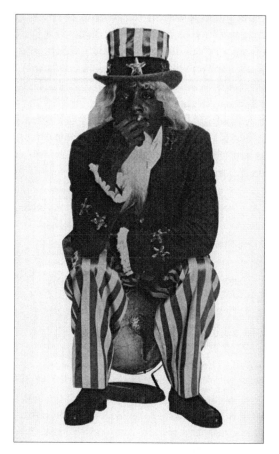

Jerry Yulsman, photograph of Dick Gregory
from *From the Back of the Bus,* by Dick Gregory.
Photograph by Jerry Yulsman, copyright © 1962,
renewed © 1990 by Dick Gregory Enterprises,
Inc. Used by permission of Dutton, a division of
Penguin Group (USA) Inc.

tender for all debts, public and private" became "Your vote is legal, sacred
and private."[107] Gregory also parodied entire genres. In his 1971 work of
revisionist American history, *Dick Gregory's Political Primer,* each chapter discusses a topic seriously but ends with a parodic section of "Review
Questions and Further Assignments." A chapter on political parties, for

example, ends with the assignment, "In an essay of five words or less, state clearly the differences between the Democratic and Republican Parties today."[108] Like Gregory's self-costuming as Uncle Sam and George Washington, this parody revised an existing form in a way that turned its very rigidity into a source of political critique.

More volatile were Gregory's reappropriations of the word "nigger." *Nigger* was the title of his first autobiography, published in 1964. In the book, he describes his need, early in his comedy career, to generate a strategy for dealing with this word when it was shouted at him by white audiences. He practiced with his wife, Lilian:

> I used to make Lilian call me a nigger over the dinner table, and I'd practice the fast comeback. Somehow, I couldn't get it right. I'd always come back with something a little bitter, a little evil.
>
> "Nigger."
>
> "Maybe you'd feel more like a man if you lived down South and had a toilet with your name on it."
>
> "No, Greg, that's not right at all."
>
> . . .
>
> "Hey, Lil."
>
> "Yes, Greg."
>
> "What would you do if from here on in I started referring to you as bitch?"
>
> She jumped out of the chair. "I would simply ignore you."
>
> I fell off the couch and started laughing so hard that old stomach of mine nearly burst. That was it. The quick, sophisticated answer. Cool. No bitterness. The audience would never know I was mad and mean inside.[109]

This story of origins begins with Gregory's frustration that he is exposing his bitterness and ends with his satisfaction that he can conceal being "mad and mean inside." The "quick, sophisticated" answer is the response of "black comedy," whose humor is inseparable from fury against racism. Gregory's account of this moment grants authority to his wife, first when she performs the role of racist audience member and then when he asks her what she would do. The parallel that this question implies between "bitch" and "nigger" acknowledges the harm inflicted by misogyny, and her answer establishes her authority as the source of his blackly comic "cool."

Building from this story of origins in *Nigger*, Gregory subsequently developed several uses of the word. The next time he was called "nigger" while performing, Gregory recalls, he said first, "You hear what that guy just called me. Roy Rogers' horse. He called me Trigger" (134). After this deliberate mishearing, he advanced his main strategy of reversal: "You know, my contract reads that every time I hear that word, I get fifty dollars more a night. I'm only making ten dollars a night, and I'd like to put the owner out of business. Will everybody in the room please stand up and yell nigger?" (135). This strategy disarmed racism by seeming to invite it, and the conceit of profiting from the word "nigger" established his authority over the entire exchange.

Gregory repeated this strategy by using "nigger" as the title of his autobiography, as he explained in a prefatory page: "Dear Momma—Wherever you are, if ever you hear the word 'nigger' again, remember that they are advertising my book." As with the anecdote about his wife, this comment positions a female interlocutor at the center of a strategy of reappropriation; here Gregory marshals the pathos implied in the image of a mother hearing the word "nigger" and reverses it. More than in the stand-up comedy routine, the use of "nigger" as a stand-alone book title challenged liberal white audiences, who would presumably have to say the word to booksellers in order to request the book.[110] Gregory himself later summarized his strategy succinctly: "I used that word so that White folks couldn't find power in it."[111]

Like the writing of Paul Laurence Dunbar, Gregory's reappropriations had multiracial origins in American culture. "Titling my book *Nigger*," he remembered, "meant I was taking it back from White folks. Mark Twain threw it up in the air and I grabbed it."[112] Gregory later named Twain, Lenny Bruce, and Richard Pryor as the three geniuses of comedy, and his approach to the word "nigger" was not dissimilar to that of Bruce. In one of Bruce's most famous routines, for example, he commented that "the word's suppression gives it the power, the violence, the viciousness. If President Kennedy got on television and said, 'Tonight I'd like to introduce the niggers in my cabinet,' and he yelled 'niggerniggerniggernig-gerniggerniggernigger' at every nigger he saw . . . till nigger didn't mean anything any more, till nigger lost its meaning—you'd never make any four-year-old nigger cry when he came home from school."[113] At the same time, Gregory's strategies had a specifically African American cultural history. Like his parodic self-costuming as Uncle Sam and George Washington, Gregory's reuse of the term "nigger" drew from the black signifying tradition. Paul Laurence Dunbar, I have argued, signified on received racist images in ways so subtle that they were often barely distinguishable from the images themselves. Gregory, by contrast, signified overtly to make a direct political intervention, one that used black comedy as both sensibility and theme. Gregory's use of the Frankenstein story is similar to his other signifying practices, but with a crucial difference: the Frankenstein story was already far more congenial for reappropriation than the toxic word "nigger."

Gregory's signifying on *Frankenstein* begins in the 1964 *Nigger*. Early in the autobiography, he describes going to see *Frankenstein* at the movies when he was a child in St. Louis: "We used to root for Frankenstein, sat there and yelled, 'Get him, Frankie baby' " (39). This memory of watching "Frankenstein"—presumably, one of the Whale films—positions the monster as both a site of psychic identification for the young black child and a source for immediate action; Gregory's shouts, in turn, both confirm the sympathy for the monster implicit in the Whale films and incorporate "Frankie baby" as an ally into his world. In the segregated theaters of 1940s St. Louis, his action counters both the racist on-screen construction of heroes and monsters and the racist ordering of theatrical space.[114]

In addition to this direct citation of *Frankenstein*, Gregory uses the metaphor of monstrosity to structure his self-representation throughout *Nigger*. When he competed in high-school track meets, he remembers, "I'd stand up real slow, and feel this thing start to take me over, this monster that started at my toes like hot water flowing upward through a cold body. . . . [Then] I knew I could crush the world" (56). When Gregory began to work as a comedian, he "hooked up with the monster again" (100): "Every time I stood on that stage I felt the monster seep right up me, and I was funny and every show was a masterpiece" (127). In the book's last quarter, the monster propels him toward involvement in the civil rights movement: when he debates whether to participate in a dangerous voter-registration campaign in Mississippi, "the race was for survival and the monster said go" (163). White journalist Robert Lipsyte, Gregory's collaborator on the autobiography, defined Gregory's "monster" as a symbol for "ego and ambition. Every man has a monster . . . but his drove him harder than most men's."[115] Gregory later confirmed Lipsyte's description: "I guess Bob was right. The life blood of the monster inside me was adrenaline, which filled my veins when there was a race to win, an audience to turn on, a civil rights struggle to engage in."[116]

Gregory ends *Nigger* with an extended metaphor of the civil rights movement as a monster:

> [The monster] wants some respect and dignity, and it wants freedom. It's willing to die for freedom.
>
> It's getting stronger every day. . . .
>
> It's not just a Negro monster. . . .
>
> . . . I saw it in New York where we marched against school segregation. . . .
>
> I saw the monster in Mississippi where we marched for voter registration. . . .
>
> I saw it in San Francisco where white doctors and lawyers marched on the lines with us. . . .
>
> . . . And now we're getting ready to change a system, a system where a white man can destroy a black man with a single word. Nigger.
>
> When we're through, Momma, there won't be any niggers any more.
> (208–9)

In this passage, Gregory recasts the monster from an individual metaphor into a collective symbol of the unstoppable force of the civil rights movement. The conclusion returns to both the figure of Gregory's mother and the word "nigger," establishing an interplay between two forms of signifying: his reappropriation of "nigger," which he aims to obliterate, and his recasting of "monster," which he aims to transforms into a symbol of collective struggle. *Frankenstein* is not named directly here, but the monster "getting ready to change a system" is continuous with the "Frankie baby" for whom the young Gregory cheered in the movie theater. Interpreting *Frankenstein* through racial frameworks, *Nigger* also understands racial struggle—Gregory's own and that of the nation—through the language of monstrosity.

Directly infusing the themes of *Nigger*, the Frankenstein story also provides a more indirect frame for the book's authorship. Gregory is not identified as the sole author of any of his works. All are "edited by" or "with" someone else, and *Nigger*'s byline was "Dick Gregory with Robert Lipsyte." In his review of the book, Nat Hentoff explained that it "was actually taped and put into form by Robert Lipsyte, but the voice is unmistakably Gregory's throughout."[117] This description is hierarchical: a black man has been "put into form" by a white one, as in the slave narrative.

Newsweek's hostile reviewer described the book as "Dick Gregory's *Nigger* (written with the shadowy assistance of *New York Times* man Robert Lipsyte)."[118] The "*New York Times* man" is relegated to parentheses but paradoxically appears all the more prominent, as the "shadowy" white figure who stands behind the black man's story.

Yet the authorial relationship between Gregory and Lipsyte was complex. As Albert Stone has analyzed, numerous African American autobiographies of the era were collaboratively authored, including those of Malcolm X and Alex Haley, and they involved a range of authorial hierarchies.[119] In the case of Gregory and Lipsyte, the hierarchy also operated in Gregory's favor: in the emerging genre of the ghostwritten celebrity autobiography, the unknown ghostwriter was ruled by his more famous subject. In a profile of Gregory for *Esquire*, Lipsyte remembered that he went into the project "hardly interested in drowning my own ego for ghosthood."[120] Although Lipsyte's profile is admiring, it also details Gregory's control over the interviewing process, and it ends with Gregory outwitting another white interlocutor, television host Mike Douglas. The complexity of the relationship between Gregory and Lipsyte is confirmed in more recent descriptions that each has given of the book. In his own memoir, Lipsyte remembers Gregory as "Dick Gregory, whose autobiography, *Nigger*, I eventually did write," a description that suggests he was the book's sole author. Conversely, Gregory remembers of *Nigger* that "I just dumped my head in a tape recorder," a description that displaces Lipsyte entirely.[121] The authorial interplay between Gregory, the self-described "monster," and Lipsyte, the man who puts him "into form," suggests a relationship of narrators not unlike that modeled by Victor and the monster in *Frankenstein*. As in *Frankenstein*, the monster's maker relays the voice of the monster to his audience, but the monster's narration also emerges distinctly. As the autobiography of a "monster," *Nigger* is not unmediated by its white interlocutor, but it is not contained by him either. The book revises the hierarchies of authorial voice inherited from the slave narrative and refracted through *Frankenstein*.[122]

Gregory expanded the Frankenstein story into an explicit political allegory a few years later, in *The Shadow That Scares Me*, a 1968 collection of "impious sermons" edited by James R. McGraw. In a section called "Dreaming in a Movie," Gregory outlines the importance of the movie theater for black audiences: "The movie theater is the only place the ghetto brother has ever had the American white man to himself for a little while without the cop looking down his back. The noise, the hooting, and the laughing in the wrong places are a protest against mental abuse."[123] This account of spectatorship as political resistance is preamble to a meditation on watching *Frankenstein* as a child, an experience he now remembers differently:

> I remember coming home from the movie theater one day in tears. I had just seen *Frankenstein*. My momma asked me what was wrong. Still crying, I told Momma, "I just saw *Frankenstein* and the monster didn't scare me." Momma couldn't explain it and I couldn't understand it. I was afraid I wasn't normal. But now that I look back, I realize why I wasn't frightened. Somehow I unconsciously realized that the Frankenstein monster was chasing what was chasing me. Here was a monster, created by a white man, turning upon his creator. The horror movie was merely a parable of life in the ghetto. The monstrous life of the ghetto has been created by the white man. Only now in the city of chaos are we seeing the monster created by oppression turn upon his creator.[124]

This is a more sustained account than the earlier description of cheering for "Frankie baby." In her study of British moviegoers, Annette Kuhn has shown that adults' memories of watching horror movies as children are distinguished by their initial bodily responses to the film; these responses anchor unusually vivid anecdotes of film spectatorship.[125] Here, Gregory's memory of watching Karloff is founded on a bodily response, not of screaming and shaking—the more usual responses to terror—but of tears. This is an account of horror that fails to register as horror; Gregory's fear is that he is not afraid enough.

By beginning his anecdote in this more abject way, Gregory can emphasize its epiphanic turn to parable, when he realizes that "the Frankenstein monster was chasing what was chasing me." Gregory's "parable of life in the ghetto" neatly maps the Frankenstein story of monstrosity and revolt onto U.S. race relations. In contrast to the 1964 *Nigger*, which celebrates the nonviolence of the civil rights movement, here he focuses on the "city of chaos," the violent urban uprisings in Watts, Detroit, Newark, and elsewhere in the 1960s. A lifelong pacifist, Gregory was injured while trying to calm rioters in Watts, an act that Eldridge Cleaver condemned in *Soul on Ice* as "an Uncle Tom cool-out."[126] Here, he uses the memory of watching *Frankenstein* to generate an explanatory parable for—but not an endorsement of—the origin of contemporary black violence.

In 1971, Gregory expanded this parable in his revisionist history, *No*

More Lies: The Myth and the Reality of American History. The book's last chapter features a section called "Horror Movies," which is another extended commentary on *Frankenstein* films. In this version, Gregory leaves behind his childhood experience and moves wholly into political allegory. In the process, he alters the story of Frankenstein significantly:

> The old *Frankenstein* movies are parables of America's destruction. . . .
>
> . . . America is the world's mad doctor. The mad doctor paid people to sail to Africa, dig up the bodies of black folks from their native soil, steal them, and bring them back to him. The mad doctor put them in chains and made them do his bidding. He made black folks his monster, trained and controlled to do his dirty work for him..
>
> . . . America has become a mad scientist's laboratory. The monster must act on his own. The monster has turned and cannot be expected to be the same again.[127]

Gregory here adds to the Frankenstein story a plot in which the doctor continues to control the monster, as his servant, after he brings him to life. This change strengthens the political parable, since it provides an account of the continuation of racial oppression rather than just its origin. This version also resituates the Frankenstein story in a global frame, with America as "the world's mad doctor." *No More Lies* elsewhere includes a critique of the Vietnam War: "Can white America really be insane enough to believe that black soldiers can be . . . [shipped] to Vietnam with orders to kill foreigners to liberate other foreigners, without realizing that those same black soldiers will return home to apply their instruction to liberate their own parents?"[128] Gregory's Frankenstein parable is one answer to this question, since it prophesies the rebellion of the black soldier against his symbolic white parents and in support of his literal black ones. This is the Frankenstein monster situated in a transpacific circuit with Vietnam, as well as a transatlantic one with Africa. The monster now stands at the center of an apocalyptic vision of imperial international violence as well as internecine civil war.

This image of the Vietnam War resembles the critique of the war that emerged implicitly in *Blackenstein* the next year, suggesting the congruence between a black artist reconfiguring *Frankenstein* for largely white audiences and a white filmmaker reconfiguring *Frankenstein* for largely black audiences. The relation of *Blackenstein* to *No More Lies* is less that of a coopted white text versus an authentic black one than that of related voices in a culture widely but unevenly influenced by antiracist and anti-war movements. Gregory's 1971 *Frankenstein* also echoes the more sustained language of violent reawakening in Black Power; as in Eldridge Cleaver's *Soul on Ice*, Gregory's monster is "already dead to begin with." Yet Gregory's account diverges from *Blackenstein* and *Soul on Ice*, not only in his antipathy to violence but also in his gender politics. Gregory got his start from Hugh Hefner, and his version of the Frankenstein story still works with male doctors and male monsters; his model of a resistant moviegoer remains that of the "ghetto brother." But he also begins to dislodge the exclusionary male focus of the Frankenstein story. His story of watching *Frankenstein* in "Dreaming at the Movies" features his mother, and his story of revising "nigger" highlights his wife; as the partner to a self-described "monster," Lilian functions, supportively, as Gregory's bride of Frankenstein. *No More Lies* goes further in its approach to women. The book devotes a section to the new women's liberation movement, or what he describes on the dedication page as "Women's Liberation, the movement of the 1970s which will make all Americans proud to call the Statue of Liberty their momma." The comedy of making the Statue of Liberty a maternal landmark does not lessen the landmark event—still unusual —of a male author dedicating a book to feminism.

Two live recordings of Gregory's stage performances from this period suggest his continued experiment with the parable of a black Frankenstein monster. A minimalist version of the parable emerges from the live recording of a 1970 performance that he gave at Bronx Community College, entitled *Dick Gregory's Frankenstein*. In this recording, Gregory makes no mention of the Frankenstein story; the audience was presumably meant to make its own connection between the title "Frankenstein" and the content of this material—in effect, to build anew the metaphor of the black man as Frankenstein monster.[129] This least visible of Frankenstein references was also, conversely, its most visible: the inside art for the double-sized album cover, stretching across both panels, is an image of a Frankenstein monster, with the square head, bolted neck, and green skin of Boris Karloff, dressed in an American flag and emerging through the threshold of a jail cell. Like Gregory's earlier self-costuming as Uncle Sam, this image—by well-known artist and designer Milton Glaser—re-appropriates American iconography, but with an additional layer of metaphor. The Uncle Sam photograph situated the black man as quintessential American; the album cover suggests both that the Frankenstein monster is an iconic American and that the monster is an iconic black man. Leaving

Milton Glaser's cover art for the album *Dick Greg-ory's Frankenstein*, 1971. Reprinted by permission.

a jail cell, free at last, this Frankenstein monster is flagged as quintessen-tially African American.

By contrast, Gregory delivered a maximalist version of his interest in *Frankenstein* in the concert performance he gave the next year at Kent State University, in the wake of the Ohio National Guard fatal shooting of antiwar student protesters there. In this recording, the performance ends with a five-minute version of the Frankenstein parable. He begins with a discussion of how children respond to the monster as a hero when they see *Frankenstein* on film and then moves to his interpretation of the film:

> Frankenstein was in the grave and Bela Lugosi . . . went and got him out, and got to hooking all kind of strange stuff to him, and no doubt created a monster. . . . [And] every time I'd see Frankie I get scared, 'cause I didn't have the wisdom to watch that movie right. You know who Frankenstein was scared of? Bela Lugosi! . . .
>
> Every time Frankie went out and killed one of them ladies, he wasn't killing for himself—that was the mad scientist wanted her. I'm so busy being hung up on Frankenstein, I let Bela Lugosi slip by.[130]

Gregory here calls the doctor "Bela Lugosi," the actor known for playing Dracula in the 1931 film contemporary with Whale's *Frankenstein* and in numerous other films.[131] This is presumably an error on Gregory's part, but it is a productive error. Frankenstein and vampire imagery combine in the black Frankenstein tradition at least as far back as Frederick Douglass's condemnations of parasitic slaveowners, which functioned effectively to condemn ongoing oppression. Indeed, Dracula is a better symbol than Dr. Frankenstein of a figure who continually coerces others "to do his dirty work." Conflating the Dracula and Frankenstein stories also helps Gregory to explain the monster's misogynist violence. This violence is now the result of white monstrosity, since Frankie "wasn't killing [ladies] for himself—that was the mad scientist wanted her." In Gregory's inadvertent amalgamation of two founding figures of gothic horror, the bloodsucker and the monster-maker conjoin as models for how white racism sustains itself: not only by creating black monsters but also by continuing to suck them dry.

Accordingly, the monster who turns against his maker is also a victim who refuses to be drained. Gregory's parable turns to resistance:

> One day [Lugosi] overshot Frankie and Frankie backed up on him. . . . Frankie reached for him and he said, "Be nonviolent, boy," and he said "OK," and he hugged him to death. And when he got to squeezing Bela Lugosi, he was trying to get away and he kicked over the lamp and the lab caught on fire. And that was the end. The lab burnt down, Bela Lugosi burn up, Frankie burn up. . . .

> . . . Well, one day in the early 1960s he overshot us. And we backed up
> on him on the streets, and now most young folks is backing up on him.
> And I say, if the man's not very careful, he might sit here and watch his
> whole lab burn.[132]

Gregory tells the story of the monster "overshot" into resistance twice. It is
first a joke about nonviolence, in which the monster parodies his maker's
racist embrace of nonviolence—"Be nonviolent, boy"—by embracing him
to death. The narration of past revolt then becomes an account of contemporary uprising, with "most young folks . . . backing up" on his maker,
and an apocalyptic portent of further destruction. As recorded, this routine prompts huge applause. In the politically raw setting of Kent State in
1971, the parable of a black Frankenstein monster may not yet burn up the
lab of America, but it does bring down the house.

Taken together, then, these five versions of the Frankenstein story from
Nigger through Kent State show the range of Gregory's strategies of reappropriation. Anchored in his own memories of the Whale films, his parables of a black Frankenstein monster encompass the civil rights movement, black urban uprising, and protests against the Vietnam War, and
they indirectly pay tribute to the emergence of contemporary feminism.
Over time, Gregory adapts the parable to foreground Frankenstein's continued oppression of the monster, thereby conjoining the narratives of
Frankenstein and Dracula. His signifying practices stress the theme of visibility in several senses. These are overt accounts of a black Frankenstein
monster, drawn from the imagery of film and reproduced in the visual
medium of stand-up comedy. Like Baldwin under surveillance in an icy
all-white town, Gregory developed his persona in response to white scrutiny, by audiences whom he did not want to leave cold. His result, in performance and then in writing and recording, was the black comedy of
"Frankie baby": not a soul on ice but a cool monster for a comedian of
cool.

As much as he exploits the figure of a black Frankenstein monster, however, Gregory finally chooses to leave the monster behind. In his second
autobiography, *Up from Nigger* (1976), the last chapter is, once again, a
long meditation on the Frankenstein story as a racial parable. "The social
and political system in the United States," writes Gregory in his signature
formulation, "is Dr. Frankenstein, and it has created monsters in slums,
ghettos, and other pockets of poverty all over this land. Like Dr. Frankenstein, the system creates the living dead."[133] But the extended metaphor

of "the monster inside me" that structured his first autobiography is gone. This is why:

> I used to think my monster was a good thing. It gave me the drive to climb to the top. But now I realize that the monster was created within me by an oppressive and unjust social and political system. . . .
>
> As I came to understand my monster's creator better, the monster itself began to disappear. . . .
>
> When I was driven by the monster, I struggled against a system which called me "nigger." . . . [Now I have] moved "up from nigger." The system no longer controls my actions or my reactions. Having ridden myself of the monster, I now see personal witness and human service as providing all the drive I ever needed.[134]

This account rejects the monster as a metaphor for Gregory's own "drive" because the monster has been "created" within him by an "oppressive and unjust political system"; instead, Gregory embraces "personal witness and human service." As in his first autobiography, Gregory charts a connection between the words "nigger" and "monster," but in 1964 he had aimed to use the latter to eradicate the former. In 1976, having moved "up from nigger," he moves up from "monster" as well. For Gregory, this project of ridding himself of the monster coincided with his turn in the 1970s toward diet and health initiatives. These included extended fasts, such as one "to call attention to the narcotics problem in America. . . . I hoped my fast would help people to recognize the poisons infecting the national body, to see the need for cleansing the nation of impurities."[135] In light of Gregory's waning interest in *Frankenstein*, we could see such impulses as alternative ways to purify the monstrous body of the nation. A recent biographical sketch of Gregory is aptly entitled "Curing the Body Politic." For Gregory, part of this cure was the elimination of *Frankenstein*.[136]

More generally, we could view his account of "outgrowing" the monster as a commentary on the limitations of the Frankenstein story as a parable of racial oppression. In *The Monster*, I suggested, Stephen Crane leaves the metaphor of a black Frankenstein monster behind because he has exhausted his aesthetic interest in it. Gregory's abandonment is for political rather than aesthetic reasons. The parable of a black Frankenstein monster provides Gregory with a powerful account of the origins of oppression; with slight adaptation, it dramatizes the continuation of oppression; and it offers an apocalyptic model of revolutionary rebellion against that oppression. It serves less well, however, as a framework for the post-revolutionary future, or as an account of black life lived apart from white oppression. Gregory's black Frankenstein stories stay locked within, even as they invert, a narrative that situates black creations in reactive relation to white creators. The most radical use of the figure of a black Frankenstein monster, his work seems to suggest, may inhere ultimately not in bringing him back to life in new ways but in killing him off for good.

Afterword

At the same moment that Dick Gregory was killing off the black Frankenstein monster, others were reanimating him anew. In 1977, for example, a comic book called *Black'nstein* featured a white Kentucky slaveowner, Colonel Victah Black'nstein, who builds a black monster-slave; conversely, a novel called *The Slave of Frankenstein* (1976) presented Victor Frankenstein's son as a white abolitionist who challenges an evil proslavery monster, just after John Brown's raid on Harper's Ferry in 1859.[1] At the same time, musician George Clinton and his band Parliament released *The Clones of Dr. Funkenstein* (1977), which signified very differently on the Frankenstein tradition, in its creation of a black doctor of funk. Clinton's costumes and makeup for Dr. Funkenstein were extravagant riffs on those in the Whale films, and his monster was "The disco fiend with the monster sound / The cool ghoul with the bump transplant."[2] In the era of the national bicentennial, some artists returned the black Frankenstein monster back to his earlier American ground of the antebellum South, but Dr. Funkenstein took him back to the future. Like Dick Gregory, George Clinton offered a Frankenstein monster who was a super-cool version of a soul on ice.

Of the numerous representations of black Frankenstein monsters that have emerged since, I end with a work of visual art from the early 1990s. *Study for Frankenstein #1* (1992) is a painting by Glenn Ligon, a visual artist who came to prominence in a period of intense interest in identity politics in American art. The work of Ligon, who is an African American gay man, was featured, for example, in two exhibitions at the Whitney Museum of American Art that were both praised and criticized for their overt focus on political themes: the 1993 Whitney Biennial and "Black Male: Representations of Black Masculinity in Contemporary Art" (1994). These exhibitions included many artists of color, and among other themes, their work responded to the longstanding depiction of black men as symbolic monsters and the corollary genealogy of representations depicting black men being punished for their perceived monstrosity. "American narratives of violence against blacks," as Elizabeth Alexander puts it, "are usually figured as male. The whipped male slave; the lynched man; Emmett Till; Rodney King: all of these are familiar and explicit in the popular imagination."[3] The story of Rodney King—a black man assaulted in 1991 by white policemen, whose subsequent acquittal by an all-white jury sparked urban uprising in Los Angeles—was one of many reminders of the continuing presence of this imagination. Indeed, the Whitney Biennial included the amateur videotape of the beating of King as part of the exhibition. Like the imagery of the townspeople mercilessly pursuing Boris Karloff, the videotape offered a narrative of monstrosity imagined, tracked, and punished en masse. The white jury who ratified this vision in their verdict and the black people who took to the streets in protest both testified, in different ways, to the violent real-life consequences of a world in which black men are still often envisioned as monsters.[4]

Questions of black monstrosity had, of course, been explored by visual artists before. For example, in the series of performances, photographs, drawings, advertisements, and other works that she entitled *The Mythic Being* (1972–75), Adrian Piper costumed herself as a man of color and explored, among other themes, the association of black masculinity with monstrosity; one poster, for example, was entitled *I Embody Everything You Most Hate and Fear*.[5] More recently, in her sexually graphic, deliberately grotesque racial scenarios, in which black and white people are depicted in the form of the paper cutout, Kara Walker has represented what might be called the silhouette of monstrosity.[6] Between Piper and Walker, the period of the early 1990s is notable for the extent to which, however briefly and controversially, the "mythic being" of black masculinity became the widespread focus of an art scene in which, as Phillip Brian Harper notes, "blacks in general and black men in particular are still considered anomalous in the sites of high-artistic production and exhibition alike."[7] In turning to Ligon's *Study for Frankenstein #1*, then, I end with a work that explicitly takes up the legacy of *Frankenstein* in a moment of heightened attention to visual representations by and of African American men.

Study for Frankenstein #1 is the work of an artist who has consistently explored black masculinity in a variety of media and styles. Ligon's contributions to the "Black Male" exhibition included paintings that retold sexually explicit jokes by Richard Pryor; in the 1993 Whitney Biennial, he exhibited *Notes on the Margin of "The Black Book,"* an installation commenting on Robert Mapplethorpe's homoerotic photographs of black men. His earlier works included paintings that reworked the form of nineteenth-century advertisements for runaway slaves and paintings that redrew twentieth-century coloring-book versions of Malcolm X. The artist remains best known for his text-based paintings, which take quotations from literary works and stencil them over and over on large canvases; the letters repeat with increasing blurriness. These works primarily cite first-person quotations by African American authors, including Zora Neale Hurston and Ralph Ellison, such as "I feel most colored when I am thrown against a sharp white background" (Hurston) and "I am an invisible man" (Ellison). A later series, quoting from James Baldwin's "Stranger in the Village," uses black paint, with coal dust, on a dark background.[8]

Study for Frankenstein #1 is one of Ligon's early text paintings, now in the collection of the Museum of Modern Art in New York. Its text consists of one sentence from Mary Shelley's *Frankenstein* stenciled in black on a white background: "Sometimes I wished to express my sensations in my own mode, but the uncouth and inarticulate sounds which broke from me frightened me into silence again." The sentence is repeated four times from the top of the painting to the bottom, with different line breaks each time and with increasing blurriness, until the words are barely legible at the bottom. The image is 31¾" × 16", oilstick on paper, with the oilstick thickly applied to create a raised, textured surface. Interpreted as part of a genealogy of black Frankenstein monsters, *Study for Frankenstein #1* is a work of great resonance. It extends the forms and themes of this genealogy, particularly in the intricate relation it posits between form and theme.[9]

To begin with, the inclusion of Mary Shelley in Ligon's oeuvre of text-based paintings alongside figures like Ellison, Hurston, and Baldwin confirms the genealogy of racially marked interpretations of *Frankenstein* that I have been tracing throughout this book. Ligon has used other quotations from white authors in his paintings, including one from the essay "White" by Richard Dyer and another from the play *The Blacks* by Jean Genet. But *Study for Frankenstein #1* seems to be his only use of a text by a white author that does not manifestly address racial themes. In choosing *Frankenstein*, he draws Shelley into the orbit of these authors, white and black, who write explicitly about race and, in so doing, confirms the racial theme implicit in *Frankenstein* itself.

The text that Ligon selects from *Frankenstein* inflects this theme in the direction of abjection. These words are taken from early in the monster's first-person story, when he has left the laboratory and awakens alone in the woods, "a poor, helpless, miserable wretch." Observing his environment, he remembers, "I was delighted when I first discovered that a pleasant sound, which often saluted my ears, proceeded from the throats of the little winged animals who had often intercepted the light from my eyes." But this happy discovery is followed by frustration, in the sentence immediately before Ligon's quotation: "Sometimes I tried to imitate the pleasant songs of the birds, but was unable."[10] The failed attempt to express "sensations in my own mode," then, follows a failed attempt even to imitate the songs of birds. The monster's potential expression of delight is arrested, repressed, and transformed into frightened silence.

This miniplot from *Frankenstein* aptly characterizes Ligon's work as a whole. "Throughout his career," Richard Meyer notes, "Ligon has investigated those moments when identity seems to slip or give way to its own erasure."[11] The title of Ligon's 1998 retrospective at the Philadelphia Institute of Contemporary Art, "Unbecoming," captures this concept of the erasure of identity; it also suggests someone whose appearance or behavior is perceived as "unbecoming" in the sense of unattractive. The quotation Ligon selects from *Frankenstein* highlights precisely these two notions of unbecoming—erasure and unattractiveness—as it moves from a desire for self-expression to the utterance of "uncouth sounds." In his version of the black Frankenstein theme—a theme emblematic of his work as a whole—a monster who tries to speak ends up frightening himself into silence.

This theme is enacted in several ways in the painting's form, beginning with its title. Like other instances of black Frankenstein metaphors, this image self-reflexively requires the viewer to construct the metaphor. As with Paul Laurence Dunbar's *The Sport of the Gods*, in which the word "Frankenstein" appears only as a chapter title, here the painting's title anchors the words to its source, naming a text that, presumably, few spectators will recognize without it.[12] The title further establishes a parallel between text and monster—akin to Mary Shelley's prefatory comment, "I bid my hideous progeny go forth and prosper"—in its implication that this is not a definitive Frankenstein but a "study for Frankenstein #1." The title suggests both a preliminary version ("study") of a finished work and an initial entry ("#1") in a longer series; in a further extension of the idea of the preliminary, Ligon has made *Study for Frankenstein #1 (Study #2)*.[13] *Study for Frankenstein #1*, like the monster, is a body under assembly from different versions. The racial component of the metaphor is implied in the

Study for Frankenstein #1, by Glenn Ligon. ©
Copyright 1992. Oilstick on paper, 30 ½" × 17"
(77.4 × 43.3 cm). Gift of The Bohen Foundation
(219.1992). The Museum of Modern Art, New
York, NY, U.S.A. Digital Image © copyright The
Museum of Modern Art/Licensed by SCALA/Art
Resources, NY.

authorial credit. This implication emerges less because the viewer who knows that Ligon is African American will assume that the "I" of the quotation is black and more because Ligon's other text-based paintings, and body of work as a whole, deal extensively with questions of race.

Anchored by the painting's title, the metaphor of the black Frankenstein monster is given literal and symbolic shape by its lettering. Ligon is interested in nineteenth-century forms of typography, as in his works that mimic the title pages of slave narratives and in his mock advertisements for runaway slaves; here, the archaic lettering of the stencils locates the viewer in the world of Shelley, whose monster, I have argued, himself refracts and contributes to representations of African American slaves.[14] As a pictorial representation of a literary monster—a "study for Frankenstein"—the lettering turns the idea of monstrosity as depicted in words into an image of words as visually monstrous. The words of the painting grow increasingly blurry, while the space around them grows ever more smudged. Thin pencil lines to guide the stencils are faintly visible beneath the words, but the oilstick exceeds these guidelines, as the Frankenstein monster himself exceeds an orderly corporeal frame. The blackness of the words, filling and overwhelming the white paper, suggests the psychological darkness—if not also the implicit racial blackness—of Ligon's version of Shelley's monster.

The texture and heft of the words also have thematic implications for the depiction of monstrosity. As the sentence repeats, the writing becomes legible less as words and more as individual letters, and the letters themselves are hard to discern. In Ligon's other text-based paintings, Thelma Golden notes, the artist provides "repeated phrases disintegrating into patches of pigment," a description that highlights dismemberment.[15] In this painting, the act of disintegration also effects a Frankensteinian process of reanimation, since the paint coalesces just enough to cohere into letters; a patchwork monster is created from "patches of pigment." Ligon has described how, in his earliest text paintings, "I spent a long time trying to get rid of all the smearing and messiness of the process of stenciling the text. Then I realized it was the most interesting thing about the paintings."[16] Here the generative "messiness" of stenciling extends vertically as well as horizontally. In the heft of the pigment, the Frankenstein monster, disembodied from actual figuration, seems to be materialized in black. He is raised from paper, if not from the dead, into the thickened height of the pigment itself.

The combination of increasing thickness in the letters and unchanged repetition in the sentence they spell out brings the work to a despairing end. For the repetition of this particular sentence deepens the failure its words signify; the speaker can only repeat that he cannot speak, in a frozen cycle that ends each time with the word "again." As the viewer reads from top to bottom, the increasing illegibility of the text—a rendering of inarticulate speech in disarticulated letters—conveys growing frustration. The painting ends midsentence and midword with the almost unreadable letters "se," splitting the word "sensations"; the phrase "express my se—" suggests that the truncated word could also be "self." Like the monster "lost in darkness" in the last line of Shelley's novel, the painting ends in a blur of black paint. In the intermingling of visual and oral registers that the quotation effects, it is as if the process of frightening the self out of speech, the painting's theme, is now formally complete.

Such questions of self-silencing are, in Ligon's work, sexual as well as racial. I have argued that twentieth-century versions of Frankenstein develop the homosocial connotations of Shelley's novel in a variety of ways, from the homosexual panic that organizes the Edison *Frankenstein* to the more affirmative queer sensibility of the James Whale films. The lineage of symbolically queer male monsters after those of Whale culminates in the film *Gods and Monsters* (dir. Bill Condon, 1998), which reimagines the last days of Whale's life in relation to the Frankenstein story. In this film— whose director, producer, screenwriter, and star are all gay men—Whale (Ian McKellen) becomes drawn to his gardener, Clay (Brendan Fraser), who resembles the monster. Meticulously re-creating scenes from *Bride of Frankenstein*, *Gods and Monsters* both confirms the queer resonances of the earlier film and uses the Frankenstein story to understand Whale's sexuality afresh.[17]

Like *Gods and Monsters*, *Study for Frankenstein #1* is a work of the 1990s by a gay artist that takes up the legacy of queerness in the Frankenstein story, but it more overtly conjoins race and sex. Since the early 1990s, a major element of Ligon's work has been his exploration of gay sexuality, including *A Feast of Scraps* (1994–98), a combination of gay pornographic images with snapshots of Ligon's family that "insert[s] questions of sexuality into the family photo album."[18] In other works, questions of sexuality are fraught with terror. For example, in *Twin* and *Colonial* (1995), installations of boys' bedrooms, Ligon stresses the potential gothic horror of gay coming-of-age by including photographs of the serial killer Jeffrey

Dahmer and of the young men of color whom Dahmer killed. In other works, Ligon claims his place in a genealogy of gay black artists, as in his series on Baldwin's "Stranger in the Village," which itself, I have argued, symbolically connotes the Frankenstein story. In this context, we could see Ligon's painting as another representation of a Frankenstein monster —himself a "feast of scraps"—situated at the intersection of gayness and blackness. With its focus on self-silencing, *Study for Frankenstein #1* signals the pain of struggling within a sexual closet and, outside the closet, of living in a homophobic world that equates gayness—as well as blackness —with monstrosity. The concluding letters of the painting suggests that this is an extremely difficult, if not impossible, space to occupy, producing a self that splits in two at the moment of its articulation.

The form of the painting shapes its representation of sexuality as well as race. "In the lower regions" of Ligon's text-based paintings, one critic observes, "the text is virtually illegible."[19] If we think of the painting as a portrait of the monster, the "lower regions" of the body could be its sexual zones, rendered illegible by their desires as well as their dark stenciling. The possibility of reading the painting as a body portrait is corroborated by its size; hung at eye level, the painting would extend to half a torso, its letters clotting into darkness around the genitals. But even if the "lower regions" of this painting do not have such precise bodily cognates, the painting's structural replacement of an embodied monster with repeating lines of words suggests a swerve away from sexuality. If sexuality, as Meyer has suggested, is most fully developed in Ligon's work through the medium of photography, then the text-based painting seems to work against that development.[20] In this case, a text-based painting does not simply avoid representing a body: by quoting from *Frankenstein*, Ligon invokes the image of a body at its most monstrous and then suppresses even that invocation through the painting's very form.

Yet although *Study for Frankenstein #1* is not photographic, it can nonetheless be interpreted as cinematic. Of his text-based paintings, Ligon has explained, "Making a painting, for me, is akin to making a film adaptation of a text: it's just one possible way out of many to responding to a given text."[21] This model of painting as film adaptation has particular significance here, since *Frankenstein* has such an extensive film tradition, and the most famous visual representation of the Frankenstein monster is that of Boris Karloff. In Ligon's painting, the words of the Frankenstein monster stand in the place of the image of Karloff. Their serial repetition echoes, but displaces, the cinematic forward movement of a strip of film passing through a projector. Here, the film stutters and blurs; it will never advance beyond this one instant. In Ligon's version of a black Frankenstein monster, then, the artist paradoxically creates the monster's voice through rendering his self-silence. Extending the monster metaphor to pictorial —and implicitly cinematic—representation, he paradoxically adds to the visual legacy of the monster by deciding not to represent him pictorially at all.

Yet Ligon's *Study for Frankenstein #1* also works against these conjoined narratives of self-silencing. In Shelley's *Frankenstein*, the period when the monster is learning to make "uncouth and inarticulate sounds" is followed by his discovery of the De Laceys and his learning of language. I have argued that his imitation of their speech forms the basis for the radical parodies that his body and behavior effect. In this sentence, his movement toward mimicry mimics his larger progression toward revenge; what follows in the novel are his rage and violence. For the viewer of the painting who has also read the novel, the spatial descent down the darkened space of the painting also evokes a literary movement forward through the novel's plot of rebellion. One critic has proposed that Ligon's techniques of repetition and darkening suggest "a build-up of anger or an accumulative deepening of thought."[22] These effects also describe the monster in Shelley's novel as he comes to rebel, with building anger and deepening thought, against his maker. The monster in Ligon's painting may be self-silenced, stopped in freeze-frame at a moment of abjection, but he is also, in Shelley's novel, about to embark on a violently powerful future.

Moreover, interpreted as an allegory of the painter's own relation to the art world, Ligon's use of *Frankenstein* provides him with some critical distance and authority. Ligon has protested "a certain misreading and territorialization around my work. Black artist, black authors, black paintings."[23] *Study for Frankenstein #1* preemptively guards against such a misreading of Ligon's work, not only because it draws from a white author rather than a black one but also because of its particularities of plot and voice. In a marketplace in which dealers, collectors, and critics have the power to "make" an artist—and in which such arbiters of value are still, primarily, white—*Frankenstein* provides a model of a creation who refuses to obey his creator. And in a context in which the "I" of a black painter is often assumed—by black as well as white viewers—to speak essential truths about blackness, *Frankenstein* offers a model of an "I" that is highly fractured and mediated. Within *Frankenstein*, the monster's narrative is retold by Victor, whose narrative is entered into through Walton; beyond *Frankenstein,* the monster's voice has been further mediated by adaptations and parodies. By identifying the source in the title, Ligon alerts viewers that this is not an unmediated expression of an African American "I," let alone a direct autobiographical utterance of the African American artist. Reaching back to Shelley's novel, Ligon inscribes an "I" without fixing that "I," as a literary first-person voice, as an image of the film monster, or as an autobiographical representation of Ligon himself.

If the painting refuses to unite the "I" of the "black painter," it also resists the assumptions that would attach to the idea of a "black painting." Ligon has recalled the period in which he emerged as an artist as one in which the art world was structured by disabling dichotomies: "If the work was engaged with politics, that became a way of marginalizing the work too: 'the work is political, it's not aesthetic or conceptual.'"[24] I have argued throughout this study that the metaphor of the black Frankenstein monster is insistently as much about aesthetic form as racial theme; the question of politics emerges from the conjunction of these terms, not from thematic concerns alone. In drawing from a work in which form, theme, and politics are so insistently intertwined, *Study for Frankenstein #1* preemptively protests against consideration as "only" a political painting—or conversely, entirely an aesthetic one. A decade after launching his text-based paintings, Ligon addressed this dichotomy in a different way, when he coined the term "post-black" to describe the newest African American artists, a generation "characterized by artists who were adamant about not being labeled as 'black' artists, though their work was steeped, in fact deeply interested, in redefining complex notions of blackness."[25] Although this term has been controversial, its coinage testifies to the intractability of the world in which the work of a painter who is black is assumed to be "political" rather than "aesthetic."

It is against this intractable world that the black Frankenstein metaphor, over nearly two centuries, has been shaped. Is there—and should there be —a world "post-Frankenstein"? Ligon's reanimation of the black Frankenstein monster testifies to the continuing vitality of this metaphor but also to the continuing need for the very category of monster metaphors. The idea of a black American Frankenstein monster remains an enduring topic for reinvention because the categories of blackness, nationality, and monstrosity remain so enduring, as well as so reciprocally defining. In a world not organized through nations and their mirror-images of monsters, there might be no need for American Frankenstein metaphors at all;

in a world not consistently devoted to demonizing blackness, there might be no need to reappropriate monstrosity. But in the meantime, the figure of the black monster—as American as Edgar Allan Poe and Nat Turner, Stephen Crane and Paul Laurence Dunbar, Dick Gregory and Glenn Ligon —at least begins to usher in the fall of the House of Frankenstein.

Notes

NOTES TO THE INTRODUCTION

1. Michael Moore, "We Finally Got Our Frankenstein . . . and He Was in a Spider Hole!" Michael Moore website, 14 December 2003, www.michaelmoore.com/words/message/index.php?messageDate=2003-12-14.

2. Carlos Fuentes, "The Invention of the Frankenstein Monster: Interview with Carlos Fuentes," originally published in *Freitag* 31, 23 July 2004, available in English at http://portland.indymedia.org/en/2004/07/293671.shtml.

3. Maureen Dowd, "White House of Horrors," *New York Times*, 28 October 2004, A29. There are many other explicit uses of Frankenstein imagery in contemporary political discourse; see, for example, Craig Unger, in *House of Bush, House of Saud: The Secret Relationship between the World's Two Most Powerful Dynasties* (New York: Scribner, 2004), who entitles a chapter "Another Frankenstein" and quotes former Pakistani prime minister Benazir Bhutto criticizing the first President Bush for his support of extremist groups: "You are creating a veritable Frankenstein" (111).

4. Chalmers Johnson, *Blowback: The Costs and Consequences of American Empire*, 2nd ed. (New York: Henry Holt, 2004), 9. This term has a longer history; see Patricia M. Thornton and Thomas F. Thornton, "Blowback," in *Collateral Language: A User's Guide to America's New War*, ed. John Collins and Ross Glover (New York: New York University Press, 2002), 27–38.

5. Louis Menand, "Faith, Hope, and Clarity," *New Yorker*, 16 September 2002, 98.

6. Michael Hardt and Antonio Negri, *Multitude: War and Democracy in the Age of Empire* (New York: Penguin, 2004), xviii, 12.

7. Ibid., 196.

8. On the origins of the nominal confusion over "Frankenstein," see Steven Earl Forry, *Hideous Progenies: Dramatizations of Frankenstein from Mary Shelley to the Present* (Philadelphia: University of Pennsylvania Press, 1990), 36–37.

9. Mary Shelley, *Frankenstein*, ed. J. Paul Hunter (New York: Norton, 1996), 173. For discussion of the different editions of the novel, see chapter 1.

10. On the use of Frankenstein imagery in discussions of reproductive technologies, see Jon Turney, *Frankenstein's Footsteps: Science, Genetics, and Popular*

Culture (New Haven, CT: Yale University Press, 1998); in discussions of cosmetic surgery, see Virginia L. Blum, *Flesh Wounds: The Culture of Cosmetic Surgery* (Berkeley: University of California Press, 2003), esp. chap. 4; and in discussions of cadavers, see Mary Roach, *Stiff: The Curious Lives of Human Cadavers* (New York: Norton, 2003), esp. 197. For a survey of recent examples of Frankenstein imagery, see Susan Tyler Hitchcock, *Frankenstein: A Cultural History* (New York: Norton, 2007), 264–322.

11. On "McFrankenstein," see Benjamin Weiser, "Your Honor, We Call Our Next Witness: McFrankenstein," *New York Times*, 26 January 2003, Week in Review section, 5. On "Frankenpine," see Eleanor Randolph, "The Cell Tower Blight: Text-Message Calder, ASAP," *New York Times*, 26 February 2005, A26. For commentary on recent permutations of the word, see William Safire, "On Language," *New York Times Magazine*, 13 August 2000, 23, reprinted as "Franken-: A Monstrous Prefix is Stalking Europe," in *Genetically Modified Foods: Debating Biotechnology*, ed. Michael Ruse and David Castle (Amherst, NY: Prometheus Books, 2002), 133–34.

12. For a description of the movement against "frankenfoods," see Bill Lambrecht, *Dinner at the New Gene Café: How Genetic Engineering Is Changing What We Eat, How We Live, and the Global Politics of Food* (New York: Thomas Dunne/St. Martin's, 2001), 232–36; for analysis of the concept, see Elaine L. Graham, *Representations of the Post/Human: Monsters, Aliens and Others in Popular Culture* (New Brunswick, NJ: Rutgers University Press, 2002), 13–14, 25–26.

13. Leon R. Kass, "The Wisdom of Repugnance," in Leon R. Kass and James Q. Wilson, *The Ethics of Human Cloning* (Washington, DC: American Enterprise Institute Press, 1998), 18; the essay was first published in the *New Republic* in 1997. For a critique of this essay, see Chris Mooney, "Irrationalist in Chief," *American Prospect*, 24 September 2001, 10–13. For a more sympathetic view of Kass, see Hitchcock, *Frankenstein*, 297–303.

14. Frederick Douglass, "Slavery and the Irrepressible Conflict" (1860), in *The Frederick Douglass Papers*, ed. John W. Blassingame et al. (New Haven, CT: Yale University Press, 1985), ser. 1, 3:370.

15. Dick Gregory, *The Shadow That Scares Me*, ed. James R. McGraw (New York: Pocket, 1968), 168.

16. The modern revival of scholarly interest in Frankenstein was initiated by U. C. Knoepflmacher and George Levine, eds., *The Endurance of Frankenstein: Essays on Mary Shelley's Novel* (Berkeley: University of California Press, 1979).

17. I expand here on Chris Baldick's definition that the "myth of Frankenstein" has two elements: "(a) Frankenstein makes a living creature out of bits of corpses" and "(b) The creature turns against him and runs amok" (*In Frankenstein's Shadow: Myth, Monstrosity, and Nineteenth-Century Writing* [Oxford, UK: Clarendon, 1987], 3). Amalgamation of body parts and reanimation from the dead are distinct enough to constitute two features rather than one.

18. Toni Morrison, *Playing in the Dark: Whiteness and the Literary Imagination* (New York: Vintage, 1993), 17.

19. Ibid., 4.

20. For overviews and examples of these developments, see Anna Brickhouse, *Transamerican Literary Relations and the Nineteenth-Century Public Sphere* (Cambridge: Cambridge University Press, 2004); Amanda Claybaugh, *The Novel of Purpose: Literature and Social Reform in the Anglo-American World* (Ithaca, NY: Cornell University Press, 2007); Shelley Fisher Fishkin, "Crossroads of Culture: The Transnational Turn in American Studies," *American Quarterly* 57:1 (March 2005): 17–65; Paul Giles, *Virtual Americas: Transnational Fictions and the Transatlantic Imaginary* (Durham, NC: Duke University Press, 2002); Amy Kaplan, *The Anarchy of Empire in the Making of U.S. Culture* (Cambridge, MA: Harvard University Press, 2002); Caroline F. Levander and Robert S. Levine, eds., "Hemispheric American Literary History," special issue, *American Literary History* 18:3 (fall 2006); and Joseph Roach, *Cities of the Dead: Circum-Atlantic Performance* (New York: Columbia University Press, 1996).

21. Paul Gilroy, *The Black Atlantic: Modernity and Double Consciousness* (Cambridge, MA: Harvard University Press, 1993). For analyses of this model, see Ian Baucum, ed., "Atlantic Genealogies," special issue, *South Atlantic Quarterly* 100:1 (winter 2002); Vincent Carretta and Philip Gould, eds., *Genius in Bondage: Literature of the Early Black Atlantic* (Lexington: University Press of Kentucky, 2001); Jonathan Elmer, "The Black Atlantic Archive," *American Literary History* 17:1 (spring 2005): 160–70; Simon Gikandi, ed., "The 'Black Atlantic,'" special issue, *Research in African Literatures* 27:4 (1996); John Cullen Gruesser, *Confluences: Postcolonialism, African American Literary Studies, and the Black Atlantic* (Athens: University of Georgia Press, 2005); Gesa Mackenthun, *Fictions of the Black Atlantic in American Foundational Literature* (London: Routledge, 2004); and Alan Rice, *Radical Narratives of the Black Atlantic* (London: Continuum, 2003).

22. Marcus Wood, *Slavery, Empathy and Pornography* (New York: Oxford University Press, 2002), 13.

23. For an overview of feminist criticism of *Frankenstein* up to 1990, see Catherine Gallagher and Elizabeth Young, "Feminism and *Frankenstein*: A Short History of American Feminist Criticism," *Journal of Contemporary Thought* (Baroda, India) 1 (1991): 97–109. For later assessments of the field, see Diane Long Hoeveler, "*Frankenstein*, Feminism, and Literary Theory," in *The Cambridge Companion to Mary Shelley*, ed. Esther Schor (Cambridge: Cambridge University Press, 2003), 45–62; Ellen Cronan Rose, "Custody Battles: Reproducing Knowledge about *Frankenstein*," *New Literary History* 26:4 (1995): 809–32; and Berthold Schoene-Harwood, "Whose Body Does the Text Display? Representations of Gender in *Frankenstein*," in *Mary Shelley: Frankenstein*, ed. Berthold Schoene-Harwood (New York: Columbia University Press, 2000), 88–130.

24. Bette London, "Mary Shelley, *Frankenstein*, and the Spectacle of Masculin-

ity," *PMLA* 108:2 (March 1993): 256. For overviews of the study of masculinity, see Rachel Adams and David Savran, eds., *The Masculinity Studies Reader* (Malden, MA: Blackwell, 2002); Steven Cohan and Ina Rae Hark, eds., *Screening the Male: Exploring Masculinities in Hollywood Cinema* (London: Routledge, 1993); and Judith Kegan Gardiner, *Masculinity Studies and Feminist Theory: New Directions* (New York: Columbia University Press, 2002).

25. See Annette Kolodny, *The Lay of the Land: Metaphor as Experience and History in American Life and Letters* (Chapel Hill: University of North Carolina Press, 1975), which responds, in part, to Henry Nash Smith, *Virgin Land: The American West as Symbol and Myth* (Cambridge, MA: Harvard University Press, 1950); and Nina Baym, "Melodramas of Beset Manhood: How Theories of American Fiction Exclude Women Authors," in *The New Feminist Criticism: Women, Literature, and Theory*, ed. Elaine Showalter (New York: Pantheon, 1985), 63–80.

26. Eve Kosofsky Sedgwick, *The Coherence of Gothic Conventions* (New York: Methuen, 1986), ix–x. For other analyses of sexuality in *Frankenstein*, see chapter 4.

27. The foundational exploration of the homoerotic dimensions of *The Adventures of Huckleberry Finn* is Leslie Fiedler, "Come Back to the Raft Ag'in, Huck Honey!" (1948), reprinted in Mark Twain, *The Adventures of Huckleberry Finn*, ed. Gerald Graff and James Phelan (Boston: Bedford/St. Martin's, 1995), 528–34; for critiques of Fiedler, see Chris Looby, "'Innocent Homosexuality': The Fiedler Thesis in Retrospect," in Graff and Phelan, *Adventures of Huckleberry Finn*, 535–50, and Robyn Wiegman, "Fiedler and Sons," in *Race and the Subject of Masculinities*, ed. Harry Stecopoulos and Michael Uebel (Durham, NC: Duke University Press, 1997), 45–68.

28. For overviews of the literary gothic that center on British traditions, see Fred Botting, *Gothic* (London: Routledge, 1996); Jerrold E. Hogle, ed., *The Cambridge Companion to Gothic Fiction* (Cambridge: Cambridge University Press, 2002); Maggie Kilgour, *The Rise of the Gothic Novel* (London: Routledge, 1995); and David Punter, ed., *A Companion to the Gothic* (Oxford, UK: Blackwell, 2000). On American gothic, see Robert K. Martin and Eric Savoy, eds., *American Gothic: New Interventions in a National Narrative* (Iowa City: University of Iowa Press, 1998); Charles L. Crow, ed., *American Gothic: An Anthology, 1787–1916* (Oxford, UK: Blackwell, 1999); and Jeffrey Andrew Weinstock, ed., *Spectral America: Phantoms and the National Imagination* (Madison: University of Wisconsin Press, 2004). For important reassessments of race and nineteenth-century American literary gothic, see Teresa A. Goddu, *Gothic America: Narrative, History, and Nation* (New York: Columbia University Press, 1997), and Teresa A. Goddu, "Vampire Gothic," *American Literary History* 11:1 (spring 1999): 125–41. On race and twentieth-century "Southern gothic," see Patricia S. Yaeger, *Dirt and Desire: Reconstructing Southern Women's Writing, 1930–1990* (Chicago: University of Chicago Press, 2000). On race and the literary gothic, see also Ruth Bienstock Anolik

and Douglas L. Howard, eds., *The Gothic Other: Racial and Social Constructions in the Literary Imagination* (Jefferson, NC: McFarland, 2004); Justin D. Edwards, *Gothic Passages: Racial Ambiguity and the American Gothic* (Iowa City: University of Iowa Press, 2003); and Elisabeth Anne Leonard, ed., *Into Darkness Peering: Race and Color in the Fantastic* (Westport, CT: Greenwood, 1997).

For useful introductions to the horror film, see Ken Gelder, ed., *The Horror Reader* (London: Routledge, 2000); Mark Jancovich, ed., *Horror: The Film Reader* (London: Routledge, 2002); and Paul Wells, *The Horror Genre from Beelzebub to Blair Witch* (London: Wallflower, 2000). An influential early analysis that calls attention to racial questions is Robin Wood, "An Introduction to the American Horror Film," in *Planks of Reason*, ed. Barry Keith Grant (Metuchen, NJ: Scarecrow, 1984), 164–200; a major rethinking of race and horror is Richard Dyer, "White," *Screen* 29:4 (autumn 1988): 44–64. See also Frances Gateward, ed., "Scared of the Dark: Race, Gender and the 'Horror Film,'" special issue, *Genders* 40 (2004); Ed Guerrero, *Framing Blackness: The African American Image in Film* (Philadelphia: Temple University Press, 1993), 41–68; and Kobena Mercer, "Monster Metaphors —Notes on Michael Jackson's 'Thriller,'" *Screen* 27:1 (January-February 1986): 26–43.

29. See Goddu, *Gothic America*, 131–52, and "Vampire Gothic," esp. 137–38. A fuller literary history of "black gothic" writing would include many other authors, such as Octavia Butler, Charles Chesnutt, Hannah Crafts, Jewelle Gomez, Rebecca Jackson, Harriet Jacobs, Toni Morrison, and John Edgar Wideman. For relevant explorations of this topic, see the essays grouped under the rubric "African American Gothic" in *In Search of Hannah Crafts: Critical Essays on "The Bondwoman's Narrative,"* ed. Henry Louis Gates, Jr., and Hollis Robbins (New York: Basic/Civitas, 2004), 195–312; and James Smethurst, "Invented by Horror: The Gothic and African American Literary Ideology in *Native Son*," *African American Review* 35:1 (2001): 29–40.

30. Angus Fletcher, *Allegory: The Theory of a Symbolic Mode* (Ithaca, NY: Cornell University Press, 1964), 55.

31. Cindy Weinstein, *The Literature of Labor and the Labors of Literature: Allegory in Nineteenth-Century American Fiction* (Cambridge: Cambridge University Press, 1995). Perhaps the most influential revaluation of allegory is from a deconstructive perspective; see Paul de Man, *Allegories of Readings: Figural Language in Rousseau, Nietzsche, Rilke and Proust* (New Haven, CT: Yale University Press, 1979). For an account of how theories of allegory have changed historically, see Theresa M. Kelley, *Reinventing Allegory* (Cambridge: Cambridge University Press, 1997).

32. For discussion of this film, see Robert Alan Crick, "Start the Operation without Me: Monsters, Madmen, and Maturity in Mel Brooks' *Young Frankenstein*," in *We Belong Dead: Frankenstein on Film*, ed. Gary J. Svehla and Susan Svehla (Baltimore: Midnight Marquee, 1997), 225–37; Dan Harries, *Film Parody*

(London: British Film Institute, 2000); and Esther Schor, "*Frankenstein* and Film," in *Cambridge Companion to Mary Shelley*, 75–76.

33. Raymond Williams, "Aesthetic," in *Keywords: A Vocabulary of Culture and Society* (New York: Oxford University Press, 1976), 28. For recent reassessments of this issue, see Michael Bérubé, ed., *The Aesthetics of Cultural Studies* (Malden, MA: Blackwell, 2005); and Christopher Castiglia and Russ Castronovo, eds., "Aesthetics and the End(s) of Cultural Studies," special issue, *American Literature* 76:3 (September 2004). For an account of this conflict from a cultural studies perspective in an earlier moment, see Ian Hunter, "Aesthetics and Cultural Studies," in *Cultural Studies*, ed. Lawrence Grossberg, Cary Nelson, and Paula A. Treichler (New York: Routledge, 1992), 347–72; for an account from the field of aesthetics, see Deborah Knight, "Aesthetics and Cultural Studies," in *The Oxford Handbook of Aesthetics*, ed. Jerrold Levinson (Oxford: Oxford University Press, 2003), 783–95. See also Terry Eagleton, *The Ideology of the Aesthetic* (Oxford, UK: Blackwell, 1990); and George Levine, ed., *Aesthetics and Ideology* (New Brunswick, NJ: Rutgers University Press, 1994).

34. On the history of monstrosity and related terms, see Jeffrey Jerome Cohen, ed., *Monster Theory: Reading Culture* (Minneapolis: University of Minnesota Press, 1996); Lorraine Daston and Katharine Park, *Wonders and the Order of Nature, 1150–1750* (New York: Zone, 2001); Marie-Hélène Huet, *Monstrous Imagination* (Cambridge, MA: Harvard University Press, 1993); Laura Lunger Knoppers and Joan B. Landes, eds., *Monstrous Bodies/Political Monstrosities in Early Modern Europe* (Ithaca, NY: Cornell University Press, 2004); Bryan D. Palmer, *Cultures of Darkness: Night Travels in the Histories of Transgression* (New York: Monthly Review Press, 2000); and Rosemarie Garland Thomson, ed., *Freakery: Cultural Spectacles of the Extraordinary Body* (New York: New York University Press, 1996).

35. The idea of a text's "afterlife" is customarily used to designate its ongoing influence; it has particular resonance for *Dracula* and *Frankenstein*, whose protagonists are themselves embodiments of life after death. For other discussions of nineteenth-century literary afterlives, see Ian Baucom and Jennifer Kennedy, eds., "Afterlives of Romanticism," special issue, *South Atlantic Quarterly* 102:1 (winter 2003); Jay Clayton, *Charles Dickens in Cyberspace: The Afterlife of the Nineteenth Century in Postmodern Culture* (New York: Oxford University Press, 2003); and John Kucich and Dianne F. Sadoff, eds., *Victorian Afterlife: Postmodern Culture Rewrites the Nineteenth Century* (Minneapolis: University of Minnesota Press, 2000).

36. Franco Moretti, *Signs Taken for Wonders: Essays in the Sociology of Literary Forms* (London: Verso, 1988), 83–108.

37. On the politics of *Dracula*, see Ken Gelder, *Reading the Vampire* (London: Routledge, 1994), 11–20, 65–85; David Glover, *Vampires, Mummies, and Liberals: Bram Stoker and the Politics of Popular Fiction* (Durham, NC: Duke University

Press, 1996); Judith Halberstam, *Skin Shows: Gothic Horror and the Technology of Monsters* (Durham, NC: Duke University Press, 1995), 86–106; and H. L. Malchow, *Gothic Images of Race in Nineteenth-Century Britain* (Stanford, CA: Stanford University Press, 1996), 124–66. For analyses of vampires and race in contemporary U.S. culture, see William Patrick Day, *Vampire Legends in Contemporary American Culture: What Becomes a Legend Most* (Lexington: University Press of Kentucky, 2002); Goddu, "Vampire Gothic"; Joan Gordon and Veronica Hollinger, eds., *Blood Read: The Vampire as Metaphor in Contemporary Culture* (Philadelphia: University of Pennsylvania Press, 1997); and Donna J. Haraway, *Modest_Witness@Second_Millennium.FemaleMan©_Meets_Oncomouse™: Feminism and Technoscience* (New York: Routledge, 1997), 213–65. For discussion of vampires, see also Nina Auerbach, *Our Vampires, Ourselves* (Chicago: University of Chicago Press, 1995); Sue-Ellen Case, "Tracking the Vampire," *Differences* 3:2 (1991): 1–19; Laurence A. Rickels, *The Vampire Lectures* (Minneapolis: University of Minnesota Press, 1999); and David J. Skal, *Hollywood Gothic: The Tangled Web of Dracula from Novel to Stage to Screen* (New York: Norton, 1990).

38. These figures each have rich cultural histories. On the hydra, see Peter Linebaugh and Marcus Rediker, *The Many-Headed Hydra: Sailors, Slaves, Commoners, and the Hidden History of the Revolutionary Atlantic* (Boston: Beacon, 2000). On the golem, see Emily D. Bilski, ed., *Golem! Danger, Deliverance and Art* (New York: Jewish Museum, 1988); and Graham, *Representations of the Post/Human*, 84–108. On King Kong, see Cynthia Erb, *Tracking King Kong: A Hollywood Icon in World Culture* (Detroit: Wayne State University Press, 1998); and notes in chapter 4. For Caliban, see note 40.

39. *New-York Mirror*, 8 June 1833, 390, reprinted in *Nineteenth-Century Literature Criticism*, vol. 14 (Detroit: Gale, 1987), 258.

40. The literature on reappropriations of Caliban is extensive: for overviews and examples, see Trevor Griffiths, "'This Island's Mine': Caliban and Colonialism," *Yearbook of English Studies* 13 (1983): 159–80; Peter Hulme and William H. Sherman, eds., *"The Tempest" and Its Travels* (Philadelphia: University of Pennsylvania Press, 2000); Rob Nixon, "Caribbean and African Appropriations of *The Tempest*," *Critical Inquiry* 13 (spring 1987): 557–78; and Alden T. Vaughan and Virginia Mason Vaughan, *Shakespeare's Caliban: A Cultural History* (Cambridge: Cambridge University Press, 1991). For an account of African American writing that draws loosely from Caliban, see James W. Coleman, *Black Male Fiction and the Legacy of Caliban* (Lexington: University Press of Kentucky, 2001). On the theatrical connections between Caliban and the Frankenstein monster, see Forry, *Hideous Progenies*, 22.

41. William Shakespeare, *The Tempest*, ed. Peter Holland (New York: Penguin, 1999), I.ii.331–32. On the political claims of Caliban, see Patricia Seed, "'This Island's Mine': Caliban and Native Sovereignty," and on Sycorax, see Marina

Warner, "'The Foul Witch' and Her 'Freckled Whelp': Circean Mutations in the New World," both in Hulme and Sherman, *"Tempest" and Its Travels*, 202–11, 97–113.

42. Audre Lorde, "The Master's Tools Will Never Dismantle the Master's House," *Sister Outsider: Essays and Speeches* (Trumansburg, NY: Crossing Press, 1984), 110–13.

43. Shelley Jackson, *Patchwork Girl* (Watertown, MA: Eastgate Systems, 1995). Discussions of this work include Clayton, *Charles Dickens in Cyberspace*, 137–41; and N. Katherine Hayles, "Flickering Connectivities in Shelley Jackson's *Patchwork Girl*: The Importance of Media-Specific Analysis," *Postmodern Culture* 10:2 (January 2000), available online at http://www3.iath.virginia.edu/pmc/text-only/issue.100/10.2hayles.txt. Jackson discusses the novel in "Stitch Bitch: The Patchwork Girl," MIT Communications Forum, http://web.mit.edu/comm-forum/papers/jackson.html.

44. See Jackson's account of this project at http://ineradicablestain.com, and for a brief description, see Daniel Pink, "Skin Literature," *New York Times Magazine* 12 December 2004, 92, 94.

45. Malchow, *Gothic Images of Race in Nineteenth-Century Britain*; Baldick, *In Frankenstein's Shadow*.

46. Ambrose Bierce, "Moxon's Master," in *Tales of Soldiers and Civilians and Other Stories*, ed. Tom Quirk (New York: Penguin, 2000), 127–35.

47. Donna J. Haraway, "A Cyborg Manifesto: Science, Technology, and Socialist-Feminism in the Late Twentieth Century," in *Simians, Cyborgs, and Women: The Reinvention of Nature* (New York: Routledge, 1991), 151. On connections between Haraway's cyborg and the Frankenstein monster, see Clayton, *Charles Dickens in Cyberspace*, 124–45; and Chris Hables Gray, Steven Mentor, and Heidi J. Figueroa-Sarriera, "Cyborgology: Constructing the Knowledge of Cybernetic Organisms," in *The Cyborg Handbook*, ed. Chris Hables Gray, with the assistance of Heidi J. Figueroa-Sarriera and Steven Mentor (New York: Routledge, 1995), 1–14.

48. Paul Gilroy, *Postcolonial Melancholia* (New York: Columbia University Press, 2005), 1, 115, and 129.

49. Katherine Dunn, *Geek Love* (New York: Warner Books, 1990); Rebecca Brown, "Dr. Frankenstein, I Presume," in *The Terrible Girls* (San Francisco: City Lights, 1992), 93–100; Achy Obejas, *Memory Mambo* (Pittsburgh: Cleis, 1996).

50. C. L. Moore, "No Woman Born" (1944), reprinted in *The Best of C. L. Moore*, ed. Lester Del Rey (New York: Ballantine, 1975), 236–88. For discussion, see Jane Donawerth, *Frankenstein's Daughters: Women Writing Science Fiction* (Syracuse, NY: Syracuse University Press, 1997), 61–63; Susan Gubar, "C. L. Moore and the Conventions of Women's Science Fiction," *Science Fiction Studies* 7:1 (March 1980): 16–25; and Debra Benita Shaw, *Women, Science and Fiction: The Frankenstein Inheritance* (New York: Palgrave, 2000), 65–89.

51. Margaret Atwood, "Speeches for Dr. Frankenstein" (1968), in *The Animals*

in That Country (Boston: Little, Brown, 1968), 42–47; Phyllis Gotlieb, "Ms. & Mr. Frankenstein," in *Son of the Morning and Other Stories* (New York: Ace, 1983), 160–63; and Marge Piercy, "Mrs. Frankenstein," *Stone, Paper, Knife* (New York: Knopf, 1983), 3–5.

52. Liz Lochhead, "Dreaming Frankenstein," in *Dreaming Frankenstein and Collected Poems* (Edinburgh, UK: Polygon, 1984), 11; Lochhead, *Blood and Ice* (Edinburgh, UK: Salamander, 1982). On Lochhead and *Frankenstein*, see E. Douka Kabitoglou, "Mary Shelley, Liz Lochhead, and the Monster," in *Mary Shelley in Her Times*, ed. Betty T. Bennett and Stuart Curran (Baltimore: Johns Hopkins University Press, 2000), 214–32.

53. Obejas, *Memory Mambo*, 59.

54. See Rachel Adams, *Sideshow U.S.A.: Freaks and the American Cultural Imagination* (Chicago: University of Chicago Press, 2001), 196–209.

55. On transgender uses of the Frankenstein story, see Susan Stryker, "My Words to Victor Frankenstein above the Village of Chamounix: Performing Transgender Rage," in *The Transgender Studies Reader*, ed. Susan Stryker and Stephen Whittle (New York: Routledge, 2006), 244–56.

56. See David Leon Higdon, "Frankenstein as Founding Myth in Gary Larson's *The Far Side*," *Journal of Popular Culture* 28:1 (summer 1994): 49–60.

57. See Gallagher and Young, "Feminism and *Frankenstein*"; Elizabeth Young, "Here Comes the Bride: Wedding Gender and Race in *Bride of Frankenstein*," *Feminist Studies* 17:3 (1991): 403–37; Elizabeth Young, "*The Silence of the Lambs* and the Flaying of Feminist Theory," *Camera Obscura* 27 (1991): 5–35; and Elizabeth Young, "Bods and Monsters: The Return of the Bride of Frankenstein," in *The End of Cinema as We Know It: American Film in the Nineties*, ed. Jon Lewis (New York: New York University Press, 2001), 225–36.

NOTES TO CHAPTER 1

1. "Monster in iniquity" is from the *Richmond Enquirer* (25 November 1831), reprinted in *The Southampton Slave Revolt of 1831*, ed. Henry Irving Tragle (Amherst: University of Massachusetts Press, 1971), 144; "a spectacle" is from Samuel Warner, *Authentic and Impartial Narrative of the Tragical Scene Which Was Witnessed in Southampton County (Virginia)* . . . (1831), reprinted in Tragle, *Southampton Slave Revolt*, 286; and "eloquently and classically expressed" is from the *Richmond Enquirer* (25 November 1831), reprinted in Tragle, *Southampton Slave Revolt*, 143. For additional documentation of the revolt, see Eric Foner, ed., *Nat Turner* (Englewood Cliffs, NJ: Prentice Hall, 1971); and Kenneth S. Greenberg, ed., *"The Confessions of Nat Turner" and Related Documents* (Boston: Bedford/St. Martin's, 1996). For analyses of the event, see Herbert Aptheker, *American Negro Slave Revolts*, foreword by John H. Bracey (1963; 5th ed., New York: International Publishers, 1983); Mary Kemp Davis, *Nat Turner before the Bar of Judgment:*

Fictional Treatments of the Southampton Slave Insurrection (Baton Rouge: Louisiana State University Press, 1999); Franny Nudelman, *John Brown's Body: Slavery, Violence and the Culture of War* (Chapel Hill: University of North Carolina Press, 2004), 59–67; Albert E. Stone, *The Return of Nat Turner: History, Literature, and Cultural Politics in Sixties America* (Athens: University of Georgia Press, 1992); Eric Sundquist, *To Wake the Nations: Race in the Making of American Literature* (Cambridge, MA: Harvard University Press, 1993), 27–83; and Peter H. Wood, "Nat Turner: The Unknown Slave as Visionary Leader," in *Black Leaders of the Nineteenth Century*, ed. Leon Litwack and August Meier (Urbana: University of Illinois Press, 1988), 21–40.

2. Thomas Dew, *Review of the Debate in the Virginia Legislature of 1831 and 1832* (1832; repr., Westport, CT: Negro Universities Press, 1970), 105; all subsequent quotations are taken from this edition and cited parenthetically in the text. For discussion, see Drew Gilpin Faust, introduction to Thomas Dew, *The Ideology of Slavery: Proslavery Thought in the Antebellum South, 1830–1860*, ed. Drew Gilpin Faust (Baton Rouge: Louisiana State University Press, 1981), 21–23; George M. Fredrickson, *The Black Image in the White Mind: The Debate on Afro-American Character and Destiny, 1817–1914* (New York: Harper and Row, 1971), 44–46; and Larry E. Tise, *Proslavery: A History of the Defense of Slavery in America, 1701–1840* (Athens: University of Georgia Press, 1987), 70–74.

3. On Canning's comment, see Chris Baldick, *In Frankenstein's Shadow: Myth, Monstrosity, and Nineteenth-Century Writing* (Oxford, UK: Clarendon, 1987), 60; Lesley Ginsberg, "Slavery and the Gothic Horror of Poe's 'The Black Cat,'" in *American Gothic: New Interventions in a National Narrative*, ed. Robert K. Martin and Eric Savoy (Iowa City: University of Iowa Press, 1998), 103; Debbie Lee, *Slavery and the Romantic Imagination* (Philadelphia: University of Pennsylvania Press, 2002), 173–74, 182; H. L. Malchow, *Gothic Images of Race in Nineteenth-Century Britain* (Stanford, CA: Stanford University Press, 1996), 33; and Miranda Seymour, *Mary Shelley* (New York: Grove, 2000), 335. On Canning and the slave trade, see Wendy Hinde, *George Canning* (New York: St. Martin's, 1973), 341–44.

4. Quoted in Sundquist, *To Wake the Nations*, 36.

5. Dew, *Review*, 6.

6. For discussions of race in these works, see J. Gerald Kennedy and Liliane Weissberg, eds., *Romancing the Shadow: Poe and Race* (New York: Oxford University Press, 2001). On *The Narrative of Arthur Gordon Pym*, see also Jared Gardner, *Master Plots: Race and the Founding of American Literature, 1787–1845* (Baltimore: Johns Hopkins University Press, 1998), 125–59; Teresa A. Goddu, *Gothic America: Narrative, History, and Nation* (New York: Columbia University Press, 1997), 73–93; Dana D. Nelson, *The Word in Black and White: Reading "Race" in American Literature, 1638–1867* (New York: Oxford University Press, 1992), 90–108; and John Carlos Rowe, "Poe, Antebellum Slavery, and Modern Criticism," in *Poe's "Pym": Critical Explorations*, ed. Richard Kopley (Durham, NC: Duke University

Press, 1992), 117–38. On Poe and race, see also Joan Dayan, "Amorous Bondage: Poe, Ladies, and Slaves," in *Subjects and Citizens*, ed. Cathy N. Davidson and Michael Moon (Durham, NC: Duke University Press, 1995), 109–43; Ginsberg, "Slavery and the Gothic Horror of Poe's 'The Black Cat'"; and Teresa A. Goddu, "Poe, Sensationalism, and Slavery," in *The Cambridge Companion to Edgar Allan Poe*, ed. Kevin J. Hayes (Cambridge: Cambridge University Press, 2002), 92–112.

7. Edgar Allan Poe, *The Narrative of Arthur Gordon Pym*, in Poe, *Poetry, Tales, and Selected Essays* (New York: Library of America, 1996), 1179.

8. Toni Morrison, *Playing in the Dark: Whiteness and the Literary Imagination* (New York: Vintage, 1993), 33.

9. On Gray, see Thomas C. Parramore, *Southampton County, Virginia* (Charlottesville: University Press of Virginia, 1978), 105–21. For discussion of the authorship of the *Confessions*, see Davis, *Nat Turner before the Bar of Judgment*, 42–76, and Sundquist, *To Wake the Nations*, 36–56. Allan Lloyd Smith notes the affinity between *Frankenstein* and the structure of the slave narrative in "'This Thing of Darkness': Racial Discourse in Mary Shelley's *Frankenstein*," *Gothic Studies* 6:2 (2005): 215.

10. On the novel's frames, see Beth Newman, "Narratives of Seduction and the Seductions of Narrative: The Frame Structure of *Frankenstein*," in *Frankenstein*, ed. Fred Botting (New York: St. Martin's, 1995), 166–90.

11. David Walker, *David Walker's Appeal, in Four Articles; Together with a Preamble, to the Coloured Citizens of the World, But in Particular, and Very Expressly, to Those of the United States of America*, ed. and introd. Sean Wilentz (1829; repr., New York: Hill and Wang, 1995), preface to the third edition, n.p.; all subsequent quotations are taken from this edition and cited parenthetically in the text. For discussion of Walker, see also Peter P. Hinks, *To Awaken My Afflicted Brethren: David Walker and the Problem of Antebellum Slave Resistance* (University Park: Pennsylvania State University Press, 1997); and Nudelman, *John Brown's Body*, 54–59. It is not clear whether Turner knew of Walker's *Appeal*; on this question, see Hinks, *To Awaken My Afflicted Brethren*, 167–69, and Stone, *Return of Nat Turner*, 336–37.

12. Mary Shelley, *Frankenstein*, ed. J. Paul Hunter (1818; repr., New York: Norton, 1996), 68, 98; unless otherwise noted, all subsequent quotations are taken from this edition, which reprints the 1818 text of the novel, and cited parenthetically in the text. I discuss the question of the novel's variant editions below.

13. Sundquist, *To Wake the Nations*, 42.

14. It is unclear what happened to Turner's body, but popular accounts of it frequently indicated dissection. See, for example, the *Norfolk Herald* (14 November 1831): "General Nat sold his body for dissection, and spent the money on ginger cakes"; and a later account by Stephen Beauregard Weeks in *The Magazine of American History* (June 1891): "His body was given to the surgeons for dissection"; both quoted in Tragle, *Southampton Slave Revolt*, 140, 366. For discussion

of this issue, see Greenberg, introduction to *"Confessions of Nat Turner,"* 19–20, and Nudelman, *John Brown's Body*, 67.

15. On the centrality of slavery to British Romanticism, see Deirdre Coleman, *Romantic Colonization and British Anti-Slavery* (Cambridge: Cambridge University Press, 2005); Peter J. Kitson and Debbie Lee, eds., *Slavery, Abolition, and Emancipation: Writings in the British Romantic Period*, 8 vols. (London: Pickering and Chatto, 1999); Lee, *Slavery and the Romantic Imagination*; and Helen Thomas, *Romanticism and Slave Narratives: Transatlantic Testimonies* (Cambridge: Cambridge University Press, 2000).

16. For introductions to Mary Shelley, see Betty T. Bennett, *Mary Wollstonecraft Shelley: An Introduction* (Baltimore: Johns Hopkins University Press, 1998); Anne K. Mellor, *Mary Shelley: Her Life, Her Fiction, Her Monsters* (New York: Routledge, 1988); Esther Schor, ed., *The Cambridge Companion to Mary Shelley* (Cambridge: Cambridge University Press, 2003); and Miranda Seymour, *Mary Shelley* (New York: Grove, 2000). On race and Mary Shelley's upbringing, see Lee, *Slavery and the Romantic Imagination*, 171–73; Malchow, *Gothic Images of Race*, 15–17; Joseph W. Lew, "The Deceptive Other: Mary Shelley's Critique of Orientalism in *Frankenstein*," *Studies in Romanticism* 30:2 (summer 1991): 256–57; and Smith, "'This Thing of Darkness,'" 208–9. On Shelley in Bristol, see Seymour, *Mary Shelley*, xii–xiii, 137–39. On Shelley and Haiti, see Smith, "'This Thing of Darkness,'" 209, 218.

17. Quoted in Malchow, *Gothic Images of Race*, 21; Malchow discusses the monster's behavior on 19–26. On Shelley and Edwards, see also Lee, *Slavery and the Romantic Imagination*, 174–75.

18. Quoted in Robert J. C. Young, *Colonial Desire: Hybridity in Theory, Culture, and Race* (London: Routledge, 1995), 113. See also Malchow, *Gothic Images of Race*, esp. 176; and Anne K. Mellor, "*Frankenstein*, Racial Science, and the Yellow Peril," *Nineteenth-Century Contexts* 23 (2001): 22–23.

19. For discussions of polygenesis, see Bruce Dain, *A Hideous Monster of the Mind: American Race Theory in the Early Republic* (Cambridge, MA: Harvard University Press, 2002), 72–75; Fredrickson, *Black Image in the White Mind*, 71–96; and Thomas F. Gossett, *Race: The History of an Idea in America* (1965; repr., New York: Oxford University Press, 1997), 58–67. On amalgamation, see Leslie M. Harris, "From Abolitionist Amalgamators to 'Rulers of the Five Points': The Discourse of Interracial Sex and Reform in Antebellum New York City," in *Sex, Love, Race: Crossing Boundaries in North American History*, ed. Martha Hodes (New York: New York University Press, 1999), 191–212; Martha Hodes, *White Women, Black Men: Illicit Sex in the Nineteenth-Century South* (New Haven, CT: Yale University Press, 1997); and Werner Sollors, ed., *Interracialism: Black-White Intermarriage in American History, Literature, and Law* (New York: Oxford University Press, 2000).

20. Malchow, *Gothic Images of Race*, 25.

21. Mary Shelley, *Frankenstein*, ed. Maurice Hindle (1831; repr., London: Penguin, 1992), 34; all subsequent quotations from the 1831 version of the novel are taken from this edition and cited parenthetically in the text.

22. On the Shelleys' sugar boycott, see Lee, *Slavery and the Romantic Imagination*, 173; Seymour, *Mary Shelley*, 138; and Smith, "'This Thing of Darkness,'" 209.

23. On *Frankenstein* and Mary Prince, see Helen Woodard, "The Two Marys (Prince and Shelley) on the Textual Meeting Ground of Race, Gender, and Genre," in *Recovered Writers/Recovered Texts: Race, Class, and Gender in Black Women's Literature*, ed. Dolan Hubbard (Knoxville: University of Tennessee Press, 1997), 15–30.

24. On *Frankenstein* and Olaudah Equiano, see Smith, "'This Thing of Darkness,'" 214–15.

25. Malchow, *Gothic Images of Race*, 31. On the use of this imagery in British and American abolitionism, see Marcus Wood, *Blind Memory: Visual Representations of Slavery in England and America, 1780–1865* (New York: Routledge, 2000); and Jean Fagan Yellin, *Women and Sisters: The Antislavery Feminists in American Culture* (New Haven, CT: Yale University Press, 1989).

26. Gayatri Chakravorty Spivak, "Three Women's Texts and a Critique of Imperialism" (1985), reprinted in Botting, *Frankenstein*, 235–60. Spivak later amended this argument; her revision is reprinted in the Botting anthology as "Postscript," 254–56. See also Elizabeth A. Bohls, "Standards of Taste, Discourses of 'Race,' and the Aesthetic Education of a Monster: Critique of Empire in *Frankenstein*," *Eighteenth-Century Life* 18:3 (November 1994): 23–36; Lew, "Deceptive Other"; Mary Lowe-Evans, "Sweetheart of Darkness: Kurtz's Intended as Progeny of *Frankenstein*'s Bride," in *Critical Essays on Mary Wollstonecraft Shelley*, ed. Mary Lowe-Evans (New York: G. K. Hall, 1998), 203–13; Mellor, "*Frankenstein*, Racial Science, and the Yellow Peril"; Zohreh T. Sullivan, "Race, Gender, and Imperial Ideology in the Nineteenth Century," *Nineteenth-Century Contexts* 13 (spring 1989): 19–32; Rajani Sudran, *Fair Exotics: Xenophobic Subjects in English Literature, 1720–1850* (Philadelphia: University of Pennsylvania Press, 2002), 117–47; and Woodard, "Two Marys."

27. Bohls, "Standards of Taste," 25; and Lew, "Deceptive Other," 256–57.

28. Mellor, "*Frankenstein*, Racial Science, and the Yellow Peril," 11.

29. On Walton, see Lew, "Deceptive Other," 257–62.

30. Spivak, "Postscript," 255.

31. Burke quoted in Baldick, *In Frankenstein's Shadow*, 18. Connections between *Frankenstein* and Burke were first articulated by Lee Sterrenburg, "Mary Shelley's Monster: Politics and Psyche in *Frankenstein*," in *The Endurance of Frankenstein: Essays on Mary Shelley's Novel*, ed. George Levine and U. C. Knoepflmacher (Berkeley: University of California Press, 1979), 143–71.

32. Quoted in Sterrenburg, "Mary Shelley's Monster," 143.

33. Quoted in Baldick, *In Frankenstein's Shadow*, 18.

34. See Peter Linebaugh and Marcus Rediker, *The Many-Headed Hydra: Sailors, Slaves, Commoners, and the Hidden History of the Revolutionary Atlantic* (Boston: Beacon, 2000).

35. See Franco Moretti, *Signs Taken for Wonders: Essays in the Sociology of Literary Forms* (London: Verso, 1988), 83–108; Paul O'Flinn, "Production and Reproduction: The Case of *Frankenstein*," in *Popular Fictions: Essays in Literature and History*, ed. Peter Humm, Paul Stignant, and Peter Widdowson (London: Methuen, 1986), 196–221; and Baldick, *In Frankenstein's Shadow*, 121–40. A summary of connections between Marx and *Frankenstein* is provided by Elsie B. Michie, "*Frankenstein* and Marx's Theories of Alienated Labor," in *Approaches to Teaching Mary Shelley's "Frankenstein,"* ed. Stephen C. Behrendt (New York: MLA, 1990), 93–98. See also Margo V. Perkins, "The Nature of Otherness: Class and Difference in Mary Shelley's *Frankenstein*," *Studies in the Humanities* 19:1 (June 1992): 27–42.

36. Tim Marshall, *Murdering to Dissect: Grave-Robbing, "Frankenstein," and the Anatomy Literature* (Manchester: Manchester University Press, 1995).

37. Marcus Wood, *Slavery, Empathy and Pornography* (New York: Oxford University Press, 2002), 149–51, 157–59; Luke Gibbons, *Edmund Burke and Ireland: Aesthetics, Politics, and the Colonial Sublime* (Cambridge: Cambridge University Press, 2003), 183–85.

38. For many years, modern editions of the novel reprinted the 1831 version, but recently there has been a scholarly return to the 1818 edition. It is now often seen as both a better expression of the author's intentions and an aesthetically superior work; see Anne K. Mellor, "Choosing a Text of *Frankenstein* to Teach," in Shelley, *Frankenstein*, ed. Hunter, 160–66. I use the 1818 text here as well, less to defend it aesthetically than to mark it as the clearest point of departure, a first iteration of the Frankenstein story, which later versions adapt. See the similar claim by Baldick for "isolating the [1818] text from its offspring . . . to highlight the subsequent process of transformation from text to myth" (*In Frankenstein's Shadow*, 62).

For a contrasting emphasis on the 1831 text, see Nora Crook, "In Defence of the 1831 *Frankenstein*," in *Mary Shelley's Fictions: From Frankenstein to Falkner*, ed. Michael Eberle-Sinatra (New York: St. Martin's, 2000), 3–21. For a summary of changes to the 1831 edition, see Marilyn Butler's edition of the novel (Oxford: Oxford University Press, 1998), 198–228); for a detailed collation of the 1818 and 1831 texts, see the edition edited by James Rieger (*Frankenstein; or, The Modern Prometheus: The 1818 Text* [Chicago: University of Chicago Press, 1974]). For an analysis of the novel emphasizing the extremity of its textual instability, see Fred Botting, *Making Monstrous: Frankenstein, Criticism, Theory* (Manchester: Manchester University Press, 1997).

39. William St. Clair, *The Reading Nation in the Romantic Period* (Cambridge: Cambridge University Press, 2004), 364–65.

40. Baldick, *In Frankenstein's Shadow*, 4.

41. On the conservatism of these changes, see Baldick, *In Frankenstein's Shadow*, 61–62; and Mary Poovey, *The Proper Lady and the Woman Writer: Ideology as Style in the Works of Mary Wollstonecraft, Mary Shelley, and Jane Austen* (Chicago: University of Chicago Press, 1984), 133–42.

42. Steven Earl Forry, *Hideous Progenies: Dramatizations of Frankenstein from Mary Shelley to the Present* (Philadelphia: University of Pennsylvania Press, 1990), 3–42. For discussion of *Frankenstein's* theatrical history, see also Louis James, "Frankenstein's Monster in Two Traditions," in *Frankenstein, Creation and Monstrosity*, ed. Stephen Bann (London: Reaktion Books, 1994), 77–94; Albert J. LaValley, "The Stage and Film Children of *Frankenstein*: A Survey," in Levine and Knoepflmacher, *Endurance of Frankenstein*, 243–89; and Elizabeth Nitchie, *Mary Shelley, Author of "Frankenstein"* (Westport, CT: Greenwood, 1970), 218–31.

43. Richard Brinsley Peake, *Presumption; or, The Fate of Frankenstein*, reprinted in Forry, *Hideous Progenies*, 136; Forry discusses orientalism in stage productions of *Frankenstein* on 14–15. *Presumption* is also discussed in Stephen C. Behrendt, ed., *Presumption; or, The Fate of Frankenstein*, http://www.rc.umd.edu/editions/peake; and Jeffrey N. Cox, ed., *Seven Gothic Dramas, 1789–1825* (Athens: Ohio University Press, 1992), 66–71, 385–425.

44. Richard Brough and Barnabas Brough, *Frankenstein; or, The Model Man* (1849). For discussion, see James, "Frankenstein's Monster in Two Traditions," 84–87.

45. On the "Irish Frankenstein" and other nineteenth-century British political caricatures of the monster, see Baldick, *In Frankenstein's Shadow*, 90–91, 100; L. Perry Curtis, Jr., *Apes and Angels: The Irishman in Victorian Caricature*, rev. ed. (Washington, DC: Smithsonian Institution Press, 1997), 31–32, 38, 42, 48–49, 79–80; Forry, *Hideous Progenies*, 47–54; and Malchow, *Gothic Images of Race*, 34–35.

46. The 1818 edition of the novel was reprinted in the United States in 1833 and again in 1845 and 1869; American audiences also had access to imported copies of British editions, both in 1818 and 1831; and an 1845 American reprint used the 1818 text but included Mary Shelley's introduction to the 1831 edition, described in a publisher's note as being as "intensely interesting as the work itself" ("Preface to the Present American Edition," *Frankenstein* [New York: Henry Daggers, 1845], vi). For discussion of American editions of *Frankenstein*, see Ruth Mortimer, "*Frankenstein*: A Publishing History," in Mary Shelley, *Frankenstein; or, The Modern Prometheus* (West Hatfield, MA: Pennyroyal, 1983), 276–82; for a compilation of these editions, see Leonard Wolf, "A Survey of British, American, and Foreign-Language Editions of *Frankenstein*," in *The Annotated Frankenstein*, ed. Leonard Wolf (New York: Clarkson N. Potter, 1977), 345–46. The theatrical premiere of *Frankenstein* is noted in Joseph N. Ireland, *Records of the New York Stage from 1750 to 1860* (1866–67; repr., New York: Burt Franklin, 1968), 1:437; and George C. Odell, *Annals of the New York Stage* (New York: Columbia University Press, 1928), 3:145–46.

47. C. F. Volney, *Les Ruines; ou, Méditations sur les Révolutions des Empires*, reprinted as *The Ruins of Empire* (Baltimore: Black Classic Press, 1991). For a discussion of the *Ruins* that emphasizes its radicalism, see Linebaugh and Rediker, *Many-Headed Hydra*, 341–44.

48. Shelley's journals, which meticulously detail her reading, do not list Volney; on the probability that she learned about Volney from Percy Shelley, see Mellor, *Mary Shelley*, 232n8.

49. I leave unaddressed here the important questions of how the Frankenstein story was received in the Americas outside the United States and of how the Americas, more broadly conceived, are represented within the novel. See, for example, an earlier passage in the novel: "[I]f no man allowed any pursuit whatsoever to interfere with the tranquillity of his domestic affections, Greece had not been enslaved; Caesar would have spared his country; America would have been discovered more gradually; and the empires of Mexico and Peru had not been destroyed" (33).

50. Michael Sappol, *A Traffic of Dead Bodies: Anatomy and Embodied Social Identity in Nineteenth-Century America* (Princeton, NJ: Princeton University Press, 2002), 216–37. Sappol notes that "*Marietta*, obviously, is greatly indebted to *Frankenstein*," 367n12.

51. Gary Laderman, *The Sacred Remains: American Attitudes toward Death, 1799–1883* (New Haven, CT: Yale University Press, 1996), 81.

52. Russ Castronovo, *Necro Citizenship: Death, Eroticism, and the Public Sphere in the Nineteenth-Century United States* (Durham, NC: Duke University Press, 2001).

53. I am leaving undiscussed numerous other traces of *Frankenstein* in American literature. For example, H. Bruce Franklin offers a list of nineteenth-century short stories influenced by *Frankenstein* under the general category of "medicine men"; see *Future Perfect: American Science Fiction of the Nineteenth Century*, ed. H. Bruce Franklin (New York: Oxford University Press, 1966), 219, and the different list in the revised edition of this anthology under the same title (New York: Oxford University Press, 1995), 203. Susan Tyler Hitchcock offers other examples of nineteenth-century American monsters, in *Frankenstein: A Cultural History* (New York: Norton, 2007), 112–16.

54. Stuart Curran, "The Political Prometheus," *Studies in Romanticism* 25:3 (fall 1986): 429–55; Barlow and Northmore are discussed on 436–42. On Prometheus and *Frankenstein*, see also David Armitage, "Monstrosity and Myth in Mary Shelley's *Frankenstein*," in *Monstrous Bodies/Political Monstrosities in Early Modern Europe*, ed. Laura Lunger Knoppers and Joan B. Landes (Ithaca, NY: Cornell University Press, 2004), 200–226; and Botting, *Making Monstrous*, 79–80.

55. Armitage and Botting note that Franklin was known as a "modern Prometheus"; see Armitage, "Monstrosity and Myth," 210; and Botting, *Making Monstrous*, 80, 184. The idea that Mary Shelley modeled the name "Frankenstein" on

Benjamin Franklin was apparently generated by Samuel Rosenberg in the "Letters" section of *Life* in 1968; see Donald F. Glut, *The Frankenstein Legend* (Metuchen, NJ: Scarecrow, 1973), 10; and Radu N. Florescu, *In Search of Frankenstein* (Boston: New York Graphic Society, 1975), 14. On Franklin and national iconography, see Lester C. Olson, *Benjamin Franklin's Vision of American Community: A Study in Rhetorical Iconology* (Columbia: University of South Carolina Press, 2004). D. H. Lawrence compared Franklin to the Frankenstein monster, as a "production or fabrication of the human will, which projects itself upon a living being, and automatises that being." Lawrence, "Benjamin Franklin," in *The Symbolic Meaning: The Uncollected Versions of "Studies in Classic American Literature,"* ed. Armin Arnold (London: Centaur, 1962), 37; for discussion of this comparison, see Baldick, *In Frankenstein's Shadow*, 179–80.

56. On filial rebellion and the American Revolution, see Jay Fliegelman, *Prodigals and Pilgrims: The American Revolution against Patriarchal Authority, 1750–1800* (Cambridge: Cambridge University Press, 1982); and Michael Kammen, *A Season of Youth: The American Revolution and the Historical Imagination* (Ithaca, NY: Cornell University Press, 1978). On paternal metaphors in antebellum America, see George B. Forgie, *Patricide in the House Divided: A Psychological Interpretation of Lincoln and His Age* (New York: Norton, 1979); and Russ Castronovo, *Fathering the Nation: American Genealogies of Slavery and Freedom* (Berkeley: University of California Press, 1995).

57. Margaret Fuller, letter to James F. Clarke, 25 October 1833, in *The Letters of Margaret Fuller*, ed. Robert N. Hudspeth (Ithaca, NY: Cornell University Press, 1983), 1:196.

58. For emphasis on the international dimensions of Fuller's "American Literature," see Colleen Glenney Boggs, "Margaret Fuller's American Translation," *American Literature* 76:1 (March 2004): 50–51; and Anna Brickhouse, *Transamerican Literary Relations and the Nineteenth-Century Public Sphere* (Cambridge: Cambridge University Press, 2004), 33–34. For a focus on Fuller's relation to America, see Jeffrey Steele, *Transfiguring America: Myth, Ideology, and Mourning in Margaret Fuller's Writing* (Columbia: University of Missouri Press, 2001). For a useful overview of scholarship on Fuller, see Mary Loeffelholz, "Essential, Portable, Mythical Margaret Fuller," in *Challenging Boundaries: Gender and Periodization*, ed. Joyce W. Warren and Margaret Dickie (Athens: University of Georgia Press, 2000), 159–84.

59. Margaret Fuller, "American Literature," in *The Writings of Margaret Fuller*, ed. Mason Wade (New York: Viking, 1941), 358; all subsequent quotations are taken from this edition and cited parenthetically in the text.

60. Baldick, *In Frankenstein's Shadow*, 73–74.

61. For discussions of Fuller's feminism, see Bell Gale Chevigny, *The Woman and the Myth: Margaret Fuller's Life and Writings* (1976; rev. ed., Boston: Northeastern University Press, 1994); and Christina Zwarg, *Feminist Conversations:*

Fuller, Emerson, and the Play of Reading (Ithaca, NY: Cornell University Press, 1995).

62. Margaret Fuller, "Modern British Poets" (1846), in *Writings of Margaret Fuller*, 320–25.

63. On Hutchinson's legacy, see Amy Schrager Lang, *Prophetic Woman: Anne Hutchinson and the Problem of Dissent in the Literature of New England* (Berkeley: University of California Press, 1987); on Hutchinson's multiple births as political metaphors, see also Linebaugh and Rediker, *Many-Headed Hydra*, 90–92.

64. On the racial connotations of Fuller's vocabulary, see Steele, *Transfiguring America*, 253–55.

65. Nudelman, *John Brown's Body*, 41, 42.

66. See Alan C. Braddock, "'Jeff College Boys': Thomas Eakins, Dr. Forbes, and Anatomical Fraternity in Postbellum Philadelphia," *American Quarterly* 57:2 (June 2005): 355–83.

67. Frank Bellew, "The American Frankenstein," *New York Daily Graphic* 14 April 1874, reprinted and discussed in American Social History Project, *Who Built America? Working People and the Nation's Economy, Politics, Culture, and Society* (New York: Pantheon, 1989), 1:522. Bellew was born in India, where his father was an officer in the British Army, and in 1853 came to the United States, where he spent the rest of his career, largely in New York; he co-founded *Vanity Fair* and published regularly in *Harper's Weekly*. On nineteenth-century caricature, see Joshua Brown, *Beyond the Lines: Pictorial Reporting, Everyday Life, and the Crisis of Gilded Age America* (Berkeley: University of California Press, 2002), esp. 66; for a range of examples, see Bernard F. Reilly, Jr., *American Political Prints, 1766–1876: A Catalogue of the Collections in the Library of Congress* (Boston: G. K. Hall, 1991).

68. Sarah Burns, *Painting the Dark Side: Art and the Gothic Imagination in Nineteenth-Century America* (Berkeley: University of California Press, 2004), 114; I am indebted to this work for drawing my attention to both "The Modern Frankenstein" and "The New Frankenstein," discussed in the next section.

69. See Leonard Cassuto, *The Inhuman Race: The Racial Grotesque in American Literature and Culture* (New York: Columbia University Press, 1997).

70. On the visual depiction of the runaway slave, see Wood, *Blind Memory*, 78–142.

71. George Fitzhugh, *Cannibals All! or, Slaves without Masters*, ed. C. Vann Woodward (1857; repr., Cambridge, MA: Harvard University Press, 1960), 22. For discussion, see Fredrickson, *Black Image in the White Mind*, 59–60, 68–70.

72. Fitzhugh, *Cannibals All!* 260.

73. Fredrickson, *Black Image in the White Mind*, 92. For discussion of Van Evrie, see also Gossett, *Race*, 262–63; Samuel Otter, *Melville's Anatomies* (Berkeley: University of California Press, 1999), 122–23; and Forrest G. Wood, *Black Scare:*

The Racist Response to Emancipation and Reconstruction (Berkeley: University of California Press, 1968), 58–68.

74. J[ohn] H. Van Evrie, *Negroes and Negro "Slavery": The First an Inferior Race, the Latter Its Normal Condition,* 3rd ed. (New York: Van Evrie, Horton & Co., 1863), 328–29; all subsequent quotations are taken from this edition and cited parenthetically in the text.

75. Castronovo, *Fathering the Nation,* 6.

76. On Melville reading *Frankenstein,* see Andrew Delbanco, *Melville: His World and Work* (New York: Knopf, 2005), 129–30; on *Frankenstein* and "The Bell-Tower," see Baldick, *In Frankenstein's Shadow,* 74–75.

77. For discussion of this image, see Cox, *Seven Gothic Dramas,* 67.

78. On "The Bell-Tower" and *Benito Cereno* as complementary commentaries on slavery, see Carolyn L. Karcher, *Shadow over the Promised Land: Slavery, Race, and Violence in Melville's America* (Baton Rouge: Louisiana State University Press, 1990), 143–59.

79. Herman Melville, "The Bell-Tower" (1855), in *The Piazza Tales and Other Prose Pieces, 1839–1860* (Evanston and Chicago: Northwestern University Press and the Newberry Library, 1987), 174; all subsequent quotations are taken from this edition and cited parenthetically in the text.

80. Karcher, *Shadow over the Promised Land,* 156–57.

81. See Cindy Weinstein, *The Literature of Labor and the Labors of Literature: Allegory in Nineteenth-Century American Fiction* (Cambridge: Cambridge University Press, 1995), esp. 87–128.

82. Harriet A. Jacobs, *Incidents in the Life of a Slave Girl, Written by Herself,* ed. Jean Fagan Yellin (1861; repr., Cambridge, MA: Harvard University Press, 1987), 27, 54. On Jacobs and the language of the gothic, see Goddu, *Gothic America,* 140–52. For discussions of Jacobs and sexuality, see Deborah M. Garfield and Rafia Zafar, eds., *Harriet Jacobs and "Incidents in the Life of a Slave Girl": New Critical Essays* (Cambridge: Cambridge University Press, 1996).

83. Cassuto, *Inhuman Race,* 118.

84. See John W. Blassingame et al., "Introduction to Series One," *The Frederick Douglass Papers: Series One: Speeches, Debates, and Interviews,* vol. 1: 1841–46 (New Haven, CT: Yale University Press, 1979), xxiii.

85. Eduardo Cadava, "The Monstrosity of Human Rights," *PMLA* 121:5 (October 2006): 1558–65; on "echolalia," see 1560.

86. Frederick Douglass, *My Bondage and My Freedom,* intro. Philip S. Foner (1855; repr., New York: Dover, 1969), 59; all subsequent quotations are taken from this edition and cited parenthetically in the text.

87. Frederick Douglass, *Douglass' Monthly,* December 1860; this passage is discussed in Sundquist, *To Wake the Nations,* 133.

88. Frederick Douglass, "Slavery and the Irrepressible Conflict" (1 August

1860), reprinted in *The Frederick Douglass Papers*, ed. John W. Blassingame et al. (New Haven, CT: Yale University Press, 1985), ser. 1, 3:370–71. The "pet monster" image is discussed briefly in David W. Blight, *Frederick Douglass's Civil War: Keeping Faith in Jubilee* (Baton Rouge: Louisiana State University Press, 1989), 44.

89. See Elisa Tamarkin, "Black Anglophilia; or, The Sociability of Antislavery," *American Literary History* 14:3 (fall 2002): 444–78. On Douglass and Britain, see also R. J. M. Blackett, *Building an Antislavery Wall: Black Americans in the Atlantic Abolitionist Movement, 1830–1860* (Baton Rouge: Louisiana State University Press, 1983), 67–117; Audrey A. Fisch, *American Slaves in Victorian England: Abolitionist Politics in Popular Literature and Culture* (Cambridge: Cambridge University Press, 2000); Paul Giles, *Virtual Americas: Transnational Fictions and the Transatlantic Imaginary* (Durham, NC: Duke University Press, 2002), 22–46; and Alan J. Rice and Martin Crawford, eds., *Liberating Sojourn: Frederick Douglass and Transatlantic Reform* (Athens: University of Georgia Press, 1999).

90. Douglass, "Slavery and the Irrepressible Conflict," 368–69.

91. John Lothrop Motley, "The Causes of the American Civil War: A Paper Contributed to the London *Times*" (1861), reprinted in *Union Pamphlets of the Civil War, 1861–1865*, ed. Frank Freidel (Cambridge, MA: Harvard University Press, 1967), 1:42.

92. Emma Willard, "Via Media: A Peaceful and Permanent Settlement of the Slavery Question" (1862), reprinted in Freidel, *Union Pamphlets of the Civil War*, 1:346.

93. Lisa Herschbach, "Prosthetic Reconstructions: Making the Industry, Re-Making the Body, Modelling the Nation," *History Workshop Journal* 44 (autumn 1997): 22–57.

94. Lisa A. Long, *Rehabilitating Bodies: Health, History, and the American Civil War* (Philadelphia: University of Pennsylvania Press, 2004).

95. Burns, *Painting the Dark Side*, 114. This cartoon was first published in *Vanity Fair*, 10 May 1862, 227.

96. On images of Jefferson Davis cross-dressed, see Nina Silber, *The Romance of Reunion: Northerners and the South, 1865–1900* (Chapel Hill: University of North Carolina Press, 1993), 29–37; and Elizabeth Young, *Disarming the Nation: Women's Writing and the American Civil War* (Chicago: University of Chicago Press, 1999), 132–33, 183–88. On political caricature of the Civil War, see also Mark E. Neely, Jr., Harold Holzer, and Gabor S. Boritt, *The Confederate Image: Prints of the Lost Cause* (Chapel Hill: University of North Carolina Press, 1987); Mark E. Neely, Jr., and Harold Holzer, *The Union Image: Popular Prints of the Civil War North* (Chapel Hill: University of North Carolina Press, 2000); Shirley Samuels, *Facing America: Iconography and the Civil War* (New York: Oxford University Press, 2004); and Kristen M. Smith, ed., *The Lines are Drawn: Political Cartoons of the Civil War* (Athens, GA: Hill Street, 1999). For a foundational account of

images of inversion, see Christopher Hill, *The World Turned Upside Down: Radical Ideas during the English Revolution* (New York: Viking, 1972).

97. Charles Sumner, letter to George S. Hilliard, 4 December 1838, in *Memoir and Letters of Charles Sumner* (Boston, 1893), 2:21; this passage is reprinted in Betty T. Bennett, ed., *Lives of the Great Romantics III: Godwin, Wollstonecraft, and Mary Shelley by Their Contemporaries* (London: Pickering and Chatto, 1999), 3:137–38.

98. "A Few Thoughts on Slavery," *Southern Literary Messenger* (April 1854): 201 (accessed online through American Periodical Series); all quotations are taken from this edition and cited parenthetically in the text. Sumner's words are truncated from their original speech, "The Landmark of Freedom: No Repeal of the Missouri Compromise," in *The Works of Charles Sumner*, vol. 3 (Boston: Lee and Shepard, 1895), 291.

99. Harriet Beecher Stowe, *Uncle Tom's Cabin* (1852; repr., New York: Penguin, 1981), 356.

100. Charles Sumner, "Our Foreign Relations" (1863), in *The Works of Charles Sumner*, vol. 7 (Boston: Lee and Shepard, 1880), 444. This passage was quoted by William Wheeler to illustrate the term "Frankenstein" in *An Explanatory and Pronouncing Dictionary of the Noted Names of Fiction*, 23rd ed. (Boston: Houghton Mifflin, 1894), 138–39, and it is also noted in Florescu, *In Search of Frankenstein*, 14, and Bennett, *Lives of the Great Romantics III*, 137.

101. Sumner, "Our Foreign Relations," 450.

102. Charles Sumner, "The Rebellion, Its Origin and Mainspring" (1861), in *The Works of Charles Sumner*, vol. 6 (Boston: Lee and Shepard, 1880), 99.

103. Charles Sumner, "Our Domestic Relations; or, How to Treat the Rebel States" (1863), reprinted in Freidel, *Union Pamphlets of the Civil War*, 2:828, 833–34.

104. Ibid., 841.

105. Ibid., 854.

106. Ibid., 855.

107. Sumner, "Our Foreign Relations," 447.

108. Charles Sumner, letter to the Duchess of Argyll, 7 April 1863, in Edward L. Pierce, *Memoir and Letters of Charles Sumner* (Boston: Roberts Brothers, 1893), 4:153.

109. Charles Sumner, letter to John Bright, 28 October 1862, in Pierce, *Memoir and Letters*, 4:106.

110. Brooks allegedly attacked Sumner because Sumner had denounced his fellow South Carolinian, pro-slavery senator Andrew Butler, during the debate; for an account of this attack and its aftermath, see David Donald, *Charles Sumner and the Coming of the Civil War* (New York: Knopf, 1960), 288–347.

111. Ibid., 301.

112. Charles Sumner, letter to Julia Kean Fish, 27 September 1856, in *The Selected Letters of Charles Sumner*, ed. Beverly Wilson Palmer (Boston: Northeastern University Press, 1990), 1:468; Charles Sumner, letter to Samuel Gridley Howe, 23 April 1857, in ibid., 1:475.

113. Charles Sumner, letter to Samuel Gridley Howe, 1 July 1858, in ibid., 1:510.

114. Ibid.

115. Charles Sumner, letter to Frances Lieber, 2 May 1865, in ibid., 2:300.

116. Frederick Douglass, "The Speech of Senator Sumner," *Douglass' Monthly*, July 1860.

117. Frederick Douglass, "The Fall of Sumter," *Douglass' Monthly*, May 1861, reprinted in *Black Writers and the American Civil War*, ed. Richard A. Long (Secaucus, NJ: Blue and Grey, 1988), 265, 266.

118. Frederick Douglass, "The Slaveholders' Rebellion" (4 July 1862), reprinted in *Frederick Douglass Papers*, 3:541, 542–43.

119. Frederick Douglass, "Nemesis," *Douglass' Monthly*, May 1861, reprinted in ibid., 268–69 (erroneously dated 1860).

120. Frederick Douglass, "The Mission of the War" (January 1864), in *The Frederick Douglass Papers*, ed. John W. Blassingame and John R. McKivigan (New Haven CT: Yale University Press, 1991), ser. 1, 4:6; all subsequent quotations are taken from this edition and cited parenthetically in the text. This speech is discussed in Blight, *Frederick Douglass's Civil War*, 175, 176.

121. [David Goodman Croly and George Wakeman], *Miscegenation: The Theory of the Blending of the Races, Applied to the American White Man and Negro* (New York, 1864), 18. For discussion, see Sidney Kaplan, "The Miscegenation Issue in the Election of 1864," *Journal of Negro History* 34:3 (July 1949): 274–343; and Wood, *Black Scare*, 53–79.

122. Hodes, *White Women, Black Men*.

123. New York *World* (November 1864), quoted in Kaplan, "Miscegenation Issue," 331.

124. Samuel S. Cox, *Miscegenation or Amalgamation: Fate of the Freedmen* (Washington, DC, 1864), 5.

125. J[ohn] H. Van Evrie, preface to *White Supremacy and Negro Subordination; or, Negroes a Subordinate Race, and (so-called) Slavery its Normal Condition* (1867; repr. New York: Garland, 1993), 6.

126. [Croly and Wakeman], *Miscegenation*, 20.

127. On the myth of the black rapist, see Gail Bederman, *Manliness and Civilization: A Cultural History of Gender and Race in the United States, 1880–1917* (Chicago: University of Chicago Press, 1995); Angela Y. Davis, *Women, Race, and Class* (New York: Vintage, 1983), 172–201; Sandra Gunning, *Race, Rape, and Lynching: The Red Record of American Literature, 1890–1912* (New York: Oxford University Press, 1996), 3–17; Glenda Elizabeth Gilmore, *Gender and Jim Crow:*

Women and the Politics of White Supremacy in North Carolina, 1896–1920 (Chapel Hill: University of North Carolina Press, 1996), 61–89; Jacqueline Dowd Hall, "'The Mind That Burns in Each Body': Women, Rape, and Racial Violence," in *Powers of Desire: The Politics of Sexuality,* ed. Ann Snitow, Christine Stansell, and Sharon Thompson (New York: Monthly Review Press, 1983), 328–49; Hodes, *White Women, Black Men,* 176–208; and Robyn Wiegman, *American Anatomies: Theorizing Race and Gender* (Durham, NC: Duke University Press, 1995), 95–113.

128. Thomas Dixon, *The Leopard's Spots* (New York: Grosset and Dunlap, 1902), 375; all subsequent quotations are taken from this edition and cited parenthetically in the text. For discussion of this novel, see Gunning, *Race, Rape, and Lynching,* 19–47; Mason Stokes, *The Color of Sex: Whiteness, Heterosexuality, and the Fictions of White Supremacy* (Durham, NC: Duke University Press, 2001), 133–57; and Joel Williamson, *The Crucible of Race: Black-White Relations in the American South since Emancipation* (New York: Oxford University Press, 1984), 140–79.

129. George T. Winston, "The Relation of the Whites to the Negroes" (1901), quoted in Fredrickson, *Black Image in the White Mind,* 278.

130. Eleanor Tayleur, "The Negro Woman I.—Social and Moral Decadence," *The Outlook* 76 (30 January 1904): 267; all subsequent quotations are taken from this edition and cited parenthetically in the text. For brief discussions of the *Frankenstein* passage in Tayleur's essay, see Mia Bay, *The White Image in the Black Mind: African-American Ideas about White People, 1830–1925* (New York: Oxford University Press, 2000), 191; Anne Ruggles Gere, *Intimate Practices: Literary and Cultural Work in U.S. Women's Clubs, 1880–1920* (Urbana: University of Illinois Press, 1997), 164; and Elizabeth McHenry, *Forgotten Readers: Recovering the Lost History of African-American Literary Societies* (Durham, NC: Duke University Press, 2002), 223.

131. Frederick Douglass, introduction to *The Reason Why the Colored American Is Not in the World's Columbian Exposition* (1893), reprinted in Ida B. Wells-Barnett, *Selected Works,* ed. Trudier Harris (New York: Oxford University Press, 1991), 56. This pamphlet was coauthored by Douglass, Ida B. Wells, F. L. Barnett, and J. Garland Penn, with the authorship of each chapter designated.

132. Wells-Barnett et al., *Reason Why,* 79–80. For discussion of Wells's antilynching writing, see Bederman, *Manliness and Civilization,* 45–76; Jacqueline Goldsby, *A Spectacular Secret: Lynching in American Life and Literature* (Chicago: University of Chicago Press, 2006), 43–104; and Gunning, *Race, Rape, and Lynching,* 81–89.

133. A. T. Worden, "The Modern Sphinx," in "Exposition Number," special issue, *Bulletin of the Atlanta University* 48 (July 1893): 1; the poem has no title as it appears on the front page, but it is listed as "Poetry–The Modern Sphinx" in the index, p. 8. The goal of the *Bulletin* is stated in an anonymous editorial on p. 2. All subsequent quotations from the poem and the *Bulletin* are taken from this

edition and cited parenthetically in the text. For brief discussions of the poem, see Robert W. Rydell, "A Cultural Frankenstein? The Chicago World's Columbian Exposition of 1893," in *Grand Illusions: Chicago's World's Fair of 1893*, ed. Neil Harris, Wim de Wit, James Gilbert, and Robert W. Rydell (Chicago: Chicago Historical Society, 1993), 149; and Bill Brown, *The Material Unconscious: American Amusement, Stephen Crane, and the Economies of Play* (Cambridge, MA: Harvard University Press, 1996), 229. For discussion of the racial politics of the Exposition, see also Robert W. Rydell, *All the World's a Fair: Visions of Empire at American International Expositions, 1876–1916* (Chicago: University of Chicago Press, 1984), 38–71; and Alan Trachtenberg, *The Incorporation of America: Culture and Society in the Gilded Age* (New York: Hill and Wang, 1982), 208–34.

134. See Willis Goth Regier, *Book of the Sphinx* (Lincoln: University of Nebraska Press, 2004), esp. 157–59; and Scott Trafton, *Egypt Land: Race and Nineteenth-Century American Egyptomania* (Durham, NC: Duke University Press, 2004), 55–56, 63.

135. A short contemporary biography of Worden appears in an untitled article in *Current Literature* 2:4 (April 1889): 285 (accessed online through American Periodical Series). I am indebted to Christen Mucher for uncovering information about Worden.

136. A. T. Worden, "Tabitha Hoke on the New Woman," *Washington Post*, 8 September 1895, 15 (accessed online through ProQuest).

137. A. T. Worden, "February Twenty-Second," *Washington Post*, 17 February 1895, 19.

138. For discussion of African American uses of dialect in this period, see Gavin Jones, *Strange Talk: The Politics of Dialect Literature in Gilded Age America* (Berkeley: University of California Press, 1999).

139. Rydell, "A Cultural Frankenstein?" 129. Brown cites this poem's Frankenstein image as a form of antiracist critique (*Material Unconscious*, 229).

140. J. W. Hincks, "The Work of Atlanta University," in "Exposition Number," *Bulletin*, 2.

141. See Kevin K. Gaines, *Uplifting the Race: Black Leadership, Politics, and Culture in the Twentieth Century* (Chapel Hill: University of North Carolina Press, 1996).

142. Mary C. Jackson, "Failing to See," in "Exposition Number," *Bulletin*, 6.

143. "What Our Students Read," in ibid., 6.

144. Spivak, "Postscript," 255.

145. "Atlanta University Boys at the Exposition," in "Exposition Number," *Bulletin*, 7.

146. J. W. Johnson, quoted in "Atlanta University Boys at the Exposition," in ibid., 7.

147. Douglass, introduction to *Reason Why*, 52, 54.

NOTES TO CHAPTER 2

1. See I. A. Richards, "Metaphor" and "The Command of Metaphor," in *The Philosophy of Rhetoric* (New York: Oxford University Press, 1936), 89–138.

2. Dale Pesmen, "Reasonable and Unreasonable Worlds: Some Expectations of Coherence in Culture Implied by the Prohibition of Mixed Metaphor," in *Beyond Metaphor: The Theory of Tropes in Anthropology*, ed. James W. Fernandez (Stanford, CA: Stanford University Press, 1991), 225. For discussion of how to assess metaphors as bad or good, see Wayne Booth, "Metaphor as Rhetoric: The Problem of Evaluation," in *On Metaphor*, ed. Sheldon Sacks (Chicago: University of Chicago Press, 1979), 47–70.

3. The simile is itself often treated pejoratively, as a less elegant version of metaphor; for a summary of this treatment, see Jacqueline Vaught Brogan, *Stevens and Simile: A Theory of Language* (Princeton, NJ: Princeton University Press, 1986), 12–14.

4. Aristotle, *Rhetoric* 3.11.1411b28, trans. M. E. Hubbard, in *Ancient Literary Criticism: The Principal Texts in New Translations*, ed. D. A. Russell and M. Winterbottom (Oxford: Oxford University Press, 1972), 152–53; Quintilian, *The Orator's Education, Books 6–8*, 8.6.11, ed. and trans. Donald A. Russell (Cambridge, MA: Harvard University Press, 2001), 431. For recent discussion of classical theories of metaphor, see Doreen Innes, "Metaphor, Simile, and Allegory as Ornaments of Style," in *Metaphor, Allegory, and the Classical Tradition: Ancient Thought and Modern Revisions*, ed. G. R. Boys-Stones (Oxford: Oxford University Press, 2003), 7–27.

5. For discussion of dead metaphors, see Raymond W. Gibbs, Jr., "Why Idioms Are Not Dead Metaphors," in *Idioms: Processing, Structure, and Interpretation*, ed. Cristina Cacciari and Patrizia Tabossi (Hillsdale, NJ: Erlbaum, 1993), 57–77; George Lakoff and Mark Johnson, *Metaphors We Live By* (Chicago: University of Chicago Press, 1980), 52–55; George Lakoff and Mark Turner, *More Than Cool Reason: A Field Guide to Poetic Metaphor* (Chicago: University of Chicago Press, 1989), 128–31; M. Reimer, "The Problem of Dead Metaphors," *Philosophical Studies* 82 (1996): 13–25; and Elizabeth Closs Traugott, "'Conventional' and 'Dead' Metaphors Revisited," in *The Ubiquity of Metaphor: Metaphor in Language and Thought*, ed. Wolf Paprotté and René Dirven (Amsterdam/Philadelphia: John Benjamins, 1985), 17–53.

6. See *The Oxford Dictionary of Idioms*, ed. Jennifer Speake (Oxford: Oxford University Press, 1999), 149, 314.

7. Paraphrased from M. H. Abrams and Geoffrey Galt Harpham, "Figurative Language," in *A Glossary of Literary Terms*, 8th ed. (Boston: Thomson Wadsworth, 2005), 103.

8. Ambrose Bierce, *The Unabridged Devil's Dictionary*, ed. David E. Schultz

and S. T. Joshi (Athens: University of Georgia Press, 2000), 221. For discussion of this work, see James Milton Highsmith, "The Forms of Burlesque in *The Devil's Dictionary*," in *Critical Essays on Ambrose Bierce*, ed. Cathy N. Davidson (Boston: G. K. Hall, 1982), 123–35; and Roy Morris, Jr., *Ambrose Bierce: Alone in Bad Company* (New York: Oxford University Press, 1998), 182–85.

9. Donald Hall, "Hall's Index," in *Breakfast Served Any Time All Day: Essays on Poetry New and Selected* (Ann Arbor: University of Michigan Press, 2003), 180; Max Black, "More about Metaphor," in *Metaphor and Thought*, ed. Andrew Ortony (Cambridge: Cambridge University Press, 1979), 26.

10. Lakoff and Johnson, *Metaphors We Live By*, 72–75.

11. Quoted and discussed in Terence Hawkes, *Metaphor* (London: Methuen, 1972), 32.

12. Percy Bysshe Shelley, "A Defense of Poetry," in *Shelley's Poetry and Prose*, ed. Donald H. Reiman and Sharon B. Powers (New York: Norton, 1977), 482.

13. The history of metaphor in this period is further complicated by its relation to contemporary literary theory: Paul de Man notes that in the writings of Condillac, the French Enlightenment philosopher, "The story [of metaphor] is like the plot of a Gothic novel in which someone compulsively manufactures a monster on which he then becomes totally dependent and does not have the power to kill. Condillac . . . bears a close resemblance to . . . Mary Shelley" ("The Epistemology of Metaphor," in Sacks, *On Metaphor*, 21). De Man does not develop this comparison, but it suggests both a historical overlap between Condillac and Shelley and a structural overlap between deconstructive theories of metaphor, as articulated by de Man, and *Frankenstein*.

14. Brainerd Kellogg, *A Text-Book on Rhetoric*, introd. Charlotte Downey (1882; repr., Delmar, NY: Scholars' Facsimiles and Reprints, 1990); Adams Sherman Hill, *The Principles of Rhetoric and Their Application*, introd. Charlotte Downey (1888; repr., Delmar, NY: Scholars' Facsimiles and Reprints, 1994). Other examples include Alexander Bain, *English Composition and Rhetoric*, introd. Charlotte Downey (1871; repr., Delmar, NY: Scholars' Facsimiles and Reprints, 1996); James De Mille, *The Elements of Rhetoric*, introd. Charlotte Downey (1878; repr., Ann Arbor: Scholars' Facsimiles and Reprints, 2000); John H. Genung, *The Practical Elements of Rhetoric with Illustrative Examples*, introd. Charlotte Downey (1887; repr., Delmar, NY: Scholars' Facsimiles and Reprints, 1995); Thomas W. Harvey, *A Practical Grammar of the English Language*, introd. Charlotte Downey (1878; repr., Delmar, NY: Scholars' Facsimiles and Reprints, 1987); David Jayne Hill, *The Science of Rhetoric: An Introduction to the Laws of Effective Discourse*, introd. Charlotte Downey (1877; repr., Delmar, NY: Scholars' Facsimiles and Reprints, 1999); Theodore W. Hunt, *The Principles of Written Discourse* (New York, 1884); Simon Kerl, *Elements of Composition and Rhetoric*, introd. Charlotte Downey (1869; repr., Ann Arbor: Scholars' Facsimiles and Reprints, 2000); Simon Kerl, *A Common-School Grammar of the English Language*, introd. Charlotte Downey (1878;

repr., Delmar, NY: Scholars' Facsimiles and Reprints, 1985); and Alonzo Reed and Brainerd Kellogg, *Higher Lessons in English* (New York, 1877). For discussion of this material, see Dennis W. Baron, *Grammar and Good Taste: Reforming the English Language* (New Haven, CT: Yale University Press, 1982); Jean Ferguson Carr, Stephen L. Carr, and Lucille M. Schultz, *Archives of Instruction: Nineteenth-Century Rhetorics, Readers, and Composition Books in the United States* (Carbondale: Southern Illinois University Press, 2005); Nan Johnson, *Nineteenth-Century Rhetoric in North America* (Carbondale: Southern Illinois University Press, 1991); and Charles Paine, *The Resistant Writer: Rhetoric as Immunity, 1850 to the Present* (Albany: State University of New York Press, 1999).

15. Baron, *Grammar and Good Taste*, 140–68; Michel Foucault, *Discipline and Punish: The Birth of the Prison*, trans. Alan Sheridan (New York: Vintage, 1979), 170.

16. A. Hill, *Principles of Rhetoric and Their Application*, 96.

17. Kellogg, *Text-Book on Rhetoric*, 118.

18. Mark Seltzer, *Bodies and Machines* (New York: Routledge, 1992), 3.

19. Kerl, *Elements of Composition and Rhetoric*, 3.

20. Kellogg, *Text-Book on Rhetoric*, 134.

21. D. Hill, *Science of Rhetoric*, 218.

22. Hunt, *Principles of Written Discourse*, 95.

23. De Mille, *Elements of Rhetoric*, 116.

24. Gail Bederman, *Manliness and Civilization: A Cultural History of Gender and Race in the United States, 1880–1917* (Chicago: University of Chicago Press, 1995).

25. Ibid., 77–120.

26. On the codification of homosexuality in this period, see John D'Emilio and Estelle B. Freedman, *Intimate Matters: A History of Sexuality in America,* 2nd ed. (New York: Harper and Row, 1997), 223–29, and notes in chapter 4.

27. Hunt, *Principles of Written Discourse*, 120.

28. Quintilian, *Orator's Education*, 8.prooemium.19–20.

29. De Mille, *Elements of Rhetoric*, 118.

30. See Suzanne Bordelon, *A Feminist Legacy: The Rhetoric and Pedagogy of Gertrude Buck* (Carbondale: Southern Illinois University Press, 2007); and Jo Ann Campbell, ed., *Toward a Feminist Rhetoric: The Writing of Gertrude Buck* (Pittsburgh: University of Pittsburgh Press, 1996).

31. Gertrude Buck, *The Metaphor: A Study in the Psychology of Rhetoric* (Ann Arbor, MI: Inland Press, 1899), 35; all subsequent quotations are taken from this edition and cited parenthetically in the text. This work is also excerpted and briefly discussed in Campbell, *Toward a Feminist Rhetoric*, 31–44; and Jane Donawerth, ed., *Rhetorical Theory by Women before 1900* (Lanham, MD: Rowman and Littlefield, 2002). See also Bordelon, *Feminist Legacy*, 63–65; and Pesmen, "Reasonable and Unreasonable Worlds," 217–18.

32. Stephen Crane, *The Monster*, in *Harper's New Monthly Magazine*, August 1898, reprinted in *Stephen Crane: Prose and Poetry* (New York: Library of America, 1984), 389–448; all subsequent quotations are taken from this edition and cited parenthetically in the text. There is some critical disagreement as to whether the work is a short story or a novella. *The Monster* is roughly twenty-one thousand words, and Crane called it "a novelette" (letter to Edmund B. Crane, 9 September 1897, in *The Correspondence of Stephen Crane*, ed. Stanley Wertheim and Paul Sorrentino [New York: Columbia University Press, 1988], 1:296). For an assessment of why it is best termed a short story, see Michael W. Schaefer, *A Reader's Guide to the Short Stories of Stephen Crane* (New York: G. K. Hall, 1996), x–xi. I follow the Library of America edition in terming *The Monster* a novella.

33. Critical discussion of *The Monster* includes the following: Bill Brown, *The Material Unconscious: American Amusement, Stephen Crane, and the Economies of Play* (Cambridge, MA: Harvard University Press, 1996), 199–245; Joseph Church, "The Black Man's Part in Crane's *Monster*," *American Imago* 45:4 (winter 1989): 375–88; John R. Cooley, "'The Monster': Stephen Crane's 'Invisible Man,'" *Markham Review* 5 (1975): 10–14; Malcolm Foster, "The Black Crepe Veil: The Significance of Stephen Crane's *The Monster*," *International Fiction Review* 3 (1976): 87–91; Justin D. Edwards, *Gothic Passages: Racial Ambiguity and the American Gothic* (Iowa City: University of Iowa Press, 2003), 110–13; Michael Fried, *Realism, Writing, Disfiguration: On Thomas Eakins and Stephen Crane* (Chicago: University of Chicago Press, 1987), 94–96, 98–101, 132–36, 140–44; Jacqueline Goldsby, *A Spectacular Secret: Lynching in American Life and Literature* (Chicago: University of Chicago Press, 2006), 105–63; Thomas A. Gullason, "The Symbolic Unity of 'The Monster,'" *Modern Language Notes* 75:8 (December 1960): 663–68; James Hafley, "'The Monster' and the Art of Stephen Crane," in *Stephen Crane's Career: Perspectives and Evaluations*, ed. Thomas A. Gullason (New York: New York University Press, 1972), 440–46; David Halliburton, *The Color of the Sky: A Study of Stephen Crane* (Cambridge: Cambridge University Press, 1989), 182–200; J. C. Levenson, introduction to Stephen Crane, *Tales of Whilomville*, vol. 7 of *The University of Virginia Edition of the Works of Stephen Crane* (Charlottesville: University Press of Virginia, 1969), xi–lx; Nick LoLordo, "Possessed by the Gothic: Stephen Crane's 'The Monster,'" *Arizona Quarterly* 57:2 (summer 2001): 33–56; Elaine Marshall, "Crane's 'The Monster' Seen in the Light of Robert Lewis's Lynching," *Nineteenth-Century Literature* 51:2 (September 1996): 205–24; Price McMurry, "Disabling Fictions: Race, History, and Ideology in Crane's 'The Monster,'" *Studies in American Fiction* 26:1 (spring 1998): 51–72; Lee Clark Mitchell, "Face, Race, and Disfiguration in Stephen Crane's *The Monster*," *Critical Inquiry* 17:1 (autumn 1990): 174–92; Robert A. Morace, "Games, Play, and Entertainments in Stephen Crane's 'The Monster,'" *Studies in American Fiction* 9:1 (spring 1981): 65–81; William M. Morgan, "Between Conquest and Care: Masculinity and Community in Stephen Crane's *The Monster*," *Arizona Quarterly* 56:3 (autumn

2000): 63–92; James Nagel, "The Significance of Stephen Crane's 'The Monster,'" *American Literary Realism, 1870–1910* 31:3 (spring 1999): 48–57; Alice Hall Petry, "Stephen Crane's Elephant Man," *Journal of Modern Literature* 10:2 (June 1983): 346–52; John Carlos Rowe, *Literary Culture and U.S. Imperialism: From the Revolution to World War II* (New York: Oxford University Press, 2000), 141–63; Ruth Betsy Tenenbaum, "The Artful Monstrosity of Crane's Monster," *Studies in Short Fiction* 14:4 (fall 1977): 403–5; Michael Warner, "Value, Agency, and Stephen Crane's 'The Monster,'" *Nineteenth-Century Fiction* 40:1 (June 1985): 76–93; and Max Westbrook, "Whilomville: The Coherence of Radical Language," in *Stephen Crane in Transition: Centenary Essays*, ed. Joseph Katz (DeKalb: Northern Illinois University Press, 1972), 86–105. The only mentions of *The Monster* in relation to *Frankenstein* are Chris Baldick, *In Frankenstein's Shadow: Myth, Monstrosity, and Nineteenth-Century Writing* (Oxford, UK: Clarendon, 1987), 196–97; Brown, *Material Unconscious*, 234–35; and Levenson, introduction to Crane, *Tales of Whilomville*, xx.

34. The man "eaten by cancer" was the suggestion of Crane's niece, Edna Crane, quoted in Levenson, introduction to Crane, *Tales of Whilomville*, xiiin4. On the "Elephant Man," see Petry, "Stephen Crane's Elephant Man." For a summary of possible real-life cognates for *The Monster*, see Schaefer, *Reader's Guide*, 235–38.

35. Brown, *Material Unconscious*, 199–245.

36. Brown discusses the connections between William Henry Johnson and Crane's Henry Johnson in *Material Unconscious*, 217–19. On William Henry Johnson, see also Rachel Adams, *Sideshow U.S.A.: Freaks and the American Cultural Imagination* (Chicago: University of Chicago Press, 2001), 36–37; Robert Bogdan, *Freak Show: Presenting Human Oddities for Amusement and Profit* (Chicago: University of Chicago Press, 1988), 134–42; James W. Cook, Jr., "Of Men, Missing Links, and Nondescripts: The Strange Career of P. T. Barnum's 'What Is It?' Exhibition," in *Freakery: Cultural Spectacles of the Extraordinary Body*, ed. Rosemarie Garland Thomson (New York: New York University Press, 1996), 140–44; and Thomas Fahy, "Exotic Fantasies, Shameful Realities: Race in the Modern American Freak Show," in *A Modern Mosaic: Art and Modernism in the United States*, ed. Townsend Ludington (Chapel Hill: University of North Carolina Press, 2000), 67–92.

37. Marshall, "Crane's 'The Monster' Seen in the Light of Robert Lewis's Lynching." William Crane's account is reprinted in Stanley Wertheim and Paul Sorrentino, *The Crane Log: A Documentary Life of Stephen Crane, 1871–1900* (New York: G. K. Hall, 1994), 73. For an analysis of *The Monster* that foregrounds Lewis's lynching, see Goldsby, *Spectacular Secret*.

38. This episode is detailed in the entries for 3 and 4 April 1883 in Wertheim and Sorrentino, *Crane Log*, 28–29.

39. Alan C. Braddock, "'Jeff College Boys': Thomas Eakins, Dr. Forbes, and

Anatomical Fraternity in Postbellum Philadelphia," *American Quarterly* 57:2 (June 2005): 355–83.

40. Fried, *Realism, Writing, Disfiguration.* Fried shows that Eakins and Crane develop similar themes, but he does not explore the implications of this similarity beyond noting that it "is obviously a matter of some significance" (xiv).

41. Stephen Crane, "The Art Students' League Building," *The Notebook of Stephen Crane*, ed. Donald J. Grenier and Ellen B. Grenier (Kingsport, TN: Bibliographical Society of the University of Virginia, 1969), 12–13. For discussion of this sketch, see Christopher Benfey, *The Double Life of Stephen Crane* (New York: Knopf, 1992), 144–45; and Stanley Wertheim, *A Stephen Crane Encyclopedia* (Westport, CT: Greenwood, 1997), 11–12.

42. Bones was one of two "endmen," along with "Tambo" or "Brother Tambo"; see Robert Toll, *Blacking Up: A History of Blackface Minstrelsy; The Minstrel Show in Nineteenth-Century America* (New York: Oxford University Press, 1974), 54–55.

43. Peter Newell, illustration for *The Monster, Harper's*, August 1898, 353. On the popularity of the household laboratory in nineteenth-century American fiction, see Rowe, *Literary Culture and U.S. Imperialism*, 153, 335n30.

44. For relevant interpretations of this scene, see Church, "Black Man's Part"; Cooley, "'The Monster': Stephen Crane's 'Invisible Man'"; Foster, "Black Crepe Veil"; and Rowe, *Literary Culture and U.S. Imperialism.*

45. On Crane and Ellison, see Cooley, "'The Monster': Stephen Crane's 'Invisible Man.'" Ellison himself liked *The Monster* and praised it in "Stephen Crane and the Mainstream of American Fiction," in *Shadow and Act* (New York: Signet, 1964), 88.

46. Crane's focus on a judge as the arbiter of authority in race relations may also be a comment on the codification of racial segregation into law in *Plessy v. Ferguson* in 1896. See Foster, "Black Crepe Veil," 89; and McMurry, "Disabling Fictions," 52–53.

47. On the *Huck Finn* echoes of this passage, see Cooley, "'The Monster': Stephen Crane's 'Invisible Man,'" 10.

48. Warner, "Value, Agency, and Stephen Crane's 'The Monster,'" 77.

49. On the emergence of the dandy, see James Eli Adams, *Dandies and Desert Saints: Styles of Victorian Manhood* (Ithaca, NY: Cornell University Press, 1995); and Ellen Moers, *The Dandy: Brummell to Beerbohm* (New York: Viking, 1960).

50. Shane White and Graham White, *Stylin': African American Expressive Culture from Its Beginnings to the Zoot Suit* (Ithaca, NY: Cornell University Press, 1998), 92.

51. On the "Zip Coon," see Dale Cockrell, *Demons of Disorder: Early Blackface Minstrels and Their World* (Cambridge: Cambridge University Press, 1997), 92–139. On the black dandy, see Eric Lott, *Love and Theft: Blackface Minstrelsy and the American Working Class* (New York: Oxford University Press, 1995), 131–35;

Monica Miller, "W. E. B. Du Bois and the Dandy as Diasporic Race Man," *Callaloo* 26:3 (2003): 738–65; and White and White, *Stylin'*, 116–18.

52. *Indianapolis Freeman* (2 February 1898), quoted in David Krasner, *Resistance, Parody, and Double Consciousness in African American Theatre, 1895–1910* (New York: St. Martin's, 1997), 82. For discussion of the cakewalk in this period, see Eric Sundquist, *To Wake the Nations: Race in the Making of American Literature* (Cambridge, MA: Harvard University Press, 1993), 276–94.

53. For an elaboration of this argument, see Krasner, *Resistance, Parody, and Double Consciousness*, esp. 75–98.

54. Sexual connotations may be seen elsewhere in the novella as well. For example, in *The Monster's* opening section, Crane describes Jimmie Trescott's accidental destruction of a peony: "Finally he went to the peony and tried to stand it on its pins, resuscitated, but the spine of it was hurt, and it would only hang limply in his hand" (391). For interpretation of such images, see Church, "Black Man's Part."

55. For discussions of style in *The Monster*, see Hafley, "'The Monster' and the Art of Stephen Crane"; Tenenbaum, "Artful Monstrosity of Crane's 'The Monster'"; Warner, "Value, Agency, and Stephen Crane's 'The Monster'"; and Westbrook, "Whilomville."

56. On mechanical imagery in *The Monster*, see Tenenbaum, "Artful Monstrosity of Crane's 'The Monster,'" 404–5.

57. Genung, *Practical Elements of Rhetoric*, 101.

58. Bain, *English Composition and Rhetoric*, 38.

59. See Fried, *Realism, Writing, Disfiguration*, esp. 132: "Johnson's defacement in the burning laboratory may be read as imaging the very act of inscription. . . . a metaphorics of inscription is in play in *The Monster* from first to last." Fried does not analyze the story's racial content; he asserts that "approaching *The Monster* in terms of a thematics of writing precisely doesn't yield an understanding of the novella as a whole" (143–44). He elaborates these ideas in "Impressionist Masters: H. G. Wells's 'The Island of Dr. Moreau,'" in *Frankenstein, Creation and Monstrosity*, ed. Stephen Bann (London: Reaktion, 1994), 95–112. For a critique of Fried's approach to Crane, see Bill Brown, "Writing, Race, and Erasure: Michael Fried and the Scene of Reading," *Critical Inquiry* 18 (winter 1992): 387–402; and for Fried's response, see Michael Fried, "Response to Bill Brown," *Critical Inquiry* 18 (winter 1992): 403–10.

60. On the bombers as symbols of the Confederacy, see Foster, "Black Crepe Veil," 88. For other interpretations of this passage, see LoLordo, "Possessed by the Gothic," 33–34; McMurry, "Disabling Fictions," 62–64; and Rowe, *Literary Culture and U.S. Imperialism*, 151–52.

61. Bain, *English Composition and Rhetoric*, 37.

62. Hunt, *Principles of Written Discourse*, 105.

63. See Pauline Maier, *American Scripture: Making the Declaration of Independence* (New York: Knopf, 1997); and Garry Wills, *Inventing America: Jefferson's Declaration of Independence* (Garden City, NY: Doubleday, 1978).

64. Church, "Black Man's Part," 386.

65. Mary Shelley, *Frankenstein*, ed. J. Paul Hunter (1818; repr., New York: Norton, 1996), 189–90.

66. Both "Johnson" and "Dick" were in use as slang terms for the penis at this time. For discussion of the role of race in representations of the penis, see David M. Friedman, *A Mind of Its Own: A Cultural History of the Penis* (New York: Free Press, 2001), 103–47.

67. On women in *The Monster*, see Carol Hurd Green, "Stephen Crane and the Fallen Woman," in *Stephen Crane: Modern Critical Views*, ed. Harold Bloom (New York: Chelsea House, 1987), 112–14; and Rowe, *Literary Culture and U.S. Imperialism*, 159–60.

68. W. E. B. Du Bois, *The Souls of Black Folk*, ed. Donald B. Gibson (1903; repr., New York: Penguin, 1989), 5. For a different interpretation of Crane's veil image, see Goldsby, *Spectacular Secret*, 151.

69. On this image of the eye, see also Brown, *Material Unconscious*, 232–34.

70. Foster, "Black Crepe Veil," 90.

NOTES TO CHAPTER 3

1. On Reynolds, see Stanley Wertheim, *A Stephen Crane Encyclopedia* (Westport, CT: Greenwood, 1997), 293–94. *The Sport of the Gods* was first published in *Lippincott's* in 1901, and then in book form in 1902.

2. Linda Hutcheon, *A Theory of Parody: The Teachings of Twentieth-Century Art Forms* (Urbana: University of Illinois Press, 2000), 32, 20.

3. Fredric Jameson, *Postmodernism, or, The Cultural Logic of Late Capitalism* (Durham, NC: Duke University Press, 1991), 17. The most extensive discussions of pastiche are Richard Dyer, *Pastiche* (London: Routledge, 2007); and Ingeborg Hoesterey, *Pastiche: Cultural Memory in Art, Film, Literature* (Bloomington: Indiana University Press, 2001).

4. Travesty, in turn, is often defined in relation to burlesque. From the Italian *burla*, "ridicule," burlesque can operate, like travesty, by lowering an elevated original. Conversely, in the "high burlesque" mode, a low topic can be ridiculously elevated, as in the mock-heroic mode of Pope's *The Rape of the Lock*. As a theatrical genre, burlesques emerged in the nineteenth century, when they were comic theatrical entertainments akin to vaudeville; in the twentieth century, they became associated with sexually explicit stage shows. For discussions of travesty and burlesque, see Margaret A. Rose, *Parody: Ancient, Modern, and Post-Modern* (Cambridge: Cambridge University Press, 1992), 54–68; and John D. Jump, *Burlesque* (London: Methuen, 1972), 3–11.

5. Isaac D'Israeli, *Curiosities of Literature* (Boston: William Veazie, 1864), 3: 213–14; all subsequent quotations are taken from this edition and cited parenthetically in the text. *Curiosities of Literature* was a multivolume collection of essays that D'Israeli kept expanding; the first edition was published in 1791 and the fourteenth one in 1849, after his death. "Parodies" was published in the 1823 edition. For discussion of this essay, see Rose, *Parody*, esp. 10–11, 26–28; and James Ogden, *Isaac D'Israeli* (Oxford, UK: Clarendon, 1969), 95–106.

6. For an overview of parody in the age of *Frankenstein*, see John Strachan, ed., "Romantic Parody: A Special Issue of Romanticism on the Net," *Romanticism on the Net* 15 (August 1999), http://www.erudit.org/revue/ron/1999/v/n15.

7. Both *Presumption* and *Another Piece of Presumption* are reprinted in Steven Earl Forry, *Hideous Progenies: Dramatizations of Frankenstein from Mary Shelley to the Present* (Philadelphia: University of Pennsylvania Press, 1990), 135–60, 161–76; all subsequent quotations from the plays are taken from this edition and cited parenthetically in the text. For discussion of *Presumption*, see notes to chapter 1; there is little critical analysis of *Another Piece of Presumption*.

8. William St. Clair, *The Reading Nation in the Romantic Period* (Cambridge: Cambridge University Press, 2004), 372.

9. Joyce Carol Oates, afterword to Shelley, *Frankenstein*, ill. Barry Moser (Berkeley: University of California Press, 1984), 249.

10. Ebenezer Cobham Brewer, *Dictionary of Phrase and Fable* (1870), discussed in Chris Baldick, *In Frankenstein's Shadow: Myth, Monstrosity, and Nineteenth-Century Writing* (Oxford, UK: Clarendon, 1987), 3–4.

11. An even more overtly comic version of the blazon occurs in Frankinstitch's song about creating the monster (166–67), an elaborate discussion of body parts which reads, in part,

Look all who can
At this made man

Legs	Coat
Pegs	Throat
Eyes	Wrists
Thighs	Fists
Hair	Hips
Stare	Lips
Ears	Face
Tears	Grace
Wig	Arms
Jig	Charms
Nose	Knees
Toes	Ease
Joints	Points
Nail	Tail

12. Mary Shelley, *Frankenstein*, ed. J. Paul Hunter (New York: Norton, 1996), 32; all subsequent quotations are taken from this edition and cited parenthetically in the text.

13. Thomas Dew, *Review of the Debate in the Virginia Legislature of 1831 and 1832* (1832; repr., Westport, CT: Negro Universities Press, 1970), 105.

14. Simon Dentith, *Parody* (London: Routledge, 2000), 27.

15. George Canning, "Prospectus of *The Anti-Jacobin*" (1797), in *Poetry of the Anti-Jacobin* (New York: Putnam's, 1890), 6, 7. For discussion of *The Anti-Jacobin*, see Dentith, *Parody*, 26–27; Wendy Hinde, *George Canning* (New York: St. Martin's, 1973), 58–65; and Jump, *Burlesque*, 19–21.

16. On the complex politics of mimicry, see Homi Bhabha, "Of Mimicry and Man: The Ambivalence of Colonial Discourse," in *The Location of Culture* (London: Routledge, 1994), 85–92.

17. M. M. Bakhtin, *Rabelais and His World*, trans. Helene Iswolsky (Bloomington: Indiana University Press, 1984), 370. For discussion of Bakhtin and parody, see Rose, *Parody*, 125–70.

18. Bakhtin, *Rabelais and His World*, 20.

19. Ibid., 317–18. On the relation between the grotesque individual and the larger body politic, see Peter Stallybrass and Allon White, *The Politics and Poetics of Transgression* (Ithaca, NY: Cornell University Press, 1986).

20. Thomas Harvey, *A Practical Grammar of the English Language*, introd. Charlotte Downey (1878; repr., Delmar, NY: Scholars' Facsimiles and Reprints, 1987), 234.

21. For discussions of the animal-fable tradition, see Gillian Brown, *The Consent of the Governed: The Lockean Legacy in Early American Culture* (Cambridge, MA: Harvard University Press, 2001), 57–82; Louis Marin, "The Fabulous Animal," in *Food for Thought*, trans. Mette Hjort (Baltimore: Johns Hopkins University Press, 1989), 44–53; and Thomas Noel, *Theories of the Fable in the Eighteenth Century* (New York: Columbia University Press, 1975).

22. For example, La Fontaine is cited as the source in the annotations to the Chicago, Oxford, and Penguin editions of *Frankenstein* (Shelley, *Frankenstein*, ed. James Rieger [Chicago: University of Chicago Press, 1982], 110; Shelley, *Frankenstein*, ed. Marilyn Butler [Oxford: Oxford University Press, 1994], 256; Shelley, *Frankenstein*, ed. Maurice Hindle [London: Penguin, 1992], 259). The reference is most fully glossed in Shelley, *Frankenstein*, ed. Nora Crook (London: William Pickering, 1996), 86. This is the fable in Aesop:

> There was a man who owned a Maltese lap-dog and an ass. He was always playing with the dog. When he dined out, he would bring back titbits and throw them to the dog when it rushed up, wagging its tail. The ass was jealous of this and, one day, trotted up and started frisking around his master. But this resulted in the man getting a kick on the foot, and he grew

very angry. So he drove the ass with a stick back to its manger, where he tied it up.

The moral—added, like all the morals to Aesop's fables, at a later date—is, "This fable shows that we are not all made to do the same things" (*Aesop: The Complete Fables*, trans. Olivia and Robert Temple [London: Penguin, 1998], 204). The fable appears in La Fontaine as "L'Ane et le Petit Chien," in *The Complete Fables of Jean de La Fontaine*, ed. and trans. Norman B. Spector (Evanston, IL: Northwestern University Press, 1988), bk. 4, chap. 5, 154–57; all subsequent quotations from La Fontaine are taken from this edition, which presents the French original and English translation of each fable on facing pages.

23. William Godwin, "The Ass and the Lap-Dog," *Fables Ancient and Modern*, ed. David L. Greene (1805; repr., New York: Garland, 1976), 2:92–96. On Mary Shelley's relation to this book, see David Armitage, "Monstrosity and Myth in Mary Shelley's *Frankenstein*," in *Monstrous Bodies/Political Monstrosities in Early Modern Europe*, ed. Laura Lunger Knoppers and Joan B. Landes (Ithaca, NY: Cornell University Press, 2004), 212.

24. Linda Davidson, "The Use of *Blanchete* in Juan Ruiz's *Fable of the Ass and the Lap-Dog*," *Romance Philology* 33:1 (August 1979): 160. The argument that the lap-dog symbolizes erotic desire has been advanced in other contexts; see, for example, Robert Rosenblum, *The Dog in Art: From Rococo to Post-Modernism* (New York: Harry N. Abrams, 1988), 13–14.

25. The political resonances of the relationship between Caliban and Ariel have been interpreted in numerous ways. For example, Aimé Césaire's *Une Tempête* envisions both figures as slaves, with Caliban black and Ariel mulatto. For discussion of the political dimensions of the Ariel-Caliban relationship, see Rob Nixon, "Caribbean and African Appropriations of *The Tempest*," *Critical Inquiry* 13 (spring 1987): 572–74; and Alden T. Vaughan and Virginia Mason Vaughan, *Shakespeare's Caliban: A Cultural History* (Cambridge: Cambridge University Press, 1991), esp. 148–57.

26. La Fontaine, "The Ass and the Lap-Dog," 155.

27. La Fontaine, "The Ass Wearing the Lion's Skin," 239.

28. Brown, *Consent of the Governed*, 76.

29. Bakhtin, *Rabelais and His World*, 368–436.

30. Godwin, "The Ass in the Lion's Skin," in *Fables Ancient and Modern*, 1: 123–24.

31. Ibid., 127–28.

32. Godwin, "The Ass and the Lap-Dog," in *Fables Ancient and Modern*, 2:94.

33. Ibid., 94–95.

34. There is no comprehensive recent biography of Dunbar. For useful biographical perspectives, see Eleanor Alexander, *Lyrics of Sunshine and Shadow: The Tragic Courtship and Marriage of Paul Laurence Dunbar and Alice Ruth Moore*

(New York: New York University Press, 2001); Felton O. Best, *Crossing the Color Line: A Biography of Paul Laurence Dunbar, 1872–1906* (Dubuque, IA: Kendall/ Hunt, 1996); Benjamin Brawley, *Paul Laurence Dunbar: Poet of His People* (Chapel Hill: University of North Carolina Press, 1936); Dickson W. Bruce, *Black American Writing from the Nadir: The Evolution of a Literary Tradition, 1877–1915* (Baton Rouge: Louisiana State University Press, 1989), 56–98; Addison Gayle, *Oak and Ivy: A Biography of Paul Laurence Dunbar* (Garden City, NJ: Doubleday, 1971); Jay Martin, ed., *A Singer in the Dawn: Reinterpretations of Paul Laurence Dunbar* (New York: Dodd, Mead, 1975); and Peter Revell, *Paul Laurence Dunbar* (Boston: Twayne, 1979). Dunbar's writings are collected in *The Sport of the Gods and Other Essential Writings*, ed. Shelley Fisher Fishkin and David Bradley (New York: Modern Library, 2005); *The Paul Laurence Dunbar Reader*, ed. Jay Martin and Gossie H. Hudson (New York: Dodd, Mead, 1975); *The Collected Poetry of Paul Laurence Dunbar*, ed. Joanne M. Braxton (Charlottesville: University Press of Virginia, 1993); and *In His Own Voice: The Dramatic and Other Uncollected Works of Paul Laurence Dunbar*, ed. Herbert Woodward Martin and Ronald Primeau (Athens: Ohio University Press, 2002). His journalism is discussed in Fishkin and Bradley, *The Sport of the Gods and Other Essential Writings*, 233–43; J. Martin and Hudson, *Paul Laurence Dunbar Reader*, 31–35; J. Martin, *Singer in the Dawn*, 13–35; and Revell, *Paul Laurence Dunbar*, 47–51.

35. Paul Laurence Dunbar, "Chrismus on the Plantation," in *Collected Poetry*, 138.

36. On Dunbar's changing reputation, see Best, *Crossing the Color Line*, 137–57; Shelley Fisher Fishkin, "Race and the Politics of Memory: Mark Twain and Paul Laurence Dunbar," *Journal of American Studies* 40:2 (2006): 283–309; Keneth Kinnamon, "Three Black Writers and the Anthologized Canon," in *American Realism and the Canon*, ed. Tom Quirk and Gary Scharnhorst (Newark: University of Delaware Press, 1994), 143–53; and Ralph Story, "Paul Laurence Dunbar: Master Player in a Fixed Game," *CLA Journal* 27:1 (September 1983): 30–55.

37. William Dean Howells, "Paul Laurence Dunbar" (1896), reprinted in *The Heath Anthology of American Literature*, 4th ed., ed. Paul Lauter (Boston: Houghton Mifflin, 2002), 2:264–65. This passage appeared in Howells's introduction to Dunbar's *Lyrics of a Lowly Life*; Howells had previously praised Dunbar's *Majors and Minors*, his first volume of poetry, in *Harper's Weekly*.

38. Dunbar also had another white mentor, James Newton Matthews, prior to Howells; see J. Martin, foreword to *Singer in the Dawn*, 14–20.

39. Paul Laurence Dunbar, "Our New Madness" (1898), reprinted in *In His Own Voice*, 182.

40. On these freak-show figures, see Rachel Adams, *Sideshow U.S.A.: Freaks and the American Cultural Imagination* (Chicago: University of Chicago Press, 2001), 219–26; Robert Bogdan, *Freak Show: Presenting Human Oddities for Amusement and Profit* (Chicago: University of Chicago Press, 1988), 224–29; and Leslie

Fiedler, *Freaks: Myths and Images of the Secret Self* (New York: Simon and Schuster, 1978), 143–49.

41. Adams, *Sideshow U.S.A.*, 3.

42. Saunders Redding, "Portrait against Background," in J. Martin, *Singer in the Dawn*, 41, 42.

43. Quoted in Redding, "Portrait against Background," 42.

44. Alexander, *Lyrics of Sunshine and Shadow*, esp. 112–75.

45. Thomas Nelson Page, "Marse Chan" (1887), in *The Literature of the American South*, ed. William L. Andrews et al. (New York: Norton, 1998), 314, 311, 311; for discussion of Page, see David W. Blight, *Race and Reunion: The Civil War in American Memory* (Cambridge, MA: Harvard University Press, 2001), 222–27.

46. Paul Laurence Dunbar, "We Wear the Mask," in *Collected Poetry*, 71.

47. On Dunbar's favorite authors, see Alexander, *Lyrics of Sunshine and Shadow*, 13, 37. On his use of multiple forms of dialect, see Fishkin, "Race and the Politics of Memory," 299–307; Gavin Jones, *Strange Talk: The Politics of Dialect Literature in Gilded Age America* (Berkeley: University of California Press, 1999), 182–207; and Myron Simon, "Dunbar and Dialect Poetry," in J. Martin, *Singer in the Dawn*, 114–34.

48. [Paul Laurence Dunbar], "Negro in Literature" (1898), reprinted in *In His Own Voice*, 207. For discussion of Harris, see Blight, *Race and Reunion*, 225–31; and Eric Sundquist, *To Wake the Nations: Race in the Making of American Literature* (Cambridge, MA: Harvard University Press, 1993), 323–59.

49. Paul Laurence Dunbar, "The Old Cabin," in *Collected Poetry*, 260–61.

50. On Dunbar's theatrical writing, see David Krasner, *Resistance, Parody, and Double Consciousness in African American Theatre, 1895–1910* (New York: St. Martin's, 1997), 55–63; Martin and Primeau, "Introduction to the Dramatic Pieces," *In His Own Voice*, 3–16; and Revell, *Paul Laurence Dunbar*, 94–106. On the theatrical context for Dunbar, see Annemarie Bean, "Black Minstrelsy and Double Inversion, Circa 1890," in *African American Performance and Theater History: A Critical Reader*, ed. Harry J. Elam, Jr., and David Krasner (New York: Oxford University Press, 2001), 171–91.

51. Paul Laurence Dunbar, *Jes Lak White Fo'ks* (1900), in *In His Own Voice*, 141.

52. Shane White and Graham White, *Stylin': African American Expressive Culture from Its Beginnings to the Zoot Suit* (Ithaca, NY: Cornell University Press, 1998), 101. For scholarship on the dandy, see notes in chapter 2.

53. Paul Lawrence Dunbar, *The Fanatics*, ed. Lisa A. Long (1901; repr., Acton, MA: Copley, 2001), 10; all subsequent quotations are taken from this edition and cited parenthetically in the text.

54. Lisa A. Long, critical introduction to *The Fanatics*, xxxv.

55. Hutcheon, *A Theory of Parody*, xiv. See also Linda Hutcheon, *Irony's Edge: The Theory and Politics of Irony* (London: Routledge, 1994).

56. Hutcheon, *A Theory of Parody*, 6.

57. James Weldon Johnson, quoted in Gayle, *Oak and Ivy*, 145. On Dunbar as a dandy, see Alexander, *Lyrics of Sunshine and Shadow*, 2, 95, 127, and 145.

58. Paul Laurence Dunbar, letter to William Dean Howells, 13 July 1896, in *Paul Laurence Dunbar Reader*, 435.

59. Paul Laurence Dunbar, letter to William Dean Howells, 21 August 1896, quoted in Best, *Crossing the Color Line*, 74. This story appeared in biographies of Dunbar from very early. Lida Keck Wiggins, for example, recounted it as follows: "The next morning, Dunbar returned the coat with a note in which he said: 'In wearing your coat, I felt very much like the long-eared animal in the fable of the ass clad in the lion's skin'" (*The Life and Works of Paul Laurence Dunbar* [Naperville, IL: J. L. Nichols, 1907], 64).

60. Paul Laurence Dunbar, letter to Alice Dunbar, 18 March 1898, in "The Letters of Paul and Alice Dunbar: A Private History," ed. Eugene Wesley Metcalf, Jr. (Ph.D. diss., University of California Irvine, 1973), 2:523.

61. Paul Laurence Dunbar, letter to Alice Dunbar, 3 February 1898, in Metcalf, "Letters of Paul and Alice Dunbar," 2:422.

62. Paul Laurence Dunbar, letter to Matilda Dunbar, 6 June 1893, in *Paul Laurence Dunbar Reader*, 421. On Dunbar's experience at the Columbian Exposition, see Fishkin and Bradley, general introduction to *The Sport of the Gods and Other Essential Writings*, ix–xxv.

63. Paul Laurence Dunbar, "Representative American Negroes," in *Paul Laurence Dunbar Reader*, 51, 58.

64. On the idea of the "representative man" in African American culture, see Robert Levine, *Martin Delany, Frederick Douglass, and the Politics of Representative Identity* (Chapel Hill: University of North Carolina Press, 1997).

65. Arnold Rampersad, "*Adventures of Huckleberry Finn* and Afro-American Literature," in *Satire or Evasion? Black Perspectives on "Huckleberry Finn,"* ed. James S. Leonard, Thomas A. Tenney, and Thadious Davis (Durham, NC: Duke University Press, 1992), 226. On similarities between Ed and Jim, see Long, critical introduction to *The Fanatics*, xxxii; and Williams, "The Masking of the Novelist," in J. Martin, *Singer in the Dawn*, 186. On affinities between Dunbar and Twain, see Fishkin, "Race and the Politics of Memory."

66. On Twain's relation to black culture, see Shelley Fisher Fishkin, *Was Huck Black? Mark Twain and African-American Voices* (New York: Oxford University Press, 1993).

67. On trickster motifs in this era, see Elizabeth Ammons and Annette White-Parks, eds., *Tricksterism in Turn-of-the-Century American Literature: A Multicultural Perspective* (Hanover, NH: University Press of New England, 1994).

68. Many African American writers have engaged in this project directly. See, for example, versions of *Aesop's Fables* by Jacob Lawrence (*Aesop's Fables* [1970;

repr., Seattle: University of Washington Press, 1997]), and Toni and Slade Morrison (*Poppy or the Snake?* [New York: Scribner, 2003]).

69. Godwin, "Ass in the Lion's Skin," 125.

70. Dunbar's parodies also suggest the influence of a second African American trickster tradition. The folktales known as the Master-John stories feature a slave named John, who is the master's confidant. Historically, John is aligned with the black slave foreman, who was positioned in a supervisory role above other slaves; in the folktale, he uses this position to outwit the master in various ways. The figure of the slave foreman who exploits his intimacy with the master is parallel with what I have been characterizing as a lap-dog role. These two positions differ in important ways: the lap-dog is lazy, whereas the slave foreman led a life of enforced labor and was vulnerable if he failed to perform his duties. But the Master-John stories nonetheless provide another indigenous model for a trickster figure who, like Dunbar, operates at a level of relative but highly contingent privilege. On the Master-John tradition, see Lawrence W. Levine, *Black Culture and Black Consciousness: Afro-American Folk Thought from Slavery to Freedom* (Oxford: Oxford University Press, 1977), 127–33; John W. Roberts, *From Trickster to Badman: The Black Folk Hero in Slavery and Freedom* (Philadelphia: University of Pennsylvania Press, 1989), 44–61; and Sundquist, *To Wake the Nations*, 327–32.

71. Henry Louis Gates, Jr., *The Signifying Monkey: A Theory of African-American Literary Criticism* (New York: Oxford University Press, 1988), 52, xxiv. Gates argues that Dunbar's dialect poetry "signified upon the white racist textual tradition" (176); see also Gates's discussion of Dunbar's poetry in *Figures in Black: Words, Signs, and the "Racial" Self* (New York: Oxford University Press, 1987), 167–95. For examples of Signifying Monkey stories, see Roger D. Abrahams, *Afro-American Folktales: Stories from Black Traditions in the New World* (New York: Pantheon, 1985), 101–5; and Roger D. Abrahams, *Deep Down in the Jungle . . . : Negro Narrative Folklore from the Streets of Philadelphia* (1963; rev. ed., Chicago: Aldine, 1970), 142–56.

72. On the "badman," see Abrahams, *Deep Down in the Jungle*, 61–85; Levine, *Black Culture and Black Consciousness*, 407–20; Roberts, *From Trickster to Badman*; and H. Nigel Thomas, *From Folklore to Fiction: A Study of Folk Heroes and Rituals in the Black American Novel* (Westport, CT: Greenwood, 1988), 43–79. There is some disagreement about the relation between the "badman" and "bad nigger" figures: for example, Thomas asserts that they are synonymous (*From Folklore to Fiction*, 43), but Roberts sharply differentiates them (*From Trickster to Badman*, 171–82). On Stagolee, see also Cecil Brown, *Stagolee Shot Billy* (Cambridge, MA: Harvard University Press, 2003).

73. Quoted in Abrahams, *Deep Down in the Jungle*, 77.

74. Paul Laurence Dunbar, "The Lynching of Jube Benson," in *The Heart of*

Happy Hollow, introduction by Eleanor Alexander (1904; repr., New York: Harlem Moon/Broadway Books, 2005), 111; all subsequent quotations are taken from this edition and cited parenthetically in the text. There has been little discussion of this story; for brief assessments, see Bert Bender, "The Lyrical Short Fiction of Dunbar and Chesnutt," in J. Martin, *Singer in the Dawn*, 215–17; Bruce, *Black American Writing from the Nadir*, 88–89; Fishkin and Bradley, *The Sport of the Gods and Other Essential Writings*, 100–101; Jean M. Lutes, "Lynching Coverage and the American Reporter-Novelist," *American Literary History* 19:2 (summer 2007): 456; and Revell, *Paul Laurence Dunbar*, 123–24.

75. Paul Laurence Dunbar, foreword to *The Heart of Happy Hollow*, 3.

76. William Shakespeare, *King Lear*, ed. Stephen Orgel (New York: Penguin, 1999). The allusion suggests the richness of *King Lear* for Dunbar, who had cited it in the title of *The Sport of the Gods*, as I discuss in the next section. Political reappropriations of *King Lear* customarily involve a feminist reclamation of the daughters, especially Cordelia. Dunbar's interest in "happy hollow" suggests a different political project: the adaptation of Edgar's language of disguise—and the play's larger vocabulary of nothingness—in response to turn-of-the-century racial constraints. On feminist adaptations of *King Lear*, including those of Jane Smiley and Margaret Atwood, see Marianne Novy, ed., *Transforming Shakespeare: Contemporary Women's Re-Visions in Literature and Performance* (New York: St. Martin's, 1999). On the legacy of *Lear* more generally, see Peter Holland, ed., *King Lear and Its Afterlife*, *Shakespeare Survey* 55 (Cambridge: Cambridge University Press, 1992).

77. William Shakespeare, *The Tempest*, ed. Peter Holland (New York: Penguin, 1999), V.i.275–76. This line is important to much recent scholarship on *The Tempest*; see, for example, Paul Brown, "'This Thing of Darkness I Acknowledge Mine': *The Tempest* and the Discourse of Colonialism," in *Political Shakespeare: New Essays in Cultural Materialism*, ed. Jonathan Dollimore and Alan Sinfield (Ithaca, NY: Cornell University Press, 1985), 48–71.

78. Paul Laurence Dunbar, *The Sport of the Gods*, introd. William L. Andrews (New York: Signet, 1999), 148; all subsequent quotations are taken from this edition and cited parenthetically in the text. For discussion of the novel, see the following: William L. Andrews, introduction to *The Sport of the Gods*, v–xx; Houston A. Baker, Jr., *Blues, Ideology, and Afro-American Literature: A Vernacular Theory* (Chicago: University of Chicago Press, 1984), 114–38; Susan Bausch, "Inevitable or Remediable? The Historical Connection between Slavery, Racism, and Urban Degradation in Paul Laurence Dunbar's *The Sport of the Gods*," *CLA Journal* 45:4 (June 2002): 497–522; Jennifer Costello Brezina, "Public Women, Private Acts: Gender and Theater in Turn-of-the-Century American Novels," in *Separate Spheres No More: Gender Convergence in American Literature, 1830–1930*, ed. Monika M. Elbert (Tuscaloosa: University of Alabama Press, 2000), 225–42; Bruce, *Black American Writing from the Nadir*, 93–98; Gregory L. Candela, "We

Wear the Mask: Irony in Dunbar's *The Sport of the Gods*," *American Literature* 48:1 (March 1976): 60–72; Kevin K. Gaines, *Uplifting the Race: Black Leadership, Politics, and Culture in the Twentieth Century* (Chapel Hill: University of North Carolina Press, 1996), 179–208; Casey Inge, "Family Functions: Disciplinary Discourses and (De)Constructions of the 'Family' in *The Sport of the Gods*," *Callaloo* 20:1 (1997): 226–42; Revell, *Paul Laurence Dunbar* 153–61; Lawrence R. Rodgers, "Paul Laurence Dunbar's *The Sport of the Gods*: The Doubly Conscious World of Plantation Fiction, Migration, and Ascent," *American Literary Realism* 24:3 (spring 1992): 42–57; and Williams, "Masking of the Novelist," 195–99.

79. Dunbar is absent, for example, from the detailed chronology of realist and naturalist writing given in *The Cambridge Companion to American Realism and Naturalism: Howells to London*, ed. Donald Pizer (Cambridge: Cambridge University Press, 1995), ix–xvi, and from the following studies: Walter Benn Michaels, *The Gold Standard and the Logic of Naturalism: American Literature at the Turn of the Century* (Berkeley: University of California Press, 1987; Lee Clark Mitchell, *Determined Fictions: American Literary Naturalism* (New York: Columbia University Press, 1989); and Mark Seltzer, *Bodies and Machines* (New York: Routledge, 1991).

80. Shakespeare, *King Lear*, Iv.i.37–38. On the novel's title, see Baker, *Blues, Ideology, and Afro-American Literature*, 124–25; and Gaines, *Uplifting the Race*, 193.

81. Gaines, *Uplifting the Race*, 193. On the novel's relation to naturalism, see also Bausch, "Inevitable or Remediable?" 497.

82. On Frank Oakley as a dandy, see also Farah Jasmine Griffin, "*Who Set You Flowin'?*": *The African-American Migration Narrative* (New York: Oxford University Press, 1995), 25.

83. This association was certainly in place by the 1920s, when an area of Central Park was nicknamed the "Fruited Plain"; see George Chauncey, *Gay New York: Gender, Urban Culture, and the Making of the Gay Male World, 1890–1940* (New York: Basic Books, 1994), 182, 204.

84. On Kitty, see Brezina, "Public Women, Private Acts."

85. Paul Laurence Dunbar, letter to Alice Ruth Moore, 5 December 1897, in Metcalf, "Letters of Paul and Alice Dunbar," 1:269. This passage is quoted and discussed in Alexander, *Lyrics of Sunshine and Shadow*, 164.

86. Frank Norris, *McTeague*, in *Novels and Essays* (New York: Library of America, 1986), 524–25. On this scene and *The Sport of the Gods*, see Revell, *Paul Laurence Dunbar*, 159. On gender in *McTeague*, see Jennifer L. Fleissner, *Women, Compulsion, Modernity: The Moment of American Naturalism* (Chicago: University of Chicago Press, 2004), 201–31.

87. Jack London, *The Call of the Wild* (1903) and *White-Fang* (1906), in *The Call of the Wild, White Fang, and Other Stories*, ed. Andrew Sinclair (Harmondsworth, UK: Penguin, 1981), 65, 344. For discussion of London's dog stories, see Jonathan Auerbach, *Male Call: Becoming Jack London* (Durham, NC: Duke Uni-

versity Press, 1996); Marjorie Garber, *Dog Love* (New York: Touchstone, 1996), 86–88, 120–21; and Seltzer, *Bodies and Machines*, 166–70.

88. Paul Laurence Dunbar, letter to Alice Dunbar, 25 November 1897, in Metcalf, "Letters of Paul and Alice Dunbar," 1:253.

89. W. E. B. Du Bois, "The Black North," *New York Times*, 17 November 1902, in Paul Laurence Dunbar Papers, Ohio Historical Society, microfilm edition, reel 4, frame 603.

90. Review of *The Sport of the Gods*, *Athenaeum*, 29 November 1902, 1918.

91. Review of *The Sport of the Gods*, *North American* (Philadelphia), 8 June 1902, in Dunbar Papers, reel 4, frame 622.

92. Review of *The Sport of the Gods*, *Capital* (Los Angeles), 4 May 1901, in Dunbar Papers, reel 5, frame 389.

93. "New Lippincott," [illegible] (Rochester), 3 May 1901, Dunbar Papers, reel 5, frame 396.

94. Review of *Sport of the Gods*, *Bulletin* (San Francisco), 11 March 1901, in Dunbar Papers, reel 5, frame 341.

95. Pioneering critiques of racial representation in *Uncle Tom's Cabin* are James Baldwin, "Everybody's Protest Novel," in *Notes of a Native Son* (Boston: Beacon, 1955), 13–23; and J. C. Furnas, *Goodbye to Uncle Tom* (New York: William Sloane, 1956). More recent critiques include Gillian Brown, *Domestic Individualism: Imagining Self in Nineteenth-Century America* (Berkeley: University of California Press, 1990), 38–60; P. Gabrielle Foreman, "'This Promiscuous Housekeeping': Death, Transgression, and Homoeroticism in *Uncle Tom's Cabin*," *Representations* 43 (summer 1993): 51–72; and Hortense J. Spillers, "Changing the Letter: The Yokes, the Jokes of Discourse, or, Mrs. Stowe, Mr. Reed," in *Slavery and the Literary Imagination*, ed. Deborah E. McDowell and Arnold Rampersad (Baltimore: Johns Hopkins University Press, 1989), 25–61. For recent reassessments of this criticism, see Cindy Weinstein, ed., *The Cambridge Companion to Harriet Beecher Stowe* (Cambridge: Cambridge University Press, 2004).

96. Paul Laurence Dunbar, "Harriet Beecher Stowe," in *Collected Poetry*, 119. On Dunbar's father reading Stowe to him, see Best, *Crossing the Color Line*, 17.

97. Anna Julia Cooper, *A Voice from the South*, ed. Mary Helen Washington (1892; repr., New York: Oxford University Press, 1988), 222–23.

98. For an influential account of the actual gold standard in relation to literature of this era, see Michaels, *Gold Standard and the Logic of American Naturalism*.

99. Melville was not famous at that time; at most, Melville would have been familiar to Dunbar only from *Typee*, which was then better known than *Moby-Dick*. I am grateful to Carolyn Karcher for discussion of this point.

100. For discussion of this project, see Richard Yarborough, introduction to Richard Wright, *Uncle Tom's Children* (New York: Harper Perennial, 2004), ix–xxix.

101. Richard Wright, "How 'Bigger' Was Born," in Wright, *Early Works: Lawd Today!, Uncle Tom's Children, Native Son* (New York: Library of America, 1991), 874.

102. For discussion of gender in *Native Son*, see Farah Jasmine Griffin, "On Women, Teaching, and *Native Son*," in *Approaches to Teaching Wright's "Native Son*," ed. James A. Miller (New York: MLA, 1997), 75–80; Sondra Guttman, "What Bigger Killed For: Rereading Violence against Women in *Native Son*," *Texas Studies in Literature and Language* 43:2 (summer 2001): 169–93; and Trudier Harris, "Native Sons and Foreign Daughters," in *New Essays on "Native Son*," ed. Keneth Kinnamon (Cambridge: Cambridge University Press, 1990), 63–84.

103. James Smethurst, "Invented by Horror: The Gothic and African American Literary Ideology in *Native Son*," *African American Review* 35:1 (spring 2001): 32.

104. For Wright's view of Dunbar, see Richard Wright, "The Literature of the Negro in the United States," in *White Man, Listen!* (New York: Doubleday, 1957), 122.

105. This quotation is from Wright's prefatory paragraph to *Uncle Tom's Children*, in Wright, *Early Works*, 224.

106. Thomas F. Gossett, *"Uncle Tom's Cabin" and American Culture* (Dallas: Southern Methodist University Press, 1985), 388.

107. Gossie Hudson, quoted in Best, *Crossing the Color Line*, 147; Best also discusses this charge on pp. 2, 137, and 152, where he concludes that "any study which concludes that Dunbar was an accommodationist 'Uncle Tom' must be thoroughly re-examined."

NOTES TO CHAPTER 4

1. Robert Bridges, *Life*, 1 September 1898, reprinted in *Stephen Crane: The Critical Heritage*, ed. Richard M. Weatherford (London: Routledge and Kegan Paul, 1973), 258.

2. On the etymology of "monster," see Marie-Hélène Huet, *Monstrous Imagination* (Cambridge, MA: Harvard University Press, 1993), 6. On visuality in Shelley's *Frankenstein*, see Bill Brown, *The Material Unconscious: American Amusement, Stephen Crane, and The Economies of Play* (Cambridge, MA: Harvard University Press, 1996), 234–35; James A. W. Heffernan, "Looking at the Monster: *Frankenstein* and Film," *Critical Inquiry* 24 (autumn 1997): 133–58; Scott J. Juengel, "Face, Figure, Physiognomics: Mary Shelley's *Frankenstein* and the Moving Image," *Novel* 33 (summer 2000): 353–75; and Lee Zimmerman, "*Frankenstein*, Invisibility, and Nameless Dread," *American Imago* 60:2 (2003): 135–58.

3. See Juengel, "Face, Figure, Physiognomics," esp. 354.

4. William Nestrick, "Coming to Life: *Frankenstein* and the Nature of Film Narrative," in *The Endurance of Frankenstein: Essays on Mary Shelley's Novel*, ed. George Levine and U. C. Knoepflmacher (Berkeley: University of California Press,

1979), 303. For a relevant discussion of *Dracula* as an enactment of the properties of cinema, see Ronald R. Thomas, "Specters of the Novel: *Dracula* and the Cinematic Afterlife of the Victorian Novel," in *Victorian Afterlife: Postmodern Culture Rewrites the Nineteenth Century*, ed. John Kucich and Dianne F. Sadoff (Minneapolis: University of Minnesota Press, 2000), 288–310.

5. Andy Warhol's actual involvement with *Flesh for Frankenstein* was minimal, but the film was associated with him in various ways, and its alternate release title was *Andy Warhol's Frankenstein*. For discussion, see Maurice Yacowar, *The Films of Paul Morrissey* (New York: Cambridge University Press, 1993), 3–7, 71–80. Christopher Isherwood co-wrote the script for *Frankenstein: The True Story* with his partner, Don Bachardy. For discussion, see Albert J. LaValley, "The Stage and Film Children of *Frankenstein*," in Levine and Knoepflmacher, *Endurance of Frankenstein*, 279–80.

6. For discussion of these works, see the afterword. This genealogy might also include texts whose authors were not gay, such as the story "Moxon's Master" by Ambrose Bierce (1898), which is a revision of *Frankenstein* that can be interpreted as a panicked account of the sexual closet, and the illustrations to a 1934 edition of Shelley's *Frankenstein* by Lynd Ward, which offer graphically erotic woodcuts of a naked male monster (New York: Harrison Smith and Robert Haas, 1934; repr., New York: Portland House Illustrated Classics, 1988).

7. For many years, the single extant copy of the film was privately held by a collector, Alois Dettlaff, who refused to make it available for the public. It was finally screened at the Loew's Jersey Theatre in April 2003 (when I viewed it) and was then released on DVD as *Edison's 1910 "Frankenstein": The Lost Original, together with Murnau's 1922 "Nosferatu": First Dracula* (Cudahy, WI: A. D. Ventures/Father-Time Reproductions, 2003). For a recent account of the film and its distribution history, see Susan Tyler Hitchcock, *Frankenstein: A Cultural History* (New York: Norton, 2007), 123–32. The most detailed discussion of the film is Frederick C. Wiebel, Jr., *Edison's Frankenstein* (Hagerstown, MD: Frederick C. Wiebel, Jr., Fine Arts Studio, 2003); see also Frederick C. Wiebel, Jr., "Edison's *Frankenstein*," in *We Belong Dead: Frankenstein on Film*, ed. Gary J. Svehla and Susan Svehla (Baltimore: Midnight Marquee, 1997), 18–27. Materials related to the film are excerpted in "Frankenstein Meets the Edison Company," in *Focus on the Horror Film*, ed. Roy Huss and T. J. Ross (Englewood Cliffs, NJ: Prentice-Hall, 1972), 66–69. For scholarly discussions, which are hampered by lack of access to the film, see Tracy Cox, "*Frankenstein* and Its Cinematic Translations," in *Critical Essays on Mary Wollstonecraft Shelley*, ed. Mary Lowe-Evans (New York: G. K. Hall, 1998), 217–20; Wheeler Winston Dixon, "The Films of *Frankenstein*," in *Approaches to Teaching Shelley's "Frankenstein,"* ed. Stephen C. Behrendt (New York: MLA, 1990), 166–69; Steven Earl Forry, *Hideous Progenies: Dramatizations of Frankenstein from Mary Shelley to the Present* (Philadelphia: University of Pennsylvania Press, 1990), 80–85; LaValley, "Stage and Film Children of Frankenstein,"

250–52; and David J. Skal, *Screams of Reason: Mad Science and Modern Culture* (New York: Norton, 1998), 94–99.

8. Thomas Elsaesser, "Early Cinema: From Linear History to Mass Media Archaeology," in *Early Cinema: Space Frame Narrative*, ed. Thomas Elsaesser with Adam Barker (London: British Film Institute, 1990), 1. Alan Trachtenberg suggests that Edison was "a character part Prometheus, bringing light, and part Faust, tainted with satanic association" (*The Incorporation of America: Culture and Society in the Gilded Age* [New York: Hill and Wang, 1982], 66). On Edison and cinema, see Charles Musser, *Thomas A. Edison and His Kinetographic Motion Pictures* (New Brunswick, NJ: Rutgers University Press, 1995); and on his career as a whole, see Paul Israel, *Edison: A Life of Invention* (New York: Wiley, 1998).

9. Press release for *Frankenstein*, in "Frankenstein Meets the Edison Company," 67.

10. Eve Kosofsky Sedgwick, *The Coherence of Gothic Conventions* (New York: Methuen, 1986), ix.

11. Eve Kosofsky Sedgwick, *Epistemology of the Closet* (Berkeley: University of California Press, 1990), 187. See also Sedgwick's discussion of homosexuality and the gothic in *Between Men: English Literature and Male Homosocial Desire* (New York: Columbia University Press, 1985), 83–96.

12. Mary Shelley, *Frankenstein*, ed. J. Paul Hunter (New York: Norton, 1996), 68, 17.

13. For discussions of male homosexual possibility in the novel, see also Siobhan Craig, "Monstrous Dialogues: Erotic Discourse and the Dialogic Constitution of the Subject in *Frankenstein*," in *A Dialogue of Voices: Feminist Literary Theory and Bakhtin*, ed. Karen Hohne and Helen Wussow (Minneapolis: University of Minnesota Press, 1994), 83–96; Judith Halberstam, *Skin Shows: Gothic Horror and the Technology of Monsters* (Durham, NC: Duke University Press, 1995), 28–52; James Holt McGavran, "'Insurmountable Barriers to Our Union': Homosocial Male Bonding, Homosexual Panic, and Death on the Ice in *Frankenstein*," *European Romantic Review* 11:1 (winter 2000): 46–67; Anne K. Mellor, *Mary Shelley: Her Life, Her Fiction, Her Monsters* (New York: Routledge, 1988), 121–22; and Robert Samuels, *Writing Prejudices: The Psychoanalysis and Pedagogy of Discrimination from Shakespeare to Toni Morrison* (Albany: State University of New York Press, 2001), 73–86. On the question of lesbian possibilities in the novel, see Frann Michel, "Lesbian Panic and Mary Shelley's *Frankenstein*," in Mary Shelley, *Frankenstein*, 2nd ed., ed. Johanna M. Smith (Boston: Bedford/St. Martin's, 2000), 349–67.

14. For an overview of the codification of homosexuality in this period, see John D'Emilio and Estelle B. Freedman, *Intimate Matters: A History of Sexuality in America*, 2nd ed. (New York: Harper and Row, 1997), 223–29; for a sustained analysis of this codification, see Siobhan B. Somerville, *Queering the Color Line: Race and the Invention of Homosexuality in American Culture* (Durham, NC:

Duke University Press, 2000); for discussion of gay male subcultures at this time, see George Chauncey, *Gay New York: Gender, Urban Culture, and the Making of the Gay Male World, 1890–1940* (New York: Basic Books, 1994).

15. According to Chauncey, the metaphor of the homosexual "closet" emerged later: "Nowhere does [the term 'closet'] appear before the 1960s in the records of the gay movement or in the novels, diaries, or letters of gay men and lesbians. The fact that gay people in the past did not speak or conceive of themselves as living in a closet does not preclude us from using the term retrospectively as an analytic category, but it does suggest that we need to use it more cautiously and precisely" (*Gay New York*, 6). However, the idea of the closet as an illicit space containing secrets had emerged centuries before. For discussion of this formulation in a much earlier period, see Richard Rambuss, *Closet Devotions* (Durham, NC: Duke University Press, 1998); for an influential theorization of the closet, see Sedgwick, *Epistemology of the Closet*.

16. Tom Gunning, "What I Saw from the Rear Window of the Hôtel des Folies-Dramatiques, or, The Story Point of View Films Told," in *Ce que je vois de mon ciné . . . : La représentation du regard dans le cinéma des premiers temps*, ed. André Gaudreault (Paris: Méridiens Klincksieck, 1988), 37. The Edison *Frankenstein* emerges from a transitional period in cinema, roughly 1906–1913, between what Gunning has characterized as the "cinema of attractions," centered on the creation of spectacle in individual shots, and film narrative, centered on the editing of shots into character-driven stories. See Tom Gunning, "The Cinema of Attractions: Early Film, Its Spectator and the Avant-Garde," in Elsaesser with Barker, *Early Cinema*, 56–62.

17. On the peephole and sexuality in early cinema, see Miriam Hansen, *Babel and Babylon: Spectatorship in American Silent Film* (Cambridge, MA: Harvard University Press, 1991), 39–42; on pornography and early cinema, see Linda Williams, *Hard Core: Power, Pleasure, and the "Frenzy of the Visible"* (Berkeley: University of California Press, 1989), 58–92.

18. See Michel Foucault, *The History of Sexuality*, vol. 1, trans. Robert Hurley (New York: Vintage, 1980), 17–35.

19. An ethnically marked version of the Frankenstein story in early cinema can be found in the German film *The Golem* (dir. Paul Wegener, 1920), which drew on Jewish folklore, long predating *Frankenstein*, about a rabbi in Prague who makes a giant out of clay to combat religious persecution of Jews, only to find that the monster turns on him. Mary Shelley may well have known of golem folklore when she wrote *Frankenstein*; film versions of *The Golem*, in turn, have influenced film versions of *Frankenstein*. The relation between early-twentieth-century film versions of *The Golem* and *Frankenstein*, like that between their source texts, is one of ongoing conversation and mutual influence. For discussion of the film *Golem*, see LaValley, "Stage and Film Children of *Frankenstein*," 252–62. There were also two other, little-seen film adaptations of *Frankenstein* in this

period: *Life without Soul* (dir. Joseph W. Smiley, 1915) and *Il Mostro di Franken-stein* (dir. Eugenio Testa, 1920). For descriptions of these films, see Stephen Jones, *The Frankenstein Scrapbook: The Complete Movie Guide to The World's Most Famous Monster* (New York: Citadel, 1995), 18, 19.

20. For an exception, see Charlene Regester, "The Cinematic Representation of Race in *The Birth of a Nation*: A Black Horror Film," in *Thomas Dixon, Jr., and the Birth of Modern America*, ed. Michele K. Gillespie and Randal L. Hall (Baton Rouge: Louisiana State University Press, 2006), 164–82. Horror is also an important touchstone in analyses of the film by Ed Guerrero, *Framing Blackness: The African American Image in Film* (Philadelphia: Temple University Press, 1993), 8–17; and James Snead, *White Screens, Black Images: Hollywood from the Dark Side* (New York: Routledge, 1994), 37–45. Other discussions of *Birth of a Nation* include Donald Bogle, *Toms, Coons, Mammies, Mulattoes and Bucks: An Interpretive History of Blacks in American Films*, 3rd ed. (New York: Continuum, 1994), 10–18; Susan Courtney, *Hollywood Fantasies of Miscegenation: Spectacular Narratives of Gender and Race, 1903–1967* (Princeton, NJ: Princeton University Press, 2005), 61–99; Thomas Cripps, *Slow Fade to Black: The Negro in American Film, 1900–1942* (1977; repr., New York: Oxford University Press, 1993), 41–69; Richard Dyer, "Into the Light: The Whiteness of the South in *The Birth of a Nation*," in *Dixie Debates: Perspectives on Southern Cultures*, ed. Richard H. King and Helen Taylor (London: Pluto, 1996), 165–76; Jane Gaines, "*The Birth of a Nation* and *Within Our Gates*: Two Tales of the American South," in King and Taylor, *Dixie Debates*, 177–92; Robert Lang, ed., *The Birth of a Nation* (New Brunswick, NJ: Rutgers University Press, 1994); Michael Rogin, "'The Sword Became a Flashing Vision': D. W. Griffith's *The Birth of a Nation*," in *Ronald Reagan, the Movie and Other Episodes in Political Demonology* (Berkeley: University of California Press, 1987), 190–235; Mason Stokes, *The Color of Sex: Whiteness, Heterosexuality, and the Fictions of White Supremacy* (Durham, NC: Duke University Press, 2001), 158–77; Clyde Taylor, "The Re-Birth of the Aesthetic in Cinema," in *The Birth of Whiteness: Race and the Emergence of U.S. Cinema*, ed. Daniel Bernardi (New Brunswick, NJ: Rutgers University Press, 1996), 15–37; and Linda Williams, *Playing the Race Card: Melodramas of Black and White from Uncle Tom to O. J. Simpson* (Princeton, NJ: Princeton University Press, 2001), 109–32.

21. Lang, *Birth of a Nation*, 94; all quotations from the film are taken from the continuity script reprinted in this book and are cited parenthetically in the text.

22. Snead, *White Screens, Black Images*, 39.

23. Manthia Diawara, "Black Spectatorship: Problems of Identification and Resistance," *Screen* 29:4 (autumn 1988): 74.

24. Quoted in Lang, introduction to *Birth of a Nation*, 19.

25. On the lighting and other aspects of whiteness in the film, see Dyer, "Into the Light"; and Stokes, *Color of Sex*, 158–77. On the white robes of the Klan, see

Judith Jackson Fossett, "(K)night Riders in (K)night Gowns: The Ku Klux Klan, Race, and Constructions of Masculinity," in *Race Consciousness: African-American Studies for the New Century*, ed. Judith Jackson Fossett and Jeffrey A. Tucker (New York: New York University Press, 1997), 35–49.

26. Review of *Bride of Frankenstein, New York Times*, 11 May 1935, "Amusements" sec., 21; Donald Glut, *The Frankenstein Legend* (Metuchen, NJ: Scarecrow, 1973), 132; Radu N. Florescu, *In Search of Frankenstein* (Boston: New York Graphic Society, 1975), 193; Chris Steinbrunner and Burt Goldblatt, *Cinema of the Fantastic* (New York: Saturday Review Press, 1972), 106. For discussion of the Whale films, see Rhona J. Berenstein, *Attack of the Leading Ladies: Gender, Sexuality and Spectatorship in Classic Horror Cinema* (New York: Columbia University Press, 1996), 84–87, 136–47; Michael Brunas, John Brunas, and Tom Weaver, *Universal Horrors: The Studio's Classic Films, 1931–1946* (Jefferson, NC: McFarland, 1990), 20–30, 114–23; Syndy M. Conger and Janice R. Welsch, "The Comic and the Grotesque in James Whale's *Frankenstein* Films," in *Planks of Reason: Essays on the Horror Film*, ed. Barry K. Grant (Metuchen, NJ: Scarecrow, 1984), 290–306; William K. Everson, *Classics of the Horror Film* (Secaucus, NJ: Citadel, 1974), 36–62; Alberto Manguel, *Bride of Frankenstein* (London: British Film Institute, 1997); Martin F. Norden, "Sexual References in James Whale's *Bride of Frankenstein*," in *Eros in the Mind's Eye: Sexuality and the Fantastic in Art and Film*, ed. Donald F. Palumbo (Westport, CT: Greenwood, 1986), 141–50; Paul O'Flinn, "Production and Reproduction: The Case of *Frankenstein*," in *Popular Fictions: Essays in Literature and History*, ed. Peter Humm, Paul Stigant, and Peter Widdowson (London: Methuen, 1986), 196–221; Lyn Phelan, "Artificial Women and Male Subjectivity in *42nd Street* and *Bride of Frankenstein*," *Screen* 41:2 (summer 2000): 161–82; Caroline Joan ("Kay") S. Picart, *The Cinematic Rebirths of Frankenstein: Universal, Hammer, and Beyond* (Westport, CT: Praeger, 2002), 25–98; David J. Skal, *The Monster Show: A Cultural History of Horror* (New York: Penguin, 1993), 182–91; Skal, *Screams of Reason*, 148–54; and Elizabeth Young, "Here Comes the Bride: Wedding Gender and Race in *Bride of Frankenstein*," *Feminist Studies* 17:3 (fall 1991): 403–37.

For discussions of the larger *Frankenstein* film tradition, see Jean-Pierre Bouyxou, *Frankenstein* (Paris: Editions Premier Plan, 1969); Cox, "*Frankenstein* and Its Cinematic Translations"; Dixon, "Films of *Frankenstein*"; Forry, *Hideous Progenies*; Heffernan, "Looking at the Monster"; Hitchcock, *Frankenstein*; Jones, *Frankenstein Scrapbook*; LaValley, "Stage and Film Children of *Frankenstein*"; Gregory William Mank, *It's Alive! The Classic Cinema Saga of Frankenstein* (San Diego: A. S. Barnes, 1981); Caroline Joan ("Kay") S. Picart, Frank Smoot, and Jayne Blodgett, *The Frankenstein Film Sourcebook* (Westport, CT: Greenwood, 2001); Esther Schor, "*Frankenstein* and Film," in *The Cambridge Companion to Mary Shelley*, ed. Esther Schor (Cambridge: Cambridge University Press, 2003), 63–83; and Svehla and Svehla, *We Belong Dead*. On the multimedia circulation of *Frankenstein* in twentieth-century culture, see Florescu, *In Search of Franken-stein*; Glut, *Frankenstein Legend*; Peter Haining, ed., *The Frankenstein File* (London: New English Library, 1977); John Stoker, *The Illustrated Frankenstein* (New York: Sterling, 1980); Martin Tropp, *Mary Shelley's Monster: The Story of Frankenstein* (Boston: Houghton Mifflin, 1976); Tomás Fernández Valentí and Antonio José Navarro, *Frankenstein: El Mito de la Vida Artificial* (Madrid: Nuer Ediciones, 2000); and esp. Donald F. Glut, *The Frankenstein Catalog: Being a Comprehensive Listing of Novels, Translations, Adaptations, Stories, Critical Works, Popular Articles, Series, Fumetti, Verse, Stage Plays, Films, Cartoons, Puppetry, Comics, Satire and Humor, Spoken and Musical Recordings, Tape, and Sheet Music Featuring Frankenstein's Monster and/or Descended from Mary Shelley's Novel* (Jefferson, NC: McFarland, 1984).

27. I. Maurice Wormser, *Frankenstein, Incorporated* (New York: Whittlesey House, 1931), v. For discussion of this work, see Hitchcock, *Frankenstein*, 144–45.

28. Ibid., 229.

29. *Louis K. Liggett Co. et al. v. Lee, Comptroller et al.*, 288 U.S. 517 (1933). This comparison has reappeared in recent critiques of corporations; see Joel Bakan, *The Corporation: The Pathological Pursuit of Profit and Power*, rev. ed. (London: Constable, 2005), 149.

30. Skal, *Monster Show*, 132–33.

31. O'Flinn, "Production and Reproduction," 213–14.

32. The monster was also pressed into allegorical service in the 1930s in other political contexts, presumably because of the popularity of the Whale films. For example, *Hitler as Frankenstein* (1933) compared the new leader of Germany to the monster: "A monster has been created, and let loose ostensibly to arrest the march of Communism and Marxism. But the ghost has become the master of its conjurer. What will there be AFTER Hitler?" (Johannes Steel, *Hitler as Frankenstein*, pref. Harold Laski [London: Wishart, 1933], 176).

33. Jessie Daniel Ames, *The Changing Character of Lynching: Review of Lynching, 1931–41, with a Discussion of Recent Developments in the Field* (1942; repr., New York: AMS Press, 1973), 2. On Ames, see Jacquelyn Dowd Hall, *Revolt against Chivalry: Jessie Daniel Ames and the Women's Campaign against Lynching* (New York: Columbia University Press, 1979). On campaigns against lynching in this period, see also Dora Apel, *Imagery of Lynching: Black Men, White Women, and the Mob* (New Brunswick, NJ: Rutgers University Press, 2004); Christopher Waldrep, ed., *Lynching in America: A History in Documents* (New York: New York University Press, 2006); and Robert L. Zangrando, *The NAACP Crusade against Lynching, 1909–50* (Philadelphia: Temple University Press, 1980).

34. Bogle, *Toms, Coons, Mammies, Mulattoes, and Bucks*, 36.

35. On black roles in this period, see Bogle, *Toms, Coons, Mammies, Mulattoes, and Bucks*, 35–100; and Cripps, *Slow Fade to Black*, 263–308. On protest campaigns, see Leonard Archer, *Black Images in the American Theatre: NAACP*

Protest Campaigns—Stage, Screen, Radio, and Television (Brooklyn: Pageant-Poseidon, 1973), 183–224.

36. Lawrence Reddick, "Of Motion Pictures" (1944), reprinted in *Black Films and Filmmakers: A Comprehensive Anthology from Stereotype to Superhero*, ed. Lindsay Patterson (New York: Dodd, Mead, 1975), 4n3.

37. Quoted in Glut, *Frankenstein Legend*, 100.

38. Quoted in Denis Gifford, *Karloff: The Man, the Monster, the Movies* (New York: Curtis, 1973), 41.

39. Berenstein, *Attack of the Leading Ladies*, 160–97.

40. Cripps, *Slow Fade to Black*, 278. On *King Kong*, see Berenstein, *Attack of the Leading Ladies*, 184–97; Cynthia Erb, *Tracking King Kong: A Hollywood Icon in World Culture* (Detroit: Wayne State University Press, 1998); E. Ann Kaplan, *Looking for the Other: Feminism, Film, and the Imperial Gaze* (New York: Routledge, 1997), 69–75; Fatimah Tobing Rony, *The Third Eye: Race, Cinema, and Ethnographic Spectacle* (Durham, NC: Duke University Press, 1996), 157–91; Snead, *White Screens, Black Images*, 1–36; and Thomas E. Wartenberg, "Humanizing the Beast: *King Kong* and the Representation of Black Male Sexuality," in *Classic Hollywood, Classic Whiteness*, ed. Daniel Bernardi (Minneapolis: University of Minnesota Press, 2001), 157–77.

41. On *Fury*, see Cripps, *Slow Fade to Black*, 295, and Barbara Mennel, "White Law and the Missing Black Body in Fritz Lang's *Fury* (1936)," *Quarterly Review of Film Studies* 20:3 (2003): 203–23.

42. "Lynch Victim's Corpse May Have Been Dug Up," *Birmingham News*, 29 November 1933, reprinted in Ralph Ginzburg, *100 Years of Lynchings* (Baltimore: Black Classic Press, 1962), 203. For a discussion of Armwood, see Sherrilyn A. Ifill, *On the Courthouse Lawn: Confronting the Legacy of Lynching in the Twenty-First Century* (Boston: Beacon, 2007), 33–42, 78–83, 88–92.

43. "Suspect Hanged from Oak on Bastrop Public Square," *New Orleans Tribune*, 10 July 1923, reprinted in Ginzburg, *100 Years of Lynchings*, 220.

44. See James Allen et al., *Without Sanctuary: Lynching Photography in America* (Santa Fe, NM: Twin Palms, 2000). These photographs have prompted much new scholarship; see, for example, Dora Apel and Shawn Michelle Smith, *Lynching Photography* (Berkeley: University of California Press, 2008).

45. Richard Wright, "How 'Bigger' Was Born," in Wright, *Early Works: Lawd Today!, Uncle Tom's Children, Native Son* (New York: Library of America, 1991), 881. For discussion of Wright and the gothic, see James Smethurst, "Invented by Horror: The Gothic and African American Literary Ideology in *Native Son*," *African American Review* 35:1 (spring 2001): 29–40.

46. James Curtis, *James Whale: A New World of Gods and Monsters* (London: Faber and Faber, 1998), 270; on *Black Majesty*, see ibid., 272. On the friendship between Whale and Robeson, see also Martin Bauml Duberman, *Paul Robeson*

(New York: Knopf, 1998), 196–97; and Paul Robeson, Jr., *The Undiscovered Paul Robeson: An Artist's Journey* (New York: Wiley, 2001), 233–34.

47. On *Show Boat*, see Cripps, *Slow Fade to Black*, 293–94; and Miles Krueger, *Show Boat: The Story of a Classic American Musical* (New York: Oxford University Press, 1977).

48. Wells's intentions are remembered by screenwriter R. C. Sherriff, quoted in Curtis, *James Whale*, 200; on Whale and *Invisible Man*, see ibid., 196–210.

49. Ralph Ellison, *Invisible Man* (New York: Vintage, 1972), 3.

50. On Whale's sexuality, see Curtis, *James Whale*; David Ehrenstein, *Open Secret: Gay Hollywood, 1928–1998* (New York: Morrow, 1998), 58–71; and Mark Gatiss, *James Whale: A Biography* (London: Cassell, 1995). On David Lewis, see Boze Hadleigh, *Hollywood Gays* (New York: Barricade, 1996), 309–42; and William J. Mann, *Behind the Screen: How Gays and Lesbians Shaped Hollywood, 1910–69* (New York: Penguin, 1991), 188–93.

51. Richard Barrios, *Screened Out: Playing Gay in Hollywood from Edison to Stonewall* (New York: Routledge, 2003), 64. The pioneering gay interpretation of the *Frankenstein* films is Vito Russo, *The Celluloid Closet: Homosexuality in the Movies* (1981; rev. ed., New York: Harper and Row, 1987), 49–52. See also Harry M. Benshoff, *Monsters in the Closet: Homosexuality and the Horror Film* (Manchester: Manchester University Press, 1997), 46–51; Berenstein, *Attack of the Leading Ladies*, 136–47; and Mark Bronski, "*Gods and Monsters*: The Search for the Right Whale," *Cineaste* 24:4 (1999): 10–14.

52. On Thesiger, see Curtis, *James Whale*, 250; Hadleigh, *Hollywood Gays*, 321–22; and Mann, *Behind the Screen*, 187. On Laughton, see Simon Callow, *Charles Laughton: A Difficult Actor* (New York: Grove, 1987). For an overview of gay Hollywood at this time, see Ehrenstein, *Open Secret*, 161–237.

53. *Variety* quoted in Mann, *Behind the Screen*, 126.

54. Berenstein, *Attack of the Leading Ladies*, 85–87.

55. Vidal quoted in an interview with Mann, *Behind the Screen*, 208.

56. Cripps notes that the German title of the film was *King Kong und die Wiesse Frau* ("King Kong and the White Woman"), which foregrounds the possibility of interracial rape even more fully (*Slow Fade to Black*, 278).

57. Sedgwick notes the sexual implications of this passage in *Between Men*, 10.

58. Jacqueline Dowd Hall, "'The Mind That Burns in Each Body': Women, Rape, and Racial Violence," in *Powers of Desire: The Politics of Sexuality*, ed. Ann Snitow, Christine Stansell, and Sharon Thompson (New York: Monthly Review Press, 1983), 335.

59. Valerie Smith, "Split Affinities: The Case of Interracial Rape," in *Conflicts in Feminism*, ed. Marianne Hirsch and Evelyn Fox Keller (New York: Routledge, 1990), 276.

60. Curtis, *James Whale*, 243.

61. For discussions of the "tragic mulatta," see Judith Berzon, *Neither White nor Black: The Mulatto Character in American Fiction* (New York: New York University Press, 1978); Elaine K. Ginsberg, ed., *Passing and the Fictions of Identity* (Durham, NC: Duke University Press, 1996); Eve Allegra Raimon, *The "Tragic Mulatta" Revisited: Race and Nationalism in Nineteenth-Century Antislavery Fiction* (New Brunswick, NJ: Rutgers University Press, 2004); Debra J. Rosenthal, *Race Mixture in Nineteenth-Century U.S. and Spanish American Fictions: Gender, Culture, and Nation Building* (Chapel Hill: University of North Carolina Press, 2004); and Werner Sollors, *Neither Black nor White yet Both: Thematic Explorations of Interracial Literature* (Cambridge, MA: Harvard University Press, 1997), 220–45. On *Imitation of Life*, see Lauren Berlant, "National Brands/National Body: *Imitation of Life*," in *Comparative American Identities: Race, Sex, and Nationality in the Modern Text*, ed. Hortense J. Spillers (New York: Routledge, 1991), 110–40; Courtney, *Hollywood Fantasies of Miscegenation*, 142–90; and Valerie Smith, "Reading the Intersection of Race and Gender in Narratives of Passing," *Diacritics* 24:2–3 (summer–fall 1994): 43–57. On *Show Boat*, see note 47 above. For examples of the "tragic mulatta" figure in other film genres, see, for example, Lei Lani Nishime, "The Mulatto Cyborg: Imagining a Multiracial Future," *Cinema Journal* 44:2 (winter 2005): 34–49, and Stephen Jay Schneider, "Mixed Blood Couples: Monsters and Miscegenation in U.S. Horror Cinema," in *The Gothic Other: Racial and Social Constructions in the Literary Imagination*, ed. Ruth Bienstock Anolik and Douglas L. Howard (Jefferson, NC: McFarland, 2004), 72–89.

62. Norden, "Sexual References in James Whale's *Bride of Frankenstein*," 150.

63. Moe Meyer, "Introduction: Reclaiming the Discourse of Camp," *The Politics and Poetics of Camp*, ed. Moe Meyer (London: Routledge, 1994), 1; Fabio Cleto, "Introduction: Queering the Camp," *Camp: Queer Aesthetics and the Performing Arts: A Reader*, ed. Fabio Cleto (Ann Arbor: University of Michigan Press, 1999), 5.

64. Quoted in Hadleigh, *Hollywood Gays*, 323.

65. Interview with Gregory Mank, in *The Bride of Frankenstein*, ed. Philip J. Riley (Absecon, NJ: Universal Filmscripts, 1989), 23.

66. For discussion of the relation between camp and race, see Pamela Robertson, "Mae West's Maids: Race, 'Authenticity,' and the Discourse of Camp," in Cleto, *Camp*, 393–408.

67. See, for example, Skal, *Monster Show*, 182.

68. Eric Lott, "The Whiteness of Film Noir," in *Whiteness: A Critical Reader*, ed. Mike Hill (New York: New York University Press, 1997), 81–101.

69. Mel Watkins, *On the Real Side: Laughing, Lying, and Signifying—The Underground Tradition of African-American Humor That Transformed American Culture, from Slavery to Richard Pryor* (New York: Simon and Schuster, 1994), 485.

70. Jules Feiffer and Watergate cartoons reprinted in Haining, *Frankenstein File*, 121, 122.

71. John Tytell, *The Living Theatre: Art, Exile and Outrage* (London: Methuen, 1987), 207. This is a description based on 1965 performances of the play, which was revised throughout the decade. On the Living Theatre *Frankenstein*, see also Pierre Biner, *The Living Theatre* (New York: Horizon, 1972), 111–41.

72. This example is drawn from a videotaped production of the Living Theatre *Frankenstein* staged for German television in 1965 (New York Public Library for the Performing Arts NCOX 954).

73. James Baldwin, *The Devil Finds Work* (1976), reprinted in *Collected Essays* (New York: Library of America, 1998), 530. For discussion of *Guess Who's Coming to Dinner*, see Guerrero, *Framing Blackness*, 75–78; and Thomas Wartenberg, *Unlikely Couples: Movie Romance as Social Criticism* (Boulder, CO: Westview, 1999), 111–30. On blaxploitation, see Harry M. Benshoff, "Blaxploitation Horror Films: Generic Reappropriation or Reinscription?" *Cinema Journal* 39:2 (winter 2000): 31–50; Bogle, *Toms, Coons, Mammies, Mulattoes, and Bucks*, 231–42; Joe Bob Briggs, "Who Dat Man? *Shaft* and the Blaxploitation Genre," *Cineaste* 28:2 (spring 2003): 24–29; Thomas Cripps, *Black Film as Genre* (Bloomington: Indiana University Press, 1978), 50–55, 128–40; Manthia Diawara, "Blaxploitation in Africa," in *Back to Black: Art, Cinema and the Racial Imaginary*, ed. Richard J. Powell, David A. Bailey, and Petrine Archer-Straw (London: Whitechapel Gallery, 2005), 162–65; Guerrero, *Framing Blackness*, 69–111; Darius James, *That's Blaxploitation! Roots of the Baadasssss 'Tude (Rated X by an All-Whyte Jury)* (New York: St. Martin's, 1995); Leerom Medovoi, "Theorizing Historicity, or the Many Meanings of *Blacula*," *Screen* 39:1 (spring 1998): 1–21; Mikel J. Koven, *Blaxploitation Films* (Harpenden, UK: Pocket Essentials, 2001); Paula J. Massood, *Black City Cinema: African American Urban Experiences in Film* (Philadelphia: Temple University Press, 2003), 79–116; Mark Anthony Neal, *Soul Babies: Black Popular Culture and the Post-Soul Aesthetic* (New York: Routledge, 2002), 23–55; Mark A. Reid, *Redefining Black Film* (Berkeley: University of California Press, 1993), 69–91; Richard Simon, "The Stigmatization of 'Blaxploitation,'" in *Soul: Black Power, Politics, and Pleasure*, ed. Monique Guillory and Richard C. Green (New York: New York University Press, 1998), 236–49; Yvonne D. Sims, *Women of Blaxploitation: How the Black Action Film Heroine Changed American Popular Culture* (Jefferson, NC: McFarland, 2006); Joe Wlodarz, "Beyond the Black Macho: Queer Blaxploitation," *Velvet Light Trap* 53 (spring 2004): 10–25; and the documentary film *BaadAsssss Cinema* (dir. Isaac Julien, 2002).

74. For discussions of Black Power, see William L. Van Deburg, *New Day in Babylon: The Black Power Movement and American Culture, 1965–76* (Chicago: University of Chicago Press, 1992); Eddie S. Glaude, Jr., ed., *Is It Nation Time? Contemporary Essays on Black Power and Black Nationalism* (Chicago: University of Chicago Press, 2002); and Guillory and Green, *Soul*.

75. Huey Newton, "He Won't Bleed Me: A Revolutionary Analysis of *Sweet Sweetback's Baadasssss Song*" (1971), in *To Die for the People: The Writings of Huey P. Newton*, ed. Toni Morrison (New York: Writers and Readers, 1995), 113.

76. Blaxploitation has come under affectionate revival in such Hollywood films as *I'm Gonna Git You Sucka* (dir. Keenen Ivory Wayans, 1988), *Original Gangstas* (dir. Larry Cohen, 1996), *Jackie Brown* (dir. Quentin Tarantino, 1997), *Undercover Brother* (dir. Malcolm D. Lee, 2002), and *Austin Powers in Goldmember* (dir. Jay Roach, 2002). On recent uses of blaxploitation in independent cinema, see Wlodarz, "Beyond the Black Macho," 20–22.

77. James, *That's Blaxploitation!* xx.

78. William Paul, *Laughing Screaming: Modern Hollywood Horror and Comedy* (New York: Columbia University Press, 1994); on blaxploitation, see ibid., 141–43.

79. Medovoi, "Theorizing Historicity," 18; both Medovoi and Benshoff, "Blaxploitation Horror Films," offer valuable accounts of the politics of blaxploitation horror. For discussions of the racial politics of film horror, see also Frances Gateward, ed., *Scared of the Dark: Race, Gender and the "Horror Film,"* special issue, *Genders* 40 (2004); Guerrero, *Framing Blackness*, 41–68; Kobena Mercer, "Monster Metaphors: Notes on Michael Jackson's 'Thriller,'" *Screen* 27:1 (January/February 1986): 26–43; Annalee Lewitz, *Pretend We're Dead: Capitalist Monsters in American Pop Culture* (Durham, NC: Duke University Press, 2006), 108–21; and Mark Reid, *Black Lenses, Black Voices: African American Film Now* (Lanham, MD: Rowman and Littlefield, 2005), 61–78.

80. There has been no sustained scholarly analysis of *Blackenstein*. For brief celebrations, see James, *That's Blaxploitation!* 161; and Koven, *Blaxploitation Films*, 75–76. For more-characteristic dismissals, see David H. Smith, "*Blackenstein*," in Svehla and Svehla, *We Belong Dead*, 144–55; and Jimmy Green, "*Blackenstein . . . The Black Frankenstein*: No Tagline—It's Too Awful to Deserve One," 70s Movies Rewind website, http://70s.fast-rewind.com/blackenstein.htm.

81. The film's alternate title was the more straightforward but less evocative "The Black Frankenstein."

82. Eldridge Cleaver, "*Playboy* Interview with Nat Hentoff" (1968), in *Post-Prison Writings and Speeches*, ed. Robert Scheer (New York: Ramparts/Vintage, 1969), 179.

83. Susan Jeffords, *The Remasculinization of America: Gender and the Vietnam War* (Bloomington: Indiana University Press, 1989).

84. Ibid., 116.

85. These parodies literally used materials from the originals: the equipment in the film's laboratory sequences was that of Kenneth Strickfaden, who had done the special effects for the Whale *Frankenstein* films (Smith, "*Blackenstein*," 148, 153).

86. Angela Y. Davis, "Afro Images: Politics, Fashion, and Nostalgia," in Guillory and Green, *Soul*, 23.

87. Van Deburg, *New Day in Babylon*, 201–2. On the Afro wig in black popular culture of this era, see also Richard J. Powell, "Racial Imaginaries, from Charles White's *Preacher* to Jean-Paul Goude's and Grace Jones' *Nigger Arabesque*," in Powell, Bailey, and Archer-Straw, *Back to Black*, 9.

88. James, *That's Blaxploitation!* 161.

89. Richard Dyer, "White," *Screen* 29:4 (autumn 1988): 59–63; see also Richard Dyer, *White* (London: Routledge, 1997). For other interpretations of this film as a political allegory, see Barry Keith Grant, "Taking Back *The Night of the Living Dead*: George Romero, Feminism and the Horror Film," *Wide Angle* 14:1 (January 1992): 64–76; Sumiko Higashi, "*Night of the Living Dead*: A Horror Film about the Horrors of the Vietnam Era," in *From Hanoi to Hollywood: The Vietnam Era in American Film*, ed. Linda Dittmar and Gene Michaud (New Brunswick, NJ: Rutgers University Press, 1990), 175–88; J. Hoberman and Jonathan Rosenbaum, "George Romero and the Return of the Repressed," in *Midnight Movies* (New York: Harper and Row, 1983), 110–35; and Gregory Waller, *The Living and the Undead* (Urbana: University of Illinois Press, 1986), 272–327. For discussion of race in relation to the film's distribution, see Kevin Heffernan, *Ghouls, Gimmicks, and Gold: Horror Films and the American Movie Business, 1953–1968* (Durham, NC: Duke University Press, 2004), 202–19.

90. This resemblance is noted by Waller, who describes the zombie as "running with a lurching, pigeon-toed gait so that he seems almost a caricature of the creature in James Whale's *Frankenstein*" (*Living and the Undead*, 272).

91. See *A Stranger in the Village: Two Centuries of African-American Travel Writing*, ed. Farah J. Griffin and Cheryl J. Fish (Boston: Beacon, 1998).

92. James Baldwin, "Stranger in the Village" (1953), in *Collected Essays*, 118; all subsequent quotations are taken from this edition and cited parenthetically in the text.

93. This account also darkens, in both psychological and racial senses, the famous description of Chartres written in 1904 by Henry Adams: "The church was built for [the Virgin Mary] . . . exactly as a little girl sets up a doll-house for her favourite blonde doll" (*Mont Saint Michel and Chartres*, introd. Raymond Carney [New York: Penguin, 1986], 88). On Baldwin's revision of Adams, see Michel Fabre, *From Harlem to Paris: Black American Writers in France, 1840–1980* (Urbana: University of Illinois Press, 1991), 203–4.

94. Baldwin, *Devil Finds Work*, 571.

95. Frantz Fanon, *Black Skin, White Masks*, trans. Charles Lam Markmann (1952; repr., New York: Grove, 1967), 113, 114, 115. Discussions of this work include Anthony C. Alessandrini, ed., *Frantz Fanon: Critical Perspectives* (London: Routledge, 1999); Gwen Bergner, *Taboo Subjects: Race, Sex, and Psychoanalysis* (Minneapolis: University of Minnesota Press, 2005), 1–18; Homi K. Bhabha, "Remembering Fanon: Self, Psyche, and the Colonial Condition," in *Remaking History*, ed. Barbara Kruger and Phil Mariani (New York: New Press, 1989), 131–48; Nigel

C. Gibson, *Fanon: The Postcolonial Imagination* (Cambridge, UK: Polity, 2003); Lewis R. Gordon, T. Denean Sharpley-Whiting, and Renee T. White, eds., *Fanon: A Critical Reader* (London: Blackwell, 1996); and Maurice O. Wallace, *Constructing the Black Masculine: Identity and Ideality in African American Men's Literature and Culture, 1775–1995* (Durham, NC: Duke University Press, 2002), 170–78.

96. On parallels between Baldwin and Fanon, see Kobena Mercer, "Busy in the Ruins of a Wretched Fantasia," in Alessandrini, *Frantz Fanon*; and Wallace, *Constructing the Black Masculine*.

97. Eldridge Cleaver, *Soul on Ice*, introd. Maxwell Geismar (New York: Delta, 1968), 11; all subsequent quotations are taken from this edition and cited parenthetically in the text.

98. See, for example, Cleaver's 1968 interview in *Playboy*: "I came to realize that the particular women I had victimized had not been involved in actively oppressing me or other black people. I was taking revenge on them for what the whole system was responsible for" (Cleaver, "*Playboy* Interview with Nat Hentoff," 204).

99. David L. Dudley, *My Father's Shadow: Intergenerational Conflict in African American Men's Autobiography* (Philadelphia: University of Pennsylvania Press, 1991), 164.

100. Michele Wallace, *Black Macho and the Myth of the Superwoman* (New York: Warner Books, 1980), 101. For a critique of Wallace's critique of Cleaver, see Robyn Wiegman, *American Anatomies: Theorizing Race and Gender* (Durham, NC: Duke University Press, 1995), 85–86, 108–10.

101. On the relationship between Cleaver and Baldwin, see Dudley, *My Father's Shadow*, 137–65; Robert F. Reid-Pharr, "Tearing the Goat's Flesh," in *Black Gay Man: Essays* (New York: New York University Press, 2001), 99–134; Marlon B. Ross, "White Fantasies of Desire: Baldwin and the Racial Identities of Sexuality," in *James Baldwin Now*, ed. Dwight A. McBride (New York: New York University Press, 1999), 13–55; William J. Spurlin, "Culture, Rhetoric, and Queer Identity: James Baldwin and the Identity Politics of Race and Sexuality," in McBride, *James Baldwin Now*, esp. 112–15; and Stokes, *Color of Sex*, 187–92.

102. Leroi Jones, "American Sexual Reference: Black Male" (1965), in *Home: Social Essays* (1966; repr., Hopewell, NJ: Ecco, 1998), 216. Marlon Ross stresses that not all Black Power writers were homophobic, citing Huey Newton as a counterexample; see Ross, "White Fantasies of Desire," 47–48n16; and Newton, "The Women's Liberation and Gay Liberation Movements: August 15, 1970," in *To Die for the People*, 152–55.

103. James Baldwin, "History as Nightmare," in *Collected Essays*, 580.

104. On the composition of "Stranger in the Village," see David Leeming, *James Baldwin: A Biography* (New York: Knopf, 1994), 78–79, 99–105.

105. Watkins, *On the Real Side*, 498; for an excellent survey of Gregory's early comedy career, see ibid., 495–503. A more recent discussion of Gregory is Gerald

Nachman, *Seriously Funny: The Rebel Comedians of the 1950s and 1960s* (New York: Pantheon, 2003), 480–508.

106. Dick Gregory, *From the Back of the Bus*, ed. Bob Orben, introd. Hugh Hefner (New York: E. P. Dutton, 1962), 20.

107. This dollar is reproduced as an illustration in Gregory's most recent autobiography, Dick Gregory with Sheila P. Moses, *Callus on My Soul: A Memoir* (Atlanta: Longstreet, 2000), photo insert, n.p., and discussed in his second autobiography, Dick Gregory with James R. McGraw, *Up from Nigger* (Greenwich, CT: Fawcett, 1976), 189–90. He details his campaign platform in Dick Gregory, *Write Me In!* ed. James R. McGraw (New York: Bantam, 1968).

108. Dick Gregory, *Dick Gregory's Political Primer*, ed. James R. McGraw (New York: Harper and Row, 1971), 81.

109. Dick Gregory with Robert Lipsyte, *Nigger* (1964; repr., New York: Pocket, 1965); all subsequent quotations are taken from this edition and cited parenthetically in the text.

110. Hilton Als also suggests that the title is "a joke on the tradition [Gregory] was working against—protest literature, with its typically raw titles ('Black Boy,' 'No Name in the Street,' 'Daddy Was a Number Runner'). By calling his book 'Nigger,' Gregory replaced rhetoric with candor" ("More Harm than Good," *New Yorker,* 22 February 2002, 88).

111. Gregory, *Callus on My Soul*, 120.

112. Ibid., 258. Randall Kennedy surveys the cultural history of the word in *Nigger: The Strange Career of a Troublesome Word* (New York: Pantheon, 2002). Although Gregory's effort to recast the word was one of the most prominent, Kennedy mentions him only briefly, as someone who was called "nigger" in his youth (20–21), and he writes inexplicably that "[w]hile the hip comedians of the 1950s and 1960s—Dick Gregory [and others]—told sexually risqué or politically barbed jokes, *nigger* for the most part remained off-limits" (39).

113. Lenny Bruce, "Blacks," in *The Essential Lenny Bruce*, ed. John Cohen (New York: Ballantine, 1967), 16. Gregory praises Twain, Bruce, and Pryor in *Callus on My Soul*, 255–57. For discussion of Bruce, see Kennedy, *Nigger*, 38–39; John Limon, *Stand-Up Comedy in Theory, or, Abjection in America* (Durham, NC: Duke University Press, 2000), 11–27; and Watkins, *On the Real Side*, 482–86.

114. See also Gregory's childhood memory of watching Tarzan movies: "Once we had a riot in the movies when Tarzan jumped down a tree and grabbed a hundred Africans. . . . we took that movie house apart, ran up on the stage and kicked the screen and fought the guys who still dug Tarzan" (*Nigger*, 39).

115. Robert Lipsyte, "You Gits a Little Uppity and You Lands in Jail," *Esquire* 68 (August 1967): 73.

116. Gregory, *Up from Nigger*, 283.

117. Nat Hentoff, "Pulling the Fangs of a Poisonous Word," *Book Week,* 1 November 1964, 5.

118. "Where the Bread Is," *Newsweek*, 19 October 1964, 113. See also Peter de Lissovoy's review in the *Nation*: "Robert Lipsyte probably put it all to paper, but the storyteller's voice is Gregory" ("Comedy's Cold Sustenance," *Nation*, 23 November 1964, 383).

119. Albert Stone, *Autobiographical Occasions and Original Acts: Versions of American Identity from Henry Adams to Nate Shaw* (Philadelphia: University of Pennsylvania Press, 1982), 231–64.

120. Lipsyte, "You Gits a Little Uppity," 73.

121. Robert Lipsyte, *In the Country of Illness: Comfort and Advice for the Journey* (New York: Knopf, 1998), 42. Dick Gregory is quoted in Wil Haygood, "The Pain and Passion of Dick Gregory," *Boston Globe*, 24 August 2000, available online at http://www.commondreams.org/views/082400-104.htm.

122. See also Gerald Nachman's account of his relationship to Gregory: "Easily the most slippery [to interview] was Dick Gregory. We finally met and had a good heart-to-heart, but not until I had proved my mettle by telephoning him nearly a dozen times in various cities where he was speaking—merely to arrange a time to talk. After chasing him to Los Angeles, I eventually cornered him at midnight in the deserted lobby of a Radisson Hotel in Century City" (*Seriously Funny*, 40).

123. Dick Gregory, *The Shadow That Scares Me*, ed. James R. McGraw (New York: Pocket, 1968), 168.

124. Ibid.

125. Annette Kuhn, *Dreaming of Fred and Ginger: Cinema and Cultural Memory* (New York: New York University Press, 2002), 66–99, esp. 68, 80.

126. Cleaver, "Lazarus, Come Forth," in *Soul on Ice*, 90.

127. Richard Claxton Gregory, *No More Lies: The Myth and the Reality of American History*, ed. James R. McGraw (New York: Harper and Row, 1971), 279.

128. Ibid., xii.

129. Dick Gregory, *Dick Gregory's Frankenstein* (1970; reissued by Collectable Records, 1997).

130. Dick Gregory, "Frankenstein," *Dick Gregory at Kent State* (1971; reissued by Collectable Records, 1997).

131. Lugosi did play the Frankenstein monster in *Frankenstein Meets the Wolf Man* (dir. Roy William Neill, 1943), and he played Ygor, the doctor's assistant, in *Son of Frankenstein* (dir. Rowland W. Lee, 1939) and *Ghost of Frankenstein* (dir. Erle C. Kenton, 1942).

132. Gregory, "Frankenstein," *Dick Gregory at Kent State*.

133. Gregory, *Up from Nigger*, 284.

134. Ibid., 283–84.

135. Dick Gregory, *Dick Gregory's Natural Diet for Folks Who Eat: Cookin' with Mother Nature*, ed. James R. McGraw with Alvenia M. Fulton (New York: Perennial, 1974), 21.

136. Nachman, *Seriously Funny*, 480–508; Gregory's diet and health initiatives are discussed on 504–8. For Gregory's current activities, see his website, www. dickgregory.com.

NOTES TO THE AFTERWORD

1. Donald F. Glut describes the comic book as follows: "In Kentucky, 1859, Colonel Victah Black'nstein wants to create the perfect plantation worker. Brought to life with liquor, the monster gets drunk with the Colonel's black assistant, then goes off to find women" (*The Frankenstein Catalog: Being a Comprehensive Listing of Novels, Translations, Adaptations, Stories, Critical Works, Popular Articles, Series, Fumetti, Verse, Stage Plays, Films, Cartoons, Puppetry, Radio and Television Programs, Comics, Satire and Humor, Spoken and Musical Recordings, Tape, and Sheet Music Featuring Frankenstein's Monster and/or Descended from Mary Shelley's Novel* [Jefferson, NC: McFarland, 1984], 310). Robert J. Myers's *The Slave of Frankenstein* (Philadelphia: Lippincott, 1976) is the sequel to his *The Cross of Frankenstein* (Philadelphia: Lippincott, 1975), which brings the monster and the son of Victor Frankenstein to antebellum America but does not discuss racial issues.

2. *Clones of Dr. Funkenstein* (New York: Polygram Records, 1976). On Dr. Funkenstein, see John Corbett, *Extended Play: Sounding Off from John Cage to Dr. Funkenstein* (Durham, NC: Duke University Press, 1994). Other musical references to the Frankenstein story include those of Sam Cooke, Alice Cooper, Aimee Mann, the New York Dolls, and the Edgar Winter Group. For brief discussion, see Susan Tyler Hitchcock, *Frankenstein: A Cultural History* (New York: Norton, 2007), 262–63.

3. Elizabeth Alexander, "'Can You Be BLACK and Look at This?' Reading the Rodney King Video(s)," in *Black Male: Representations of Masculinity in Contemporary American Art,* ed. Thelma Golden (New York: Whitney Museum/Harry N. Abrams, 1994), 105. On the "Black Male" exhibition, see the essays in ibid., and, for an early response, see Linda Nochlin, "Learning from 'Black Male,'" *Art in America* 83:3 (March 1995): 86–91. On the 1993 Whitney Biennial, see the exhibition catalogue (Elizabeth Sussman et al. [New York: Whitney Museum/Harry N. Abrams, 1993]); for commentaries, see the special section of *Artforum* devoted to the exhibition (*Artforum* 31 [May 1993]: 7–17); and for a curator's reassessment, see Elisabeth Sussman, "Then and Now: Whitney Biennial 1993," *Art Journal* 64:1 (spring 2005): 74–79.

4. For discussion of Rodney King, see Robert Gooding-Williams, ed., *Reading Rodney King/Reading Urban Uprising* (New York: Routledge, 1993); for a comparison between representations of King and the Frankenstein monster, see Thomas L. Dumm, *United States* (Ithaca, NY: Cornell University Press, 1994), 112.

5. See *Adrian Piper: A Retrospective*, ed. Maurice Berger (Baltimore: Fine Arts

Gallery, University of Maryland Baltimore County, 1999); for images from the "Mythic Being" series, see ibid., 120, 142–53. For a recent reappraisal of this project, see Cherise Smith, "Re-member the Audience: Adrian Piper's Mythic Being Advertisements," *Art Journal* 66:1 (spring 2007): 46–58.

6. Gwendolyn DuBois Shaw, *Seeing the Unspeakable: The Art of Kara Walker* (Durham, NC: Duke University Press, 2004).

7. Phillip Brian Harper, *Are We Not Men? Masculine Anxiety and the Problem of African-American Identity* (New York: Oxford University Press, 1996), 172. Other analyses of representations of black men in the 1990s include Marcellus Blount and George P. Cunningham, eds., *Representing Black Men* (New York: Routledge, 1996); Robert F. Reid-Pharr, *Black Gay Man: Essays* (New York: New York University Press, 2001); and Maurice Wallace, *Constructing the Black Masculine: Identity and Ideality in African American Men's Literature and Culture, 1775–1995* (Durham, NC: Duke University Press, 2002).

8. For introductions to Glenn Ligon, see Wayne Baerwaldt et al., *Glenn Ligon: Some Changes* (Toronto: Power Plant, 2005); and Judith Tannenbaum, ed., *Unbecoming* (Philadelphia: Institute of Contemporary Art, 1997). On his most recent work, see Richard Meyer, "Light It Up, or How Glenn Ligon Got Over," *Artforum* 44:9 (May 2006): 240–47; and Matthew Guy Nichols, "Ligon's Color Theory," *Art in America* 95:3 (March 2007): 154–59, 189. On Ligon's central place in the "Black Male" exhibition, see Thelma Golden, "My Brother," in Golden, *Black Male*, 28–29, 34.

9. I have not located any sustained analysis of *Study for Frankenstein #1*, which I identify as a painting. Ligon has produced works centered on quoted words in a variety of media; these are commonly referred to as his "text-based paintings." For a brief discussion, see Holland Cotter, review of "The Evidence of Things Not Seen," *New York Times*, 18 October 1996, C29.

10. Mary Shelley, *Frankenstein*, ed. J. Paul Hunter (New York: Norton, 1996), 68, 69.

11. Richard Meyer, "Borrowed Voices: Glenn Ligon and the Force of Language," in Tannenbaum, *Unbecoming*, 32.

12. Ligon's most recent work foregrounds literary quotation; for example, the title and text of his recent neon sculpture, *Warm Broad Glow* and "negro sunshine," are quotations from the novella *Melanctha* by Gertrude Stein.

13. This painting uses the same text from *Frankenstein* but with different line breaks; this image may be found in *New Observations* 114 (spring 1997): 20, available online at www.plexus.org/newobs/114/pg20.html.

14. On this work by Ligon, particularly the series *To Disembark*, see Kimberly Rae Connor, *Imagining Grace: Liberating Theologies in the Slave Narrative Tradition* (Urbana: University of Illinois Press, 2000), 157–93; Darby English, "Committed to Difficulty," in Baerwaldt et al., *Glenn Ligon*, 57–60; and Meyer, "Borrowed Voices," 13–17.

15. Thelma Golden, *Good Mirrors Are Not Cheap* (New York: Whitney Museum of Art, 1992), 1–2.

16. Glenn Ligon, interview with Stephen Andrews, in Baerwaldt et al., *Glenn Ligon*, 173.

17. Elizabeth Young, "Bods and Monsters: The Return of the Bride of Frankenstein," in *The End of Cinema as We Know It: American Film in the Nineties*, ed. Jon Lewis (New York: New York University Press, 2001), 225–36. On *Gods and Monsters*, see also Mark Bronski, "*Gods and Monsters*: The Search for the Right Whale," and Richard Porton, "*Gods and Monsters*: An Interview with Ian McKellen," both in *Cineaste* 24:4 (1999): 10–15.

18. Byron Kim, "An Interview with Glenn Ligon," in Tannenbaum, *Unbecoming*, 54. On sexuality in Ligon's work, see Meyer, "Borrowed Voices"; and Meyer, "Light It Up."

19. Nichols, "Ligon's Color Theory," 156.

20. Meyer, "Light It Up."

21. Kim, "Interview with Glenn Ligon," 53.

22. Ken Johnson, "Glenn Ligon at Max Protetch," *Art in America* 80 (November 1992): 131.

23. Lori Firstenberg, "Neo-Archival and Textual Modes of Production: An Interview with Glenn Ligon," *Art Journal* 60:1 (spring 2001): 45.

24. Rhea Anastas, Gregg Bordowitz, Andrea Fraser, Jutta Koether, and Glenn Ligon, "The Artist Is a Currency," *Grey Room* 24 (2006): 113.

25. This is the account of Ligon's coinage of the term given by Thelma Golden, introduction to *Freestyle*, by Thelma Golden with Christine Y. Kim, Hamza Walker, et al. (New York: Studio Museum in Harlem, 2001), 14.

Index

Page numbers in italics indicate figures or illustrations on the page.

abolitionism: British abolitionism, 46, 52; Canning and, 20; Douglass and, 8, 46; *Frankenstein* (Shelley), 27–28, 40, 43–44, 52; Shelley and, Mary, 27, 61; Sumner and, 48, 51–52; in West Indies, 46

Adams, Henry, 285n93

Adams, Rachel, 123–124

Aesop, *Fables*, 119–120, 264n22

aesthetics: black American Frankenstein monster, 228; Crane and, 106; isolation from culture, 12–13; race and, 228

African Americans: 1930s, 175–176; badman/outlaw tradition, 133–134, 188; monster tradition, 134; signifying by, 108, 126, 133, 152, 204, 207–209; trickster tradition, 108, 126, 132–133, 136, 269n70

Alexander, Eleanor, 124–125, 149

Alexander, Elizabeth, 220

allegory: of America in Vietnam, 192, 196; class allegories, 174; legibility of, 93; in *The Monster*, 92–94, 99; political allegory, 80, 94, 192, 196; racial allegory, 160–161, 174–175; similarities to Frankenstein monster, 11

"American Frankenstein," 26

"The American Frankenstein" (Bellew), 38

American literature: antebellum literature, 33, 34–38, 42–43; antislavery writing, 42–44; dissection, fascination with, 33; as freak show, 124; literary nationalism, 34–38, 74; rhetoric guidebooks, 73–75, 91

"American Literature" (Fuller), 25, 34–38

"American Sexual Reference: Black Male" (Baraka), 202–203

American Studies, 8

Ames, Jessie Daniel, 175

Anatomy Act (Great Britain, 1832), 30

Andy Warhol's Frankenstein (film), 274n5

animals: animal fables, 120, 132–133; apes, 150; ass, 117–121, 125, 130; "The Ass and the Lap-Dog" (fable), 117–119, 264n22; "The Ass in the Lion's Skin" (Godwin), 119, 120–121, 130, 132–133, 268n59; birds, 22, 222; dogs, 126, 135, 141–142, 147, 150, 151, 196; elephants, 81; fish, 73; foxes, 117, 132; gorillas, 182–183; lap-dogs, 117–119, 121, 125, 128, 129, 151, 157, 269n70; lions, 117, 119, 120, 121, 125, 130; monkeys, 81, 90–91, 92; orangutans, 21; panthers, 95; rabbits, 132; sex with, 4; Signifying Monkey, 133, 152

Another Piece of Presumption (Peake), 111–116, 129

The Anti-Jacobin (journal), 115, 129

antiracist rhetoric, 66–67

Appeal to the Coloured Citizens of the World (Walker), 23–24, 44

Ariel, 119, 265n25

Aristotle, 70

Armwood, George, 178–179

"The Ass and the Lap-Dog" (fable), 117–119, 264n22

"The Ass in the Lion's Skin" (Godwin), 119, 120–121, 130, 132–133, 268n59

Atlanta University, 60, 64, 65

Atlanta University *Bulletin* (July 1893), 60–61, 61, 63–67, 253n133

Atwood, Margaret, 17

Austin Powers in Goldmember (film), 284n76

The Autobiography of an Ex-Colored Man (Johnson), 65–66

badman/outlaw tradition, 133–134, 188–189

Bain, Alexander, 92, 93

Bakhtin, Mikhail, 116, 120

Baldick, Chris, 15, 30–31, 232n17, 244n38

Baldwin, James: black American
    Frankenstein monster, 7; on Chartres
    cathedral, 199–200; civil rights move-
    ment, 198; Cleaver compared to, 202;
    on the devil, 200; Frankenstein story in,
    161; gothic literature and, 11; Gregory
    compared to, Dick, 216; on *Guess Who's
    Coming to Dinner*, 188; Happersberger
    and, 203; "History as Nightmare," 203; ice
    in, 198; *Notes of a Native Son*, 198; slavery
    and its aftermath, 7; "Stranger in the
    Village," 198–200, 203, 221, 226
Baraka, Amiri (Leroi Jones), "American
    Sexual Reference: Black Male," 202–203
Barlow, Joel, *The Columbiad*, 34
Baron, Dennis, 73
Barrios, Richard, 181, 186
Bederman, Gail, 75–76
"The Bell-Tower" (Melville), 26, 42–44,
    46, 92
Bellew, Frank: "The American
    Frankenstein," 38; birthplace, 248n67;
    black American Frankenstein monster,
    38–39, *39*; "The Modern Frankenstein,"
    38–40, *39*, 48; publishers of his
    works, 248n67; racial connotations of
    Frankenstein story, 25
Benito Cereno (Melville), 42
Berenstein, Rhona, 176
Bhutto, Benazir, 231n3
Bierce, Ambrose: *The Devil's Dictionary*,
    68, 71, 73; "Moxon's Master," 15, 274n6;
    Orientalism, 15; on "symbol," 68, 71
bin Laden, Osama, 1
The Birth of a Nation (film), 168–172;
    blackness as monstrous, 6; *Bride of
    Frankenstein* and, 174, 176, 184; con-
    demnations of racial amalgamation and
    black revolt, 170; Edison *Frankenstein*
    compared to, 171–172; homosexuality in,
    171–172; interracial rape, images of, 183;
    as a monster movie, 168–171; racism,
    160–161; slavery and its aftermath, 7;
    stills from, *171*
Black, Max, 71
black American Frankenstein monster;
    aesthetics and race, 228; Baldwin
    and, 7; Bellew's monster as, 38–39, *39*;
    Blackenstein in tradition of, 190; in
    Civil War, 47–55; Cleaver and, 7; Crane
    and, 5, 6; demonization of interracial
    contact, 56; Douglass and, 6; Dunbar
    and, 5, 6; Fuller and, 6; Ligon and, 7;

masculinity, fantasies/anxieties about,
    5, 10; Melville and, 6; myth of the black
    rapist, 56–58; need for, 228–229; in "The
    New Frankenstein," 47–48, *49*; origin of,
    19; parables of, 161–162; sexual violence,
    56–58; Sumner and, 6; Turner as, 19; in
    U.S. literature, film, culture, 4–7; vampire
    imagery, 215; Van Evrie and, 6; visual
    reappropriation strategies, 162; in Whale
    films, 6. See also *The Monster*; *The Sport
    of the Gods*
"black Atlantic," 8
"black comedy," 187, 188, 206
black dandy: in *Jes Lak White Fo'ks*, 128; in
    The Monster, 80, 87–88, 104; in *The Sport
    of the Gods*, 109, 142–143
"black gothic" writing, 235n29
Black Majesty (James), 179–180
Black Power movement, 7, 189, 194–195, 201
Black Skin, White Masks (Fanon), 200–201
Blackenstein (film), 190–198; Afro haircut
    in, 194–195; as allegory of America in
    Vietnam, 192, 196; badman/outlaw tradi-
    tion, 188; as "black comedy," 188; dis-
    embowelment in, 196–197; *Frankenstein*
    (Shelley) and, 196–197; humor in, 197;
    importance, 190; misogyny in, 196–197;
    No More Lies and, 212–213; poster, *195*;
    stills from, *191*, *193*, *194*; Whale films and,
    6, 161, 190, 197; white orderly in, 190–194,
    196
blackness as monstrous, 6, 228–229
The Blacks (Genet), 221
Black'stein (comic book), 219
Blacula (film), 189–190
blaxploitation films, 188–190, 194–195,
    284n76
Blood and Ice (Lochhead), 17
blowback, 2, 3
Bogle, Donald, 175
Bram, Christopher, *Father of Frankenstein*,
    162
Brandeis, Louis, 174
Br'er Rabbit, 133
Brewer, Ebenezer Cobham, *Dictionary of
    Phrase and Fable*, 111
Bride of Frankenstein (film), 172–187; as
    antilynching narrative, 177; *Birth of a
    Nation* and, 174, 176, 184; as "black com-
    edy," 187; as black Frankenstein story, 6;
    black men in, 176; blind hermit in, 177–
    178; bride in, 184–186; Byron in, 172, 181;
    campiness and, 186–187; comedy/humor

in, 187; critical reception, 173; Edison *Frankenstein* and, 174; female monsters since, 17–18; in *Gods and Monsters*, 225; homosexuality in, 181–182; interracial rape, images of, 183; Lewis and, David, 182; lynch mob in, 177; monster's skin color, 176; *New York Times* on, 172; popular understanding of Frankenstein story, 172, 173; popularity, 173; as racial allegory, 160–161, 174–175; reanimation as Christian martyr, 179; Shelley in, Mary, 172, 181; Shelley in, Percy Bysshe, 172, 181; stills from, *178, 185*; sympathy for monsters, 186; tragic mulatta in, 185–186
Bronx Community College, 213–214
Brooks, Mel, *Young Frankenstein*, 12
Brooks, Preston, 53, 251n110
Brophy, Bob, 190
Brown, Bill, 81
Brown, Gillian, 119
Brown, H. Rap, 189
Brown, John, 219
Brown, Rebecca, "Dr. Frankenstein, I Presume," 17
Browning, Tod, *Dracula*, 173, 215
Bruce, Lenny, 207
Buck, Gertrude, 77–80, 106
Burke, Edmund, 29–30
burlesque, 262n4
Burns, Sarah, 38, 48
Bush, George W., 4, 231n3
Butler, Andrew, 251n110
Butler, Octavia, 235n29
Byron, Lord, 172, 181

Cadava, Eduardo, 44–45
cakewalk, 88–89, 91
Caliban, 13–14, 119, 138, 265n25
The Call of the Wild (London), 150
camp, 186–187
cannibalism, 4
Cannibals All! (Fitzhugh), 40
Canning, George: abolitionism, 20; *The Anti-Jacobin* (journal), 115, 129; on Jacobinism, 115; Peake and, 20, 115; visual embodiment of language of, 38–39; West Indian social rebellion, 19–20, 22, 31–31, 50, 114–115
carnivalesque, 116–117
Carr, Raymond, 81–82
Cassuto, Leonard, 39, 44
Castronovo, Russ, 33, 42
Césaire, Aimé, 13, 265n25

Chartres cathedral, 199, 285n93
Chauncey, George, 276n15
Cheney, Dick, 1–2
"Cheneystein," 2, 3
Chesnutt, Charles, 122, 235n29
"Chrismus on the Plantation" (Dunbar), 122
Church, Joseph, 94
civil rights movement: Baldwin and, 198; blaxploitation films, 188; Gregory and, Dick, 204, 208–209, 211, 216; as a monstrosity, 208–209; nonfiction of, 7, 161; as second Civil War, 4
Civil War, 47–55
Clarke, James, 34
Cleaver, Eldridge, 201–203; Baldwin compared to, 202; black American Frankenstein monster, 7; Black Power movement, 201; Frankenstein story in, 161; gothic literature and, 11; on Gregory, 211; homophobia, 202–203; ice in, 198; pacifism, 211; Shelley compared to, Mary, 201; *Soul on Ice*, 201–203, 211; on Vietnam War, 191
Cleto, Fabio, 186, 187
Clinton, George, *The Clones of Dr. Frankenstein*, 219
Clive, Colin, 172
The Clones of Dr. Frankenstein (album), 219
cloning, 3, 4
Cohen, Larry, *Original Gangstas*, 284n76
Colonial (Ligon), 225–226
colonialism, 27–28, 32, 52
The Columbiad (Barlow), 34
Columbian Exposition (Chicago, 1893), 60–61, 63, 66, 131
Condillac, Etienne Bonnot de, 256n13
Condon, Bill, *Gods and Monsters*, 162, 225
Confederacy: Douglass on, 54, 55; as Frankenstein monster, 51–52, 53; Sumner on, 51–52, 53, 54
The Confessions of Nat Turner (Gray), 22–23
The Confessions of Nat Turner (Styron), 19
"coon shows," 127
Cooper, Anna Julia, *A Voice from the South*, 154–155
Cooper, Merian C., *King Kong* (with Schoedsack), 177, 182–183
cosmetic surgery, 3
Cox, Samuel, 56
Crafts, Hannah, 235n29
Crain, William, 189–190

Crane, Stephen: agent, 107; black American Frankenstein monster, 5, 6; Dixon compared to, 98; Dunbar and, 107; intimacy between natural and technological, 73–74; *The Monster* (see *The Monster*); reanimation of metaphors, 80; Reynolds and, 107; Shelley compared to, Mary, 94; Twain and, 87; white anxiety, language of, 9

Crane, Wilbur, 82

Crane, William, 81–82, 100

Cripps, Thomas, 176–177

Croly, David, *Miscegenation* (with Wakeman), 55–56

cultural theory, 16, 114

Curiosities of Literature (D'Israeli), 110, 124

Curran, Stuart, 33–34

"A Cyborg Manifesto" (Haraway), 15

Dahmer, Jeffrey, 225–226

dandies. *See* black dandy

Davis, Angela, 189, 195

Davis, Jefferson, 47–48

Dawley, J. Searle, 160

de Man, Paul, 256n13

De Mille, James, *The Elements of Rhetoric*, 75, 77

De Sue, Joe, 190

Dean, John, 188

Demme, Jonathan, *The Silence of the Lambs*, 17

Dentith, Simon, 115

desecration of corpses, 4

Dettlaff, Alois, 274n7

The Devil's Dictionary (Bierce), 68, 71, 73

Dew, Thomas: College of William and Mary, 24; Frankenstein story, 20, 25; on slave revolts, 19–21, 22; white anxiety, language of, 9

Diawara, Manthia, 169

Dick Gregory's Frankenstein (album, performance), 213–214

Dick Gregory's Political Primer (Gregory), 205–206

Dickens, Charles, 44

Dictionary of Phrase and Fable (Brewer), 111

Discipline and Punish (Foucault), 73

D'Israeli, Benjamin, 110

D'Israeli, Isaac: *Curiosities of Literature*, 110, 124; Godwin and, 115; on mimicry, 115–116, 119; "Parodies," 110–112, 113, 115, 126; *Vaurien*, 115

Dixon, Thomas: Crane compared to, 98;

language of black monstrosity, 168; *The Leopard's Spots*, 57–58, 98, 170–171; racist rhetoric, 26; white anxiety, language of, 9

Dr. Black and Mr. Hyde (film), 189

"Dr. Cheneystein," 2, 3

"Dr. Frankenstein, I Presume" (Brown), 17

Douglas, Mike, 210

Douglass, Frederick: black American Frankenstein monster, 6; British abolitionism, 8, 46; Columbian Exposition (Chicago, 1893), 66, 131; on Confederacy, 54, 55; Crane and, 107; Dickens and, 44; in *Douglass' Monthly*, 45; Dumas and, 44; Dunbar and, 121, 131; favorite novelists, 44; gothic literature and, 11; "The Mission of the War," 55; *My Bondage and My Freedom*, 45; myth of the black rapist, 60; *Narrative of the Life of Frederick Douglass*, 22, 44–45; "Our New Madness," 107, 123; racial connotations of Frankenstein story, 25–26; *The Reason Why the Colored American Is Not in the World's Columbian Exposition* (with Wells), 60, 66; regeneration through war, 55; Reynolds and, 107; on secession, 54, 55; on slavery, 4, 19, 54, 66; slavery and its aftermath, 7; slavery and monstrosity, association of, 45–46; "Slavery and the Irrepressible Conflict," 19, 45–46, 52; on Sumner, 53–54; United States as Frankenstein monster, 54–55; use of Frankenstein and vampire images, 13, 215; on white fathers of mixed-race children, 45

Dowd, Maureen, 1–2, 3

Dracula (film), 173, 215

Dracula (Stoker), 13, 216, 236n35

"Dreaming Frankenstein" (Lochhead), 17

Dreiser, Theodore, 74

Du Bois, W. E. B.: Dunbar and, 121, 131, 153; *The Souls of Black Folk*, 132; veils in, 101

Dudley, David L., 201–202

Dumas, Alexandre, 44

Dunbar, Paul Laurence, 121–158; African cultural forms, 8; agent, 107; alcoholism, 125, 146, 149; on "The Ass in the Lion's Skin," 130; authority figures/white masters in, 108, 125, 128, 134; badman/outlaw tradition, 133–134; on being a celebrity, 130; black American Frankenstein monster in, 5, 6; black dandy figures in, 109, 128, 142–145; on black intellectuals, 123; black subservience in, 108, 125, 128, 134,

135; "Chrismus on the Plantation," 122; Columbian Exposition (Chicago, 1893), 131; as a commodity, 123; depression, 125; dialect poetry, 121–122, 125, 126–127, 157; Douglass and, 121, 131; dramatic pieces, 127; Du Bois and, 121, 131, 153; essays, 121; *The Fanatics*, 128–129; favorite authors, 126–127; Frankenstein in, 125, 135, 138, 141; as a Frankenstein monster, 125; as a freak, 123–124; gothic literature and, 11; Gregory and, Dick, 204; "Harriet Beecher Stowe," 154–155; Harris and, 127; *The Heart of Happy Hollow*, 135, 136–137; Herrick, 127; "The Hottest Coon in Dixie," 127; Howells and, 122–123, 124, 130, 268n59; influences on, 153; irony in, 129–130, 131–132, 139, 140–141, 142, 151, 152; *Jes Lak White Fo'ks*, 128, 132; Johnson and, James Weldon, 130; journalism by, 129, 131; *King Lear* and, 270n76; "The Lynching of Jube Benson" (*see* "Lynching of Jube Benson"); lyrics for black vaudeville shows ("coon shows"), 127–128; marriage, 121, 125, 149; Melville and, 155, 272n99; mimicry in, 127; minstrelsy in, 127–128; myth of the black rapist, 135; naturalism, 140, 149–150; "The Old Cabin," 127; parody and, 108, 121, 125–133, 134; parody of naturalism, 150; parody of racist nostalgia, 126–127, 135–136; poetry readings by, 124; racial equality, 108, 121; "Representative American Negroes," 131–132; Riley and, 127; as self-described ass, 125, 130, 132; self-hatred, 125; Shakespeare and, 127, 136, 138, 140; Signifying Monkey in, 133, 152; signifying tradition in, 108, 126, 133, 204, 208; *The Sport of the Gods* (see *Sport of the Gods*); Stowe and, 153, 154, 156–158; targets of, 125; Tennyson and, 127; trickster tradition in, 108, 126, 132–133, 136, 269n70; Twain and, 132; as "Uncle Tom," 157; *Uncle Tom's Cabin* and, 178; violence against women in his writing, 153, 156; Washington and, Booker T., 121, 131; "We Wear the Mask," 126; Wordsworth and, 127; Wright and, 157

Dunbar-Nelson, Alice: Dunbar letters to, 130, 149, 151; marriage, 121, 149; physical abuse of, 125, 149; on a poetry reading by Dunbar, 124

Dunn, Katherine, *Geek Love*, 16, 17

Dyer, Richard, 197, 221

Eakins, Thomas, *The Gross Clinic*, 82

Edison, Thomas, 162–163

Edison *Frankenstein* (film), 162–168; availability, 162, 274n7; *Birth of a Nation* compared to, 171–172; *Bride of Frankenstein* and, 174; homosexuality in, 162, 163–168; period of production, 276n16; stills from, *164, 165, 166, 167*

Edwards, Bryan, *History, Civil and Commercial, of the British Colonies in the West Indies*, 26, 27

Elements of Composition and Rhetoric (Kerl), 74

The Elements of Rhetoric (De Mille), 75, 77

Ellison, Ralph, 7, 86, 180, 221

Elsaesser, Thomas, 163

Emerson, Ralph Waldo, 36

Enlightenment, 72, 120

Equiano, Olaudah, 28

Erlichman, John, 188

Esquire (magazine), 210

The Exorcist (film), 200

fables, 120, 132–133

Fables (Aesop), 119–120

Fables Ancient and Modern (Godwin), 118, 120

The Fanatics (Dunbar), 128–129

Fanon, Frantz, *Black Skin, White Masks*, 200–201

Father of Frankenstein (Bram), 162

Faust, 163

A Feast of Scraps (Ligon), 225

"February Twenty-Second" (Worden), 63

Feiffer, Jules, 187

femininity and metaphors, 77–78

feminism, 4, 37. *See also* women's liberation

Fetchit, Stepin, 175

figurative language: in *The Monster*, 12, 90–92, 95–96; "savage" in, 75

"film noir," 162, 187

Fitzhugh, George, 25, 40, 50

Fleming, Victor, *Gone with the Wind*, 175–176, 182–183

Flesh for Frankenstein (film), 162, 274n5

Fletcher, Angus, 11

Forry, Steven, 31

Foucault, Michel, 73, 168

Founding Fathers, 24, 33–34

"frankenfoods," 3–4

Frankenhooker (film), 17

"Frankenstein" (the term), 3, 31, 246n55

Frankenstein, Incorporated (Wormser), 173–174

Frankenstein; or, The Monster (1830s play), 31

Frankenstein: The True Story (film), 162

Frankenstein, Victor (monster's creator): Crane's version of, 84; death of, 114; Elizabeth (character) and, 31; Founding Fathers and, 34; Frankenstein monster as self-parody of, 113–114; Franklin and, 34; as polymath, 47; in *Presumption*, 42, 112; as Prometheus, 173; as story's mediator, 22; U.S. foreign policy as, 1–2

Frankenstein as metaphor: in American literature, film, culture, 4–7, 18; antiblack racism, 15–16; of metaphors, 12, 72; of slave revolts, 20–23; transatlantic circulation of, 8–9; vitality of, 2–3, 4; women writers, 16–17

Frankenstein (Edison Company silent film). *See* Edison *Frankenstein*

Frankenstein (film): as black Frankenstein story, 6; class disruptions of Depression-era America, 183; Gregory on, 4, 159, 208, 211, 212, 215–216; Igor (character), 3; interracial rape, images of, 183–184; lynch mob in, 177, 179; *Night of Living Dead* compared to, 197–198; as parable of life in the ghetto, 4; popular understanding of Frankenstein story, 172; as racial allegory, 160–161

Frankenstein (Living Theatre adaptation), 188

Frankenstein monster: African American men equated to, 68–69; allegory, similarities to, 11; amalgamation from body parts, 5, 71–72; antiracist rhetoric, 66–67; as automaton/mechanical monster, 42; badman/outlaw tradition, 134; bin Laden as, 1; blowback as embodiment of, 2, 3; Caliban and, 13–14; Cheney as, 1–2; class politics, 15; color of, 5, 28, 116–117; Columbian Exposition (Chicago, 1893) as, 63; Confederacy as, 51–52, 53; corporations as, 173–174; cyborg compared to, 16; dead metaphors, 69–72, 79; as a dependent victim, 28; Dunbar as, 125; fame of, 1; fears of interracial rape, 27; fears of racial mixture ("amalgamation"), 27, 40–41; fears of the mechanical, the savage, 76–77; fleshiness of, 116–117; in *Frankenstein* (Shelley), 2; Franklin compared to, 246n55; Hitler compared

to, 279n32; Hussein as, 1; hydra and, 13, 29; as icon created by a woman writer, 9; immature works of American literature as, 50–51; inability to reproduce, 27; Irish nationalism as, 32; Karloff and, 69; learning to talk, 227; Luddites, 30; lynch mob as, 58, 60; mechanical components, 42; as metaphor (*see* Frankenstein as metaphor); mimicry by, 117; most famous visual form, 69; namelessness in the novel, 31; Negro women as, 58–60; "outgrowing" of, 217–218; as parodist, 113–114; as a parody, 111, 116–117; as personification of personification, 70; Pinochet as, 1; placelessness, 66; in *Playing in the Dark* (Morrison), 7; in political discourse, 1–4, 13–14, 231n3; polygenesis, sterility hypothesis of, 27; proletariat as, 30; in racial discourse in U.S., 5–6, 14 (*see also* black American Frankenstein monster); racial meanings, 15; racist rhetoric, 66; railroad industry as, 38; Reid as, 16; sectional revolt as, 51; as self-parody of Victor Frankenstein, 113–114; Shah of Iran as, 1; Signifying Monkey and, 133; slaves as, 43, *49*, 49–50; Somoza as, 1; stereotypes of Africans and West Indians, 27; Sumner as, 49–50; as symbol of American literature, 36; as symbol of the "multitude," 2; as sympathetic figure, 2–3, 28, 177, 186; synecdoche and, 70; travesty by, 117; Turner as, 6, 19–20; United States as, 34–35, 47, 54–55; unwaged labor, 44; vampires and, 13; violence by in the novel, 22; white fears about black power, 27; in "Wild Man" dramas, 31

Frankenstein (Shelley): 1818 edition, 30, 32, 244n38, 245n46; 1831 edition, 27, 29, 30, 32, 244n38, 245n46; 1934 edition, 274n6; abolitionism, 27–28, 40, 43–44, 52; "afterlife" of, 236n35; amalgamation from body parts, 5, 71–72; America in, 32–33; Americas in, 246n49; animal fable and, 117; antebellum rhetoric of national self-making, 25; availability of, 30; Bakhtin and, 116; to black writers, 198; *Blackenstein* and, 196–197; Burke and, 29; Captain Walton (character), 22, 28, 228; carnivalesque in, 117; cinematic qualities, 160, 163; class allegories in, 174; colonialism, 27–28, 32; conservative vocabularies of repugnance and fear, 41; dismemberment, language of, 51;

Dracula and, 215–216; elements of the story, 5, 14, 232n17; Elizabeth (character), 27, 31, 134, 149, 172, 181; error in, 32–33; Felix De Lacey (character), 32–33, 117, 118, 160; feminist criticism of, 9; filial revolt, language of, 51; first film version (1910) (*see* Edison *Frankenstein*); as a Founding Father story, 24, 33–34; golem folklore, 276n19; graverobbing controversies, 30, 38, 82; Henry Clerval (character), 28–29, 31; homosexuality in, 6, 163; humor in, 11; "I" in, 227–228; imperialism, 27–28; influence of, 33, 51; influences on, 33; "making" as a topic, 72; masculinity in, specularization of, 9–10; misogyny in, specularization of, 9; monster character (*see* Frankenstein monster); *The Monster* compared to, 94; name "Frankenstein," source of, 34, 246n55; *Narrative of the Life of Frederick Douglass* and, 44–45; North Pole in, 22; Orientalism, 15–16, 28–29, 31; parodies of, 12, 109, 111, 115, 138, 140, 149, 152; parody in, 108, 112–114, 117–118, 129; pastiche in, 112; political meanings, 28–32; preface, 3; prefatory comment in, 222; racial connotations, 25–26, 31, 86; racial significance to American culture, 8; reanimation from corpses, 5, 69–72; revolt against its creator, 5; Safie (character), 28, 31, 32–33, 118, 121; setting, 20, 22; sexual connotations, 10; slave narratives' structure and, 28, 241n9; sources/origins, 25, 29; *The Sport of the Gods* and, 152; *Study for Frankenstein #1* and, 221, 222; theatrical adaptations, 15, 30–31, 160, 186; travesty in, 112; twentieth-century versions, 161; updates by others, 6, 174; Victor Frankenstein (character) (*see* Frankenstein, Victor); violations of white women, 57–58; white anxiety about slave rebellion, 21–22

Franklin, Benjamin, 34, 162, 246n55

Fraser, Brendan, 225

freaks: American literature as freak show, 124; American writers as, 124; Buck and, 79, 80; Dunbar as freak, 123–124; freak shows, 17, 81, 101, 123–124, 147; writers' association with, 123–124; Zip Coon and, 88

Fredrickson, George, 40

Fried, Michael, 82, 92, 95, 261n59

Friedkin, William, *The Exorcist*, 200

From the Back of the Bus (Gregory), 204, 205

Fuentes, Carlos, 1, 3

Fuller, Margaret: "American Literature," 25, 34–38; black American Frankenstein monster, 6; Clarke and, 34; Emerson and, 36; female monsters, monster-makers, 46; feminism of, 37; literary nationalism, 34–38; reaction against British influence, 35, 52; Shelley and, Percy Bysshe, 37; slavery and its aftermath, 7; *Woman in the Nineteenth Century*, 37

Fury (film), 177

Gaines, Kevin, 140

Garrison, William Lloyd, 22, 40, 50

Gates, Henry Louis, Jr., 133

gay rights, 4. *See also* homosexuality

Geek Love (Dunn), 16, 17

Genet, Jean, *The Blacks*, 221

genetically modified foods, 3

Genung, John, *The Practical Elements of Rhetoric*, 91

Gilroy, Paul, 8, 16

Glaser, Milton, 213, *214*

Gobineau, Joseph Arthur, Comte de, 27

Goddu, Teresa, 11

Gods and Monsters (film), 162, 225

Godwin, William: antislavery rhetoric, 26; "The Ass in the Lion's Skin," 119, 120–121, 130, 132–133, 268n59; D'Israeli and, Isaac, 115; *Fables Ancient and Modern*, 118, 120

"The Gold Bug" (Poe), 21

Golden, Thelma, 224

The Golem (film), 276n19

golem folklore, 2, 276n19

Gomez, Jewelle, 235n29

Gone with the Wind (film), 175–176, 182–183

Gone with the Wind (Mitchell), 7, 182

Gossett, Thomas, 157

gothic literature, 10–11, 25, 72

Gotlieb, Phyllis, 17

graverobbing controversies, 30, 38, 82

Gray, Thomas, *The Confessions of Nat Turner*, 22–23

Greeley, Horace, 38–40, 48

Gregory, Dick, 203–218; on America, 212, 216; *From the Back of the Bus*, 204, 205; Baldwin compared to, 216; black Frankenstein monsters, parables of, 161–162; at Bronx Community College (1970), 213–214; Bruce compared to, 207;

Gregory, Dick (*continued*)
civil rights movement, 204, 208–209, 211, 216; Cleaver on, 211; comedy career, 203–204; *Dick Gregory's Frankenstein,* 213–214; *Dick Gregory's Political Primer,* 205–206; diet and health initiatives, 217; Douglas and, Mike, 210; Dunbar and, 204; Frankenstein story, 204, 210; on *Frankenstein* (the film), 4, 159, 208, 211, 212, 215, 215–216; Glaser and, 213, *214*; gothic literature and, 11; Hefner and, 203, 213; at Kent State University (1971), 214–216, *216*; on life in the ghetto, 4; Lipsyte and, 208, 209–210; Nachman interview, 288n122; *Nigger,* 206–210; "nigger," use of, 287n112; *No More Lies,* 211–213; "outgrowing" the Frankenstein monster, 217–218; parody in, 204–206; Peace and Freedom Party, 204; political activism, 204; presidential candidacy (1968), 204; Pryor to, 207; self-costuming as Uncle Sam and George Washington, *205,* 206, 213; *The Shadow That Scares Me,* 159, 210–211; signifying tradition, 204, 207–209; slavery and its aftermath, 7; Tarzan, reaction to, 287n114; Twain compared to, 207; *Up from Nigger,* 216–217; use of Frankenstein and vampire images, 13, 215; Whale films, 204, 208, 216; wife (Lilian), 206, 213; on women's liberation, 213
Gregory, Lilian, 206, 213
Griffith, D. W. See *The Birth of a Nation*
The Gross Clinic (Eakins), 82
Guess Who's Coming to Dinner (film), 188
Gunning, Tom, 165, 276n16

Haldeman, H. R., 188
Haley, Alex, 210
Hall, Donald, 71
Hall, G. Stanley, 75–76
Hall, Jacqueline Dowd, 183
Happersberger, Lucien, 203
Haraway, Donna, "A Cyborg Manifesto," 15
Hardt, Antonio, *Multitude* (with Negri), 2
Harper, Frances, 122, 128
Harper, Phillip Brian, 220
Harper's (magazine), 84, *85,* 198
"Harriet Beecher Stowe" (Dunbar), 154–155
Harris, Joel Chandler, 127, 133
Hart, John, 190
Harvey, Thomas, 117
"haunting back," 11

The Heart of Happy Hollow (Dunbar), 135, 136–137
Hearts of Dixie (film), 175
Hefner, Hugh, 203, 213
Henenlotter, Frank, *Frankenhooker,* 17
Hentoff, Nat, 209
Herrick (Dunbar), 127
Hill, Adams Sherman, *The Principles of Rhetoric and Their Application,* 73
Hill, David Jayne, 74
History, Civil and Commercial, of the British Colonies in the West Indies (Edwards), 26, 27
"History as Nightmare" (Baldwin), 203
Hitler as Frankenstein (Steel), 279n32
Hobson, Valerie, 172
Hodes, Martha, 56
homosexuality: in *Birth of a Nation,* 171–172; black dandies, 87; in *Bride of Frankenstein,* 181–182; campiness and, 186–187; Cleaver on, 202; "closet" as metaphor for, 276n15; in Edison *Frankenstein,* 162, 163–168; of *Frankenstein* (Shelley), 6, 163; *Gods and Monsters* (film), 162, 225; as monstrosity, 226; "overcivilization" and, 75–76; in *The Sport of the Gods,* 145; "Stranger in the Village" (Baldwin), 198–200, 203, 221, 226; *Study for Frankenstein #1* (Ligon), 219–229, *223*
"Hop Frog" (Poe), 21
Hopkins, Pauline, 122
horror films, 189
"The Hottest Coon in Dixie" (Dunbar), 127
House of Bush, House of Saud (Unger), 231n3
Howells, William Dean, 123–124, 130, 268n59
Huck Finn (Twain), 7, 10, 87, 132
Hunt, Theodore, 75–76, 93
Hurston, Zora Neale, 221
Hussein, Saddam, 1, 3
Hutcheon, Linda, 109, 129
Hutchinson, Anne, 37
hydra, many-headed, 13, 29, 46, 52

I Embody Everything You Most Hate and Fear (Piper), 220
idioms, reanimation of, 71
Igor (character), 1, 3, 112
Il Mostro di Frankenstein (film), 276n19
I'm Gonna Git You Sucka (film), 284n76
Imitation of Life (film), 185

imperialism, 27–28
Invisible Man (Ellison), 180
Invisible Man (film), 180
Iola Leroy (Harper), 128
irony: control of, 91; in Dunbar, 129–130, 131–132, 139, 140–141, 142, 151, 152; parody and, 129; self-directed, 139
Irving, Washington, 65
Isherwood, Christopher, 162

Jackie Brown (film), 284n76
Jackson, Rebecca, 235n29
Jackson, Roosevelt, 196
Jackson, Shelley, 15
Jacobs, Harriet, 44, 235n29
Jamaica, 50
James, C. L. R., *Black Majesty*, 179–180
James, Darius, 189, 197
Jameson, Fredric, 110
Jefferson Medical College (Philadelphia), 38, 82
Jeffords, Susan, 192, 193
Jes Lak White Fo'ks (Dunbar), 128, 132
Johnson, Chalmers, 2
Johnson, James Weldon, 65–66, 130
Johnson, Mark, 72
Johnson, Samuel, 72
Johnson, William Henry ("Monkey Man," "Zip"), 81, 88
Jones, Leroi. *See* Baraka, Amiri
jungle-horror films, 176

Karcher, Carolyn, 43, 272n99
Karloff, Boris (born William Henry Pratt): campiness, 187; as Frankenstein monster, 69, 161, 198, 226; Gregory on watching, 211; parody of, 194
Kass, Leon, 4
Kellogg, Brainerd, *A Text-Book on Rhetoric*, 73, 74
Kennedy, John F., 207
Kennedy, Randall, *Nigger: The Strange Career of a Troublesome Word*, 287n112
Kent State University, 214–215, 216
Kerl, Simon, *Elements of Composition and Rhetoric*, 74
King, Rodney, 220
King Kong, 13, 176–177
King Kong (1933 film directed by Cooper and Schoedsack), 177, 182–183
King Lear (Shakespeare), 136, 140, 270n76
Kirkland, Caroline, 37
Kissinger, Henry, 187

Kramer, Stanley, *Guess Who's Coming to Dinner*, 188
Ku Klux Klan, 92, 122, 168, 170–171
Kuhn, Annette, 211

La Fontaine, Jean de, 119, 264n22
Laderman, Gary, 33
Lakoff, George, 72
Lamming, George, 13
Lanchester, Elsa: in *Bride of Frankenstein*, 173, 174, 184–185, 187, 194; Laughton and, 182
Lang, Fritz, *Fury*, 177
Larson, Gary, 18
Laughton, Charles, 182, 187
Lawrence, D. H., 246n55
Lee, Malcolm D., *Undercover Brother*, 284n76
The Leopard's Spots (Dixon), 57–58, 98, 170–171
Levey, William, See *Blackenstein*
Lewis, David, 181, 182, 186
Lewis, Robert, lynching of, 81–82, 100
Life (magazine), 123–124
Life without Soul (film), 276n19
Ligon, Glenn, 219–229; black American Frankenstein monster, 7; *Colonial*, 225–226; Dahmer and, 225–226; Dyer and, 221; *A Feast of Scraps*, 225; gay sexuality, 225–226; Genet and, 221; at Museum of Modern Art (New York), 221; *Notes on the Margin of "The Black Book,"* 220–221; at Philadelphia Institute of Contemporary Art, 222; "post-black" art, 228; self-silencing, 225, 2227; "Stranger in the Village" and, 221, 226; *Study for Frankenstein #1*, 219–229, 223; *Study for Frankenstein #1 (Study #2)*, 222; text-based paintings, 221, 224, 226, 290n9; *Twin*, 225–226; "Unbecoming," 222; at Whitney Museum of American Art, 219, 220
Lippard, George, *The Quaker City*, 33
Lipsyte, Robert, 208, 209–210
Living Theatre, 188
Lochhead, Liz, 17
London, Bette, 9
London, Jack, 74, 150
Long, Lisa, 47, 129
Lorde, Audre, 14
Lott, Eric, 187
Luddites, 30
Lugosi, Bela, 215

lynching: dismemberment, 178–179; horror films and, 179; lynch mobs as monsters, 58, 60, 99–100; lynch mobs in Whale films, 177, 179; in *The Monster*, 99–100; myth of the black rapist, 135; of Robert Lewis, 81–82, 100
"The Lynching of Jube Benson" (Dunbar), 135–140; imitation of black subservience, 135; irony in, 139; making black men into monsters, 152; myth of the black rapist, 135; parody in, 109, 135–136, 138–139; tricksters in, 136; *Uncle Tom's Cabin*, parody of, 153, 155–156, 157; visual revelation in, 159; white man as monster, 139; women excluded from, 139

Mailer, Norman, "The White Negro," 202–203
Malchow, H. L., 15, 26, 27, 28
Malcolm X, 210, 221
Mapplethorpe, Robert, 221
Marietta (Robinson), 33
"Marse Chan" (Page), 126, 127, 135
Marshall, Elaine, 81–82
Marshall, John, 43
Marshall, Tim, 30
Marx, Groucho, 71
Marx, Karl, 30
masculinity: fantasies/anxieties about, 5, 10; metaphors and, 75–76; specularization of, 9–10; in stories about Vietnam War, 192–193
Maslansky, Paul, *Sugar Hill*, 189
Master-John stories, 269n70
McDaniel, Hattie, 175
McDonald's Chicken McNuggets, 3
McDowell, James, 21
McGraw, James R., 210
McKellen, Ian, 225
McTeague (Norris), 149–150
Medovoi, Leerom, 189–190
Mellor, Anne K., 28, 244n38
Melville, Herman: "The Bell-Tower," 26, 42–44, 46, 92; *Benito Cereno*, 42; black American Frankenstein monster, 6; Dunbar and, 155, 272n99; *Moby Dick*, 155, 272n99; racial connotations of Frankenstein story, 25–26; slavery and its aftermath, 7; *Typee*, 272n99
Memory Mambo (Obejas), 17
Merrick, John (the "Elephant Man"), 81
metaphor: bad metaphors, 69; "closet" as metaphor for homosexuality, 276n15;

dead metaphors, 69–72, 79, 94, 106; Enlightenment approaches to, 72; femininity and, 77–78; Frankenstein as (*see* Frankenstein as metaphor); "frigid metaphors," 78; history of, 12, 256n13; identification with children, savages, 75–76, 77–78; identification with "overcivilization," 75–76; Igor as, 1; masculinity and, 75–76; as mechanical products, 77; for metaphor, 12, 72, 101–102; metaphor-making, 10, 68, 90, 98, 100; mixed metaphors, 69, 73, 79, 96, 144; in *The Monster*, 90–92, 94, 95–96, 101–102, 104–106, 159–160; monsters and, 6, 12, 68–72, 73, 79, 80, 94, 96 (see also *The Monster*); national identity and, 74; "Oriental" writing, 75; reanimation of, 69–71, 79, 80, 94, 97; Richards on, 69; Romantic poets, 72; Shakespeare and, 77; Shelley and, Percy Bysshe, 72; simile and, 69, 255n3; teachers of, 74; tenor of, 69, 105, 106, 108; vehicle of, 69, 105, 106, 108
The Metaphor (Buck), 77–80
metaphoraphobia, 106
metaphorophilia, 106
Meyer, Richard, 222, 226
mimicry: in "The Ass and the Lap-Dog," 119; D'Israeli on, Isaac, 115–116, 119; in Dunbar, 127; by Frankenstein monster, 117
minstrelsy, 88–89, 127–128
Miscegenation (Croly and Wakeman), 55–56
"miscegenation" (the term), 55–56
misogyny: in *Blackenstein*, 196–197; in *Frankenstein* (Shelley), 9; in *The Monster*, 103–104; in *Native Son*, 156; in *The Sport of the Gods*, 151
"The Mission of the War" (Douglass), 55
"Mr. Bones," 83
Mitchell, Margaret, *Gone with the Wind*, 7, 182
Moby Dick (Melville), 155, 272n99
"The Modern Frankenstein" (Bellew), 38–40, 39, 48
"The Modern Sphinx" (Worden), 61–66, 253n133
"Monkey Man" (William Henry Johnson), 81, 88
"monster" (the term), 160, 217
The Monster (Crane), 80–106; as allegory of allegory, 92–94, 99; black dandy as monster, 80, 87–88, 104; cakewalk, 88–89, 91; Declaration of Independence

in, 93; figurative language, 12, 90–92, 95–96; first publication, 80; *Frankenstein* (Shelley) compared to, 94; *Harper's* illustrations for, 84, 85; interracial rape in, 97; irony in, 91–92; Johnson and, William Henry, 81; judge as arbiter of authority in race relations, 86, 260n46; *The Leopard's Spots* (Dixon) compared to, 98; lynch mob in, 99–100; metaphor-making in, 68, 90, 98, 100; metaphorophilia, 106; metaphors in, 90–92, 94, 95–96, 101–102, 104–106, 159–160; minstrelsy tradition, 88–89; misogyny in, 103–104; "Mr. Jolton Bones" in, 83; as political allegory, 80, 94; racism making black men into monsters, 80, 85, 97–99; racist stereotypes in, 87–90, 96, 102–103; reanimation in, 84, 86; resemblance between monsters and metaphors, 6, 68–69; as rewriting of *Frankenstein* (Shelley), 102; sexual connotations, 89, 261n54; *The Sport of the Gods* (Dunbar) compared to, 107–108; veils in, 101; women in, 98, 103–104, 105
monsters/monstrosity: in antebellum slave narratives, 44; black dandy as, 80, 87–88, 104; black men as, 80, 85, 94, 97–99, 102, 107, 109, 137; blackness as monstrous, 6, 228–229; Burke and, 29; civil rights movement as, 208–209; Confederacy as, 51–52, 53; failed masculinity as, 144–145; fallen women as, 146; female monsters/monster-makers, 17–18, 46, 58–60; gayness as, 226; Hutchinson and, 37; lynch mob as, 58, 60, 99–100; metaphors and, 6, 12, 68–72, 73, 79, 80, 94, 96 (see also *The Monster*); minstrelsy as, 88–89; mixed-race children as, 40–41; mulattos as, 56; reinvention by African Americans, 134; slaveowners as, 44, 50; slavery as, 42, 43, 45–46, 49, 49–50; social construction of, 22, 78, 80, 85, 97–99, 109, 150; sympathy for, 186; texts equated to, 69; visual art, 220; Watergate figures as, 188; white man as, 139
Moore, C. L., "No Woman Born," 17
Moore, Michael, "We Finally Got Our Frankenstein," 1, 2, 3
Moretti, Franco, 13
Morrison, Toni, 7–8, 22, 235n29
Morrissey, Paul, *Flesh for Frankenstein*, 162, 274n5
Motley, John Lothrop, 47
"Moxon's Master" (Bierce), 15, 274n6

mulattos, 41, 56, 185–186
Multitude (Hardt and Negri), 2
"The Murders in the Rue Morgue" (Poe), 21
My Bondage and My Freedom (Douglass), 45
myth of the black rapist: in 1930s Hollywood films, 182–183; black American Frankenstein monster, 56–58; Douglass and, 60; Dunbar and, 135
The Mythic Being (Piper), 220

NAACP, 175
Nachman, Gerald, 288n122
Napoleon Smith (Worden), 62
Narrative of Arthur Gordon Pym (Poe), 21–22
Narrative of the Life of Frederick Douglass (Douglass), 22, 44–45
Native Son (Wright), 156–157, 179
naturalism, 140, 149–150
Negri, Michael, *Multitude* (with Hardt), 2
"The Negro Woman" (Tayleur), 58–60
Negroes and Negro "Slavery" (Van Evrie), 40–41, 56
Nestrick, William, 160
"The New Frankenstein" (Stephens), 47–48, 49
"New Woman" (Worden), 63
New York World (newspaper), 56
Newell, Peter, 84, 85
Newsweek (magazine), 210
Newton, Huey, 188–189, 190
Nigger: The Strange Career of a Troublesome Word (Kennedy), 287n112
Nigger (Gregory), 206–210
Night of the Living Dead (film), 197–198
Nixon, Richard, 187–188
No More Lies (Gregory), 211–213
Norris, Frank, 74, 149–150
North American (newspaper), 153
Northmore, Thomas, *Washington, or Liberty Restored*, 34
Notes of a Native Son (Baldwin), 198
Notes on the Margin of "The Black Book" (Ligon), 220–221
Nudelman, Franny, 38

Oates, Joyce Carol, 111
Obejas, Achy, *Memory Mambo*, 17
O'Flinn, Paul, 174
"The Old Cabin" (Dunbar), 127
orangutans, 21

Orientalism: Bierce and, 15; *Frankenstein*
(Shelley), 15–16, 28–29, 31; metaphor
and, 75; *Presumption; or, The Fate of
Frankenstein* (Peake), 31
Original Gangstas (film), 284n76
"Our Domestic Relations" (Sumner), 51–52
"Our Foreign Relations" (Sumner), 50,
51–52
"Our New Madness" (Dunbar), 107, 123
The Outlook (journal), 58

Page, Thomas Nelson, "Marse Chan," 126,
127, 135
Park, Mungo, *Travels in the Interior
Districts of Africa*, 26
Parks, Gordon, Jr., *Super Fly*, 188
Parks, Gordon, Sr., *Shaft*, 188
"Parodies" (D'Israeli), 110–112, 113, 115, 126
parody: in *Another Piece of Presumption*,
111–116; in black cultural practice, 12;
Black Power movement, 194–195; blaxploitation films, 194–195; conservative
use of, 114–115; in cultural theory, 114;
definition, 109, 110; Dunbar and, 108,
121, 125–133, 134, 135–136, 150; as a form,
12; Frankenstein monster as, 111, 116–117;
in *Frankenstein* (Shelley), 108, 112–114,
117–118, 129; of *Frankenstein* (Shelley), 12,
109, 111, 115, 138, 140, 149, 152; Gregory
and, Dick, 204–206; irony and, 129; of
Karloff's Frankenstein monster, 194; in
"The Lynching of Jube Benson," 109, 135–
135, 138–139; of naturalism, 150; political
possibilities of, 121; of racist nostalgia,
126–127, 135–136; self-directed, 112–114,
131–132; in *The Sport of the Gods*, 109; of
Uncle Tom's Cabin, 109, 153–154, 155–156,
157
pastiche, 109–110, 111–112
Patchwork Girl (Jackson), 15
Paul, William, 189
Peake, Richard Brinsley: *Another Piece of
Presumption*, 111–116, 129; Canning and,
20; *Presumption* (see *Presumption; or, The
Fate of Frankenstein*)
personification, 70
Pesmen, Dale, 69
Phillips, Wendell, 22
Pierce, Jack, 176
Piercy, Marge, 17
Pinochet, Augusto, 1
Piper, Adrian, *The Mythic Being*, 220
Playing in the Dark (Morrison), 7–8

Plessy v. Ferguson, 260n46
Poe, Edgar Allan, 7, 21–22, 179
Poitier, Sidney, 188
polygenesis, 27, 40, 56
"post-black" art, 228
"post-Frankenstein" world, 228–229
Postcolonial Melancholia (Gilroy), 16
The Practical Elements of Rhetoric
(Genung), 91
Pratt, William Henry. *See* Karloff, Boris
Presumption; or, The Fate of Frankenstein
(Peake): Bakhtin and, 116; Canning and,
115; Frankenstein monster as automa-
ton/mechanical monster, 42, 77; Fritz
(Igor character) in, 112; Orientalism of,
31; parody of, 111; success, 30; Victor
Frankenstein in, 42, 112
Prince, Mary, 28
*The Principles of Rhetoric and Their
Application* (Hill), 73
Prometheus: Edison and, 163; Founding
Fathers as, 33–34; Franklin as, 246n55;
Sumner and, 53; Victor Frankenstein as,
173
Prospero, 14, 138
Pryor, Richard, 207, 220

The Quaker City (Lippard), 33
Quintilian, 70, 76

racism: fears of interracial rape, 27; fears
of racial mixture ("amalgamation"),
27, 40–41; first professional racist in
American history, 40; internalization
of racist norms, 150; making black men
into monsters, 80, 85, 97–99, 109, 142,
143–144, 152; orangutans, likeness to,
21; racist nostalgia, parody of, 126–127,
135–136; racist rhetoric, 66; *Uncle Tom's
Cabin* and, 154; white fears about black
power, 27
Rampersad, Arnold, 132
rape, interracial, 27, 97, 98. *See also* myth of
the black rapist
*The Reason Why the Colored American Is
Not in the World's Columbian Exposition*
(Douglass and Wells), 60, 66
Reddick, Lawrence, 176
Redding, J. Saunders, 124, 131
Reid, Richard, 16
"Representative American Negroes"
(Dunbar), 131–132
Reynolds, Paul Revere, 107

rhetoric guides, 73–75
Richards, I. A, 69
Riley, James Whitcomb, 127
Roach, Jay, *Austin Powers in Goldmember,*
  284n76
Robeson, Paul, 179–180
Robinson, John Hovey, *Marietta,* 33
Romero, George, *Night of the Living Dead,*
  197–198
Roosevelt, Theodore, 76
The Ruins (Volney), 32–33
Rydell, Robert, 63

St. Clair, William, 111
Saletri, Frank, 190
Sappol, Michael, 33
"savage" (the term), 75
Schoedsack, Ernest B., *King Kong* (with
  Cooper), 177, 182–183
Scottsboro case (1931), 175
Sedgwick, Catherine Maria, 37
Sedgwick, Eve Kosofsky, 10, 163
Seltzer, Mark, 73–74
The Shadow That Scares Me (Gregory), 159,
  210–211
Shaft (film), 188
Shah of Iran, 1
Shakespeare, William: Dunbar and, 127,
  136, 138, 140; *King Lear,* 136, 140, 270n76;
  metaphor, use of, 77; *The Tempest,* 138.
  See also Ariel; Caliban; Prospero;
  Sycorax
Shelley, Mary: abolitionism, 27, 61; anti-
  slavery rhetoric, 26; "The Ass and the
  Lap-Dog" (fable), 118; boycott of sugar,
  27; in *Bride of Frankenstein,* 172, 181;
  British discussions of race, 26–27;
  Cleaver compared to, 201; Condillac
  and, 256n13; Crane compared to, 94;
  Dunbar and, 153; East India Company,
  28; equation of monsters and texts, 69;
  Fables Ancient and Modern (Godwin),
  118; *Frankenstein,* (see *Frankenstein*
  (Shelley)); gothic literature, 25; parents,
  26; Stowe and, 158; Sumner and, 48
Shelley, Percy Bysshe: boycott of sugar,
  27; in *Bride of Frankenstein,* 172, 181;
  Franklin and, 34; Fuller and, 37; meta-
  phors and, 72; Volney's *The Ruins,* 32–33
Shelton, Lee (Stagolee), 134
Show Boat (film), 179–180, 185
signifying, 108, 126, 133, 204
Signifying Monkey, 133, 152

Signing of the Declaration of Independence
  (Trumbull), 93
The Silence of the Lambs (film), 17
simile, 69, 255n3
single-parenting, 4
Skal, David, 174
"Skin" (Jackson), 15
slave narratives, 22–23, 28, 44, 209–210,
  241n9
Slave of Frankenstein (novel), 219
slave revolts, 19–23. *See also* Turner, Nat
slaveowners as monsters, 44, 50
slavery: aftermath of, 7; Douglass on, 4,
  19, 54, 66; in Jamaica, 50; as monster/
  monstrosity, 42, 43, 45–46, 49, 49–50; in
  West Indies, 20; white American writers'
  response to, 9
"Slavery and the Irrepressible Conflict"
  (Douglass), 19, 45–46, 52
Sloan, Paul, *Hearts of Dixie,* 175
Smethurst, James, 157
Smight, Jack, *Frankenstein: The True Story,*
  162
Smiley, Joseph W., *Life without Soul,* 276n19
Smith, Allan Lloyd, 241n9
Smith, Valerie, 183
Snead, James, 169
Somoza, Anastasio, 1
Soul on Ice (Cleaver), 201–203, 211
The Souls of Black Folk (Du Bois), 132
Southern Literary Messenger, 49–50
Spivak, Gayatri Chakravorty, 28, 29, 65
The Sport of the Gods (Dunbar), 140–158;
  black dandy in, 109, 142–145; critique
  of white men, 143; failed masculinity in, 144–145; "Frankenstein" in,
  125; *Frankenstein* (Shelley) and, 152;
  Frankenstein story in, 141, 147–152;
  homosexuality in, 145; internalization of
  racist norms, 150; irony in, 140–141, 142,
  151, 152; making black men into monsters, 109, 142, 143–144, 152; master-slave
  story in, 147, 148; *McTeague* and, 150;
  misogyny in, 151; mixed metaphors in,
  144; *The Monster* compared to, 107–108;
  naturalism, 140; *North American* on, 153;
  parody in, 109; protagonist in, 6; reception of, 153–154; social construction of
  monstrosity, 150; temperance narrative
  in, 146; title, 140; *Uncle Tom's Cabin,*
  parody of, 109, 153–154, 155–156, 157;
  women in, 145–151
Stagolee (Lee Shelton), 134

Stahl, John, *Imitation of Life*, 185
Steel, Johannes, *Hitler as Frankenstein*, 279n32
stem-cell research, 3
Stephens, Henry Louis, 6, 26, 47–48, 49
Stoker, Bram, *Dracula*, 13, 216, 236n35
Stone, Albert, 210
Stone, Ivory, 190
Stowe, Harriet Beecher: black critiques of, 154–155; daughter, 155; Dunbar and, 153, 154, 156–158; Shelley and, Mary, 158; *Uncle Tom's Cabin* (see *Uncle Tom's Cabin*); Whale and, 178; Wright and, 156
"Stranger in the Village" (Baldwin), 198–200, 203, 221, 226
Study for Frankenstein #1 (Ligon), 219–229, 223
Study for Frankenstein #1 (*Study #2*) (Ligon), 222
Styron, William, *The Confessions of Nat Turner*, 19
Sugar Hill (film), 189
Sumner, Charles, 48–55; abolitionism, 48, 51–52; black American Frankenstein monster, 6; Brooks's attack on, 52–53, 251n110; Butler and, Andrew, 251n110; colonialism, 52; on Confederacy, 51–52, 53, 54; Douglass on, 53–54; as Frankenstein monster, 49–50; Indian uprising (1857), 52; "Our Domestic Relations," 51–52; "Our Foreign Relations," 50, 51–52; Prometheus and, 53; racial connotations of Frankenstein story, 26; regeneration through war, 55; on sectional revolt, 51; Shelley and, Mary, 48; slaveowners as monsters, 50; *Southern Literary Messenger* on, 49–50
Sundquist, Eric, 24
Super Fly (film), 188
Sweet Sweetback's Baadasssss Song (film), 188
Sycorax, 14
"symbol" (the term), 68, 71
synecdoche, 70

Tarantino, Quentin, *Jackie Brown*, 284n76
Tarzan, 287n114
Tayleur, Eleanor, 26, 58–60, 63
The Tempest (Shakespeare), 138
Tennyson, Alfred, 127
Testa, Eugenio, *Il Mostro di Frankenstein*, 276n19
A Text-Book on Rhetoric (Kellogg), 73, 74

Thesiger, Ernest, 172, 182, 186–187
Till, Emmett, 220
Travels in the Interior Districts of Africa (Park), 26
travesty: in *Another Piece of Presumption*, 116; burlesque and, 262n4; definition, 110; by Frankenstein monster, 117; in *Frankenstein* (Shelley), 112
tricksters, 108, 269n70
Trumbull, John, *Signing of the Declaration of Independence*, 93
Turner, Nat: crimes committed by, 19; dissection of his body, 24, 38, 241n14; fate of, 24; as Frankenstein monster, 6, 19–20; Gray and, 22–23; McDowell on, 21
Twain, Mark: Crane and, 87; Dunbar and, 132; as a freak, 123–124; Gregory and, Dick, 207; *Huck Finn*, 7, 10, 87, 132; slavery and its aftermath, 7
Twin (Ligon), 225–226
Typee (Melville), 272n99

"Unbecoming" (Ligon), 222
Uncle Remus, 127, 133
"Uncle Tom" (the term), 157, 273n107
Uncle Tom's Cabin (Stowe): Dunbar and, 178; parodies of, 109, 153–154, 155–156, 157; racism and, 154; slavery and its aftermath, 7; Topsy (character), 50; Whale's films, 178
Uncle Tom's Children (Wright), 156, 157
Undercover Brother (film), 284n76
Unger, Craig, *House of Bush, House of Saud*, 231n3
Universal Studios, 173
Up from Nigger (Gregory), 216–217
uplift ideology, 64

vampires, 13, 215
Van Evrie, John, 40–42; black American Frankenstein monster, 6; English abolitionism, 46; on mulattos, 41; *Negroes and Negro "Slavery,"* 40–41, 56; polygenesis, 40; proslavery polemics, 25; racial connotations of Frankenstein story, 25; *White Supremacy and Negro Subordination*, 56
van Peebles, Melvin, *Sweet Sweetback's Baadasssss Song*, 188
Variety (newspaper), 182
Vaurien (D'Israeli), 115
Veblen, Thorstein, 74
Vidal, Gore, 182
Vietnam War, 191, 192–193

A Voice from the South (Cooper), 154–155
Volney, Constantin-François, *The Ruins*,
   32–33

Wakeman, George, *Miscegenation* (with
   Croly), 55–56
Walker, David, 23–24, 25, 44
Walker, Kara, 220
Wallace, Michele, 201–202
Ward, Lynn, 274n6
Warhol, Andy, 162, 274n5
Warner, Michael, 87
Washington, Booker T., 121, 131
Washington, George, 43
Washington, or Liberty Restored
   (Northmore), 34
Watergate scandal, 188
Watkins, Mel, 187
Wayans, Keenen Ivory, *I'm Gonna Git You
   Sucka*, 284n76
"We Finally Got Our Frankenstein"
   (Moore), 1, 2, 3
"We Wear the Mask" (Dunbar), 126
Wegener, Paul, *The Golem*, 276n19
Weinstein, Cindy, 11, 44
Wells, H. G., 180
Wells, Ida B., *The Reason Why the
   Colored American Is Not in the World's
   Columbian Exposition* (with Douglass),
   60, 66
West Indies, slavery in, 20, 46
Whale, James: background, 180–181; *Black
   Majesty* and, 179–180; *Blackenstein*
   compared to his films, 197; *Bride of
   Frankenstein* (see *Bride of
   Frankenstein*); comedy in films of, 187; as depicted in
   Gods and Monsters, 162, 225; *Frankenstein*
   (see *Frankenstein* (film)); Frankenstein's
   fame, 1; Gregory and, Dick, 204, 208,
   216; homosexuality in his films, 181–182;
   Invisible Man, 180; Lancaster and, 184–
   185; Lewis and, David, 181, 186; lynch
   mobs in films of, 177, 179; popular
understanding of Frankenstein story,
   172, 173; queer sensibility of, 225; racial
   allegory in films of, 160–161, 174–175;
   Robeson and, 179–180; *Show Boat*, 179–
   180, 185; Stowe and, 178; Thesiger and,
   186–187; *Uncle Tom's Cabin* and, 178;
   white anxiety, language of, 9
White, Graham, 87, 128
White, Shane, 87, 128
"white Atlantic," 8–9
"White" (Dyer), 221
White Fang (London), 150
"The White Negro" (Mailer), 202–203
White Supremacy and Negro Subordination
   (Van Evrie), 56
whiteness, 7, 22
Wideman, John Edgar, 235n29
"Wild Man" dramas, 31
Wilks, William, 45
Willard, Emma, 47
Williams, Raymond, 12
Witchcraft, a Tragedy (a play), 37
Wollstonecraft, Mary, 26
Woman in the Nineteenth Century (Fuller),
   37
women: in *The Monster*, 98, 103–104; in
   naturalistic fiction, 149–150; Negro
   women, 58–60; violations of white
   women, 57–58; women writers, 16–17.
   See also feminism; misogyny
women's liberation, Gregory on, 213
Wood, Marcus, 9
Worden, A. T., 61–66, 253n133
Wordsworth, William, 127
Wormser, I. Maurice, *Frankenstein,
   Incorporated*, 173–174
Wray, Fay, 182
Wright, Richard, 7, 156–157, 179

Young Frankenstein (film), 12

Zip Coon, 88, 128
"Zip" (William Henry Johnson), 81, 88

About the Author

Elizabeth Young is Professor of English at Mount Holyoke College. She is the author of *Disarming the Nation: Women's Writing and the American Civil War* and coauthor of *On Alexander Gardner's "Photographic Sketch Book" of the Civil War.*

Lightning Source UK Ltd.
Milton Keynes UK
UKOW02f1917250416

272958UK00004B/211/P